The Birds Fall Down

Rebecca West, author of a multitude of books of both fiction and non-fiction, is rightly regarded as one of Britain's leading literary celebrities.

Amongst many other honours and academic degrees, she was awarded the DBE in 1949 and became a Chevalier of the Legion of Honour in 1957.

Her novel *The Birds Fall Down* was first published in 1966.

THE BIRDS
FALL DOWN

REBECCA WEST

We are all bowmen in this place.
The pattern of the birds against the sky
Our arrows overprint, and then they die.
But it is also common to our race
That when the birds fall down we weep.
Reason's a thing we dimly see in sleep.

CONWAY POWER, *Guide to a Disturbed Planet*

Pan Books
in association with Macmillan London

First published 1966 by Macmillan & Company Ltd
This edition published 1967 by Pan Books Ltd,
Cavaye Place, London SW10 9PG
3rd printing 1978
in association with Macmillan London Ltd
© Rebecca West 1966
ISBN 0 330 30037 7
Printed and bound in Great Britain by
Hazell Watson & Viney Ltd, Aylesbury, Bucks

Foreword

THIS NOVEL IS founded on a historical event: perhaps the most momentous conversation ever to take place on a moving railway train. Students of modern history will recognise the necessity for specifying that it was moving. The Armistice which ended the First World War was signed in a stationary train. The conversation in this book takes place on a slow train making its way up through Northern France at the very beginning of the twentieth century, just after the close of the South African War; the conversation which historians have recorded took place, nearly ten years later, on the Eastern Express between its departure from Berlin and its arrival at Cologne. The real participants differed from my characters in many respects, but not in their interests and emotions; and their exchange of information had the same effect on the Russian political scene. There were certainly other factors at work. But it is true that because of this conversation the morale of the powerful terrorist wing of the revolutionary party crumbled. As Theodore Dan puts it in his authoritative work *The Origins of Bolshevism*, the results of this strange encounter 'dealt a blow to the tactic of political terror that it never recovered from'. It is also true that the Russian bureaucracy found the affair gravely disillusioning, and the defences of the Tsardom were breached. From then on the door of opportunity slowly swung open before the cool-headed Lenin.

Most of the characters in these pages are portraits of people who were living at this period and seriously involved in this situation, though they bore other names, and I have drawn heavily on their recorded sayings and their writings. I think I can claim to have told a true story, as it may have happened on a parallel universe, differing from ours only by a time-system which every now and then gets out of true with our own. Sometimes my story may surprise only because the changes in our society have been so rapid and so fundamental.

7

It would have been inevitable in 1900 that a girl like Laura would have spoken and understood, as of nature, Russian, the Old Slavonic of the Liturgy, French and English; and she would probably have been a fair German and Italian scholar as well. And it would not have been surprising at that time that a French professor in a medical college was an enthusiastic Latinist. It is also to be noted that I have exaggerated neither the bloody score of the terrorists, nor the number of executions and imprisonments for which the Tsarist Government must bear responsibility, as well as its astounding interferences with liberty such as the violation of the mails, known as perlustration.

I would like to acknowledge my indebtedness to the writings of Boris Nikolaievsky, of whose death I heard with much regret while I was writing the last chapter of this book. I would also like to send a word of thanks to the ghosts of Ford Madox Ford, and his sister, Juliet Soskice, wife of a Russian revolutionary who took refuge in England, and a pioneer translator of Russian literature, from whom I first heard the story which I have transformed into this novel, so long ago that the leading participants were still alive.

1

ONE AFTERNOON, IN an early summer of this century, when Laura Rowan was just eighteen, she sat, embroidering a handkerchief, on the steps leading down from the terrace of her father's house to the gardens communally owned by the residents in Radnage Square. She liked embroidery. It was a solitary pastime and nobody bothered to interfere with it. The terrace had been empty till ten minutes before, when her father had come out of the house. She had known without looking up that it was he. He had shifted a chair quite a distance to a new position and as he settled in it he had grumbled at its failure to comply with his high standards of comfort; and as he had thereafter kept up a derisive mutter she assumed he was reading a book. He could not see her, she was sitting on the bottom step, and she was content that it should be so, as otherwise he would have told her either to sit up straight or not so straight. His criticism was not so urgent as other people's was apt to be, and never demanded instant action, but it was continuous. Presently she heard the click of the french window which opened on the terrace, and she set down her embroidery and prepared to eavesdrop. For the last year or so everybody in the house had been eavesdropping whenever they had a chance.

Her unseen mother's voice said with a curious formality, as if she were reading the words out of a book, 'Edward, I'm writing to my mother, I'd like to be able to say that I'm taking Laura over to Paris for a fortnight quite soon.' Of late her English accent had deteriorated. Anyone could have told she was a foreigner.

After a pause Edward Rowan answered, 'You know quite well, Tania, that I don't think it's good for any of the children to go over there. It's too heavily charged an atmosphere. It's also not very sensible to go among the French when they haven't yet got over their feelings about the Boer War. And I wish you yourself didn't have to make such a long visit.'

'A long visit?' repeated Tania ironically. 'A fortnight!'

'Long enough, in the circumstances,' her husband told her.

'In your circumstances or mine?' asked Tania.

Laura thought, 'It's no use pretending that they're fond of each other any more. They were, but they aren't. Is that unusual, I wonder? Are other people's parents happy together? They all pretend to be, of course. But is it true?' The cat from Number 13 walked along the gravel path and paused beside her, but she did not dare to pet it, lest she missed something.

'It doesn't suit the boys, I know,' Tania went on in a conciliating tone, as if she were already sorry for her sharpness. 'Osmund likes nothing except Eton and cricket and summer at Torquay, and Paris makes a perfect little clown of Lionel. They don't like being half-Russian. They're wholly your children,' she said bitterly. 'But Laura can sail through anything, she never notices what's going on round her. And as for me,' she said, all attempt at conciliation abandoned, 'as for me, if I might put forward my own claims, I think it my duty to visit my father and mother. After all, they're lonely and unhappy.'

'Why lonely? They know everybody.'

'Not now.'

'Oh, not everybody can have turned their backs on them, there must be a lot of decent Russians —'

'You don't appreciate their position. How should you? You've always put off going to see it for yourself. You're a busy man. I do not blame you. But you haven't even thought of them, tried to imagine what it's like to be them, for quite a long time. You've been so extremely, so excessively occupied with other things. Well, there isn't anybody my parents can see. They'd rather die than have a liberal exile inside the house, and the Russians of their own sort who come abroad merely to travel are equally out of the question. Either they think that my father did something wrong and deserves to be disgraced, in which case they sincerely don't want to see him, or they think he's innocent, in which case they might pay such a price for showing their faith in him that he wouldn't dream of allowing them to run the risk. And also,' she added, hesitantly, 'my father doesn't want to be considered innocent if the Tsar thinks him guilty. You don't allow for that, Edward. My father can't quarrel with what the Tsar has done any more than he could quarrel with God.'

'Perhaps, perhaps,' said Edward Rowan. 'But no, I really can't swallow that. He can't honestly be such a believer in juju. I remember perfectly well what he used to be like when we were first married, oh, and long after, when he was a Minister, all that good talk, and those excellent speeches. He wasn't quite like an Englishman but he wasn't much different from a top man at the Quai d'Orsay or the Ballplatz. I can't believe all this stuff about Holy Russia. I believe it's the same sort of humbug we have over here. I go to church every Sunday and say, "All we like sheep", and so do all the rest of us, but I don't believe any of us really thinks that we closely resemble four-legged animals covered with wool. But even if your father does carry it so far as to feel that the Tsar is always right, I can't think he couldn't stop feeling it tomorrow if he chose. Anyway, he ought to come over here. He's apparently kept a firm grip on most of his income and he could easily find a place in the country with some shooting.'

'The shooting here in England seems contemptible to all Russians,' said Tania. 'Even at Sandringham and Welbeck we have to laugh. Our people only come because they like the English and their gossip. You should know that, you lived long enough in Russia. And anyway it would make things worse for him with his Government if he came here.'

'Then he should forget the Russian Government,' said Edward. 'I should think he'd be glad to be free of it. Such nonsense —'

Tania said through her teeth, 'If you mention the Duke of Fife I shall scream.'

The conversation was going very wrong. Laura wondered if it were time for her to stand up and show them she was there. The name of the duke was never uttered in the house. It had happened that when Tania and Edward were first married they went to stay with her parents, who were spending a winter month at their villa in Nice, and Edward, walking in the town, had met the Duke of Fife and brought him back to luncheon. Afterwards the members of the Russian Secret Police guarding Tania's father presented an adverse report on the visit, reporting that the duke was a member of the Liberal Party, and disregarding the fact that he was also the son-in-law of Queen Victoria. Edward Rowan always loved telling this story, and the children had laughed with him over it, till they noticed as they moved through their teens that their mother hated hearing it; and then there had been a Sunday supper when Edward brought it out to amuse a lethargic guest, and Tania had gone white and stood up very straight like somebody in opera and said she had a headache and must go and lie down. Since then the story had not been heard again.

Choking, Tania went on: 'I've explained to you, again and again and again, that we don't think of things that way. One of our grand dukes was actually sent to Siberia. But you can't be expected to understand our conventions regarding royalty when you don't understand your own. You haven't got a Siberia here in England, but there are circumstances in which English people do suddenly find that Queen Victoria's sons-in-law don't know them any more.' There was a further silence which she broke by saying, in that reading-aloud tone she had used when she began the conversation: 'My father and mother are old and exiled and unhappy. I wish to go and stay with them for a fortnight and I wish to take my daughter with me. They are always asking for her. She's only been over once, when they first got there.'

'That sounds like a request drafted to sound reasonable by a solicitor and rehearsed before him,' said Edward, and his wife made no answer.

Laura stood up and said, 'Oh, Mummie, that will be lovely.' As she had been sitting on one of the lower steps this brought her head just about level of the terrace. Her parents stared down at her, and she stared back with a smile at once false and sincere. She was humbugging them, but it was in their interests. Tania's cheeks burned, but Edward Rowan took only a second to reassume his public calm. He said didactically, 'I trust you to take care of your mother. You must spare her all the trouble you can. It's on that understanding that I'll let you go.' His eyes left her face and looked far into the distance, he turned round and began to walk up and down the terrace. Already he was thinking of something else. Tania watched him incredulously. Smiling, he paused, regretfully shook off the pleasant thought which had preoccupied him, picked up his book off his chair, sat down and started reading again.

Laura slipped her arm round her mother's waist. 'Come and show me what clothes I ought to take.' As they went through the drawing-room she dropped a kiss on Tania's cheek. 'How soon can we go?'

'Four days, I suppose. Oh, less. I'll send telegrams to people telling them I've gone. Then what can they do? Nothing. Would you mind it if we hurried off?'

'Roughly speaking,' said Laura, 'I don't mind anything. Particularly not this touch. It's no penance to see Grandfather and Grandmother. They're awfully grand. And it's no penance to go to Paris. You might stand me my first real Paris hat.'

'They don't make hats for unmarried girls in Paris,' said Tania. She banged into the newel-post at the bottom of the staircase. She really must be very unhappy. This was the way that when one was little one bumped into things after one had been crying till one was half-blind. 'They just cover the poor little things with cornflowers and marguerites, turn them into tidied-up Ophelias.' They laughed immoderately at the little joke.

It was only two days afterwards, for Tania was phrenetic once she went into action, that Edward Rowan took his wife and his daughter and the lady's maid, Hélène, down to Victoria and put them on the boat-train. He hardly looked at them once he had settled them in their carriage, and stared along the platform at the engine as if he were waiting for the very first detectable sign that it was getting up steam; and indeed he was waiting for that signal. When the puffing began he turned round, raised his hat, and spoke through the window. 'Good-bye, Tania,' he said, 'I hope you find things better than you fear. And I rely on you – to come back soon. I do ask you not to stay away too long.' He spoke easily, as if he were exercising the command over his wife's good nature which it was natural he should have, and as the train started to move he put his hat back on his head and walked quickly away.

Tania sank back in her seat, fierce as she had been on the terrace, her cheeks as hot. Laura was feeling angry with her father because he had not said good-bye to her at all. There came back to her a morning, some years before, when he had seen them off to Torquay and had whispered through the window to her that she was his plain Jane, his ugly little thing, his monster, and begged her not to come back any more hideous than she was. That would have been silly now she was grown-up, but he might have said something. She had not forgotten having overheard her mother say of her the other afternoon that she never noticed what was going on, and while she thought this opinion untrue, she supposed her mother held it because she would have liked it to be true. So, to show she had been blind to the remoteness of her father's farewell, she said calmly, 'How wonderful Papa looks. Always so much better than other men. Only he frightens me, he's so fastidious. I was terrified in the carriage, look, I've one button off this glove.'

It didn't go well. Her mother said in a cold and dreaming tone, 'Yes. So fastidious. Why, he can't endure being touched. It's quite an ordeal for him to be fitted by his tailor or his shoemaker. It's all very extraordinary.' Shuddering, she picked up *The Times* from her lap and spread out its pages with uncertain and blindish gestures.

Laura hoped her mother would not cry, for of course the other people in the carriage were taking as good a look at her as politeness permitted. They had recognised Papa, that had been obvious, and people always did; none of the younger Members of Parliament was as often photographed as he was. And for another thing, Mummie was so unusual-looking, with her dark-gold hair, her long grey-green eyes, her high cheekbones, her honey-coloured pallor, her royal and incapable air, her splendid clothes. Laura had found that even she was stared at, because she had the same hair and eyes and skin, and of course she was nothing like as good-looking as her mother. But she need not have worried because Tania was being stared at, Tania kept her secrets. Her way of emotion was as unusual as her appearance, simply she looked as if she had been roughly aroused from sleep and was not yet quite awake. She might have been just a woman who had had to break her custom of sleeping on till noon.

The carriage swung about. Laura could not read, and though she usually liked looking out of a railway train, the countryside along the line always seemed of a different sort than was accessible by walking, greener and more unspoiled, but it appeared that one had to have nothing to worry about to be able to enjoy that. She had a lump in her throat and a pain behind her breast-bone – her father might have said good-bye to her. What was it that her father was doing that had spoiled the way he had seen them off, and everything in the house at Radnage Square? Now when she came back with her governess from her afternoon classes at tea-time the house was forbidding like barracks full of troops divided against themselves. It was not that her father and mother were quarrelling. They could not have done that, her father was not even there to be quarrelled with, for except when Parliament was in recess he was never at home on week-day afternoons, except on Friday. It was as if life had slowed down and gone muddy. The books from Mudie's Lending Library were not changed for weeks together, and her mother often forgot to take tickets for concerts and the opera, even when she could have heard the music and musicians that she most liked. Also the flowers were nothing like as good as they had been before. All other winters, it had been wonderful to go into the drawing-room and find Tania in a tea-gown by a bright fire, with mounds of bronze and gold chrysanthemums piled cunningly where they were reflected in the chinoiserie mirrors, one curtain left undrawn so that one could see the bare trees against the night sky and the yellow street-lamps shining on the further side of the gardens, which for no reason at all shone with the aching sweetness of sad music, sad verse. But this winter even if Tania had remembered to buy flowers, she might leave them to be arranged by the parlourmaid or the governess, and many times she had had tea in her own room and did not come down till dinner, and then with swollen eyes. And her father always seemed to be thinking of something else. He did not say amusing things any more.

Laura knew that husbands could do several sorts of things which angered their wives, and though she did not care to think of them too exactly, she could not imagine her father doing any of them. Such husbands 'ran way'. Her father could not have moved an inch from where he was. His friends had all sprung up round him in a crowd, at Eton, at New College, in the Commons. When he travelled he was invited to stay with people he knew; his appropriate hosts had scattered themselves everywhere. The house in Radnage Square had been built for his father, and he could walk about it in the dark without bumping into anything. Alone in a strange place, what could he do? In any case, surely such husbands 'ran away' towards gaiety. But her father, though not dull, had committed himself to dullness for life and liked it; he enjoyed Blue Books, General Elections, questions in the House, Ministerial Posts.

Anyway Tania was going to be away from whatever the trouble was for a fortnight. And she was better already. She seemed to be actually reading *The Times* as the train slid through Kent, and as it drew near Dover she emerged from her sorrow into a distress which Laura found not in the least distressing, because it was familiar and idiotic. When Tania was young in Russia she had hardly ever seen the sea, except the Baltic and the Black Sea in high summer, and the English Channel was to her a mentally deranged piece of water attended by a fellow-maniac, sea-sickness, which she saw as a separate and uncontrollable entity, capable of intruding even into harbours. She could not go down to her cabin at once because Hélène had mislaid the ticket, and she fell into a comfortable irritation, not likely to last more than ten minutes, just as she did at home when meals were late or Osmund was snobbish or Lionel got over-excited and showed off, or rather as she had done when she was still happy enough to know such minor unhappinesses. This holiday would be just what she needed.

But things were not as they should have been. When they got down into the cabin and Hélène brought out the blanket and pillow from the soft red leather holdall and laid them on the sofa, Tania breathed with an absurd urgency, 'Well, when we get to the Gare du Nord we'll have the little Kamensky to meet us.' Laura thought this tactless of her mother. Of course the little secretary man, or whatever he was, would not lose any tickets and would be much more efficient then Hélène, but her mother need not have said so. Hélène put up with a great deal; she had to spend hours in brushing Tania's hair, and Laura's too now, and they both had an awful lot of hair. Also Monsieur Kamensky was an educated man, he had worked for her grandfather in his Ministry, of course he would know how to do things better than Hélène. But Tania had evidently meant something different, for Hélène answered without rancour, 'Yes, indeed, Monsieur Kamensky will tell us all we want to know.'

They both spoke of the little secretary (she thought he was little but could not really remember with certainty) in voices softened by trust, and she thought guiltily of an occasion on their last visit to Paris, two years before, when she had been ungrateful for his devotion to the family. Somebody had come from the Russian Embassy to question her grandfather about something that had happened when he was still a Minister, her grandmother had shut herself up in her bedroom to rage and cry, Tania had had to share this angry vigil, and Monsieur Kamensky had very kindly offered to take her a drive. On their way home they had been going along the odd cemetery-feeling road that runs along the back gardens of the houses on the Rue St Honoré, including the British Embassy, on the one side, and the Champs Elysées, on the other, when she caught sight of the open-air stamp-market. There the grave men were sitting on little iron chairs with their portfolios spanning their knees or lying on the ground at their feet, and she remembered that Osmund had said that if she had a chance she might buy him some French colonials. She asked Monsieur Kamensky to stop, and he had helped her a lot, he had found the man with the brindled moustache who was the specialist in such issues; and then, when she had found just what Osmund had wanted, she had asked the man if he had any Russian stamps. She did not collect stamps, they did not interest her at all, but she would have liked to have some Russian stamps. She knew

Osmund had a number of them, but she wanted some of her very own. She was proud of being half-Russian, though she loved England; it was not only that it had done a lot for her with the other girls at school, it was that she felt, while knowing it was against reason, all that Tania felt about Russia.

The man with the brindled moustache told her that he had no Russian stamps, and that she would do best to go to two men sitting some distance away, nearer the street, the men with the borzoi lying at their feet. She had started to walk towards them when Monsieur Kamensky caught her by the arm and said, 'Please, Miss Laura, you cannot have any dealings with those people.' She was enraged because he spoke to her as she thought that no man should speak to any woman, even if she was a schoolgirl: in command. She was also resentful of the strength of the grip of his hand on her arm. She threw back her head and tore herself away and started again towards the two men with the borzoi lying at their feet. But her arm was gripped again, more firmly than before. One would never have thought he was so strong. She said crossly, 'Why shouldn't I buy those stamps?' Her anger had broken on the polished stone of his unchanging face. He had told her sadly that people dealing in Russian goods in Paris were often revolutionaries, even terrorists, and that dangerous consequences might follow if any of them got a clue to her identity.

'What,' Laura had asked, 'is it as bad as that?' and he had answered gently, 'It is as bad as it can be. Have your parents never told you why you and your brothers were never allowed to visit your grandparents while they still lived in Russia? No? With all due respect to them, I think that wrong. I will take the responsibility of telling you. Three times the terrorists attempted Count Diakonov's life, and the wing of his country house was mined. The last time your mother's old English governess was killed.' The horror stilled her. 'I am sorry,' she said. They walked soberly to the carriage, and she stopped to ask him in a horrified voice, 'But are the terrorists here? In France? In Paris?' He had answered softly, so that she could scarcely hear him, 'They are everywhere.' In silence they had driven home along the Champs Elysées, towards a blood-red sunset.

They were at Calais, and Laura thanked a saint because she had not been sea-sick, though she never was. After the pushing and snapping in the French customs there was the long train-journey with its good moments; the estuary where a wide sweep of ghost-coloured dunes fell to a tidal river, no more than a string of pools white in the fawn mud, a piney wilderness on the further bank running seawards to the golden haze of the horizon; and the green and glassy outskirts of Amiens, where someone had planned waterways as a child might do it, with canals cutting across one another like open scissors, and perfectly round little ponds encircling perfectly round islands. A young man kept on walking up and down the corridor so that he could look in as he passed their carriage and stare at her. She thought men dull. Next year she would be presented, and she would have to go through the season and dance with a lot of men, and she did not know how she would bear it. She supposed she would have to get married, but she could not imagine herself getting to know a man well enough for that. She did not believe there was much in men to know.

At last there was the screaming, hurrying Gare du Nord, but no Monsieur Kamensky, only the bull-necked Pyotr, who kissed Tania's hand and wept over it, and kissed her own and wept some more, and took them out to the carriage where the giant coachman, Vissarion, kissed their hands and wept again. Laura could not remember that there had been quite so much emotion when she was in Paris before. Then they drove off into the boulevards, into the whiteness which follows the sun-set of a clear June day, with crowds of people hurrying along not as if they feared to be late but as if they were eager to reach some place where they were going to enjoy themselves, past cafés where other people seemed to have reached that goal of contentment, the women smiling under huge cartwheel hats, so much larger than were worn in England, the men tilting forward bowler hats, so much smaller than were worn in England. The carriage spun on while the gas-standards came into yellow flower and the sky was pierced with stars, until they turned up the long low hill of the Avenue des Champs Elysées, between the stout rich private houses that were nearly palaces, towards the Arc de Triomphe, proud and black against the silver ending of the sunset.

Then they turned into the sombre breadth of the Avenue Kléber, and came to a halt at the most sombre building there; and that was the end of pleasure, of Paris. They drove across the pavement through an open double gateway into a court-yard where a circle of shrubs grew round a fountain flowing from a vase held by a plaster naiad, and they were met in a dark hall by a yellow-faced concierge, who, as she remembered, was half-French and half-Japanese. The Diakonovs had made their home in this building solely because it was owned, and the lower floors occupied, by a commercial syndicate of so many and such bizarre nationalities, including a substantial Japanese participation, that they could trace no connection with Russia and therefore feared no curiosity from their land-lords. Hélène stayed to look after the luggage, and Tania and Laura stepped into a lift made of iron grilles and red mahogany, which rose moaning and whistling up a pole shining like a slate-pencil; and on the fourth storey they got out at an open door, and Laura saw that the place was as awful as she remembered it. There was no actual difficulty in seeing that the hall was lined with tapestries and rugs, and gorgeously coloured, but the gloom took them to itself, the walls were dull as if they had been panelled with deal. Laura followed Tania as she hurried through one sitting-room after another, pushing aside portières of fringed and bobbled bottle-green velvet, penetrating a darkness intensified by weak shaking circles of light emanating from the lamps burning before the icons in the corners of each room. Tania paused at the last doorway and exclaimed, 'They aren't here, yet surely, surely they can't have gone out.' But in this last room an old man was huddled at a little round table, pondering over a game of patience and looking too weak to do anything else, to rise or to speak, but who sprang to his feet, overturning the table and sending the cards spinning across the floor, and shouted, 'Tania, my daughter Tania!'

'He's just what I remembered, I didn't exaggerate,' thought Laura with admiration, with distaste. He was so huge. Her father was six feet, Nikolai Nikolaievitch must have been four inches taller, and even for that he was broad. Though his roar was loving, in his embrace Tania appeared the victim of a great beast of prey. His head was too massive; when he bent to kiss his daughter first on one cheek and then on the other, it seemed terrible that she should have to suffer the second blow. He was not growing old in a way young people like to see; his white hair and his beard were streaked with the barbaric gold glowing as it glowed on his daughter's head. His features were nearly classical yet were thickened as if by some blood not European, and the colour of his skin sent the mind to Asia. It made him look all the taller and stranger and yellower that he was wearing a long fawn garment cut like a monk's robe. But it was the change in him that was so alarming. Before he had been a wilder, stronger version of other and quite familiar kinds of people. There were Members of Parliament who came to the house for dinner and looked quite like Nikolai Nikolaievitch, allowing for a difference in size and vehemence, and when her grandfather came to London he frequented the Distinguished Strangers' Galleries in the Lords and Commons, and had been to dinner at Downing Street and stayed at Hatfield and Chatsworth, and it had all gone very well. But now he could not have set foot outside the apartment without being followed by a crowd, and without gratifying their anticipations, for his movements were strange as signals to another star.

'Darling Papa, where is Mamma?' asked Tania, freeing herself from his arms.

The old man's great amber eyes went to Laura. She was engulfed in his hugeness, smothered by the softness of his robe. It was some kind of wool, but soft as silk. He let her go, then caught her hands. 'Were you anxious to see us? Did you have a good journey? Did the Channel make your mother ill?'

He wanted to know none of these things. He was testing her Russian, making sure that her mother saw to it that she spoke it as well as she spoke English. It did not matter that he and his wife often spoke French. If she spoke Russian, it would mean that his blood was somehow bound to Russia. She answered as quickly as she could get the words out, 'We have been speaking of nothing else for days. The journey did not seem long at all. Mother was better than I have ever known her on the sea.'

But she thought, in English, 'How I wish I was not here. I wanted to come, but now I wish I was back in Radnage Square.' These walls were lined from floor to ceiling with pictures in swollen gilt frames, shallow portraits of bearded and moustachioed generals with giant chests barred and crossed with insignia, abundant women wearing high tiaras and carrying wide feather fans, landscapes showing larches and birches and pines standing lifeless as metal among their cobalt shadows on the snow. On the chimney-piece a huge clock showed the time in gross diamond figures on a gold globe fixed to a lapis lazuli firmament, and it was flanked by lines of small objects such as an alexandrite bulldog with ruby eyes and a number of gold and silver jewel-studded Easter eggs. Several small tables were covered with cloisonné jardinières and others with glass tops contained rose bushes made of coral and jade, and many miniatures and snuff-boxes, all repellent to interest. On each side of the fireplace stood a malachite vase as high as herself. All these things were getting old, as people get old; and bad taste seemed present, as a separate entity, like dust. Yet it had been delicious to touch her grandfather's robe. It was as different from ordinary material as something sung from something spoken. In a way she liked her grandfather. Once she had seen children crawling under a circus-tent so that they could see the elephant, and she would have done that to see her grandfather; and what she liked in him was the upside-downness of him, as this inverted luxury which gave him an everyday possession – for she supposed this robe was just a dressing-gown – which was uniquely exquisite, while the pictures and bric-à-brac round him were dull as china dogs and shell picture-frames from Margate.

But it was infuriating of him to pay no attention to Tania's twice-repeated question, 'Father, where is Mamma?' He simply went on trying out Laura's Russian, holding her hands powerless in his, staring at her, and telling her that her accent was good, that she held herself well, that he was glad that she had inherited the family golden hair. Tania exclaimed softly, 'Everything seems to go wrong at the same time,' and took off her coat and held it in her arms as if it were a baby or a little dog or her own anxiety. Laura felt frightened to see her mother suddenly becoming young and defenceless, even younger than she was herself. She pulled her hands out of her grandfather's grasp and asked him loudly, 'Where's Grandmamma?'

Nikolai seemed to think the question odd. 'Why, child,' he said kindly, 'she has been pacing up and down her room all day, actually crying with eagerness for your arrival and praying that your mother should not be too sea-sick.'

'Is she there now?' asked Tania.

'How should I know?' he asked in indulgent rebuke. 'She might be. In any case they will have told her that you are here, and she'll be coming in a minute. Sit down and rest, it's you and not she who has been doing the travelling.'

'I must go and find her,' said Tania, going towards the door. But she halted, breathed deeply, and nerved herself to ask: 'How is she? Is she well?'

'Is she well? Really I can't say that,' said Nikolai. 'We're none of us in very good health. We don't want to be here in Paris, so it doesn't suit us. There's an old Russian proverb —'

'Yes, yes,' said Tania, and turned to the door, but was met by Hélène, followed by the two women servants whom the Diakonovs had brought from Russia: Pyotr's wife, Katinka, the stout old cook, and Vissarion's sister, Aglaia, the Countess's elegant and jaundiced maid. Laura thought they looked like characters out of those boring Marivaux plays that she always tried to dodge being taken to see at the Comédie Française, for in the house they wore dresses belonging to another age, with full skirts and tight bodices made of thick grey cotton, with neckerchiefs of white linen and white stockings. Now they seemed more like players than ever, for they looked at Tania with great eyes before they kissed her hand, and there was an emphasised devotion in their kisses, while they cast sidelong glances at Nikolai, so plainly pitying him for his ignorance of some impending calamity that he would certainly have ceased to be ignorant of it had he not been sealed in himself. When they kissed Laura's hand they mimed the same sort of fear, and she stiffened with fear. Was her mother perhaps going to leave her father? But she was wrong. There was some other calamity here. As Hélène took her mother's coat from her she said in an undertone, 'They say the Countess will be back in a minute and you must not worry. It appears there is a vigil service in their Church, in your Church, this evening, it's one of your saint's days.'

'It's the day of Constantine and Helena, the Great Monarchs,' murmured Aglaia, an inch or two above Laura's hand.

'Isn't Laura Eduarevna like her mother?' Nikolai asked them.

'The image, the image,' the two servants chanted together, and Katinka murmured to Tania, 'the Countess didn't feel like going to our church in the Rue Darou, so she's just stepped round to the chapel in the Countess von Krehmunden's house in the Avenue du Bois —'

'Do you mean to say she's well enough to go out alone?'

Katinka and Aglaian exchanged another dramatic glance. 'Oh, there's no question of that. Even if she'd felt like doing anything so rash, we wouldn't have let her. But she was taken by Monsieur Kamensky.'

'Ah, that excellent little Kamensky,' sighed Tania.

'Indeed, we don't know where we'd all be without him. It's a pity he can't be here all the time. But he has to follow his profession. Well, he's out with her, and he'll bring her back as soon as he can. But you know how devout she is. He wouldn't like to cut short her devotions.'

'Not even to remind her about you,' said Aglaia.

'Soon we will have to give a great ball for our little Laura,' said Nikolai. 'Your grandmother will stand beside your mother at the head of the staircase as she stood beside your mother at her first great ball, and you will stand beside your mother.'

'Madame Tania hasn't changed since her first ball,' Katinka said to him, in the tone nurses use to children when they are telling them to eat up something, and Aglaia spoke in the same style. 'Nobody will know which is the mother and which the daughter.'

'Laura will be wasted in England,' Nikolai told Tania.' The English have next to no ceremonies. She should have been coming to us in St Petersburg now. She might have stayed with

24

us for a long time. She might have been a *demoiselle d'honneur*
at Court as you were.'

'I couldn't do it,' said Laura, looking up into his clouded
amber eyes. She felt she had to make him understand that. She
knew he was disgraced and had now no influence at Court, yet
he had this magicianly air, she was afraid he might be able to
bring about impossible things, including this. 'I wouldn't be
any good at the Russian Court or the English. I've got to be
presented next year and I hate it. I'm frightened. I'll do the
wrong thing and we'll —', she was going to say, 'we'll all be
sent to the Tower', and then checked herself. Nikolai had been
sent to the Tower.

The servants, seeing that things were going better, were
backing out. 'You wouldn't do the wrong thing, Laura,' said
Tania. 'I thought I would, but something comes and takes
over. After all the family has been doing it for so long, we're
wound up.' She went to stand by the fireplace, rested her elbow
on the chimney-piece, between a chalcedony frog and an agate
tortoise. Her small hat, trimmed with a bird, her close-fitting
blouse, and her long skirt, cut in the slanting lines of a tacking
yacht, gave her the shape of a swift force prepared to go into
action. 'After all, Laura,' she said in an undertone, 'Grand-
mamma can't be so bad if she goes out at all. And to one of our
services. You have to be pretty strong for that. The Almighty
always feels he can't outstay his welcome with us.' To Nikolai
she said, 'The silly girl doesn't realise one can do anything
one really wants to.'

'She would have looked superb in the *demoiselle*'s ruby vel-
vet dress,' said Nikolai.

'Laura doesn't want to look superb,' said Tania. 'Do remem-
ber she's half-English, and so doesn't care much about drama.
But the English are a sentimental people. Laura prefers to love
people rather than to be a person. She's prepared to love you
and Mamma though she doesn't know you as well as I would
like. She loves me,' she said, in a sudden flight of rapture, look-
ing in the glass as if the reflection of her face confirmed what
she said. 'I don't want to look as I did at my first great ball.
I'd be grateful enough if I could look like myself, if I don't
just fall to pieces and be nobody, be dust. But I'm kept

together because my children love me. Laura loves me quite a lot. Papa, does it mean a great deal to you that your children love you?' When he vaguely smiled and nodded, she turned round and begged him, 'Hasn't it meant a great deal to you that we love you so much, in this time, in this bad time, since all this has happened to you? Haven't you found it true that the love of your children makes up for anything that can happen to you?'

Nikolai answered, 'Yes, yes, it means a lot. A family life is one of the few real joys we're vouchsafed here on earth. Sit down and rest, presently, they'll bring you some tea, some Russian tea. I hope your brothers send you tea regularly as they do to us, real tea from Russia. But they may not, they've never been in England and they don't know how dreadful English tea is. Much that's drunk there is that rubbish from India. Even that appalling stuff from Ceylon.'

'We love you so much,' Tania went on. She had turned again to the glass and was combing her hair with one of her hat-pins. 'I didn't know till this last year how much I loved you. You and Mamma on the one hand, the children on the other. Nothing,' she said, her face distorted with pain, 'can really hurt me, because of that love.' She spun round, crying, 'Isn't that Mamma talking out there in the corridor?'

It was frightening, when one wanted one's mother, for her to want her mother too. But that was being a selfish beast. The door did not open at once. There was a weak twisting of the handle as if someone outside was trying to turn its massiveness with one hand, and then a call for help, then Pyotr held the door open and her grandmother came in, leaning heavily on the arm of a small bearded man whom Laura recognised as Monsieur Kamensky, though chiefly because she remembered that he had looked very like a lot of other people, and so did this man. Whoever he was, Madame Diakonova pushed him away when she saw Tania and Laura, stretched out her hands and took a step towards them, and then came to a halt, shaking her head and smiling shyly, as if she expected a scolding.

'Mother!' said Tania in a whisper. 'Mother!' She caught her hat to her bosom and drove her hat-pin through the bird

26

which trimmed it, as if she were killing something which must not be permitted to exist for one more moment.

'Well, I warned you I wasn't feeling as healthy as a peasant,' said Sofia Andreievna, with a little laugh, and the two women stood quite still, looking at each other.

Laura hated her grandfather for what his grief had made of this apartment. It was horrible to see what breathing the poisoned air had done to her grandmother. In the past, before her grandfather had gone into exile, Sofia Andreievna had visited them often in Radnage Square. Then she had been almost as beautiful as Tania, though in a quite different way, for her hair was black and her face a smooth oval and she was not at all barbaric; and she was very grand, prodigiously so, considering that she was small and slight. She had an immense amount of jewellery, all the stones very large, and she had furs that were as weightless and warm as good weather, and she possessed only what would have been – for anybody else – best clothes. Even in bed she was grand, wearing jackets frothing over with feathers between sheets she brought from Russia, sheets of linen so fine that it was dark, under bed-covers that dripped heavy Venetian lace to the floor. But within all this magnificence, and under the other weight of her years, she remained supple as a young animal. On her very last winter visit she had hunted regularly in Leicestershire, rushing back to town glittering with well-being, ready for whatever was going in the way of operas and theatres and dinner-parties and balls. They said she owed her vitality to her descent on her mother's side from a Polish family famous for strength and longevity; an ancestress of hers had ridden out at the head of an army of her serfs to do battle against an army commanded by her own great-grandson.

None of that stock died before eighty, or lost their health before they died. She could not be much more than sixty, Laura calculated. She had been married at seventeen to her middle-aged bridegroom, her eldest son was a little over forty. But now she might have been an ugly and weakly old woman. Her neck had been round and white, but now the flesh had shrunk away under her chin and her neck was a narrow fluted tube, and her face was like a mask of stretched hide stuck on top of it. She did not look only ugly and old, she looked poor, like the women in the slums between Radnage Square and the Fulham Road. Her hair had lost its colour and its lustre. It might not have been washed or brushed for a long time. Her eyes, which had been heavy-lidded and almost vacuously serene, stared anxiously out of deep sockets, as if she were wondering where the rent would come from. She must be got away at once, back to Radnage Square, fed on butter and cream and allowed to rest, and given a chance to swim at the Bath Club. She would soon be all right. She was so very strong. It was all a question of getting her out of this apartment.

Her grandfather said, with mild patriarchal censure, 'My dear wife, where have you been?' Having received a murmured apology, he went on, 'Now look at our Tania and see how well she is, and look at our little Laura and say who she is like.'

'My darling Tania,' said Sofia Andreievna, 'don't make such a sad face. It's not so bad really.'

'Oh, Mother, Mother,' whispered Tania. She let her hat slide out of her hands on to the floor, crossed the room and laid her arms about her mother's wasted body, resting her golden head on the thin shoulder.

'It's not so bad,' repeated Sofia Andreievna, 'and during the last three days I am much, much better. Ask Monsieur Kamensky.'

'Oh, without a doubt the Countess has improved lately,' agreed the small bearded man, in a pleasant voice. She had forgotten his voice as she had forgotten nearly everything about him, yet it was so charming, so unhurried, so good-humoured. 'But I've been away, I've been being an engineer instead of doing what I like and being a humble friend, and now I'm back I see a great improvement.'

'But isn't Laura exactly like her mother, Sofia? And doesn't that mean that she's exactly like my mother?' cried Nikolai, exultantly. Then concern sallowed his skin, dimmed his eyes, made him petitioning and humble. He was sorry for his wife after all. But no. 'Kamensky. Alexander Gregorievitch. While you were out I thought of something. I once had some correspondence with a man named Botkin. It might have some bearing on my case. I thought of a little, little thing, which might have some significance. Could you get me out the file?'

'I will have pleasure in doing that, Excellency,' said Monsieur Kamensky. 'But I'm afraid you'll have to wait till morning. That file was sent down to the Bank with the Muravlev material. A mistake in judgment, mine more than yours. But in the meantime read what I have here for you. It's a copy of a letter from Souvorin about the way things are going in St Petersburg. You'll see from the envelope who received it. As an indirect gesture of respect to you, he sent it to me yesterday, with obvious indications that it wasn't for my eyes but for yours.' Nikolai gave a sigh of pleasure and snatched the letter from his hand and sat down in an armchair by a lamp. Monsieur Kamensky bent over Laura's hand and said, 'Good evening, Miss Laura,' and as soon as he sat down beside her said in a quick undertone, 'Please, Miss Laura, look happier, Sofia Andreievna is talking to your mother now, but she might look over here, and all day long she has been saying to me, "I hope the little one will not be frightened when she sees what my horrible toothache has done to me."'

'Is that all it is, toothache?' exclaimed Laura in relief. 'Is it really only toothache?'

'So she would tell you,' he said, taking off his spectacles and polishing them. 'Persistent toothache. On many nights it gives her no sleep at all. Before long she will have to have a number of teeth extracted. That is why she wanted your mother to come over and be with her for a little time.'

'You've taken a weight off my mind,' said Laura. 'I can't tell you how glad I am it's only that. I was quite frightened. It is awful for anybody to be ill, but for my grandmother of all people, it's far worse. Don't you feel that?'

'I feel it very strongly,' said Monsieur Kamensky. 'All your family is extraordinary. Sometimes I speculate whether your grandmother was as wonderful when she married your grandfather, for I think him one of the most marvellous people who has ever lived, and some of his genius might well have rubbed off on to her. But now I have watched her enduring this illness I know she brought her own genius with her.'

He believed in laying it on with a trowel. It was

embarrassing, it seemed silly, to say, 'Oh, no,' but the alternative was to say, 'Yes, we are wonderful, aren't we?' But she forgot her annoyance, for a wave of scent had broken over her. It was too medicinal to be scent out of a bottle. But it made her think of gardens. It was the scent of something which grew in a big patch by the greenhouse in the house they rented every year outside Torquay, a herb called tansy. It seemed to be coming from Monsieur Kamensky's handkerchief. And that made her want to ask him a question. But it was impertinent. She did not ask it.

Though Monsieur Kamensky had not seemed to be watching Tania and her mother he was up on his feet as soon as they started to move towards the door, and was there to open it for them. Then he sighed, looked round the room, went to the hearth-rug and picked up Tania's hat, picked two strands of wool off it, and laid it on a table. Then he paused beside Nikolai and moved the lamp, so that a brighter light fell on the sheets of paper which the old man was reading, in absorption so profound that a stranger might have thought him a peasant who had never learned to read with ease. Kamensky lingered for a second to look down on him, frowning, and he came back to Laura murmuring, 'I wonder if he should have strong spectacles. Perhaps Pyotr can remember when he last went to an oculist. Now we can sit down and make ourselves comfortable. Don't trouble about your grandfather. That's a very long letter he's reading, and an interesting one. Monsieur Souvorin is the editor and the owner of the *Novoe Vremya*, our *Times*. He is not a good man, he is a Liberal at heart, and liberalism is not for Russia, but he's intelligent and what he says will keep your grandfather's mind occupied for hours. Let me put this cushion behind your back, you've been travelling all day. Now you're grown-up you'll see that there really is some sense in the way that your elders cosset themselves. But tell me, what's the question you thought of asking me a moment ago and then didn't? It's no use denying it, Miss Laura, for I saw your eyebrows go up and your lips part, and if you'd been whole Russian the words would have been out, but your English half gagged you. See, I know everything. You must own up.'

'But it was so silly, and not the sort of thing one ought to ask people.'

'Ask me,' said Monsieur Kamensky, 'I am not people. I am Alexander Gregorievitch.'

'This is all twaddle, like tea with the headmistress or the vicar calling,' thought Laura, 'but he likes me. It's nice to be liked by almost anybody.' She said aloud with a smile, 'The truth is, I smelt your handkerchief, and I remembered how you had told me last time I was here that you went straight from your home in South Russia to Moscow High School, and it was the first time you had ever felt the cold of the North, and you got such terrible chilblains and your grandmother made up a herbal ointment for them – it was you who told me that, wasn't it?'

'Yes, it was me,' said Monsieur Kamensky. 'And I probably told you that it was the first time she had shown me any kindness since I had broken it to her that I would rather be an engineer than a priest.'

'You didn't, actually,' said Laura, untruthfully. 'You were going to tell me, and someone came into the room. Tell me now.' He might as well tell her the story over again, it would be something to talk about.

'Well, if you are so kind as to listen to me, I'll admit to you that the news made her really horrid to me. She gave me nothing to eat except *kasha* – I don't suppose you know what that is.'

'Of course I do, it's porridge.'

'And she didn't mind if she burned it. This was terrible, because up till then she had given me very good things to eat, like the beef and cabbage stew we call *stschi*, and those little stuffed pastry turnovers called *piroki*, and all sorts of wonderful soups, and she was very good with mushrooms. And all those titbits stopped the minute I chose to be an engineer. If I may speak of such things, it was as if I had declared myself in love with some undesirable girl, when all I had done was to avow a passion for nuts and bolts, dynamos, and accumulators. Then one day it all ended, as suddenly as it had begun. The weather got cold, and I started having chilblains, and they were so painful that every time I had to put on my boots or take them

31

off, the tears ran down my cheeks, and one day it happened that she was passing through the hall when I was putting on my boots and suddenly she thrust back my head and glared down at me. "You're crying," she said, "have you at last repented of your wickedness in turning away from the service of God and breaking the heart of your grandmother who so loves you?" I couldn't bear it. I shouted at her, "Don't talk nonsense, this is something real, I have chilblains." She went into the kitchen without saying a word and I thought she would write to my parents and tell them to take me home. But when I came back in the late afternoon the house was full of the smell of tansy ointment and there was *stschi* for dinner. And she put the tansy ointment on my chilblains and gave me two platefuls of *stschi*, and we never had another cross word.' He stopped, silently chuckling.

She could not understand the story and though she smiled back, she raised her eyebrows. He explained, 'About what it is to be a priest, and what it is to be an engineer, she had not the faintest idea. But chilblains, they had always been in her world, since her childhood, and she knew all about them and how they hurt. So her heart bled for me.' He nodded, looking asiatic, his drooping eyelids smooth as wax in a chemist's pot, the corners of his mouth turning up in minute folds. 'That taught me a lesson I've always found it useful to remember if I have to deal with difficult men. When they are hard they are probably dealing with things they do not understand. If one brings them back to what is familiar to them they become soft.'

Absently she thought, 'How funny. He is talking as if he were someone important, like my grandfather, like my father. But perhaps he sometimes builds things that are quite big, bridges and dams, and then he might have people under him.' Aloud she asked, 'What did she look like, your grandmother?'

'Like a wooden doll. With two red spots on her cheeks. I have often wondered since then whether she suffered from a skin disease, or was vain and had heard that great ladies had their own ways of keeping beautiful in their old age, and tried to imitate them and use rouge, without knowing how to go about it.'

'And her house, what was that like?'

'It was a village house, because it was right on the outskirts of Moscow: wooden, and built end-on to the street. There were birches by the roadside, and inside the garden lilacs and a summerhouse, big enough for us to have meals there when the family came to visit her. And quite a long path laid out in pebbles, black and white arranged in circles and diamonds, made by my grandfather with his own hands so that my grandmother could walk up and down when it was wet underfoot. And at the end of the path beyond the summerhouse some more birches, which he had planted specially. My grandmother loved birch trees, she was a sylvan creature inside her doll's body. Her great delight was to go out into the forest and picnic, even when she was very old.'

'Mother always says there aren't enough birches in England,' said Laura.

'You look as if you were dreaming when we speak of the Russia where you have never been,' said Kamensky, 'and your voice grows warm.' Laura had been congratulating herself on keeping a conversation going though it bored her, just as grown-ups did. But that was pretence. She had liked hearing about that village house. He went on, 'But you haven't told me what it was you were going to ask, and then didn't.'

'Why, that was nothing. Simply I thought, it's summertime and why should Monsieur Kamensky have chilblains in summer-time? I wondered where you'd been.'

'You have an eye for little things,' said Kamensky. 'That you don't get from your grandfather. The little things he never notices. I could surprise you if I told you how unobservant he is. I don't think he has ever had his watch stolen from his waistcoat, but I can't think why. And, Miss Laura, you were right in being ashamed to ask that question, for the answer's embarrassing. Here I am, Alexander Gregorievitch Kamensky, a grown man, and so much more than grown that my hair is getting thin and my waist is getting thick, and I've taken degrees at the Universities of Moscow and Berlin, and I've built hydro-electric installations at which nobody dared to look down their nose. But I've no sense at all. Some things make an idiot of me still. When I pass a lake shining in the sunshine, I have to swim in it, even if the wind cuts like a knife. That's

33

what I did a fortnight ago, and that's why I got chilblains in June, and reek of tansy. Now you'll despise me for being silly.'

'I don't,' said Laura. 'I got a cold last week because I woke up in the middle of the night and saw the moon was rising over the trees in the Square and I hung out of the window for hours. I just couldn't go back to bed. That was silly, if you like. I had to go to a party two days later, and I looked awful.'

'The trouble with us,' said Kamensky, smiling, 'is that we're both of us poets, and so you get a little red nose and I get chilblains. And such beautiful emotions we had, you as you watched the moon rising, I as I watched the sun sparkling on the water. But let me tell you that what we're engaged in isn't trivial. The philosophers have busied themselves with it. You and I, young lady, are exemplifying the dialectic process. The great Hegel discovered it. Life advances by contradictions, so first we surrender ourselves, you and I, to a positive state of poetic rapture, and then we pass into a negative anti-poetic state, chilblains for me and a cold in the head for you; and we should pass into a third state of synthesis, when we reconcile these two opposites. And so we have. We're sitting here agreeing that swimming in the lake and watching the moon were worthwhile, all the same.' Suddenly his hand closed over her wrists and she frowned at him in surprise. 'Your mother and your grandmother have come back into the room. I think the Countess has come back to speak to you. It would be good if you did not show her that you noticed she was not well.'

She went to meet Sofia, who said through a fixed smile, 'I've returned to bother you because I won't be seeing you again today. Tania says I must go to bed now and have my dinner there. She's right. The church made me tired. But I haven't yet said welcome to you, I haven't yet told you how I've waited for you, my little one, and thought you'd never come.' Laura lowered her face to be kissed, and a timid expression spread over her grandmother's face, as if modesty prevented her intruding her altered self on someone young. The alteration was great. In the past she had kissed the children with an official air, as if she were conferring an honour, pinning on her kisses like orders. Now Laura had to kiss her, and under her lips her grandmother's cheek felt unlike flesh, hot and dry and in texture like some thin woven material. She forced herself to give the second kiss on the other cheek slowly and placidly.

The old woman clasped the girl's hands to her breast, which felt strange, just like some bones knocked together anyhow. 'You are like your cousin Nadine, you are like my son Vladimir's Nadine,' she told her. The old man at his table in the corner suddenly cried out, and everybody turned to look at him. He threw the letter he was reading on the floor and exclaimed, 'A disgusting mind! Souvorin has a disgusting mind!' His wife turned to Tania and out of the shelter of her arms said in a thin and distant voice, 'If only we were in Russia. Oh, if we were only back in Russia.'

Nikolai, slumped deeply in his chair, growled softly, 'If only we were back in Russia,' and then Tania repeated it, in a flat, loud voice, so loudly that it was shocking. They were all still and silent for a moment. Then Sofia sighed, 'Take me to bed.' Monsieur Kamensky went to open the door for them, and Laura dropped on her knees to pick up the sheets of paper scattered at Nikolai's feet. She wished her mother had not said she wanted to go back to Russia in that voice; it had sounded like someone tearing cotton. She might have said that she would like to take her children with her. And would she not care about leaving the house in Radnage Square? Did she not love it as they all did? There was also Papa to be thought of; but now Laura seemed to herself to be saying something that was not true, just for the sake of saying it. She thought, looking round for someone to blame, 'I hate my grandfather, there is trouble all round him.' But as she stretched up to put the papers back on the table, she saw that tears were in his eyes, tears that ran down the deep furrows by his nose and shone like pale topazes on his yellow skin.

2

BY THE TIME the victoria turned out of the Rue de Rivilo into the wide Place de la Concorde, Laura had long ceased to give her mind to what her grandfather was telling Monsieur

Kamensky, not that it was uninteresting, but one cannot go on and on listening for ever. She turned her eyes on the calm stone matrons representing the French provincial capitals, long-necked and wide-breasted, on their thrones round the edge of the Place, and she uttered a sound of protest and passion. Nikolai, whose senses had long been sharpened by fear, heard, and grumbled, as if resenting an infringement of his exclusive right to distress, 'What's the matter, child?'

She answered, 'It's the statue of Strasbourg. I always feel so sorry for the French when I see that figure, draped in black. It must be awful to have part of one's country taken by the Germans.'

Nikolai growled, 'The French lost Strasbourg, they lost Alsace, they lost Lorraine, which they pretended was sacred to them because of their saint, though they are deeply infidel. A Republican people deserves to lose all, must lose all.'

'But,' objected Laura, 'when France lost Strasbourg and Alsace-Lorraine, France wasn't a Republic, it was ruled by the Emperor.'

'No matter,' said Nikolai, 'the French were a people who had once had it in them to make France a Republic, and had it in them to make it one again.'

'Have you noticed, Count,' asked Kamensky, 'that it is only the very young who look at the statues in our cities? As we get older we keep our eyes for staring at the invisible.'

'But it can't be right that we should be punished for what we're doing long before we've done it,' persisted Laura. 'We might never do it.'

'God would foresee that we were going to do it,' said Nikolai. She never remembered him talking about religion at their previous meetings, but now he never stopped alluding angrily to God. 'Thus it is right that He should punish the apparently innocent. Perhaps that is the explanation of my own destiny. Perhaps I have been rightly disgraced, though I am innocent of the offences they pretended, for the reason that before I die I am going to commit a great sin which will deserve such chastisement.'

'That none of us will believe,' said Monsieur Kamensky. 'It is more likely that you are simply being rewarded by God for your goodness and your good deeds by exceptional opportunities to be at one with His Son in suffering.'

'I do not feel the kiss of congratulation upon my cheek,' said Nikolai. 'I think I am being punished, punished as men punish other men, for my sins. God is just and I sin in doubting it. Oh, God!' he muttered. 'I have recklessly thrown aside Thy fatherly gift of glory.' He was speaking another sort of Russian now, the Old Slavonic of the Liturgy. 'And among sinners I have dissipated the wealth which Thou gavest to me, wherefore I cry to Thee with the voice of the Prodigal. I have sinned before Thee, O merciful God, receive me, a penitent, and make me as one of Thy hired servants.'

'Do you understand what your grandfather is saying, Miss Laura?' asked Monsieur Kamensky.

'Yes, most of it. Mamma's taken us all to the Embassy Church ever since we were little, and the priests used to give us lessons.'

'Wasn't that a great trouble to you, "a great bore", as you say in English?' asked Monsieur Kamensky, with a smile that offered complicity.

She did not return the smile, she thought it impertinent of him to suggest that anything which her mother made her do could be a trouble or a bore. So she kept silent and looked ahead, to the golden light of the late afternoon behind the Arc de Triomphe, while her grandfather repeated, 'Wherefore I cry to Thee with the voice of the Prodigal: I have sinned before thee, O merciful God, receive me a penitent and make me as one of Thy hired servants.' But a tremor ran through him, he drove his strong white teeth down into his lower lip. 'But to bring such an accusation against a Diakonov! When we have served Russia since the day of Monomach!' He raised his stick, leaned forward, and drove the ferrule into a soft spot of the coachman's back between the ribs and the spine. 'Drive home,' he shouted, 'drive home, and hurry.'

Monsieur Kamensky said pleasantly to the coachman, 'The route by the Rue François Premier is the quickest, if it looks clear let us go that way.'

In the unhappy apartment Sofia Andreievna was sitting in the curtained dusk, and looked up at them with the protruding eyes of one stretched on the rack, and told them that she was much better. She was giving tea to a dull, sad man and woman in poorish clothes, she rose when Nikolai came in and greeted him with long, soft, involved speeches, which he returned as lengthily and not so softly, but in a muted roar that was meant to be humble. He stood huge above these people, but he bent his hugeness, he bowed to them. Laura curtseyed and turned away and left the room, going along the dark corridors to her mother's bedroom, but in there could not at first see her. Then her ear caught a quick gabble from somewhere near the floor, and she looked down and saw her mother's hindquarters – she really did not know what one called that part of the body when it belonged to one's mother. It was up in the air, her back sloping down to her golden head, which was right down on the carpet. Laura stood and stared. Had Tania really been prostrating herself, as she had seen the wilder-looking members of the congregation doing at the Russian Church in the Rue Darou, had she been beating her forehead on the floor?

Her mother sat up on her haunches and looked at her with vague eyes which focused sharply as she cried, 'For heaven's sake, don't stand there looking so English. You have to help us. Mamma has to go into a Clinic at Passy.'

'To have her teeth out?'

Tania stood up and brushed her skirts and seemed to reflect. 'Yes. To have her teeth out.'

'How can I help?'

'We can't have your grandfather in Paris while it's going on. He'd want to visit her in the Clinic. Also he might not approve of the people who are treating her. They're Poles. You know how we Russians feel about Poles. He'd make a fuss. Grandmamma ought to be kept perfectly quiet. You must take him away. We simply must get him out into the country.'

'I quite see that. He simply roared at those people who are having tea with Grandmamma. It must have hurt her head no end. He was being quite nice to them, though.'

'Oh, he would be,' said Tania. 'He has a great respect for that couple. The man's blind and his wife has been wonderful to him.'

38

'I think this must be another lot,' said Laura, 'the man didn't look blind.'

'He doesn't but he is. He's very proud, apparently, and he hates to be helpless, so he tries to look as if he could see. Papa and Mamma do a lot for them and admire them enormously. But anyway, you've got to go and take Papa to stay with Aunt Florence at the villa at Mûres-sur-Mer. Mercifully she's settled down there for the summer already.'

'What a lark,' said Laura. 'When I bathe will the old lady still insist on that footman who is at least seventy-five standing with the surf boiling round his boots in case I drown? The only thing is I shall get fat with all those interminable meals and nobody talking so that there's nothing to do but eat. And I'll do the wrong thing all the time, you do realise that?'

'Perfectly,' said Tania. 'It's so hard to do the right thing there. It isn't fair, Uncle Konstantin having married an American. It isn't fair on us Continentals that there are Americans at all. There's this English language and one learns it, and there's this English literature and one reads that, and one learns English customs, calling things by the wrong names, somebody was at the House and it's really Christ Church. And then some accident like your uncle marrying Aunt Florence, suddenly acquaints one with the fact that there's also an American English language and a literature written in it.'

'Well, Mark Twain's lovely,' said Laura.

'I know, but there's William Dean Howells,' said Tania. 'He's a friend of Aunt Florence, and if she asks you to read his books aloud to her, you must.'

'Will that be awful?'

'Not nearly awful enough,' said Tania. 'About a life unnaturally unawful. Or is one,' she asked, going to the dressing table and looking at herself in the triple mirror, 'specially unlucky? Are other people's lives perhaps not awful at all? And there are mysteries upon mysteries about America. Thank goodness you're going to Mûres-sur-Mer, it would be worse if you had to take your grandfather to Aunt Florence's family house in the States, at a place called Newport. They attach immense importance to it being at Newport, it's like having a *palazzo* at Venice, and when you get there there's not just no

Venice, there's nothing, nothing at all. We were astonished, your father and I.' She ran a comb through her hair. 'But help all you can. Let your grandfather talk to you if he seems to bother Aunt Florence, keep on curtseying to her; she thinks that's a guarantee that you're well brought up, though why should it be, everybody can bend their knees, and try to fix your mind on the game if she wants you to play bezique, and always try to behave as if you were entirely English, it goes down best. Oh, darling,' she said, laying down the comb and resting her elbows on the table and looking at herself in the mirror censoriously, 'I should have arranged this better, but I haven't, and I've got to ask you to do this. But I know it isn't very nice for you.'

'It's not so dreadful either,' said Laura, 'and I don't suppose it'll be for very long.'

Tania took up her comb again. 'I don't know how long it'll be,' she said in a choked voice. 'I really don't understand much about your grandmother's illness.'

Laura went to the dressing-table and took the comb out of her mother's hand, and played with the abundant hair, winding bright strands of it round her fingers, and rubbed her face against her mother's shoulder. 'Don't be so worried,' she said. 'Teeth are nothing nowadays, we're not in the Middle Ages. But I wish you weren't unhappy about this when you've been so upset at home. I thought this visit was going to be lovely for you.'

Her mother repeated, 'Upset at home?'

'I am a fool,' thought Laura, 'I'll just have to go straight on.' She said aloud, 'Well, weren't you? I thought you were.'

'No,' said her mother slowly, as if she were completely bewildered. 'I haven't been upset about anything. Why should I be?'

'You've looked it sometimes. You always look beautiful, I don't mean you've ever been plain or anything like that, but once or twice I've thought you were worried about something.'

'My eyes have been getting inflamed lately,' said Tania. 'I never remember to use the prescription Dr Carey gave me. I may sometimes have looked as if I'd been crying.' She took up a powder-puff and passed it over her face and throat.

'Well, it was rather that I was thinking of,' said Laura. 'Yes, I have thought you had been crying, several times. I'm glad you weren't. And don't worry about me at Mûres-sur-Mer. I'll look after Grandfather all right, and anyway I'll get some swimming.'

'But tell me,' said Tania, 'what did you think I was upset about at home?'

'I didn't know.'

'Oh, tell the truth, Laura,' said Tania. 'It's such an odd idea to have got into your head. What could go wrong at home?'

'Well, I thought perhaps Papa had lost a lot of money,' replied Laura. 'He has seemed worried, and so have you, and people's fathers seem to lose their money. Two of the girls in my class say theirs suddenly got poor. They say it was awful, like a hurricane. One day the money was there and the next day it wasn't.'

'How absurd you are,' said Tania, turning to her looking-glass and again combing her hair as if trouble had got into it as knots get into knitting wool. 'But I suppose if you got that idea it may have been quite frightening. But never worry about that. We're very fortunate. If Papa lost all his money we should still be all right. Your grandfather was very generous to us when we married, and there'll always be a lot of money coming to us from Russia, and it's all from things that can't run away, mines and railways and oil-wells. But do tell me next time you get an idea like that. I hate to think of you worrying over nothing.'

'I didn't really worry much,' said Laura, 'except that I'd prefer you to be all right, you know. When do we go to Aunt Florence?'

'In two days' time,' said Tania. But her eyes were on Laura's like an unhappy dog's. 'But why should you suddenly have got this idea about your father losing his money? You never think of money. Osmund likes to save it and Lionel likes to spend it, but you've hardly heard of it. Why should you develop a theory that we were going to be poor and worry about it? Are you sure you weren't worried about something else? Do tell me.'

'It was the two girls in my class that made me frightened,' Laura persisted calmly. She wondered at her own power of lying. 'They mind being poor awfully. They're not going to be presented at Court. Does the Mûres-sur-Mer train leave in the morning or the afternoon?'

'Some time fairly early in the morning. And nothing can happen to you. Pyotr is going ahead with the heavy luggage and the bedlinen. Grandpapa and Grandmamma simply will not understand that that is unnecessary in the West. Then the little Kamensky will take you down to the Gare du Nord and put you in the train, a slow train that stops at Mûres-sur-Mer, and Pyotr will meet you on the platform. I can't see that anything can go wrong.'

'Can't you? You should read the Litany,' said Laura. 'There's always earthquakes, for one thing.' She felt that things had eased enough for her to kiss her mother. They clung together and Laura thought, reading the tension of the familiar body in her arms, 'She's glad to be so close to me that I can't see her face. What can have happened?' She rubbed her own face against Tania's shoulder as if she herself were the one that needed comfort. A tremor warned her that her mother was near to weeping. Laura released her and walked over to the window, saying, 'We're going to have another gorgeous sunset. Do you suppose it really is because of that earthquake in Martinique that we're having all these marvellous sunsets?'

'It wasn't an earthquake, it was a volcanic eruption,' said Tania, and Laura said, 'I was practising, I was being polite to it, just as I've got to be to Aunt Florence,' and Tania said in a sleepy and unconcerned voice, 'But it's more polite to call an earthquake a volcanic eruption than the other way round, there's something very dashing about a volcano, and now I must go to Mamma. She's been too long with those people, however admirable they are. She must lie down.'

'Do your hair first, Mummie,' Laura told her, 'you look very White Queen,' and kissed her once again before they went along the dark corridor. 'Should I hold her hand?' Laura asked herself. 'No, better not.'

But the blind man and his wife had left, and Sofia Andreievna had already gone to her room, and Tania followed her there. Laura joined her grandfather and Monsieur Kamensky,

42

who had opened the french window and were standing on the narrow balcony, watching the street below.

'You see, Count, you needn't have worried,' said Kamensky, 'she's got him across the street quite safely.'

'All the same I wish that I'd had the forethought not to let Pyotr go off for the evening,' said Nikolai. 'I'd have liked to send them home in the carriage, they've such a long way to go, and one should do such a couple honour.'

'Look at them making their way through the crowd,' said Kamensky. 'The crowd are such mediocrities, and they too look mediocre. Nobody just seeing them like that could guess that here are two who could be to Paris as the one just man might have been to Sodom. Even from here we can't easily pick them out.'

'I can't tell which they are,' said Laura. 'Are they the ones behind the two priests?'

'No, you're out by a dozen yards,' said Kamensky. 'See, stand behind me and look over my shoulder where my hand is pointing. There, you can see the glazier walking along with his pane of glass behind him. Well, they're passing him now.'

'But I think there is something special about them,' said Laura. 'But you are right about the other people, they do look alike.'

'How unjust life is,' said Kamensky, 'for I, and anyone else who knows you, could pick you out of the crowd in a second, even if you were a long way further off.'

'Why, how would you do that?' she asked to please him. It never interested her to hear anything about herself.

'Quite easily. Nobody else walking down the Avenue Kléber now, or at any other time of the day, has hair quite as golden as yours,' he said, in a gentle educative voice, as if he were a schoolmaster demonstrating a theorem on a blackboard.

'They are hurrying along like rats rushing into the granary when a sack has been spilt,' said Nikolai, resting his arms on the balcony and leaning right over. 'A people without God,' he pronounced.

'How can he tell that,' thought Laura, 'by looking down on the tops of their heads? All he can fairly say is, "A people with lots and lots of bowler hats."'

Kamensky said, 'Ah, yes, Count, a people without God or even the hunger for God.' Again he turned to Laura like a schoolmaster and said, 'Indeed, you couldn't hide from any friend, even if he couldn't see you. You know how it is when one comes up to this apartment by night. The lamp on the staircase comes on as soon as the concierge opens the front door, but the lift lumbers up so slowly that the lamp goes out before one gets to this storey, and one steps out on to a pitch-dark landing. Well, if we met there in the blackness, just the two of us, with no light coming from anywhere, I should know in a second that it was you.'

She could not have been less interested. She had just invented in her fancy a little Frenchman, the bald kind with a pointed beard, who was complaining to Nikolai, 'I asked for bowlers and you gave me a God.' Would Mummie think that funny? One never could be sure. To be polite to Monsieur Kamensky, because he was so nice, she asked, 'How would you know it was me?'

'Because, just as nobody else has hair like yours, nobody else has a voice like yours. It is rather high, but not shrill, and suddenly it cracks and it is as if a charming icicle had splintered into shining fragments.'

'Something funny happened to my voice when I had my tonsils out,' she said.

'But, of course, if I were walking down the Avenue Kléber, and your hair was hidden under a hat and you were alone and not speaking to anybody, there is another thing I would notice about you.'

Smiling as if she were eager to hear what it was, she thought, 'How odd, he would notice me. I would not notice him. How unkind of me.'

'I would say to myself,' he continued, ' "How wonderful, a minute ago I would have sworn that round me there were only Frenchmen and a few English and Americans, and I was a lonely foreigner, but now I am not alone any more, for here is a Russian young lady." '

It did not strike her at once what he had said. Then she exclaimed joyfully, 'No, you can't really mean that! Oh, I would be pleased if that were true. You actually think I look Russian?'

'Indeed I do,' said Kamensky, 'and I will even be more exact. It is not only that you have a certain resemblance to the ladies in St Petersburg and other parts of Russia who are your relatives. It is that in every Russian town there is always one young lady who makes the men of the town discontented with even the nicest of all the other young ladies; and all those special young ladies have something in common with you.'

'My head's turning round and round,' said Nikolai, pushing himself back from the balcony railing, his great head falling back on the thick column of his throat. 'I must sit down.'

They helped his rocking hugeness to his arm-chair. As the old man sank down among the cushions his loosely swinging arm struck Kamensky's spectacles from his nose. 'Go, Alexander Gregorievitch,' he panted, 'get my medicine from my night-table. Not the white tablets, the yellow.' Kamensky said, 'Yes, yes, dear Count,' and bent down to pick up his spectacles, but Nikolai cried, in a weak, howling whisper, 'What are you doing? My tablets, my tablets, I must have them.' Kamensky straightened himself, sighed, and hurried from the room.

Laura picked up the spectacles and sat down with them on her lap. 'Grandfather is being ridiculous,' she thought. 'He brought all this on himself, hanging over the balcony, it's quite a height. That's all it is. He should be ashamed to make such a fuss about nothing when it's Grandmamma who's really ill. I wish I could tell him so. I can't think why nobody ever stands up to him.' To pass the time she played with the objects on the occasional table beside her: a lapis lazuli paper-weight, a miniature of one of her ancestresses, young but many-chinned among ringlets and scarves, a snuff-box made of that spectral black and silver mixture of alloys known as niello, its design depicting the Cathedral of St Sophia at Kiev, a round box made of varnished plaited straw and containing some sugar almonds rough with age. Again she had the feeling that the bric-à-brac in this apartment were getting old in the same way as its occupants, they were tedious as if they were deafish and blindish and slow. She wondered why Kamensky had not come back, and reflected that it might be hard for him to find the tablets without his spectacles, and picked them up, ready to take them to him. But he had probably not come back because he had gone to tell Tania that her father was ill. 'He does everything that's necessary, always,' she said to herself, and for lack of anything else to do she put his spectacles on her own nose.

She burst out laughing. The lenses were plain glass. Now she liked him more than ever. Her father had told her that many Japanese and Hindus with perfect sight wore spectacles simply for the sake of looking wise, and it was delightful that Monsieur Kamensky, who was so modest and kind and self-less, should have, as his only detectable fault, this innocent vanity which did not harm a soul.

'Grandfather, grandfather,' she called, folding the gold wings over her ears, eager to let him into the joke, for she knew he was really nice, and would not laugh at Monsieur Kamensky except in a loving way.

But Nikolai stared at her icily. 'Take off those spectacles at once,' he said. 'Girl, I am ashamed of you. You are not a child, if you had been reared in Russia you would be a married woman by now. You should have learned long ago that you should never touch people's personal possessions when they are out of the room.'

There was no foundation for her dream that she could defy him. 'I am sorry, Grandfather,' she said, and took off the spectacles.

Kamensky was back in the room, carrying a little silver tray with a tube of tablets and a glass of water on it. 'You had better take two,' he told Nikolai.

'It says one on the box,' the old man grumbled, 'and medicine is not for me. Except for quinine, which I took when I was soldiering in those accursed marshes, I never tasted a pharmacist's mess till I was over fifty. No, one tablet will be enough.'

'Ah, but the doctor said you should take two when you were seriously upset. Truly, truly, he said that. I heard him say it, and so, I think, did you. It is not a matter of being ill. There is nothing wrong with your body as yet, dear Count. But your mind is troubled and that drains away your forces. And this afternoon we had a long drive.'

Nikolai swallowed the one tablet and then said, timidly, 'But there is something else which makes me not want to take this second tablet.'

'What can that be?' asked Kamensky, tenderly. He had left the tray on the table and was kneeling in front of Nikolai with the glass of water in one hand and the second tablet on the palm of the other. She wondered how he managed to look neither servile nor absurd.

'I am afraid of that little tablet,' Nikolai owned. 'I think there is a conspiracy against me. If there is, perhaps these tablets are poisoned. One I have often taken, and I have lived. But two? I'm quite simply frightened.'

'Count, you'd be very foolish, considering all things, if you didn't look warily at any tablets. But these were made up from the prescription given you in St Petersburg by our dear Dr Dervize and repeated by Dr Lefebure here, and I had it made up by a chemist in the Rue du Faubourg St. Honoré who hadn't the faintest idea who I was or for whom I was acting. I simply walked in off the street and waited till it was ready. Take this second tablet and sit for a minute with your eyes closed. Really, you'll feel much better.'

When he turned from the old man and set the tray down on the table, Laura gave him his spectacles. In case he should guess she had tried them on and knew his secret, she said, 'I was afraid you wouldn't find my grandfather's medicine when I saw you'd gone off without these,' and he answered, with a smile of complicity, 'So was I, but I didn't dare come back without it, so I got one of the servants to help me.'

It startled her that he lied so quickly and so well; as quickly as she had lied to Tania a little while before, and rather better. She supposed that this pretence must matter a great deal to him, and could not imagine why. But then she had no idea of what went on inside any human being except herself. What was happening inside Tania, inside Papa? She began to think of Susie Staunton, she could not imagine why. But now Susie seemed part of their lives, though it was only two years since they had first met her. Cousin Angus had taken Tania and Lionel and her to see his son play polo at one of those clubs out in the western distances of London, an old house and its gardens and parklands, which had got stranded in a criss-cross

47

of little greyish streets, down near that part of the Thames where one went to see the Boat Race. Between matches she and Lionel had loitered under a tulip tree, enchanted by the great white flowers which were so oddly up instead of down, while Cousin Angus and Tania did the drill, which Laura watched with half an eye, because it was pretty. Over the lawn sauntered the men with their grey top-hats and black coats and striped trousers, the women with their hats like trays of flowers and their bright fan-tailed dresses, each couple halting every now and then to greet another couple. The women did the talking, standing face to face, digging their frilly parasols into the turf a few inches in front of them and crossing their hands on the crooks of their parasols, which showed off their graceful wrists, and tilting back their heads to keep the hat-brims from nodding over their eyes, so that they all seemed to be taking a dashing, defiant conversational line. The men, standing soberly by, might have been members of another species, who kept these lively multicoloured creatures as pets and were exercising them. In each gloved male hand there might have been a lash, a collar round every female throat under the net and lace.

But if Tania had been a sheep-dog she would never have passed the obedience tests. Though her cousin's fingers hovered near his hat-brim, in readiness for farewell, she kept on talking to the woman opposite her with such absorption that she let her parasol fall, and did not pretend to mind when the two men bent to pick it up, but turned and beckoned to Laura and Lionel as if to tell them to come quick before the rainbow faded.

That was not surprising. It would have been a pity to miss the really extraordinary hair which shone under the Stranger's black hat. It was golden, but not like Tania's or her own, which was dark as the gold used by Egyptian and Roman jewellers; Susie's was like the bloom on the petals of certain flowers, the celandine and the kingcup, yellow and yet white. Her lips too were extraordinary. It was as if an artist had painted a perfect mouth and smudged it, not from carelessness, but to get a certain effect. What effect? Just that effect, just what one saw. But what did one see? One had to look again, and never was

48

sure. Everything about this woman was unexpected, like the flowers on the tulip-tree, which were up instead of down.

Nobody had ever said that Susie Staunton had anything to do with the darkness that had fallen on Radnage Square. There was no real reason to suppose that she had. When they had got home in the hot late afternoon Papa had been drinking hock and seltzer in the curtained drawing-room, and Tania had poured out her ecstasy over this beauty she had discovered. It had turned out that Papa had met her, ten or twelve years before. She was the daughter of a North-Country baronet, poor and unimportant, from whom he had once bought a horse, and had been married out of the schoolroom to the son of an equally poor and unimportant peer. Papa had been introduced to her by her father-in-law when he was giving the young couple tea on the terrace before they went off to some job in Canada. The husband, Tania supplied, was now in the Caribbean, she had had to come home because she could not stand the relaxing climate.

Tania added, 'I think she's poor. Her clothes look good, but what clothes wouldn't, on her?'

Papa shook his head and said he had thought nothing of the woman, wondered only why his single meeting should have stuck in his memory, and teased Tania about her enthusiasms. He had never said or done anything to suggest that he had changed his opinion of Susie: never, during all the time when she was in the house every day of the week from Monday to Friday, not just for parties, but like a relative, only more so, nor during the period which followed, when she did not come to see them any more. Odd as it was that Susie should have become a part of their lives though it was only two years since they had met, but it was odder still that she still seemed so, when it must be a full year since her name had been spoken in the house.

But perhaps her mother was making a mistake about something quite innocent her father had done. Tania had changed lately. In the past, if she had had one quality more than all others, it was self-control. She never lost her temper, though sometimes she decided to do without it for a time, as she sometimes decided to wear no jewels. But now she was being absurd about her mother's health. Though Sofia had taken fall after fall in the hunting-field and Tania had remained calm, now she was almost hysterical because the old lady had to have some teeth out. But just now it was as if everybody were moving away from the place where they had seemed rooted. Her grandfather had seemed to her in the past simply someone foreign and grand, one of the people wearing plumed hats who drove after the crowned heads in state processions, about whom she had the secret knowledge that Tania loved him, that he enjoyed giving presents and hugging silently as he gave them, and that when there were no other grown-ups about he could deliciously pretend to be a magician. But now he might belong to a different species, and one generally supposed to be extinct. If there had been men at the same time as there were mastodons and dinosaurs, he might have been one of them. He was also like someone in the Bible. When Monsieur Kamensky had knelt at her grandfather's feet, it was as if the older man were out of the Old Testament, the younger man out of the New.

Time passed. The white roses in a crystal vase on the table beside her shed one petal, then another, then another. Where people were unhappy the flowers were neglected. She pushed the petals together in a little pile. The old man opened his eyes, looked round him, and resumed his misery.

'I am quite well,' he said argumentatively. 'I was never ill.'

'That's what we thought,' said Kamensky. 'And now we know it. If you were, such a short sleep couldn't have refreshed you. There's a lot of evening left. Would you like to play a game of chess?'

'I haven't the time,' said Nikolai. 'The darkness awaits me, and there are many things of which we should talk.'

'About ideas?' said Kamensky.

'No, that is too dangerous a pleasure,' said Nikolai. 'How right Prince Shirinsky-Shikhmatov was! You have heard of him?'

'Minister of Education about 1850,' said Kamensky. 'I confess I might have failed to recognise his name had I not once benefited by a prize he instituted.'

'He made a wise decision afterwards reversed. He entirely

50

prohibited lectures on philosophy in all the Universities of Russia. He saw that speculations regarding the Creator are superfluous, since the revelations we have been given on divine authority are sufficient, but he saw that researches into the wonders of creation can never do any harm. So he encouraged the physical sciences. This must be right, because it is logical – though I have to admit that some of the students of physical sciences are among our most godless and subversive. No, I want to talk to you not about ideas, but about facts. You saw that I was afraid when I questioned you about that medicine?'

'Yes. But, as I say, it was not unreasonable.'

'You might answer differently if I opened my heart to you. I did not tell you everything. It wasn't only that I feared that those tablets might have been poisoned by my enemies. I had another fear. Let me tell you a story, and do not laugh at me, though it may strike you as absurd.'

'Miss Laura and I could never laugh at you.'

'It will comfort me a lot to confess what happened to me some years before my disgrace. I can't remember the exact date, even the year. But one day I was at my office and a member of the Poliakov family, the grain-dealers, came to see me. He happened to take from his pocket a letter from his son, a young lawyer who had gone to Warsaw on business. He thought it would interest me, but it didn't. My attention was caught by one thing, however. The letter was written on bright-red paper, and the envelope was bright-red too. At the moment I made nothing of it except as a sign that young people like to do things in a way which is obviously incorrect.'

'How long ago,' Laura asked herself, 'was this? Those young people are probably old now, and just what he approves of.'

'I should mention that I had heard some rumours that this young man had been seen with associates who could only be described as Liberals. Well, a few weeks later my official duties took me to Odessa. To Odessa,' he repeated and fell silent, staring at the floor.

After a moment or two Kamensky said comfortably, 'To Odessa.'

'Yes, to Odessa. But I've forgotten why I had to go there. It was to investigate a grave scandal, this is clear to me, something

51

to do with the misappropriation of public funds. But beyond that I'm not now sure of anything. I really am not myself just now. Many people were suspected, some of them my own officials, some of them bank employees, two or three land-speculators, and a couple of ship-owners. But which of them proved innocent and which guilty has gone from my mind.'

'Don't distress yourself, dear Count,' said Kamensky. 'It can't matter any more.'

'Not matter? To know of a group of men which were bad and which were good? That must always matter.'

'Yes, that that should be known matters more than anything else,' said Kamensky, 'but it is not we who need know it.'

'True, true, Alexander Gregorievitch,' said her grandfather, 'but how could the Tsar know except through his Ministers? And I was one of them.'

'But surely,' thought Laura, 'Monsieur Kamensky meant God and not the Tsar. He did. He's trying not to smile. But it serves him right. He was too pi when he said it.'

'It was my duty,' continued Nikolai, 'to see and hear for my master the Tsar. I fear now that my ears and eyes were already, even then, past such service, and had let me stray into a world of folly and suspicion in which I may now be a prisoner. You see, about that bright-red writing-paper.'

'That bright-red writing-paper,' Kamensky prompted him, after a minute.

'Yes, yes. There came a night when I wished to meet a man involved in this scandal, who seemed to me guilty, or at least to have compromised his honour; and for that reason I didn't like to ask the Governor, with whom I was staying, to admit him to his house. So I arranged a dinner for four persons, myself and my secretary – I forget his name, he was a person of your own sort – and this man and one of his associates, at a restaurant in the town. It was attached to a hotel, and one had to go in by a mediocre sort of café, a place where the tradespeople of the town went in the evening to drink beer and eat sausages. As I passed through it my eye was caught by a girl sitting all by herself at a table.'

Again he fell into silence.

'This girl.'

'As I say, she was sitting all by herself, though she was not —' he shot a look at Laura – 'not anything of that sort. And indeed it was quite a respectable place. But she was very young to be out alone, possibly under twenty, and she should not have been in such a café even with an escort, for she had an air of breeding, though she had done her best to lose it. She had thrown off her fur hat, it was lying on the table beside her. Everything about her showed that she no longer cared what people thought of her. It was very disagreeable. She had cut her hair and her head was covered with rough curls, as if she were a boy. She was bending right over the table, writing, and smiling as she wrote, putting out her tongue, just like a child getting on well with its first copy-book. I suppose she was very pretty. But that gave me no pleasure. So far as she was concerned there might have been nobody else in the room. A woman should not feel so. There was a pile of books lying beside her fur hat, and I tried to read the titles as I went by, for it struck me that she might be a medical student. You know I had some temporary success in closing all our schools for women doctors. Alas, that that too, like Prince Shirinsky-Shikhmatov's decision concerning the teaching of philosophy, was reversed. It was then that I saw that she was writing her letter on bright-red paper.'

Kamensky's brows were knitted. 'Now what would that be?' he asked softly, almost under his breath; and he shook his head.

'Ah, you too think it mysterious. That encourages me. But why? You may simply be thinking it was mysterious that I should think it mysterious. Well, I didn't enjoy my dinner. Whoever it was my guests were, I came to the worst conclusions about them. But when I got back to the Governor's House and went to bed I could not sleep and it wasn't because of these wretched criminals, it was because of that bright-red writing-paper. I couldn't imagine anybody well brought-up as that girl must have been brought-up, wanting to communicate with family or friends on such horrible glaring stuff, so unlike any writing-paper which it is natural and right to use. And I woke up in the middle of the night remembering that a Frenchman, a friend of my grandfather, had mentioned in his memoirs that just before the Revolution it became the fashion among French infidels to use bright-red writing-paper. Do you think I was foolish because the next morning I sent my secretary to go round all the stationery shops in Odessa to find out if they sold such writing-paper?'

'Why shouldn't you?' replied Kamensky. 'But did you find any?'

'It was being sold everywhere. And when I examined what he brought me back I found that the watermark was sinister. It was a cock. Well, the cock is Russia. But it's France too: France, the country of anarchy and atheism, the enemy of Holy Russia, willing host of all its exiles, among whom I now, by the most horrible irony, have to count myself. And what does "the red cock" mean in our native language, Laura? Tell her, Alexander Gregorievitch.'

'It is one of the most terrible phrases in our tongue. That's what our serfs called the arson they committed in the old days when our landowners were tyrants, and still commit, in spite of all our modern reforms, when bad men incite them. It's a terrible phrase. Innocent as the Russian peasant is, he can be seduced into burning crops, granaries, forests.'

'The terrorists would feel such evil glee in using anything inscribed with that symbol,' mourned Nikolai, 'as we would feel holy glee in handling what is marked with the cross. And this writing-paper would be a useful instrument in their conspiracy against their country. It would frustrate one of the most effective measures we take for the protection of our people, the perlustration of our mail, the examination of letters through the post, a measure which the innocent have no cause to fear and which is a hardship only to the guilty.'

'How so?' asked Kamensky. 'How could this paper help the terrorists?'

'The organisers of the terror would have no reason to write their final instructions to their dupes. The most blameless letter, written on this red paper, might be an intimation that now was the time to commit a long-planned crime. And what clue would we have?'

'Why, you're right,' said Kamensky. 'It is really a most ingenious idea, and I can believe that those fiends might conceive it.'

'So it seems to you,' said Nikolai, 'and so it seemed to me. But perhaps I am wrong, and perhaps you have allowed my influence over you to persuade you into believing what is wrong. For listen. I decided I must warn the proper authorities of this danger, and I sent some sheets and envelopes of this paper to Count Brand, who was then Minister of the Interior, pointing out the sinister significance of the colour and the watermark, telling him of the passage in the Frenchman's memoirs, and conveying that the two people whom I knew used it were tainted by suspicion.'

'Well, did they find out anything?' asked Kamensky.

'It wasn't like that at all. I noticed when I dictated the letter to my secretary that he was ill at ease. But I imagined that he might be worried about being away from St Petersburg for so long, for he had a sick child. But when the Minister answered me I realised that I had been on quite the wrong tack. Count Brand is a very old friend of mine, and all our lives we have written to each other freely. But this time Brand sent me what was little more than a formal acknowledgment of my letter, and when my secretary gave it to me I knew from his manner that he had expected and feared this. He had not wished me to bring my fine discovery about the red writing-paper before another Minister, because he had thought it ridiculous and he had quite rightly feared that Brand would find it ridiculous.'

'Ah, you are jumping at conclusions – Brand may have been preoccupied, unwell —'

'No. It was his considered opinion. The next time we met it was in the corridors of Tsarskoe Selo, and he looked at me with eyes full of pity and warned me against overwork. He presumed, he presumed! He told me that I must not let the terrorists break my nerve, since that is one of the chief aims of the terrorists. He dared say that.'

'Gently, gently,' said Kamensky. 'Remember, you aren't well, and all this happened long ago. It doesn't do any good to live it all over again.'

'He dared to say it. He dared. I can't tell you how unpleasant I found it to be pitied by a man who was certainly an old friend, but whom I had never considered as an equal. I was stronger than he'd ever been, and could work harder, and God gave me greater courage. That we had proved again and again when we were young and were in the same regiment. I rode many horses he did not trust himself to mount. Many risks that I was glad to take again and again were beyond him. I have known him ride away so that he should not see me take the big water-jump on the officer's course at Kharkov. I would be silent about such things as a rule, for they are a matter of God's gift, which He has explained to us in a parable He feels no need to make us equally. But I feel obliged to mention it now, just to make plain that if Brand's nerve had not broken it was inconceivable that mine should break.'

She was glad her father was not there to hear this. But she did not mind. Quite often one wanted to brag.

'Don't let's talk of this any more,' said Kamensky. 'Count Brand is well known to be of a peculiarly sceptical, rejecting kind of intelligence, who thought anything he had not found out for himself had never happened and could never happen. To him writing-paper would not be dangerous unless it got out of its envelope and bit his hand. But none of this is of any significance today. Chess, chess, let us play chess.'

'Later. Later. Let me finish. My secretary was a good little man, full of common sense, but he was of the same mind as Brand. He thought my great discovery about the writing-paper purely absurd, half-way to a delusion. Tell me, Alexander Gregorievitch, am I mad? I have been thrown down and disgraced because certain information known only to myself and three other officials passed out of our hands, and in consequence two sacred persons were murdered by the servants of evil. The three other officials were killed by the same bomb. We may presume them innocent. Therefore I have been presumed guilty. It seems to me that I was guiltless and that I am the victim of a conspiracy. But this may not be true. It might have been that though I kept my plans secret they were insufficiently ingenious, and that the terrorists were able to guess them, and guessed correctly the three routes we had planned, from which we chose only one at the last moment, and that thus they ambushed them all, and were able to strike when they saw the grand dukes. Look how the facts go round and round in my head. I speak in sentences like carousels, I want to tell you that all over again, but I must get on, sane men do not repeat themselves. I don't think I did fail. I think my plans were sufficiently ingenious, and I think they were efficiently executed. I believe I was betrayed. I told you about those marks on the wood of the drawer in my desk, where I kept the orders for that day. They were faint marks, and other people might have missed them, but I still have eyes like a hawk. They were like pencil-strokes which someone had rubbed out, all but the last least trace. They could have been drawn round documents so that they could be taken away and replaced exactly where they had been before. Yet the police agents said that they might have been marks left by the carpenters. But what guidance could a carpenter need on the floor of a drawer? And if they were marks made by a spy, what can that mean except that someone copied my keys? And what keys they were! That was more a safe than a drawer. Only a familiar of mine, with liberty to come and go about my office, with the right to spend hours there unchallenged, could have copied those keys. Oh, God, had those pencil-strokes any meaning which would have halted the attention of a sane man?'

'But, Count,' said Kamensky, 'don't you know quite well, as you know that you have a beard, that you are sane?'

'Well, I know that I can't be very mad. I was always a capable administrator, even to the last, and my family was happy round me, though as you're aware I have from time to time had disagreements with my sons. But you also know that that happened rarely and it was always their fault and never mine, and they were always humbled and came back to me on their hands and knees, and I raised them up by my forgiveness, and it was as if it had never happened. But I may have become a little mad as the years went on. Seeing connections, you know, between things in fact unconnected. Like the old woman you find in every village, who comes on a branch on the road blown down from a tree by a gale, and thinks it has been laid there by the butcher as a sign to the baker that the day has come for them to fulfil the plot they have long had in the hatching, and there will be arsenic in the next loaf she buys. I might be like that old woman, for God is no respecter of persons. He has turned my hair white as if I were anybody.'

'I worked under you for many years,' said Kamensky, 'and I learned that you were a man of many facets, some of which would surprise you. But none of them ever made me think of a mad old woman in a village.'

'Don't speak to me in that nurse's voice,' said Nikolai, looking at him with something almost as cold as dislike. 'Tell me the truth, I am dying for lack of it.'

'You need not die. You are right in believing yourself to be the victim of a conspiracy. Let me tell you how I know this. You've told me many things, quite trivial in themselves, which dovetail into a design we can't imagine coming into being by accident. To speak of only one thing, I was particularly impressed by what you told me about the man who came in the beginning and the end of the winter to see to the lead roof on the Ministry cupola and how you met him in the corridor, at a strange hour for a maintenance worker to be on his job and —'

'Stop, stop,' groaned Nikolai, 'we are back with the pencil-strokes in the drawer, with the bright-red writing-paper. Give me no more sympathy and sweetness, you who ought to have been a monk, be an engineer and give me real proof that I am not mad, for I am in torment.'

He was doing all the things that Laura did when she had to stop herself crying: blinking, pouting, raising his eyebrows, swallowing. She went to him and knelt at his feet and kissed his hands. It was a Russian thing to do, but she found it quite easy.

Kamensky stammered, 'Count, I have a real proof. But it has nothing to do with fact. Not with facts that one can test and make a note of for the next edition of the encyclopedia. Count, consider I could not be here if there were not a conspiracy against you. You may remember that when the grand dukes were killed I was far away, in Norway, working at that experimental power station north of Bergen. It was long before the news of your troubles reached me, and I could not understand the situation. I did not believe that the catastrophe had been caused by negligence on your part, for you are a perfect administrator, you might be a German. There were only two alternatives. Either your mind had failed you, or you were the victim of betrayal from within the Ministry, of a terrorist conspiracy, such as both you and I know so well. It was intolerable for me not to be with you in your misfortune. It was for that reason that I threw up my Norwegian post and came here to work in France. But I knew quite well that, if the first alternative was the case, my journey was in vain. If your mind was disordered, then your disgrace was the will of God, and there would be nothing anyone could do for you, except leave you to the care of God. You would have been rapt from me. I could not have reached you in the place where you would then have been, to have the honour of serving you. But if you were the victim of a conspiracy, if you were a martyr, then God was working on you through the wills of men, and my will also was a weapon. I could come close to you and fight for you with my weapons. When I came to you, you were here, you had not been caught up by the sleeve of God, you were not rapt from me. You are here, I assure you, you are here with your wife, you are with your daughter, you are with Miss Laura, you are with me, you are with Holy Russia. Therefore I know God has not disordered your mind. If he had, I should be lost and alone. But I am not. This proof lives only in my inner life, but you will have to forget all that you know before you can doubt it for that reason.'

The old man whispered, 'Alexander Gregorievitch, Alexander Gregorievitch, I believe, Alexander Gregorievitch.' He sank low in his chair and turned his face away from them, and presently was still. The dusk silted up in the room, weakly diluted by the flame before the icon in the corner. Outside the window in the tall grey houses across the avenue the lit rooms were yellow oblongs. They could hear Nikolai's breathing and the sound of the city. The clock struck a gentle quarter, and the sleeping man stirred but did not wake. The doorhandle turned and Kamensky hissed, 'Hush, Aglaia,' and she whispered, 'No light?' He whispered back, 'No light.' When the door had closed again he said softly, 'Miss Laura, that didn't wake him, you can go to your mother now.'

On the threshold she mouthed close to his ear, 'You're very good to my grandfather.'

59

'No, it is you who were good.'

'I did nothing.'

'You listened hard. He was aware of it. It is all that matters to him now.'

She went along the corridor, her eyes wet, and sat down on a carved Italian chest until she could be sure that they would stay dry. On the wall opposite hung a Persian rug, its lighter colours shining through the shadows. It was one of the oriental carpets a Polish ancestress of hers had brought with her on her marriage into the family in the middle of the eighteenth century. 'What a lot of things the Diakonovs possess,' she thought, 'but they would be lost without Monsieur Kamensky, without this man who is poor and what they would still call unimportant, I suppose.' The tears ran down her cheeks in spite of her efforts. 'How wicked the Tsar must be, and he will never be punished for the evil he does,' she told herself, and walked up and down the corridor for some minutes, wishing it were possible for her to kill him. 'Just imagine what it would be like if Queen Victoria had suddenly started persecuting Papa like this,' she thought, and remembered with awe the innocence of England. She would not even have suffered like this over there. If she had been at home at Radnage Square and had not wanted to sit in any room because she had been crying, she would have gone up to the top landing, which was flooded with strong colourless light from the high north window and Dolly the housemaid would keep on coming up, her glazed white dress giving back the brightness, to put the clean white sheets into the linen cupboard or take them out. Any conspiracy could have been blanched out of existence there or anywhere else in the house.

But here her hiding-place ran dark between treasures, from twilit room to twilit room where people were dim as if they had lived long ago, in an age smokey with tragedy, and were now foundered in the text of dull history books. It would seem that only a king, when kings had absolute power, was high enough to have fallen so far as her grandfather; and there was royalty in reverse in her grandmother's shrunken body, she might have been his queen, waiting outside the prison where they kept him. In this blackness Kamensky shone, good, exempt from greatness. She went towards her grandmother's bedroom, unafraid because he was not afraid. As she drew near Aglaia came out and held the door open for her.

Neither Sofia nor Tania heard her come in. Sofia was lying in bed, propped up on a high pile of pillows in the rosy shadow of taffeta curtains, crimson marabout feathers about her wasted wrists and corded neck; in her ears and on her fingers jewels big as the boiled sweets in a village shop, her face usurped by an old bird. Tania was standing at the end of the bed, looking like someone out of Romeo and Juliet, for her hair was loose on her shoulders and she was wearing a long clinging dress of pleated silk which her husband had bought for her at the Fortuny shop in Venice, but that was three years ago. The words which were rushing from her were English, and this showed they had been speaking about something Aglaia must not understand, for ordinarily they talked together in French or Russian. 'I shouldn't have written to you about my troubles, I see that now, Mamma,' she was saying, 'but I didn't know how ill you were, and I couldn't bear all this alone.' She had her hair brush in her hand, and she lifted it and swept it savagely down the full length of her hair, then spread wide her arms. 'It is not bearable. If this is happening now, how do I know that it hasn't happened often before and won't happen often again?'

Sofia shut her eyes and opened them again and spoke past her daughter. 'Laura, Laura. How good of you to come in and see me again.'

Tania turned round and sat down on the stool before the dressing-table and went on brushing her hair, holding herself badly, her back bent.

Laura curtseyed and said, 'I just thought I'd come and see how you were, though I knew you'd be in bed. I've been looking out of the window, and it's getting dark and the lights are coming out in all the houses, and it's very pretty, and I felt sad and very fond of everybody.'

'I know, I know,' smiled Sofia Andreievna, 'such an ache, such a rush of affection, and no reason for it either, and all enjoyable. For perfection, somebody one doesn't know should start playing Chopin in the next house.'

'Dear Laura,' said Tania, but she could hardly speak.

'How nice Laura looks,' said Sofia. 'A wide space between her eyes, and a neck long but not too long. The battle's won. I'm glad. I like my good-looking grandchildren much, much better than the plain ones.' Laughing, she raised herself in bed, drew a powder-puff from some cache and passed it over her face, and sprayed herself and her sheet with scent. 'I am feeling so much, much better, for the last three days.'

But she looked horribly ill, and she was wilting, withering, diminishing, though she still spelt magnificence, as a word retains the same meaning even if it be printed in smaller and smaller type. 'I couldn't,' Laura mourned, 'bear it if she died,' and she looked over at Tania and thought again, but in a flame, 'I couldn't bear it if she died.' She wanted to throw her arms round her mother and do what she had always done when she was little and her mother came to say good-night to her when she was in bed, she wanted to lift up her string of pearls and kiss her along the line of warmth they had left on her skin. But what she had to do now was to talk for a minute or two so that they might think she had overheard nothing, and then get out of the room. She said, 'Grandmamma, may I ask a question? That lovely fawn robe Grandpapa wears, what's it made of? It isn't wool, is it, and it isn't silk either. I don't believe we have anything like it in England.'

'Now, what is that robe made of?' Sofia pondered. 'Tania, can you remember the name of the stuff? No? Actually it's wool, but wool spun from the fleece of a strange animal, and Nikolai was given it by his cousin Vassili Sergeivitch, so I suppose the animal, whatever it was, must have existed on the big estate he had near Orenburg. But then he had property in South America, perhaps the animal was there. But it's something special, it's supposed to be to vicuna what vicuna is to ordinary sheeps' wool. If you have to buy it, it's fabulously expensive. The Indian princes like it. I remember when Prince Duleep Singh came to St Petersburg years ago to make arrangements for becoming a Russian naturalised subject in case there was war between Russia and England, your grandfather had to go and see him at his hotel, and he was wrapped round in a great cloak of this stuff, though it was well on in the year,

and he told your grandfather that it was valued by the Maha-
rajahs. They're not used to wearing heavy things, when they're
cold they like stuff that's warm and light. At the time someone
said that Baghdad Jews buy it too, they can afford anything.
I hope you told your grandfather you admired his robe. He likes
wearing it because it's like a monk's habit. To him, bless him,
he never in his life knew the cost of anything, it's part of the
ascetic life, like fasting and getting up at four in the morning
for the first service.' She laughed wickedly, sighed, dropped
her eyelids, sighed, acted drowsiness. 'Good-night, my little
darling, and thank you for coming to say good-night to me.'

As Laura closed the door she heard her mother's voice rise
like a seagull flying against the storm. She put her hands over
her ears and went back along the corridor, seeing Susie Staun-
ton's gold-white hair, her vague mouth. In the end room her
grandfather was still huddled in his chair, his deep breathing
like a long, reasoned complaint; and the curtain had not been
drawn. Across the avenue the lit windows were a brighter
yellow and the houses were nearly black. The trembling flame
before the icon seemed stronger. Monsieur Kamensky's spec-
tacles caught the light and shone like little moons laid on his
dark face. They turned towards the opening door and he
uttered a soft, wordless, welcoming sound.

3

IN THE DRAWING-ROOM after dinner, the night before
they were to leave for Mûres-sur-mer, Laura noticed, not for
the first time, a coincidence. It was when her grandfather
looked most like a prophet on an icon that her mind recalled
certain phrases used by Dolly the housemaid at home in Rad-
nage Square: 'up the pole', 'barmy on the crumpet', 'nine-
pence to the shilling'. He was talking about England, and he
was always at his dottiest when he chose that subject.

'Tania, I'm quite contented with the way you've brought
up Laura in a heretical land. She followed the Liturgy with
me quite nicely today. This can't have been an easy achievement

for my daughter, Alexander Gregorievitch. For everything is wrong in England, it must be wrong in England, corruption must be the main harvest of its fields, because the English have no religion. It is no use protesting, Tania. A wife's loyalty must not seduce her into tampering with the truth when it concerns what is sacred. The English are Protestants, and Protestantism is the negation of religion. True, Protestantism is not as obviously distasteful as Catholicism, which reeks of the vulgarity of ancient Rome, whereas we of the Orthodox faith represent the imperial spirit, born in Rome, that is true, but purged by the sufferings it endured during the long sojourn in Byzantium, even to the last defilement by the infidel. May that offence be cleansed. Laura, do you pray regularly that your mother's people may be given possession of Constantinople and restore it to its true place as our New Jerusalem?'

'Well, no,' admitted Laura, and as Nikolai flung up his great hands she amended the answer. 'Not so often as I should, I mean. There are,' she said, humbugging a bit to amuse Tania, though she would deny afterwards that she had been amused, 'there are so many other things to pray for.'

'True,' said Nikolai, 'but never neglect for long this most urgent prayer, Laura, and never let yourself be misled into luke-warmness regarding this act of restitution by the apparent violence of Byzantine history. The violence of Byzantium, and of Byzantium's child, Holy Russia, is the disguise of a healthy natural process. It is a mistake, a vulgar mistake, to regard a number of Byzantine and Russian Emperors as having been assassinated.'

'Well, they weren't alive after what happened to them had happened,' Tania interrupted.

He pretended not to have heard. 'Rather did they offer their lives as a sacrifice. They bore the burden of power on behalf of their people, and it is necessary from time to time that power be pruned, like all earthly growths.' He took a sip of brandy, twirled the glass between the palms of his hands, and said pensively, 'It is a long time since tragedy visited Buckingham Palace or Windsor Castle. I can't understand why no Indian has ever tried to assassinate Queen Victoria.'

'Certainly a pity from the point of view of the Russian Foreign Office,' said Tania. 'But go on telling us about the benefits of the Russian religion.'

'It is the greatest gift to the human soul yet given. Remember ancient Rome gave us nothing. It produced authors all too easy to remember, even impossible to forget, though the wise man would wish to do so. Now that I am wretched I am haunted by lines from that deplorable man of mean interests, Horace, that weaver of fairy-tales, Ovid, that cold heathen, Virgil, and I find no comfort in them. The Romans had sufficient insensibility to make them happy pagans, from whom nothing can be learned. The Greeks proved themselves greater by being wretched in their paganism. *Oedipus Rex* is a prolonged cry against the irrationality of a world not yet given reason by Christ. Happy are we for whom the Church took the form so inappropriately given to their religion by Roman culture, and recast it in a form purified by Greek restraint, and then had its work blessed by the progressive revelation of the Trinity which has been vouchsafed to the Slav peoples. Alexander Gregorievitch, give me some more cognac.'

As he set down his glass he said kindly: 'Tania, I am worried when I think of you sitting in that London drawing-room of yours. You must often be unhappy.'

She stared at him from under straight brows, her mouth pursed as if she had eaten something sour.

'Well, you can't find it easy to instil into our children wisdom not honoured by the community in which they live, such as the true doctrine of the procession of the Holy Ghost.'

She made a sharp derisive sound, then agreed pleasantly. 'But I've done my best.'

'You really understand that doctrine, Laura? That the Holy Ghost proceeds from the Father, and the Father alone, and that the belief that it proceeds from the Son —'

'Is man's invention,' supplied Laura. But if he were to ask her where that came from in the Church Service she was lost.

'Good. The full understanding of what that doctrine means will come to you later. Yet you should have some understanding of it now, considering the fortunate circumstances of your home. The Trinity is the means taken by God to enable man to comprehend him, for it is the image of the family, it shows God as the Father. Think of your own father. All the essence of his being is confined to his family. He would not give to the outer world any of the feelings he gives to your mother, to your brothers, to you. Love flows from him to all of you, unfailing. He turns all his wisdom and forethought to the task of contriving unbroken happiness for your mother and all her children. Even so the love and forethought of God goes out to Jesus Christ His son, and the name of that love and wisdom and forethought, which is a thing in itself, is the Holy Ghost. It cannot proceed from the Son, because if it did He would be the Father. It is not your brothers who provide you and your mother with happiness, it is your father, it is Edward Rowan. Your brothers will contrive the happiness of their families when your father is old and sits peacefully in the evening light with your mother, but now the rays of the sun are emitted by your father. Never cease to contemplate your family, Laura, it is the image of the Godhead.'

'How well you put things,' said Tania, standing up. 'It's time Laura and I went to bed. We have to say good-night to Mamma.'

Next day his mind was still in England. As usual Laura went out with him and Monsieur Kamensky for the afternoon drive, which was intended to take him to the rose-gardens at Bagatelle. But he grew tired, they had to turn back when they were not very deep in the strange amateurish forest of the Bois. His head dropped on his chest, his lids fell, but he was not asleep. 'You can't think, Alexander Gregorievitch, how difficult it must be for my Tania and her husband. For the English have no religious belief, none whatsoever. As I said, Protestantism is not a religion.'

'But surely not. I understood that there were many holy men at Oxford and Cambridge who made suitably humble enquiries into the truths of our Church. Think of Khomyakov's long correspondence with William Palmer, who belonged to a college named after the Magdalen, either at Oxford or at Cambridge.'

'An isolated soul here and there. But for the rest the piety of the English is a mockery. They want a prescription for social order and union with God means nothing to them. They love power so greedily that they cannot bear to depute it to the elect who are fitted to exercise it. They must all have their share of it, even if such a swollen electorate means that the vote becomes worthless. They want England to be a Great Power, a strong country, as they say, and a nation can be certain of strength if it be composed of industrious, sober, honest people, who do not strike or kill their enemies, who do not lie or blaspheme or beg and who keep themselves clean. So they pretend that this is what religion is for: to teach men and women to be moral. But we Russians know that religion is for the moral and the immoral. It is the love of God for man meeting with the love of man for God, and God loves the vicious and the criminal and the idle as well as He loves the industrious and the honest and the truthful and the abstinent. He humbles himself to ask for the love of the murderer, the drunkard, the liar, the beggar, the thief. Only God can achieve this sublime and insane relationship.'

Laura had been watching the equestrians who were pounding along the track beside the road, some of them in very funny clothes. She said to Monsieur Kamensky in an undertone, 'That girl in the check breeches rides so badly that she'll fall off.'

'She will not quite fall off,' said Monsieur Kamensky. 'She will nearly fall off, and that kind gentleman just behind her on the bay mare, who is a more expert horseman, will ride forward and offer his assistance. That, I think, is the plan.'

'It can be seen in our churches, the flowering of that relationship. Oh, Laura, a Russian church is so beautiful. For that alone I would be thankful to have been born a Russian, that I have had at my hand that consolation and inspiration, the Russian church, not the great body of souls, but the edifice, the actual place of worship. For that alone I would regret that I am an exile. It would be the crown of my days to take you, the best-looking of all my grand-daughters, to share in the warmth, the joy, the repose of a Russian service. In our churches all social distinctions, those ineradicable marks of the fall of man, are eradicated, privilege is annulled, and so is shame. The poorest beggar is equal to the greatest noble. The church is the only place – how happy we are to have one such place, the English have none – where the poorest man in rags will not be asked, "What are you doing here, and who are you?" It is the only place where the rich cannot say to the poor, "Your place is not beside me but behind me." Oh, Laura, if only you could see how Russians, rich and poor, good and bad, immerse themselves together in the sea of God and are washed clean.'

'You were right, Monsieur Kamensky,' said Laura. 'The gentleman on the bay is helping the girl in the check breeches. And he looks much too nice to bother about her. And the horse is good too.'

'But Alexander Gregorievitch, may you never have to enter an English church. You would be stricken to the heart. The place is devout, even pretentiously solemn, but it is a congregation not of men and women but of ladies and gentlemen. The rich sit in separate seats known as pews. A horrible word, like an exclamation of disgust. And they sit instead of standing, even the hale and hearty sit in those seats, as only the sick are allowed to do in Russia when they are in God's house, and they loll in these pews like so many subscribers to the opera in their *loges*. All use prayer-books and each has his own. It is a sign that each wants to be alone before God in his own proud isolation instead of liquefying himself in a sea of worshippers dissolved by worship. Ah, that divine liquefaction.'

He really slept. They had to wake him when they got to the Avenue Kléber. He seemed very tired, and though he would not go to bed he did not come in to dinner, but had a tray sent into his sitting-room. He was not so tired, however, for when the ice-pudding was being served he sent in a message to say he was expecting them all and hoped they would not be long. When the butler had gone out to say they were nearly finished Monsieur Kamensky looked across the table, which glittered like a Catholic altar, with all the silver and the Prague crystal, and said to Tania: 'If I may say so, you are very pale. May Miss Laura and I not make your excuses to the Count?'

'I am quite well,' she told him coldly.

'I must be rude and set aside the *glacé* cherries in this pudding,' he said, as if he had not made the suggestion and had not heard the reply. 'But I have a horror of them; they taste to me

68

like cardboard.' After a pause he added, smiling, 'Perhaps Miss Laura has told you, his mind was running on England during our drive.'

'Laura told me nothing except that you had been able to foresee the behaviour of a blonde young lady in check breeches, and we were both wondering how that came about,' said Tania, and laughed at him over the rim of her glass. But her laughter went. She asked wearily, 'But why does my father go on and on about England? Why is it always in his mind?'

'Simply because you live there.'

'There's no other reason?'

'None. That's enough, you know.'

'I wonder if he might have heard . . . have heard . . . that I was not happy living there. There comes a time, you know, when people living abroad want to go home. He might perhaps have thought that that had happened to me. But it hasn't. It hasn't.' Her voice died away.

As she opened the door into Nikolai's room she halted, threw back her head, sighed, stiffened herself and went to her seat, for he had called out: 'Alexander Gregorievitch. Alexander Gregorievitch. This afternoon we were talking of the English Church and the way it is ordered for the enjoyment of the rich. I do not think I explained how far this goes. Incredible as it may seem, in the English Church the powers of appointing priests to parishes are owned by the rich, and they appoint whom they please and pay them themselves. The Bishops are supposed to have some say in the matter, but you can imagine how much of a safeguard that is in such a corrupt society. My son-in-law took me to his club, the Athenaeum, and there were Bishops in that worldly place, behaving like any of the other prosperous shaven and combed and oiled and tailored worldlings who frequent that place. It is a horrible traffic. The office of priest can be bought by a rich person for a certain sum, calculated according to the capital value of the income, just as in Russia lawyers and stockbrokers can buy partnerships in firms. Nothing is lacking to make the arrangement disgusting. In any English newspaper you may find a series of advertisements offering these priestly appointments, which are called "Livings", an ironical name for a sign of spiritual death. There is actually a journal published in London wholly devoted to this shameless simony, and it is typical of English hypocrisy that it bears an innocuous title, the *Church Preferment Register*. What could sound more virtuous? What in fact could be more depraved?'

'Well,' said Monsieur Kamensky, placidly, 'it's always been a problem how to provide for the material needs of the clergy.'

'Nowhere else has such a deplorable solution been accepted. When I think of this shameful system, carried on under the cloak of piety, I am the more enraged by my recollections of those delegations. Those delegations! Those accursed delegations of English clergymen, which persist in presenting themselves at St Petersburg and Moscow, harping shamelessly on their sense of brotherhood with us, and impudently demanding union of their corrupt church with ours, when they should know, even though they are ignorant as children, that their creed and their practices are merely sacrilegious parodies of the true faith and valid Liturgy which are our Russian heritage. God is merciful, that He had not long ago destroyed them.'

'I must bring you a copy of a German religious journal,' said Monsieur Kamensky, 'in which a German theologian discusses this very point and suggests that we consider it calmly.' But that did not work. 'Laura,' said Nikolai, with thunder in his voice and an expression conveying benevolence and common sense, 'you must forgive me if I have spoken frankly of your father's country. But I must own that at one time it lay heavily on my conscience that I should have permitted one of my daughters to marry an Englishman, and I would like to explain to you that it wasn't lightly that I disregarded my scruples.'

'Oh, Father, don't let's talk of that,' said Tania. 'I chose to marry Edward. It was my decision.'

'It was not. How could it have been? If I hadn't wished you to marry him you wouldn't have married him. What I want you to understand, Laura, is that when I gave my consent to your parents' marriage, I realised all the arguments against it. For one thing, I realised that there can never be peace between England and Russia until we have taken India from her.'

'What on earth does he think India would do with Russians

walking about all over it being crazy about the Orthodox Church?' thought Laura.

'Until we have it, England must regard her with suspicion and fear, and this can only be replaced by resentment when the struggle comes to its inevitable end. As a Christian woman, your mother is bound to accept it as her duty to have no thought and emotions which are not her husband's, so she would be bound to side with England in this dispute did I allow her to marry an Englishman. So it might have happened that I might rejoice when we gained a bulwark for our Empire and at the same moment lost a daughter. This might yet happen in my lifetime,' he cried in sudden alarm. 'After all that has happened to me, it might very well be that this too might befall me, I might not die before Russia takes India from England, and then I would be divided from my Tania.' He looked upwards as if some enemy in the sky were eavesdropping, and scowling, crossed himself.

His roar became gentler and more reflective. 'But it was not only India which troubled me. It was the coldness of the English character, the avoidance of error and all contact with the extreme, which I fear for my Tania. Even a woman should not always stay in the garden, she should sometimes walk in the forest, for her soul's sake. I watched your father, I must confess, with something almost like dislike, certainly with apprehension, not because of his individual character, but because he was an Englishman and must limit his wife's experience to what is right and unsurprising. But presently I saw signs that he wasn't as English as all that. True, he always stood upright or sat with a straight back, and held his head up, and bowed and acknowledged greetings with formality, as if he were deliberately cooling his sentiments, but sometimes there were signs that within him burned the same fires that burn within us Russians. His eyes are light. They are blue-grey. But sometimes they appear quite dark —'

'So they do,' said Tania. 'So they do. I don't know how it can be possible, but it's so. When Edward feels anything deeply his light eyes suddenly become dark. How odd you should have seen that. I always think you don't notice things.'

'I do not trouble to notice things as a rule. But I was watching

71

a man who, if he made you unhappy, would be my enemy. So I noticed too that his voice changes when he is moved. As a rule it is clipped and shallow, but it is quite different when he cares about something. He doesn't shout, as we Russians do. On the contrary, the words cling to his lips and one can hardly hear —'

'Yes,' said Tania. 'That's true too. His words cling to his lips.' Monsieur Kamensky had put down a glass of brandy beside her, and she picked it up and sipped it.

'I knew then that if my daughter married Edward Rowan, she was not marrying a mere English Protestant, but a man who had transcended all the limitations imposed on him by his unfortunate situation. Suddenly I felt at peace. Calmly I withdrew my opposition to the marriage, feeling I was doing the will of God, Who had indeed perhaps specially contrived my daughter's curious infatuation, since, foreseeing the torments of my old age, He wished to give me a good son-in-law. I often wonder whether he hasn't some Russian blood far back in his ancestry, which has made it impossible for his Protestant upbringing to corrupt him. So I gave my daughter to your father, Laura, knowing she would have a husband beyond price, a Russian without Russian faults, an Englishman without English faults —'

'You were right, Father,' said Tania, suddenly emptying her glass down her throat. 'Edward is perfect. He has never bought a Living in his life. No copy of the *Church Preferment Register* has ever entered our house.'

'I can believe that,' said Nikolai happily, 'and like me he's also opposed to cremation.'

'There's an awful lot of cremation in India,' Laura warned him, and Tania giggled.

'That means much to me,' said Nikolai. 'How coarse and repugnant I find the English and German agitation for this new and perfunctory method of disposing of the dead. We don't find it distasteful to bend our eyes to the fleshly abode of the departed soul, we cherish it as it lies in its coffin, we reverence it and don't shrink from giving it the last climactic kiss, we watch over it for three days and three nights of praying and chanting, and we delay the surrender to earth of the beloved

72

body by the length of our beautiful funeral prayers. But these barbarians, these Anglicans, these Lutherans, these atheists, they wish to tip their dead into specially constructed furnaces, after a ceremony which by its brevity betrays that the survivors grudge their poor departed ones both their time and their tears. It's sickening to think that our own Orthodox Church refuses to condemn this infamous practice. I was so pleased when the last time I saw Edward he told me that he too was repelled by this cold and unkind method of alienating the dead from the living.'

'Yes, yes,' said Tania, 'we're a perfect couple. Innocent of the slightest taint of simony, we shall lie side by side in the Rowan family vault. Not that one can be sure of anything. But it's time we went to bed. Something tells me I shall go earlier and earlier to bed while I stay in Paris.' She knelt before her father and lifted her face to his, saying impatiently, 'Good-night, good-night.' As soon as he had kissed her she tried to free herself and rise, her face contradicting itself, as if she wanted both to cry and to make someone else cry, but he folded her in his arms, so that she was forced back on her knees.

'Thank you, my little Tania,' he said. 'Thank you very much.'

'What's this now?' she murmured. She was blinking in confusion. 'Why are you thanking me?'

'Because your marriage is the one thing that has gone right in my life,' he answered. 'The one thing not brought down in ruins by my disgrace. Your brothers and sisters are in the orbit of my shame. You're outside it and you're happy. I eat and drink your happiness.'

She sat back on her heels and stared up at him. 'How generous you are,' she said softly. 'Your thanks come gushing out like a spring. Oh, how good, how very good it is that I made a marriage that gives you such pleasure. To think that I can give you such pleasure!' She choked, she had to go on sitting on her heels till she recovered mastery over herself. Suddenly it could be recognised that only an accident of appearance made her seem proud and daring and harsh, she was really humble, a sort of saint. But of course she was that. If she took Laura and the boys anywhere she was grateful to them for enjoying themselves, when Papa brought her home a present she would take it all over the house showing it to the butler, the cook or Dolly the housemaid, going out into the Square gardens and telling the gardener about it, in a daze of wonder that she should have been so favoured. But people went usually by the high carriage of the head, the slightly raised eyebrows, and were a little afraid of her. Laura went over and pulled her to her feet and took her to her bedroom. They walked like sisters through the corridor. And as she undid the hooks and eyes at the back of her mother's dinner-dress, her mother said, 'To think that my father is happy because of us. It's a great privilege. For he is a great, great man and his sufferings are great.'

Lying in bed half an hour later Laura marvelled how it was that one looked and looked at people and then quite suddenly saw them as they were. That made her think of Susie Staunton. Why did she have to think of Susie Staunton so often, and see her so brightly against the blackness of the night or of her own shut lids? She had been quite used to Susie Staunton going and coming about the house before she realised that Tania was right enough in considering her remarkable. It had seemed to her before that time that Tania was simply being over-grateful to someone who had only the special advantage of being invariably agreeable. But that was the wrong word. It sounded as if Susie made an effort, and she was never so positive. She simply agreed to everything and anything proposed to her in the house in Radnage Square, with a gaiety which was assumed to be brave. For it was still understood that she was poor. True, she lived in a Knightsbridge square which was not cheap, but possibly the house was lent, people would enjoy being kind to such a lovely creature. Oh, she must be poor, Laura thought so too. One day she was coming downstairs while her mother's guests were arriving for a luncheon-party, and Mrs Staunton was standing in the hall while the butler was letting in the woman who had followed her by seconds. Against the light of the open doorway she was a dark silhouette, a slight movement of her wide hat showing that she was timidly looking about her, as if she were a governess come for an interview and afraid that, with her habitual ill-luck, she had strayed into the wrong house. But behind her the front door closed, and she moved forward, her skin and hair quite bright, not more visibly impoverished than the plume-crested and heavily-boa'd guest on her heels, her glacé silk skirts rustling, quite a big brooch at her throat. Yet even so there hung about her a delicate version of want. She was in need of something she had not got, though she was keeping the particulars of her poverty a secret.

So it was natural that when Tania and she arranged to ride together in the Row, Tania should reserve a quiet mare for her for the season at Smith's Stables in Sloane Square, and give her a silver-mounted switch and a new habit, and that all their companionship involved such generosity. Then, late one afternoon, during the thickening of the friendship, when Tania had had a committee meeting in her drawing-room of one of the Societies for the relief of distress among the troops returned from South Africa, Susie, whom Tania had put on the Committee, brought an evening dress and changed into it in the visitor's room. That way they could have good time to dine before they took Laura to see Barrie's new play, *Quality Street*. Tania's maid was out, so she and Laura went in to see if they could help. They found Susie standing before the cheval-glass in a prim, close dressing-gown, a hairbrush in her narrow hand, her hair loose about her shoulders in a spreading cloak of primrose light. Though everybody who met Susie noticed, and went on noticing, the unique colour of her hair, this was a surprise. It could not have been guessed, what happened to Susie when she took the pins out of the coils and bands which gave her the same shaped head as all fashionable women of the time. Now the released ethereal abundance of her hair made her a supernatural being, and odd at that, an angel whose shining wings had a span far wider than was needed to lift her fragility.

Tania's voice soared. 'Laura, look at her! Look at her hair! Ours is horsehair beside it. And look at her little, little wrists and ankles! Compared to her we're just carthorses. That's why we have horsehair. Oh, Susie, wonderful Susie!' But Susie shook her head and said, with the slight stammer which always afflicted her when she was complimented, 'No, no, I'm . . .' She

75

did not end the sentence and define what she was, but her oval face, though it remained quite smooth, was appalling in its avowal of privation. It was perhaps the blurred mouth that avowed it. She had great possessions, she had this hair, but she was racked, as if she were wandering waterless in a desert, by this phantom yet unassuageable need.

Laura got up and poured herself a glass of water, and drank it between the sheets, and told herself it was a medicine that would sweat out her fears. It was so strange that she should keep on thinking of Susie Staunton. Nobody, nobody, she must remember this, had ever said that Susie Staunton was responsible for what had happened between her mother and father. She slept and woke to a more hopeful morning, and when she dressed went to Nikolai's sitting-room, where she knew he would be, drinking the black coffee which was all his breakfast, to see if he was still talking about England. But mercifully that was at an end.

He looked up at her and said, 'Laura, I understand we are going to Mûres-sur-mer, simply because my poor wife would not stay in the clinic if she thought that you and Tania and I were in the apartment, because her dutiful nature would make her rise from her bed and come back to take care of us. See, Laura, how miserably deluded we are by our affections, for actually my dear wife's concern for me is making me do something I detest. I don't want the trouble of getting into a train unless it's going to take me somewhere in Russia. To St Petersburg. To Moscow. To Kiev. To our country house, to Datchina. Ah, Laura, you can't think how beautiful Datchina is.'

'She cannot think how beautiful Russia is,' said Monsieur Kamensky. She had not heard him come in, but he was standing just behind her. He must come to the house very early.

'Yes, Russia is beautiful. Not in the way that Europe is beautiful. We have no Acropolis, no Venice, no Bay of Naples. But our whole country is suffused with beauty which is the property of our most featureless and monotonous landscapes, it is a component part of the air in our forests and on our plains and over our lakes and on our rivers and above our mountains, there is no point where it begins and none where it ends, and every place seems its heart. I believe Datchina to be its heart, though I know it can't be so, that Datchina is just a place like many another, and each of them is thought by some Russian to be the living core of his country's beauty.'

'Will you not have a croissant, Excellency?' said Monsieur Kamensky. 'Black coffee is not enough for you now. You must begin to pamper yourself.' He set about buttering one.

'Has anybody told you, Laura, what Datchina is like?'

She knew every foot of it, from her mother's descriptions, from Grand-aunt Feodora's water-colours, and the photographs. She had even believed when she was little that she had been born there, for on the photograph of the tennis-party on the verandah there was a peasant woman with a high head-dress holding a baby, which she had taken to be herself, though of course it was Tania. She said, 'Tell me about it, Grand-father.'

'Listen, Laura. The house stands on a hill among the forests. The hill was long ago clear-felled, in the time of the Great Catherine, and never replanted. It is a park. But from all the windows we look down, over this park, on a sea of treetops, a sea of dark green pines, with the birches and maples between them, light green in the spring, a kind of singing green; but the birches are yellow in the autumn, and the maples are crimson. At the foot of the hill is a river. Your mother must have told you about the river. She used to swim there, though only the boys were supposed to bathe in it, the current was so strong. That's a strange thing, women have no need for courage, yet there is a certain charm about a courageous woman. Well, the road to the house crosses the river by an old wooden bridge, built well by our splendid serfs long ago, long ago, and the road winds about the hill up to the pillared front of the house. We knew when our guests were drawing near because we heard the horses' hooves clop-clop-clopping over the bridge. Sometimes it would be one of my dear sons who was arriving, bringing his wife and his children, your cousins, Laura, whom you have never seen, whom I shall never see again; or some of my friends, and I shall never see them again either, all people of whom I approved, whom I liked, whom I even loved.

'Let me give you a present, Laura, a good thing to remember about your father and your mother when they were young.

Early one morning I was drinking my coffee in my bedroom, and it was very early, for I rose at cockcrow in those days, and suddenly I heard the clop-clop-clop, and I asked myself, "Who can that be, crossing our bridge so early in the morning?" Then there was a knock on my door, and in came your mother in her dressing-gown, her eyes shining and her hair flowing over her shoulders, heavy, heavy gold, and she said, "That is my Englishman." I exclaimed, "What, at this hour?" and she answered, "Yes, he said he would drive all night to be with me at the first possible moment." I should have known from that moment that the marriage was meant to be.'

She had had her eyes fixed on the door for fear Tania might come in. She heard Monsieur Kamensky say, 'Excellency, it is nearly time for the doctor to come, we had better go and prepare for him.' When her grandfather had left the room Monsieur Kamensky turned back to her. 'I am arranging for the Metropolitan to dine with your grandfather tonight. They would like to be alone. So this evening your mother and you must reconcile yourselves to dining with no better company than mine.'

She said, 'But that will be delightful,' and smiled gratefully, and wondered how much he knew. But what was there to know? She drew her hand across her face to hide her spasm of anguish.

He said, 'There are not enough fountains in Paris.'

'What did you say? Not enough fountains in Paris?'

'Exactly. In Rome there are enough fountains. The water rises up into the sunlight and falls down shining, all day long, and one knows that nothing matters. But in Paris, no. It's a great lack.'

Next morning they were all three of them sitting together in the same room, waiting till it was time to start for the Gare du Nord, and Nikolai's mind was still in Russia, still at Datchina.

'It was always delightful there. It was of course supremely delightful when I was a boy, for then society was stable. We had only the sorrows laid on us by God, not those engineered by the devil, and they were outnumbered by our joys. But the place was delightful still in the last years. Indeed there seemed, except in the troublesome papers I had to bring from St Petersburg, almost no change. The young women were still playing tennis in their pretty white dresses, the boys looked strong and supple and Russian when they came up from bathing in the river. And the sport was still marvellous. The fishing and the shooting. But fishing is nothing, women can do it. Shooting's another thing. There strength tells, the true strength, not the mere brawn that a peasant has, but the strength of muscles and nerves fused into an electric current by perfect co-ordination. We had that in my young days, all the men of my kind had that. None of us was ever tired. And our strength didn't leave us with our youth. Shooting was the great test we put ourselves to. One must be able to walk for miles, get soaked to the skin and stay soaked, wait in perfect stillness for hours and then send one's aim and one's shot together in a single straight flight of the will, perfectly, without error, again and again and again. I could always pass that test. I passed it still, the very last time I was at Datchina. By the mercy of God I did not know that it was to be the last time. God, I have not thanked Thee enough for that.'

His lids dropped, he seemed to sleep, and presently Monsieur Kamensky's head nodded and fell forward. He had told Laura that he had to sit up very late with Nikolai and the Metropolitan. She went to the window and looked down on the Avenue Kléber, and of course there was something going on, there always was. The nuns at the head of a crocodile of little girls were about to take them across the road, when one thrust out a forefinger from her thicket of black draperies and counted. Panic followed. The nuns ran about scolding, the crocodile twisted and broke apart into a centipede. The two missing children were much further down the avenue, hidden from the nuns by a tree-trunk as they tore out each other's hair. They looked horrid, it was nice to think they were hurting themselves and no one else.

'Laura, Laura. I wanted to tell you about these two special shoots we had at Datchina, which were among the greatest pleasures any man could know. You have nothing like them in England. Your father was a little shocked by them. You see, in England, where everything is small and sparse, you have to preserve your game in the mating season or you would have none left. But we have so much that we can shoot as we like, it makes no mark on our abundance. So at Datchina we shoot woodcock when the snows are melting, when the spring has come, when the birds are courting. Laura, it was so beautiful when we shot the woodcock. The foresters used to send word when they had seen them coming up from the south, in their three-cornered flights, and we would make up a party, and drive out into the forest about midnight. It had to be then, for we had to go far, far into the forest, and we needed to be at the trysting-place about half past two or three in the morning. Then we would go into the brushwood shelters the foresters had built on the side of a clearing, for each gun a shelter. There was something holy about sitting there alone, looking at the dawn, which with us comes quickly, far more quickly than the dawns here in France. How slowly daylight comes in this accursed country! But in Russia the dawn is very clear and brings hope as well as light. Then we would hear the swish of many wings, and a croaking call, and a curious double whistle, and the woodcocks came dropping down into the clearing, very neatly for their size. They are larger than your English woodcock.

'You know what a woodcock is like, Laura? It's a dark bird, with a long bill and a large eye, a speaking eye, an eye such as one doesn't see in any other game bird. When one picks them up off the ground after the shoot they stare at one as if they had been baptised. And indeed what do these birds do when they alight but give proof that through all nature runs the pattern of ritual, of ceremony. Matrimony is their business then. The hen-birds settle on the bushes and dress their feathers with their beaks, and the cocks strut on the ground below, and immediately it appears that each hen is sought by more than one cock, and there's going to be trouble. Then the strangeness of the occasion makes itself felt. The birds don't go at their rivals at once. First they freeze into a kind of trance. They are active, this is the peak of their lives' activities, but their consciousness of it takes the form of unconsciousness. They go into an ecstasy, they move but they are in a sort of stillness, like dancing dervishes. They are awake, and they move, and they are asleep.

'Above, on the bushes, the hens quiver, but are hypnotised. They are impaled on the sight of the warring cocks below; and as for the cocks, they circle round and round and round one another and then they rush together and wound each other with their long bills, at once without sensation and as purposeful as fencing men. The hens they watch, the cocks they fight, they watch and fight, they watch and fight, and they hear nothing when we begin to shoot. Then some of the cocks are pierced through their nescience, not by the noise, for they do not turn their heads, but by astonishment that adversaries whom they have not killed are falling dead. They stand in shock beside the carcases, and then the spell on the hens is broken. They shriek. Then cocks and hens alike rise straight up in the air, shrieking, shrieking, shrieking in panic. It is then that we really shoot. We bring them down by hundreds. They come down like a plump feathered rain, down, down.' His voice faded away. 'I tell you, there is nothing like a woodcock shoot.'

He might be her grandfather, he might be very unhappy. All the same, she had to say, 'It sounds horrible.'

'It is only right you should think so. I should be shocked if you did not. You are a young girl. But a woodcock shoot is for men, and it is beautiful with more than its own beauty. There is an indescribable fascination in what is happening: a system, perfect in itself, and exquisitely ingenious, is destroyed at the very moment when it is implementing its perfection, by another system, just as perfect and ingenious.'

'You're always talking about God,' said Laura. 'What does he say about this? What about caring when a swallow falls?'

'He may care for each individual woodcock,' said Nikolai, 'but for the destruction of one system by another, that is part of his plan. There is such war between nations, between empires. And take heed of what this little war, this woodcock shoot, really is. Men who are threatened with a thousand perils go out with guns against birds who enjoy almost complete safety in the forest. Men, who at any moment may be displaced in the favour of God by another species. Have you never thought that may be the punishment our sinfulness brings upon us? Our system may be destroyed by another system, and perhaps it will be the system of our own sins.'

'But why would a merciful God do that?' asked Laura, feeling no mercy towards him.

'Oh, there is pity for the individual man, the individual woodcock. But not for the system. I have sometimes thought there might be such catastrophes among the stars. Galaxies might defeat each other, not by action, but by being simply what they are, by their mass, their momentum. The great may perish as the small. But why do I use such words as great and small? The galaxies may be only birds, whom we think fixed in the sky but which are falling through it at the slow pace of a larger time, while hunters to whom the universe is not knee-high level at them guns which were loaded outside infinity. But again galaxies and such hunters may be small, simply corpuscles within the bloodstream of a vaster being, which would be small itself, being itself some part of another still vaster being. Not that any of that would alter what I am telling you, that Datchina was beautiful, and the woodcock shoot one of the most beautiful things that happened there. Wasn't it so, Alexander Gregorievitch?'

'You forget that I never had the opportunity to learn to shoot,' said Monsieur Kamensky, 'and I'm rather of the opinion which I read on Miss Laura's face, that what breathes should be allowed to go on breathing. But Excellency, the Countess has come to say good-bye to you.'

She was leaning on the arm of Tania, who said, 'Papa, it's time you went.' Sofia echoed, 'Time you went,' and turned on them a strong, piercing glance and a weak smile. Her hair had been carefully marcelled and she had changed into a dress too elaborate for morning wear, and perhaps too young for her, made of honey-coloured ottoman silk with a fichu of heavy lace. She had put on rouge, not without cunning, but too much.

She held out both her hands to Laura and said, 'Dear child, remember your grandmother.'

'I won't have the chance to forget,' answered Laura. 'Grandfather talks about you all the time, just as Mummie does, when we're at home.'

'Your mother's brought you up to have good manners,' said Sofia, and regarded her steadily, even staring at her.

'I only wish you were better, Grandmamma,' said Laura, to break the silence.

'You've got your wish already,' Sofia said with sudden vivacity, 'I've been much better, much, much better, for the last three days. And now good-bye.'

The girl curtseyed deeply and raised her lips, but the old woman shook her head and simply laid the hot, dry cloth of her cheek against the young face. Straightening herself she remarked to nobody in particular, 'What's happening to me is like – what is it like? Like being on a horse that's bolted.' She moved to Nikolai and ran her fingertips over his sleeves. 'My dear one, the carriage is ready. You must go. We're no longer in Russia – you can't keep trains waiting for you here, you know.'

'I'm quite ready,' he said, patting his pockets. 'Yes, the tickets are in that envelope, my notes in the red wallet, my papers in the black, but where's my little money? And are those tickets really in that envelope? Laura, I must tell you about this other shoot we had at Datchina, better at Datchina than anywhere else —'

'Say good-bye,' said Sofia. 'Say good-bye to me.' She nuzzled in the breadth of his chest.

'Good-bye, my dear little one,' he said, kissing her while his hands were busy with the things he had taken out of his pocket. 'Why, what a sad face! Be sensible and remember that our separation is to be a short one.'

'You're right,' said Sofia. 'It can't in any case be a very long one.'

Nikolai gently pushed her away and, breaking into a little laugh, said to the others over her head, 'Do you know, just because I've travelled with secretaries all my life and had the business of tickets and baggage and passports taken out of my hands, I feel as helpless as a little child now I have to look after myself, though it was precisely because I was less helpless than other people that others were deputed to take such things out of my hands. But really I won't be happy starting till I've made sure all over again that everything's in order.'

Shaking his head at his own silliness, he sat down again and checked on everything he had taken out of his pockets. Sofia stood beside him, her great sunken eyes losing not one of his movements. 'Nikolai,' she said softly, 'Nikolai. Pay attention to me, are you paying attention to me? Nikolai, you must always remember that what is broken here on earth will be made whole in heaven.'

He replied, 'My dear, I give you my word that I need no such advice. I have forgotten everything about my disgrace for the last half hour or so, telling our dear Alexander Gregorievitch and this child here of the good times we used to have at Datchina.'

Tania uttered a sharp cry of irritation, but Sofia laughed and for a second looked well and young and mischievous. As the mischief faded from her face she raised her hand and rubbed her knuckles against her lips, watching him as he replaced in his pockets the wallet, the coin-case, the envelope, the unnecessary passport which he was carrying just as if he were still in Russia, where they cared for such things.

'Now it's really good-bye,' he said happily.

'Now it's really good-bye,' she echoed.

'A malediction on those cursed teeth, my little darling. We must be off.'

'Mummie,' said Laura, 'good-bye, Mummie. Dear Mummie. I wish I wasn't going.'

Tania looked at her with abstracted eyes. 'Nothing can happen to you,' she said. 'Monsieur Kamensky is putting you on this train that takes you all the way to Mûres, and at the other end Pyotr and perhaps Aunt Florence will be on the platform to meet you. You'll be all right. Anyway you're a pussycat. You always fall on your feet.'

4

THE LITTLE FOOTMAN shut the door of the carriage, and Laura and Nikolai settled back in their seats. 'What I was trying to tell you, Laura,' said Nikolai, 'was that many people whose judgment on sport I respect think that a woodcock shoot is as nothing compared to a capercailzie shoot.' But as he spoke they heard a deep sigh from Monsieur Kamensky; and another, which was more than that, a choked moan, and they saw that he was holding his left hand in the fingers of his right, and that his face was contorted with pain.

'Dear Sasha, what is it?' cried Nikolai. Laura had never before heard him call Monsieur Kamensky by the affectionate diminutive. Perhaps it was for the first time. The younger man, even in his agony, had to smile with pleasure, before he faintly answered, 'It's nothing. Really it's nothing. Only when the door was shut ... my hand was foolishly in the way.'

Nikolai roared like a lion. He threw open the carriage door and shouted to the little footman, who was just climbing up to the box. 'Here you, Jean, Claude! Tell Vissarion we won't start yet, and you come back here. Here. Look into the carriage. See what you've done, Claude, René!'

'I am called Louison,' said the little footman sadly. He was not a proper footman, he was only a houseboy whom the Diakonovs had taken on from the previous tenants of the apartment. Tania said that it was because her parents had never acquired the habit of dismissing servants, they thought of them as serfs bound to them by an unbreakable bond, and a boy without employment seemed to them a serf whose owners had disgracefully repudiated their obligations towards him. The boy was hidden under layer after layer of unreality by his benefactors, for not only were they wrong about his state but Nikolai always called him by the names of footmen he had employed nearly forty years ago, at the time when the family had a villa in Nice. 'What have I done, Excellency?' asked Louison.

'When you slammed the door you were a blundering little idiot,' said Nikolai. 'You hurt the gentleman's hand, you imbecile lout.'

'No, no,' protested Monsieur Kamensky, 'poor Louison was as careful as could be. It wasn't his fault, it was mine.'

The little footman drew back from the door, as if the incident were finished.

'You impudent little ass,' shouted Nikolai, 'are you not even going to say you are sorry?'

'But, Excellency, I've not done anything,' said the little

footman, 'the gentleman says it wasn't my fault, and indeed it can't have been, for I didn't shut the door until I'd made sure there was nothing in the way. Vissarion has taught me to do that, we practise it in the stables.'

'You lie, you little wretch,' said Nikolai.

'Don't, don't,' said Monsieur Kamensky, and Laura said, 'Grandfather, please, let's do something for Alexander Gregorievitch's hand. Let's go back upstairs and then Mamma's maid can put on a fomentation. She's good at that sort of thing. There must be lots of other trains.' She said to Louison, 'Tell Vissarion not to start. We're going back to the apartment to have Monsieur's hand attended to.'

Horror came into the little footman's face. 'But is the gentleman really hurt?' It was plain that till then he had attached no meaning to what Nikolai said, confident that employers were maniacs, always making trouble for trouble's sake. 'That I should have hurt Monsieur Kamensky! Monsieur Kamensky! Why, I wouldn't hurt him for anything in the world.'

'Oh I know that, Louison,' said Monsieur Kamensky, and managed to laugh affectionately. He laid his injured hand on Nikolai's arm, and said, 'Please, dear Count, let us forget this. I have a good reason for asking this. If I go back to the apartment now, the Countess would probably refuse to set out for the clinic, which she should do in a few minutes. If you came up with me, she'd be worried because you'd missed your train and would excite herself over all the plans which would have to be altered, the messages which would have to go to Mûres-sur-mer, and if you didn't, she'd distress herself because you'd have trouble in going unattended to the train. In either case —' he paused and looked steadily at Laura — 'it would add greatly to Tania Nikolaievna's anxieties.' They exchanged wise little nods, and he turned to the window, biting his lips as he shifted his position, and called out gaily to the little footman, who was staring in with appalled round eyes, 'My child, it wasn't your fault. My hand was very low down on the window, you couldn't possibly have seen it. Don't think of it again, and now ask Vissarion to drive quickly to the station.'

They were all silent as the carriage turned into the Champs Elysées. Then Nikolai broke out, 'Do you know what I am thinking of, Alexander Gregorievitch? I am thinking of the day when we drove to the station at Kiev.'

'You shouldn't think of that,' said Monsieur Kamensky, vigorously, almost as if he could bear no more of Nikolai's reminiscences, of any kind whatsoever. 'There is nothing,' he added more patiently, 'to be gained by such thoughts. Evil men have created confusion but God will one day make all things plain.'

The old man would never leave go of his bitterness. 'How did they know that it was the 10.5 and not the 11.15?' he grumbled. 'Tell me that. If you could tell me that, I could die in peace.'

Monsieur Kamensky, who was rocking himself and pressing his injured hand to his mouth, made a faint sound of dissent. 'You will die in peace, whatever you know or don't know. God is your friend. With such a friend, you have no need to know who is your enemy.' He spoke with mild censure, and the old man was for an instant abashed. But he got back into the saddle again. 'Yes, but my enemy was the enemy also of the Tsar, of God's anointed. Of God.' His voice was strong now that he had re-established the importance of his grief. 'Do you remember how the sunshine beat down on us that accursed day when they stole on us, those who love neither the Law of God nor eternity because it discloses the Will of God, but rejoice only in fleeting time, which being incomplete tells lies? How hot it was. It was so stifling that when we heard the first bomb I thought it was thunder, and I said to Miliukov —'

Monsieur Kamensky was forced to interrupt. 'Count, Count,' he said faintly, 'I am afraid I can't go on. Please stop the carriage and I'll get out.'

'You can't go on?' enquired Nikolai, mystified. 'You want to get out?'

'It's his hand,' said Laura, leaning across the carriage and tapping on the glass.

'His hand,' repeated Nikolai. 'His hand? Ah, I remember. Poor Sasha, I am so sorry! But this is nonsense, we must take you to a doctor.'

'Most warm-hearted of friends and patrons,' said Monsieur Kamensky, 'that's very kind of you, but if you stop at the next corner I'll go to a pharmacy near by. I know the proprietor very well, and he's a clever man who'll deal with me for the moment and send me to a doctor if he thinks I need one.' The carriage had stopped, and the door had been opened, but Nikolai caught at his jacket as he got out.

'Nonsense, no pharmacist is good enough,' he growled, 'Let me take you to Dr Alanov. Though his consulting-room is sure to be crowded with duchesses and Jews, he'll drive them out and see you at once for my sake, his grandfather was a serf on my father's estate.'

'This morning,' said Monsieur Kamensky gravely, swaying a little as he stood on the curb, 'you wouldn't find Dr Alanov at home. He'll already have arrived at your home in the Avenue Kléber, to take the Countess to her clinic. Good-bye, Excellency. Good-bye, dear Miss Laura.' His face was twisted by a sudden spasm of pain, and the little footman, who stood gaping at him, blubbered, 'Oh, Monsieur, Monsieur, what have I done?'

Monsieur Kamensky compelled himself to laughter.

'My dear little Louison,' he said, 'I've told you it wasn't your fault, and even if it were, it's nothing serious. I shall come up to the apartment tomorrow morning, at quarter past eleven, to take Madame Rowan to the clinic, and before I leave I'll box your ears very hard, and that with both hands, just to show you how little serious it was. Now, get up beside Vissarion as fast as you can, and off to the station.' As they drove off he stood in an attitude of courteous farewell, hat in hand, his feet at attention, and his mouth set in a smile which, as Laura craned from the window to see the last of him, faded suddenly.

'I hope the pharmacy isn't too far away,' she told her grandfather, 'he looks as if he were going to faint.'

'It's a curious thing,' Nikolai ruminated, 'people are not as strong as they used to be. I don't think that when I was his age I would have fainted just because I'd hurt my hand. I wonder if I have our tickets and my passport.'

'Of course you have,' said Laura, 'Don't you remember, you took them out and went over them and put them back in your pocket, just before we started.'

'I did? I did? You must be right, but . . .'

This had not happened before, not quite like this. Several times since she had come to Paris, he had shown forgetfulness, but what was forgotten had been eminently forgettable. It had been as if his mind were too full of memories and he had thrown away some that did not matter. But now the facts, even the most useful ones, were running out of his mind like water out of a cracked cup. The journey before her suddenly looked different. She would have to behave well, she would have to behave like Monsieur Kamensky.

But when they came to the Gare du Nord her grandfather transacted the first business of the journey better than she had expected. He gave the porters reasonable directions in a voice like anybody else's. But once they passed under the smoke-glazed vaults of the station he paused and looked around him at the hurrying and cantankerous crowds, bowed his head, folded his hands behind his back, and strode on ahead as if he were alone. She hurried at his heels, and after her hurried little Louison, carrying Nikolai's leather attaché case and her trinket-box. In the station, as in every French railway terminus she had ever seen, there was an atmosphere of threatening and causeless rancour, as of a revolution without an object. The porters pushing their barrows uttered cries less like warnings than demands for revenge, the passengers swept on in angry waves as if storming a palace to wring a constitution from an absolute monarch instead of merely boarding trains for which they had been issued tickets. It was funny, but it was not kind. Had Monsieur Kamensky been there it would have been only funny. He would have looked at the black-browed crowds without yielding an inch to their ferocity, his bearded face relaxed and lineless like the face of someone in a holy picture, but lit by hidden laughter ... When they reached their carriage her grandfather dropped an excessive number of francs into the porters' hands, muttering in Russian, 'Dear God, dear God, these creatures produced by a popular government,' and he helped her up on the high steps, while he gave Louison a farewell tip and some last instructions.

There were two women already in the carriage, sitting opposite their own reserved places, women dressed in heavy mourning, their round faces framed for contentment, but not at that moment contented. The older was saying, 'It was indelicate of them to buy us the first-class tickets. If they had given us the money for first-class tickets, the handsome gesture was there, we would have given them the credit for it. I am sensitive to generosity, I am touched by it, and the fact that we would have travelled third and kept the balance wouldn't have lessened my gratitude to them. As it is I must reconsider my view of them.'

'They meant to be kind,' said the younger woman.

'Meaning is one thing and doing is another,' said the other, 'and it's the lack of delicacy which appals me. And always,' she added, after some seconds, 'will.'

She hoped Grandfather would not hear them going on like that, popular government and God could get into the business at the drop of a hat. She wished they could go to Mûres-sur-mer as she and her father and mother and brothers went to Scotland or Torquay, with nothing much coming up except that they were going to Scotland or Torquay. But when her grandfather sat down beside her he was mild, he was back in Russia before that had become a torment to him.

'I've been trying to tell you all the morning about the capercailzie shoot, but people kept on interrupting us. The capercailzie were with us about the same time as the woodcock. In April, would it be, or was that too early? I can't remember. An exile gets confused about the seasons. But it was a time in the year when there was gaiety in the air, it was a pleasure like going to a ball when one is young, just to be alive. To get the capercailzie we had to go even further into the forest than when we were after the woodcock, we drove sledges mile after mile to where the marshes begin, then we went on foot, a long way on foot. It was a real ordeal, this shoot. I tell you I dreaded every year lest this time I should find I was too old and make a fool of myself in front of my inferiors. But I was still able to carry it off up to the last spring I spent at Datchina. I am still enormously strong.

'The capercailzie isn't like the woodcock. It is more of an aristocrat. It doesn't give itself away by fighting itself blind and dead, it keeps its sense till the very last, and till then it hears everything even to the snapping of a twig underfoot. I've seen the whole thing a failure because of some lout's single false step. Keeping absolute silence, that's it. Standing still and waiting, feet on the frozen marshland, and staring up at the tall trees, the firs and birches, silhouetted against the night sky. They are sparser here. You would hardly call it the true forest, it just straggles down into the marshes.

'The hen-birds are hidden in the branches of the trees. You can't see them. Even I, with my sight which is so much keener than other people's, even I could not see them. The capercailzie is like your grouse, you know, but of course much bigger, bigger than a pheasant, and very dark in colour. Then, suddenly, just before the dawn breaks, the cock-birds come. They fly swiftly, discharging themselves like arrows at the treetops, where they alight on the topmost branches. There they remain still, quite still, while the sun comes up. The wait seems endless, though probably it isn't ten minutes, because you daren't make the smallest movement, you hardly risk breathing. If the birds hear the faintest sound they're up and spreading all over the sky, into the distance, as quick as a woman shaking out her fan, and you've come all the way for nothing. But if you stay quiet, all at once the cocks begin to sing. They're serenading their mates in the branches below, the sun is on the cocks above, the hens are still down in the darkness. At first the song's faint, one can just hear the soft chuck-chuck-chuck, but soon it swells, it's their church choir.

'Even then you can't be sure your safe. As I told you, these birds keep their ears, they get every sound at this point, and sometimes they stop singing altogether, and there's a hush, such a hush, you hear the blood beating in your head and you think they must hear it. It's that which makes this shoot such a test. Keeping still like that exhausts a man's nervous and muscular energy before he lifts his gun. We thought a man a remarkable shot if he could bag six or seven birds with the kind of guns we had when I was young. You see, there's just one moment when one can get them, when one has to twist oneself into the right stance and blaze away, and that moment comes at full dawn, when one stops thinking, "It's getting light, hurrah, it's getting light", and thinks, "It's light, it's broad daylight" – surely it must have been light for quite a time, because the day tips into the dark sky as if someone were

91

emptying the bottle bolt upright above it, filling it up to the brim. It's then that the cock-bird's love-song rises to its height in one long note. Shrill, penetrating. It's terrible to hear in a way, that note, it's like a cold finger slowly drawn down one's spine. A very high note as it goes on. And it seems to stretch everything, one's nerves, everything, even the sky. It's then one shoots. The cocks know nothing when they're singing this extraordinary note. The hens know nothing when they're listening to this extraordinary note. They're quite defenceless, both of them. They become the note itself. They're nothing else.'

The words crumbled on his lips. A line of saliva ran down from the corner of his mouth. Distastefully he wiped it away, and said, 'It tired me to remember that note. Indeed I can't quite remember that note. Indeed I can't quite remember it. But it was wonderful, that shoot.' He sighed, his eyelids dropped.

She was not sorry. As he spoke she had been looking out of the window at Louison, who was standing in the correct position for a footman seeing off his master and family at the station, at right angles to the door, with his arms crossed and his elbows in the palms of his hands. He had a babyish profile, with a snub nose and plump cheeks falling to a little round chin, and he was looking very sad, sad because he was too young to be sad, like a grieving puppy. She leaned from the window and said, 'Louison, are you all right?' He started.

'Oh, yes, Mademoiselle. Your grandfather gave me a gold piece.'

'Well, that's nice,' she said.

'It's more than that. It's an occasion. It's the first I've ever had. In fact, it's a little awkward, it's so much more than I expected. I'm wondering if he really meant to give it to me. Sometimes at the house we think the Count and Countess don't know the value of French money.'

'I shouldn't worry,' said Laura. 'If it was an accident, it isn't likely to occur again, so take it and spend it and be happy.' That was the kind of thing her father would have said in such a situation.

'But I can't be happy,' said the little footman. 'I can't get over what I seem to have done to Monsieur Kamensky. He made light of it, but that's his way. He's always been so kind to me, I can't tell you. For I've had my difficulties at the Avenue Kléber. The last butler I was with said that every kitchen had as much intrigue in it as the Chamber of Deputies, and that's certainly true of your grandfather's establishment, there being the French and the Russians working together. I'm the youngest and I've had to bear the brunt. But Monsieur Kamensky's always helped me, and he's always made light of it. And now it seems I've hurt him quite badly.'

'Don't worry,' said Laura, 'He was going to a chemist whom he trusted. His hand will probably have stopped hurting by now.' She opened her trinket-box and took out a packet of chocolate and handed it to him. Her grandmother had told her that Louison would carry her jewellery to the train, but she had not all that much, so she had filled the vacant space in the box with chocolate and biscuits. Everybody had told her that when she grew up she would stop being hungry all the time, but it had not happened yet.

'Within ten minutes,' said Louison, 'my first gold piece and my first chocolate from Maison Rumpelmayer.'

'Your first step towards becoming President,' said Laura as the train started. She had heard her father say something like that to a gardener's boy whom he had tipped: 'Your first step towards becoming Prime Minister.' She was always imitating people. She could not think how to be kind to her grandfather except by imitating Monsieur Kamensky, and if she were to go to a grand party her only idea of behaving properly would be to imitate Tania. She suspected that she had no character of her own, which was a curious defect for a member of her family. 'Mentally, I am an albino,' she decided, 'and perhaps that is why I can't imagine myself doing all sorts of things other people want to do. I don't want to get married. If there were any other way of going down an aisle in a white satin dress I'd take it. I don't want a husband. Men talk about interesting things, but they are not interesting in themselves.' She shuddered with an apprehension of the disagreeable. 'Only women,' she thought, 'are nice to look at and worth imagining things about.' She made sure that her grandfather was still sleeping and opened one of the magazines Monsieur Kamensky had bought for her. A note on the cover proclaimed that it was designed '*pour les jeunes filles*', and it contained articles on the soppier pictures in the Louvre, particularly those by Murillo and Sassoferrato, on the childhood of the Empress Josephine, and on the construction of the atoll, all alike described in a nervously persuasive manner, as if to distract the attention of *les jeunes filles* from some powerful preoccupation.

'How sad,' she reflected, 'that after all this trouble it doesn't work, and French married women are so awful that I'm not allowed to read Paul Bourget. I wonder how long it takes for them to change over. How many years from atoll to adultery? Can I repeat that to Mummie? Perhaps not. Half my best jokes have to curdle inside me.' Lifted up by the gaiety of travel, she smiled across at the two women, they smiled back, they seemed about to speak.

But just then her grandfather woke up and turned to her with agony and embarrassment in his eyes. 'Where are we?' he whispered, then his glance became hard again and he said, as if dismissing her from intimacy. 'Ah, yes. This tedious journey'. But his hand looked miserable on his lap. She clasped it in hers and he softly pressed her fingers. They were still near Paris, just where the Nord line bridges a steeply-trenched valley slicing down to a river like a strip of mirror, which gives back the woods from its glass. The sight of it always pleased Tania, and she watched for it every time she made the journey. 'Look,' Laura said to her grandfather, 'this is the place Mummie thinks so pretty.'

To her surprise Nikolai, who talked as if he knew nothing of France outside Paris and Nice, who had once asked her where the Pont du Gard might be, nodded in recognition. 'The river is the Thève,' he said. 'I've often been in that valley. One rides under the trees to the hunting-lodge of a queen. I have forgotten which queen, a medieval queen. One breakfasts there at tables in a courtyard, the huntsmen play music on their horns.'

'When does this happen?' asked Laura.

'I don't suppose it happens any more. But it used to happen. Years ago, many years ago. When my eldest brother, Ivan, was ambassador of the Tsar in Paris.'

That sounded very grand. 'Did I know him when I was little?'

'No, God is merciful, Ivan died before the times became evil,' said the old man, and closed his eyes. At first he murmured angrily to himself, but soon he slept without disorder. His huge and delicate hands gripped the firm tables of his knees, his white and golden beard marked the exact centre of his chest, each of his bowed shoulders was like the rounded top of a strong wall. He had for the moment gone over to the other side, he was an emblem of serenity.

Laura looked at her other magazines, and found that they were all *pour les jeunes filles*. She was surprised, she thought that Monsieur Kamensky had realised that she was practically grown-up. But in one there was an article about the Angkor Vat, with beautiful photographs of the profuse jungle pressing in on a profusion of towers and domes and terraces and carved images. 'I must go there,' she thought, 'I must go there soon. I would like to see all Asia and all America.' Then the corridor door slid open and someone came into the compartment. She looked up in annoyance, supposing it would be the ticket-collector, who would wake up her grandfather. But it was a passenger, a middle-aged man, carrying one of those satchels used only by schoolchildren in England but by quite grown-up men on the Continent. She went back to her book, wondering why he remained standing when the two middle seats on each side of the carriage were free. He was probably going to be a fussy fellow-traveller, since he was changing his compartment.

Still standing, he said 'Good morning, Miss Laura.'

He had spoken in Russian. But he was not one of the Russians she knew. She had not met him in Paris or in London. Slowly she said, 'Good morning, Monsieur,' taking a good look at him, and was still sure that she had never seen him before. He was middle-sized, lean and pale, with unkempt hair and meagre beard and moustache, all mouse-brown, and grey eyes behind spectacles. He would have passed unnoticed if it had not been that he was very badly dressed. His great-coat looked like a dressing-gown, for it was made of an odd fawn-and-blue-striped material and too loosely cut, and it was worn carelessly, the belt twisted, the collar half-up, half-down. He looked

Russian, she would have known he was that even if he had never opened his mouth.

He had the high cheekbones and that air of being in the middle of thinking about something important. She knew too that he was a gentleman, like her grandfather, like her father. But neither of them would have chosen this man as their friend. She could not have said why. He was in one place, they were somewhere else; it was just that. But it was usually people less fortunate than her grandfather and father who carried such satchels, people who worked in offices and banks as clerks, and this satchel was worn and battered; and so was the hat he held in his other hand. If he were poor, she had to be polite. So, though she did not want at all to speak to him, she said, trying to smile, 'How do you know my name is Laura?'

'Well, you're Tania Nikolaievna's daughter, aren't you? Well then,' he said with an air of cold logic, 'you must be Miss Laura.'

'But how do you know anything about my mother, how do you know anything about me? Do tell me,' she said, forcing the smile, 'who you are.'

He gave no answer and stood contemplating her grandfather.

'Who are you?' she asked.

'You belong, Miss Laura,' he said, as if he had not heard, 'to a remarkably handsome family. Look how splendid Nikolai Nikolaievitch is. What a unit! His skeleton and his muscular system are so perfect that when he is relaxed not one part of them gives way, they remain in a state of equilibrium. This is because he is an aristocrat and therefore has been adequately nourished since he was an infant.' He paused and cleared his throat. 'Not so,' he said in English, 'are our Russian peasants, not so the wretched workmen who labour in our Russian cities.' He waited as if for a compliment, so she told him that his accent was remarkable. He looked happy for a second, bowed, and then went back to Russian. 'I have to admit that your grandfather is a work of art, though I think the cost of producing him has been too great. A part of me, the same part which insists on still enjoying the Imperial Ballet, when I have the opportunity of seeing it, insists on enjoying him. I would like to go on looking at him as he is now for quite a long time, and I regret that I must wake him up.'

'But you can't do that.' Suddenly she felt frightened. She knew she was talking nonsense. This shabby man could wake her grandfather and do much beside, though what that was she did not precisely know. 'My grandfather,' she said, 'isn't very well. Things worry him. He's had a bad time lately. You mustn't wake him up, really you mustn't.'

'But I must,' said the stranger. 'We have to talk about something very important.'

'Nowadays there's only one thing which is important to him,' she said, 'and I don't think you can know anything about that.'

'But that's the thing I want to talk to him about,' said the shabby man.

She said, 'But how could you know anything about it? All he wants is —' she paused. One never talked of one's family affairs to outsiders. But for the last minute or so she had suddenly become aware that all rules were suspended, and a cold feeling crept over her scalp. She went on, 'Nothing matters to him except being pardoned by the Tsar, and you can't have been sent by the Tsar, he wouldn't send somebody to speak to my grandfather in a train. So let him sleep. Please, please go away.' She found she had risen to her feet. But anything she could say or do would be inadequate. This man had some sort of advantage over her and everybody else in the carriage. It was as if they had met to perform a play and he was the only actor who had seen the script and learned his lines, while the rest of them had to improvise. The women sitting opposite were watching with intense but placid curiosity, as if he were indeed an actor and what he was doing could have no consequences in the real world. Yet it could for her and her grandfather. He had shifted his stance so that he stood between her and the corridor door, still carrying his battered satchel in the one hand, the battered hat in the other, but spreading his arms wide. He did not mean her to get past him.

'There's always the communication cord,' she thought, 'But whoever really pulled that? And he wouldn't let me get there. He's quick on his feet.' She turned her head to the window and scanned the moving landscape as if a tree, the mass of a hill on the skyline, or a church-spire might signal her instructions for her next move. Now it was no help to speculate how Edward Rowan or Tania would have met the occasion, for she did not believe they could have done so. Out of her confusion came the clear knowledge, 'This man is on the other side. Of course, Monsieur Kamensky said they were everywhere. He means to do something dreadful to my grandfather. I'll have to stop him.' Everything was glassy, time had slowed down, it was like the moment after one has dived and is deep down in the water and it has not begun to lift one to the surface. She found herself repeating, 'Let my grandfather sleep. Please let him sleep.'

She must have spoken quite loudly, for Nikolai stirred and muttered. The shabby man put down his satchel and his bowler on the seat, removed his spectacles, took another pair from his pocket, put them on very carefully – still taking care to keep between Laura and the door – and bent over Nikolai, peering down into his face. Recoiling, he made a gesture as if he were going to cross himself, but stopped it; and exclaimed softly, 'How he has altered since I last saw him!'

Laura said, 'Why, you really know him!'

The shabby man was trembling. 'Know Nikolai Nikolaievitch? Since my childhood. What have they done to him since then! I can see that he is a greater man than he set out to be. But the sight of him has sent me back to the days when I talked nonsense, and had not seen the light of reason, for of course he cannot be a great man at all, no man can be greater than his social function, and your grandfather has been deprived of any possibility of greatness by our present system. But I won't deny that, looking at him now, he appears to me as great. I'm disturbed,' he said, frowning. 'I'm even moved.'

'He liked him, he even likes him very much,' she thought. It was not the words that proved it, but the blend of pity and resentment of veneration and condescending affection in his voice. That was how all the older people in the family spoke of her grandfather. But she had heard that terrorists considered it their duty not to be influenced by their natural feelings. They even seemed to be regarded as noble for that reason, though she could not see why. Vigilantly she watched the shabby man as he pulled her grandfather's sleeve with fingers yellowed by nicotine, and spoke his name. There was something dangerous about even that. She covered her mouth with her hands and said, 'Let him sleep, oh, let him sleep.' But the old man's eyes opened, and when they saw the stranger grew as hard as stone.

'Do you recognise me?'

'Of course. You are Vassili Chubinov, Vassili Iulievitch, and your father was — your father was a noble, a very fine lawyer, and my trusted friend. You have done many things to him and to Russia which make it quite impossible that I should ever forget you or forgive you.' He looked the stranger up and down. 'You not only are a Liberal, you look like one. I would know that look anywhere.' He caught his breath, his teeth drove down into his lower lip, then he was calm again.

'Why are you here? Has my time come to die?' he asked in a full, strong voice. Laura sat down beside him and put her arms round him. He did not seem to notice.

'No, it hasn't!' exclaimed the shabby man, irritably. 'You shouldn't alarm your grand-daughter unnecessarily like this. If your subordinates have done their duty properly, you should know that I'm not one of the activist members of my organisation and never have been. From the first my task has been to depute and clarify the theory of our movement and give it a sound ideological basis, as well as to act as its historian. If your hirelings had shown as much intelligence in reading my letters, as they have assiduity, you should have known that.' More gently he added, 'So you needn't fear death, yet, Nikolai Nikolaievitch.'

'Fear death!' said her grandfather contentiously. They were already in the heart of an argument, might have been bickering for hours instead of minutes. 'I didn't say anything about fearing death. I asked if my time had come to die, so that I could put myself in the proper frame of mind to enter the presence of my Creator. But fear, no. I've always obeyed the injunctions of the Church, I've been a regular communicant and I've kept the fasts, I've served God and His instrument on earth, the Tsar, and therefore when I die the saints will protect me and bring me to the feet of God, who will forgive me my sins, and

99

I shall be raised to salvation. Why should I fear this splendid fulfilment of my destiny? I look forward to it.'

'But that can't be true,' said Chubinov, changing to his other pair of spectacles. 'The first law of animal life is self-preservation. All living things wish to live as long as possible. Therefore you must fear death.'

'I don't. Try to kill me and see.'

She hoped Chubinov would not take him up on this. It would probably be he that got killed.

'I've told you,' said Chubinov, 'that I'm not one of the activist members of my group. But even if I were, I couldn't kill you. I've a great attachment to you, Nikolai Nikolaievitch. In another form of society you might have been a remarkable person. But if you'd any of the scientific spirit you'd realise that you must fear death.'

It was odd, Laura thought, nearly all Russians who were anybody were brought up by English governesses, but they never seemed to have been taught not to argue.

'Nonsense, if science is anything, it's observation,' said Nikolai. 'I'm not an egotist, Heaven knows, I think nobody has ever charged me with that. But I am obliged to study myself by the Church, and as a result I know I haven't any trace of the fear of death. It's absurd for you, because of something you've read in a book, probably by an English or a French infidel, a Huxley or a Renan, to deny the truth of my own observations of myself; and it's not the scientific spirit which impels you to this folly, it's the spirit of godlessness, which desires that man should be indistinguishable from the brutes, and likes to imagine that a man dies like a pig or an ass or a goat, and not as a child of God.'

'I think they're talking about politics,' said one of the Frenchwoman to the other. 'But what a language. Swish-swish-swish.'

'Please don't shout, Grandfather,' said Laura, 'you'll make yourself ill. Monsieur Chubinov, don't excite him any more.'

They did not even hear her. 'You're shouting,' Chubinov told Nikolai, 'because you know perfectly well that you're defending an absurd and superstitious point of view, unworthy of a modern man.'

'Your father never beat you enough when you were a boy.'

'Your reference to violence shows that you are conscious how little you can defend that point of view by argument.'

'What folly,' said Nikolai, gasping. 'As if a sensible man with all reason on his side would not feel an inclination to strike an idiot who insisted on babbling blasphemies in his presence. And what an extraordinary thing for a terrorist to say. You and your friends must know that there is no logical justification for their arguments at all, for the resort to the extremest form of violence, known as murder. This man,' he told Laura, leaning back in his seat and panting, 'is a murderer and the friend of murderers.'

'That is an utterly inexact description of our sacrifices, Miss Laura,' said Chubinov.

Laura's temper suddenly ran away. It seemed to have nothing to do with her. It was like a flag going up on a mast.

'I don't care what you are. I want you to stop bothering my grandfather. What on earth can it matter to anybody but himself whether he is or isn't frightened of dying? I never heard of a more idiotic reason for starting a fight. Please go away. If you won't, at least stop standing in front of us, which is most irritating, and sit down, and be quiet.'

'You have the arrogance of your class,' said Chubinov as he took his seat.

'Well, you're of the same class,' said Laura.

'I wonder you didn't notice that your grandfather paused before he said my father was a noble,' snapped Chubinov. 'We are not like the Diakonovs. Our family belongs to the very minor nobility.'

'From the way you say that, it's clear you believe in the whole silly business yourself,' said Laura. She was shaking with rage and suddenly felt she wanted something to eat. She opened her trinket-box and took out the other slab of chocolate. When she had taken off the silver paper she paused and thought to herself, 'I don't think this man meant to kill us, probably he's only tiresome and wants to talk,' while she said aloud, 'Here, have half, my grandfather doesn't like it.'

'You're quite wrong about my attitude to nobility,' he told

her. 'I've no respect for such trifles, I assure you. My whole life is spent in an attempt to form a classless society.'

'Do you eat chocolate or don't you?' asked Laura.

Absently he took the bar. 'How you're wasting the opportunities open to you because you were born in England,' he said, didactically but not unkindly, 'where the call to reason has already been heard. You've chosen to carry on the obsolete traditions of your grandfather, though you are a compatriot of Darwin, Huxley, Winwood Reade —'

'I was at school with two of the Darwin family,' said Laura, 'and it's not a family which would go in for making scenes in railway trains in front of strangers.'

That was rather too rude, she reflected a minute later. She gave him some more chocolate and one of the nicer of the two sorts of biscuits the cook had given her. When he had finished munching he brushed off the crumbs with a large handkerchief, clean but with a hole in the middle, and said: 'One would think that the *bourgeois* system of bringing up girls without discipline or education solely for the marriage-market would at least produce a certain sensibility. But it doesn't seem to have struck home to you that I'm labouring under intense emotion. I'm very unhappy. I don't think I've ever been more unhappy in my life.'

'If you're so keen on being rational,' she said, 'surely you must see that I can't care whether you're unhappy, at least not very much. If I could put an end to your unhappiness, I'd do it. But I'm sure I couldn't, so we needn't worry about that. For the rest, so far as I'm concerned, you're just a nuisance. You came in and said you must wake up my grandfather, and I told you not to. I have the right to do that, he's my grandfather and not yours. I said you'd upset him and you went on and on and on, and you did upset him, and about something so idiotic. You actually started a fight about whether he was afraid of death or not. Of all things. You'd said that there was something important you wanted to talk about, and that's what you chose. And now there he is, half-dead with it all, and you're just sitting there eating chocolate and staring at the tops of your boots and you don't look as if you were even thinking of going away. But that's what you ought to do.'

Quite a long time passed before Chubinov answered her: 'You're wrong. I've something quite important to say to your grandfather. I'm sitting like this because I'm a coward. I'm staring at my boots, at your grandfather's tartan rug, though my boots are anything but beautiful – oh, I've been thinking about my boots lately, I know they're awful – and staring at that rug, which probably represents a criminal waste of money, which should have gone to the poor, because I'd like to go on for ever like this, travelling in this compartment, travelling very fast, staring down at my boots and the rug or looking up and seeing you and those two lost and villainous Frenchwomen —'

'Why lost and villainous?' asked Laura.

'They are *bourgeois* and therefore corrupt. But let that pass.'

'Yes. Let that pass as nonsense. You don't know anything about them.'

'They are *bourgeois* and therefore corrupt,' he repeated with mild obstinacy, devoid of malice. 'But I tell you, I'd rather sit like this, staring sometimes at the poplars and the farm buildings and the fields that are rushing past, for ever and ever. For if we never got to a railway station I wouldn't have to talk to your grandfather about this matter, which, as I told you, is important. I never wanted to do anything less.'

'Then don't talk about it. If you go on like this I'll go down the corridor and fetch the attendant.' Once more Chubinov took off his spectacles and brought the other pair out of his pocket. She broke off in exasperation. 'Why do you keep on doing that? Why do you keep on changing your spectacles?'

'They're not my spectacles. Not my real spectacles. Not my current spectacles. They got broken last week. I haven't had time to get them mended. That's part of it. Everything has gone so wrong during the last few days. So I've fallen back on two old pairs I had. But they're quite old, and my sight seems to have changed a lot, and I can't make out which is the better for me to use now. Both hurt my eyes after I've been wearing them for a little.'

'But you'll blind yourself if you go on wearing the wrong spectacles!' she exclaimed. He was really too silly.

'I know, I know,' he said piteously, trying on first one pair and then the other, and blinking like a child in its bath with soap in its eyes. 'When there is a great tragedy, all other things should go well,' he sighed. 'It's not fair, having to look after all sorts of secondary matters as well.'

Perhaps she ought to give him the benefit of the doubt, perhaps she was being harsh and unkind, and even careless of her grandfather's interests. 'Am I being stupid?' she asked him, giving him another biscuit. 'Would it make my grandfather happier if you talked to him about whatever it is?'

'Not happier,' said Chubinov. 'No, not happier. That we won't be. Neither him nor me. For my case, surprising as he'll find it, is the same as his. We're both going through the world manacled to a mystery. If the talk goes well we'll lose our manacles. Still, we won't be any happier.'

'Then why have the talk?'

'These manacles weigh heavy. It'll be a relief to be without them. And there's safety. I mean it in the simplest way. Staying alive, you know.'

'Nonsense,' she said, then caught her breath. 'Oh, the Russian thing. But no. We're not in Russia. We're in France. The police here aren't like the English, but there's still some of them.'

'You left behind the world where police are any good,' said Chubinov. 'You left it when you got into this train. I left it long ago, and so, in spite of everything he could do, did your grandfather.' He leaned over and laid his hand on Nikolai's sleeve, and Nikolai started to strike it away, but stopped. They looked into each other's eyes, taut like fencers.

'I wrote to you as soon as I heard you'd got to Paris,' said Chubinov, 'but you never answered me.'

'You can't have expected an answer,' said Nikolai, gently. 'You couldn't really have hoped for a second that I would contribute my memoirs to your infidel review, which stands for everything I detest, and is written and read only by renegades and haters of Russia like yourself – none of whom would be at liberty today if I had had my way.'

'Yet it's only in the pages of my review,' said Chubinov, as gently, 'that your memoirs could be published if you wrote them honestly, and of course you would, if you were to write

104

them at all. What's more, they'd do no harm, even from your point of view, if they appeared in my review, for the Tsar would appear in your memoirs just as my contributors and readers already think of him. Mean, evasive, grotesquely careless of his country and his own honour.'

'I am listening to you quietly,' said Nikolai, 'because it is necessary that I should know what the powers of evil are planning in my case.'

'Fruitful in tricks, your Tsar,' Chubinov continued, 'tricks one wouldn't expect from even the most hard-pressed of gentry fallen on evil days, and God knows we're a poor lot when we're overtaken by adversity. Tricks one would never expect from an Emperor, lord of half a continent of abundance. Tricks that would seem in character only if they were committed by a Yid money-lender coming out to rob the peasants from his den in a ghetto.'

'You and your friends charge us servants of the Tsar with unreasonable hostility to the Jews,' said Nikolai, still softly, still without passion. 'I'm interested by your allusion to those money-lenders.'

'I spit on Jewish money-lenders, not because they are Jews but because they are money-lenders, and belong to a depraved species fostered by the capitalist system,' Chubinov said, with a certain haste, but keeping his voice low.

'I am glad you have corrected your phrase to "Jewish money-lenders",' said Nikolai. 'I don't myself use the word "Yiddish", or "Yid", and have never permitted any of my officials to do so.'

'To continue,' said Chubinov, glaring, but speaking more softly than ever, 'the Tsar has to your own knowledge not shrunk on certain occasions from the lie, the lie in its most degraded form, the lie told to throw blame on another —'

'Even the foulest words,' Nikolai said sweetly through his clenched teeth, 'cannot defile the Lord's anointed.'

'Ah, forgive me,' said Chubinov, his voice suddenly breaking, while he got out his torn handkerchief and wiped his forehead, 'but I have to say this to you, for your sake as well as mine. I must go on, I must point out to you that there were moments when it must have been borne in on you that the ointment the Lord employed in this instance must have been insufficient or of an inefficaceous kind? I know that you came on many incidents which must have aroused such suspicion.'

'Never,' said Nikolai.

'But I've found testimony that you did,' murmured Chubinov, 'testimony in your own correspondence.'

Nikolai winced.

'In my stolen correspondence,' he said with remote contempt.

'No,' said Chubinov. 'In your perlustrated correspondence. Perlustration is the word you servants of the Tsar give to your practice of opening letters in the post. You do it in order to maintain your control of the social system in which you believe. We revolutionaries open letters, not in the post, but before they are posted or afterwards, in order to inaugurate the social system in which we believe. There's no moral difference between us.'

'Only the difference between heaven and hell,' said Nikolai. 'Unworthy as we are, we represent lawful authority.'

It seemed so odd, all these people reading other people's letters, like the sort of butler and lady's maid that gets sacked without a reference.

'That's your tragedy, Nikolai Nikolaievitch,' said Chubinov. 'You believe in your system, with a religious faith. You're so honest. Tears have often come into my eyes, your diaries are so honest.'

'My diaries?' asked Nikolai in a whisper. His clasped hands must have hurt each other.

'Your diaries. They are so honest. They might be written by a well-trained gun-dog, a setter or a labrador. You know, a dog trained to bring in game and keep a soft mouth and not break a feather of the bird he carries. You learned as an official to fetch home the truth without a broken feather and put it whole into your memoranda. So the most fantastically evil business came out with the clarity which a dishonest man would have reserved for the recital of the Tsardom's most virtuous acts, the spending of the apanage on schools, the gifts to hospitals, and all the fumbling rest.'

'For your father's sake, tell me what you mean by this nonsense.' She could hardly hear the faint words.

'You wrote, Nikolai Nikolaievitch, the whole truth about the Sipyagin diaries, in the barest terms, but all the shame came through. General Sipyagin's widow complained to you that after the assassination of her husband the court officials had seized his diaries and had not returned them, though months had passed. You wrote to her so naïvely, and if I may say so without patronising you, so nicely, assuring her that there must have been a breakdown in routine, and that you'd get back her lost property without delay. Then General Hesse told you that he had had the diaries and that he'd given them to the Tsar with his own hands, and hadn't seen them since. Then two days later, you were graciously received by the Tsar and you raised the question of the diaries on the poor woman's behalf, and the Lord's anointed looked you straight in the face and said, "I know nothing of these diaries, but I know that General Hesse and General Sipyagin were on bad terms, and I expect that General Hesse found much in the diaries relating to himself, and that he's destroyed them, for to tell you the truth, General Hesse has, in spite of all his good qualities, certain weaknesses which would permit him to do a thing like that." Poor gun-dog, trained to bring home the truth, your disgust wrote itself on the page in spite of all your efforts. It could be clearly seen which of the two you thought the liar, General Hesse or the Lord's anointed.'

'Your spy stole my diaries, and you read them,' whispered Nikolai Nikolaievitch. 'What would your father have said to that Vassili Iulievitch?'

'The Lord's anointed, the Lord's anointed, the things he gets up to,' said Chubinov. 'He assured you, didn't he, that though he'd accepted your resignation, he was convinced of your innocence. He said that though you alone had known beforehand the change of route by which the two grand dukes proceeded to the station at Kiev at the close of the feast of Saint Vladimir, he was certain that it wasn't through you that the terrorists had known what the best point of vantage would be. He said also that he was certain that the plot against his life accidentally uncovered by the arrest of a revolutionary group at Kharkov, had not been formed as a result of any indiscretion of yours, however much of the evidence seemed to suggest that it had. He told you that he believed you to be his loyal and devoted servant and persuaded you to believe that your disgrace was due to your fellow-Ministers and not to him, by adding that though he was glad you were going to Paris for a rest, it was a great sorrow to him that you and he could not prepare for Easter Communion together, as you had done the year before. You wrote it all down. I could see the setter's eyes growing great in adoration of his lying master.'

'I'd like to strike you,' sighed Nikolai.

'Can't you shut up?' Laura asked Chubinov.

'But he hadn't finished with you, the Lord's anointed. First of all, before you left for Paris, he wrote to you asking for the return of all the letters he had ever sent you. You obeyed. But I know what it must have cost you. For you kept them in a place which was sacred to you, where you keep the letters of your father. All the same you obeyed. And what happened then? He sent his burglars to your house on the Kammeny-Ostrov Prospect to see that none had been held back. The Lord's anointed, should he keep his private thieves? Then after you came to Paris, there was the letter from Baron Roller. I could repeat it to you word for word.'

In the hush one of the Frenchwomen said to the other, 'I thought we were in for a quarrel. But the old man's as happy as a lark. It can't have been politics, it must have been a family dispute. But it's evidently completely settled.'

'Are family disputes ever completely settled?' asked the other.

'Then,' said Chubinov, 'came the letter from Baron Roller. Please, please don't look at me like that. I must tell you. The letter from Baron Roller. This is how it went, didn't it? "I consider it necessary to share with you the impression made by a talk I have just had with his Majesty. When your name was mentioned in connection with the present political situation, his Majesty expressed himself to the effect that your return to Russia would be at the present time highly undesirable. I have judged it —" '

'Enough,' said Nikolai. 'Laura, you should not have heard all this. Do not believe what this fool has said about the Tsar. He is speaking of him as if he were a man. So he is, but he is the man chosen to be an intermediate between God and man, and he takes on himself the guilt of earthly power, so that other men, unsullied by political action, can the more easily work out the destiny which in the end brings them to reconciliation with God.'

'The only objection to that is that there is no God,' said Chubinov.

'There is a God,' said Nikolai, baring his teeth. 'Laura, Laura, you must listen. If, in the course of the Tsar's assumption of the burden of power, he is forced into an apparent loss of honour, that is to be considered as a sacrifice he has made for the sake of his people. I do not even need to forgive him. Whatever he has done against me is part of his intercessory function, it is not, it cannot be a sin. Chubinov, you will not get me off my knees before the Tsar. I perpetually pray to him as a saint, and as a martyr too. You may think this strange, Laura, for of course the Tsar will die in his bed, his people will always protect him. But there are martyrs, Laura, who die in their beds. Do not think I am not telling the solemn truth because I am gasping, I am panting, I am simply choking with rage. You are half-English, and the English over-estimate the value of calm. I am enraged, I would kill this man if I could, for about God and what He wills for Russia I enjoy perfect knowledge of the truth, and this man is blaspheming. Vassili Iulievitch, you talk repulsive nonsense of a very degraded type. A country schoolmaster with some disgusting digestive disease might think as you do. Yet I have to thank you. For you have done me a great favour, tonight I shall sleep as I have not slept for years.'

'Nikolai Nikolaievitch,' said Chubinov, 'what you are now saying shows that you haven't understood what I'm trying to tell you.'

'It's you who don't understand,' said Nikolai. 'For years I've suspected that there had been a conspiracy against me, that some descendant of Judas had wriggled on his belly into my home and into my Ministry and had stolen my secrets and distorted them so that I was disgraced. But I'd not proof and it's well known that such suspicions are often the first signs of insanity. A letter suddenly had a profaned and fingered look, my keys had or had not a tiny particle of wax on them. So I was haunted by the fear that I was mad and might do all the things that madmen do. I had heard of madmen stripping off their clothes, and was afraid that some day I might show my nakedness, perhaps to innocent children, or that I might become violent, and that would be a serious matter with a man of my strength. Nobody would be able to overcome me. Also I had heard of lunatics who turned against their families, and I love mine, though I have often had to chasten them. My dread even cast a shadow on the brightest radiance which shines upon my life. Since my disgrace God has been very good to me, He has been with me constantly, when I say His Name it is a living thing on my lips. But lunatics often believe themselves to be visited by God when that is a deception of the devil, as they show by their blasphemies and their indecorous gestures. But now you have told me that I was the victim of a conspiracy; and I am not mad. You couldn't have done me a greater kindness.'

Chubinov was on the point of weeping. 'What, you thought you were mad? Oh, my poor venerated one, oh, Nikolai Nikolaievitch, I never dreamed of this suffering! But couldn't you have gone to a good doctor, who would have told you that you weren't? The science of psychiatry has made marvellous advances in the last few years.'

'You're idiotic like an idiot in Gogol,' chuckled Nikolai. 'You're such a fool that you achieve a certain eminence by being such a supreme example of your type. I'd like to give a great party in your honour, such as I used to give when I was young, with the gipsies coming in to sing, and immense quantities of champagne and brandy, costing money which should have gone to the poor.' He laughed hugely into his beard, but Chubinov rose and stood over him.

'But you can't take it like this!'

'But I can. I'm disgraced, I can devote myself to God and forget about my disgrace, and I can thank God for letting me know through your imbecility that I am not mad. It's all over and done with.'

'But no. No. It's still going on. Listen. We have that last letter from Roller, the very last one, the one he wrote when he was taking the waters at Vichy. The one in which he said no, he could not come to visit you in Paris, because the Tsar had expressed a wish that he should not.'

'Oh, that letter,' breathed Nikolai.

'You don't like thinking of it. No wonder. He was the friend of your childhood. He didn't like writing it either. That could be told from the disorder of his handwriting, which is usually exceptionally neat.'

'Well, the poor devil has his own Judas in his own office. You have covered Russia with such Judases. It's horrible, but I don't see how it affects me.'

'But you're wrong. We didn't get that letter from him. We got it from you.'

'From me? But I got it only a month ago.' Nikolai was frozen for a moment, then he cried out in a cracked shout, 'How do you know that whoever copied it for you got it from me and not from Roller? He may have told you so. But all spies, even the ones who spy for the right side, are liars.'

'Believe me, you must believe me, we got it from you.'

'It can't be so. I am in exile, and exile is the misery which even other forms of misery pity as truly miserable, but it has one source of contentment, I am alone now with those I know and can trust. Vassili Iulievitch, you have been cheated. Dealing with cheats, you are bound to be cheated – was it not so with me? Your Judas got the letter from Roller.'

'No. No. It came from you, from your home.'

'You cannot prove it.'

'Oh, yes, I can prove it. But don't make me do it. Miss Laura, try to get him to believe me. Oh, don't look at me like that, Nikolai Nikolaievitch. How is it that I still feel I must obey you? Well, it was the tear-mark which proved it. There, I've said it. The great tear-mark in the middle of the page. The man who copied it told me about it. Court officials aren't much given to weeping before they are disgraced. Roller hasn't been disgraced, and never will be. He is a lesser man than you, and nothing great and tragic and beautiful will ever happen to him as it happens to you. But reading that letter from your old schoolfellow in your study in the apartment on the Avenue Kléber, of course you wept. Don't you remember shedding that tear? I'm sure you do. You're ashamed when you weep, you don't forget it. Oh, Nikolai Nikolaievitch, now do you believe me? And do you see what it means? You're still being spied on. Not, as you may perhaps have suspected, by people who hang about your doors, who look at you through binoculars from a window across the street. But inside your own house, in your own rooms, you're watched all the time. Oh, don't look at me like that. I have to tell you. I have a reason.'

5

'I REPEAT, MISS LAURA, you are arrogant like your grandfather. I don't deserve your reproaches. Yes, I see that your grandfather is looking very ill, though I don't think he's actually had a stroke. But no, I could not have stopped my story at the point where it simply dispelled his fear that he is mad. Yes, you may have been making signals, but I was doing what I have to do. I have to do it, will you not understand, I have to do it. I must tell your grandfather a long and complicated story, for both our sakes. I am not, as you put it, talking and talking and talking, I am telling the story in an orderly fashion. I spent hours last night in taking full notes of what I have to say and arranging them under the headings of 1, 2, 3 and 4. We've now reached the end of section 1. By the time we've reached the end of 4, though he will be no happier, as I warned you, he will at least have the relief of understanding what has happened to him, and you'll be grateful, yes, even you will thank me. And what was the meaning of that expression you applied to me in English? What you said to me in French was disgraceful. Disgraceful. The upbringing of such girls as you is even worse than I had supposed. But I demand to know the meaning of that English expression. I demand.'

'It doesn't matter. But as for 1, 2, 3 and 4, my grandfather will be dead before you're half-way through it.'

'I will not. This miserable son of an admirable father could not possibly kill me. Sit down, both of you.' Nikolai took his time, when they had obeyed him, smoothing the knees of his trousers with shaking hands, putting his fingers behind his beard to straighten his tie, breathing slowly in and out of his great nostrils. 'I wish I had a secretary to take notes of all this,' he murmured, and Laura knew he was thinking of Monsieur Kamensky. But perhaps that was not such a good idea. Then he said in a business-like tone, 'Vassili Iulievitch, you and your terrorist friends have over a long period been receiving information about me and you are here because you wish to discuss your informant.'

Chubinov would not speak until he had moistened his lips. 'I know and I do not know.'

Nikolai said, 'You have the desperate aspect of a man who has at last decided to tell the truth after a lifetime of lies.' He reflected, and nodded. 'I see the situation. A. tells you he's getting information about C. through B. But really he's getting it from D., whom he wishes to shield from enquiry. This often happens to us on our side of the fence. We've found that it's no reason for doubting the honesty of A. or the validity of the information he brings in.'

'It often happens to us too,' said Chubinov. 'Deception is there but the truth also. One can't always work by the book.' They exchanged nods. They were speaking quietly again and with a comradely air. Laura was reminded of the way the policemen had talked to each other when they went round the house in Radnage Square the morning after burglars had taken the silver. It was a curious thing to find one's family talking like that. 'The affair, however,' Chubinov went on, 'is more complicated than that. Indeed – indeed, Nikolai Nikolaievitch, it might save us both much pain if you could tell me whether you yourself have any idea who it can be that's spying on you. Is there any man who comes and goes about your house, and yet absents himself so often that he might be living another life somewhere else?'

'There's one such man,' said Nikolai. 'You, Laura, know who I mean —' She nodded and they smiled at each other – 'but he's not the spy.'

'Why do you say that?' asked Chubinov. 'It isn't,' he went on apprehensively, 'that you feel that the man is good and loves you very much and wouldn't betray you?'

'It's partly that.'

'I might have guessed it. People who are very cruel – and you've made countless hundreds, no, thousands, weep – they're always sentimentalists.'

'How utterly you are abandoned to evil. The mere mention of goodness and trust confuses you. But these are side-issues. The man of whom I speak couldn't be the spy for quite another reason than his noble simplicity and his devotion to me: an official reason.'

'Can't you tell me what it is?' asked Chubinov piteously. 'I wouldn't repeat it. I give you my word for that. After all, my father was your friend.'

'What have you not done,' asked Nikolai, 'since my friend begot you?'

'Since I was born,' replied Chubinov, 'I've lived as much like you as possible. My father admired you above all other men, and it's been my aim to be a second you; but I've done my imitation, as you put it a moment ago, on the other side of the fence.'

One of the Frenchwomen said to the other, 'You said they'd settled their family dispute. Now listen to them yapping. I tell you, that's how family disputes always get settled. We'll never be real friends with Melanie again.'

'This is what I told you,' said Laura, 'You talk and talk and talk. Do get to the point. You mayn't think my grandfather's ill, but I do.'

'Arrogance, sheer arrogance,' said Chubinov. 'Miss Laura, you are deformed by your class. Well, Nikolai Nikolaievitch, if you will not help me, I'll have to give you the whole story. Tell me, does the name of Gorin mean anything to you?'

'It does indeed,' said Nikolai. 'I've never been able to forget a disreputable connection between you and him. When you were still at Moscow University and had just begun breaking your father's heart by joining the Union of Social Revolutionaries, you started a seditious journal named the *Morning Star*. In its first number, which I am pleased to say I contrived should be the last, you published an article calling for the assassination of the Tsar. The only sympathetic response you received was from a man named Gorin, who was then an engineering student at the polytechnic in Karlsruhe in Germany, and played a prominent part in a Union of Expatriate Social Revolutionaries which had been started by the Russian students there, God forgive them.'

'That's the man,' sighed Chubinov. 'But did you ever meet him?'

'No. I never even saw him. He came to Moscow shortly after he wrote to you, but we didn't arrest him. We hardly troubled to watch him. It was ascertained that he was of no importance.'

'Of no importance?' repeated Chubinov, raising his eyebrows.

'Quite negligible. He was one of the older men in the Movement, older than you, much older than you, and in such poor health that he was always retiring to somewhere in the south, to a certain sanatorium.'

'Now why do you say that?'

'As to his age, we had his birth certificate. He was born in Baku. I don't know why I remember that, but I do. As for the sanatorium, it regularly reported his admission and his discharge. He was visited there by the police on one or two occasions.'

Chubinov said, 'No. At some point your men went wrong. Gorin wrote to me about my call for the assassination of the Tsar, yes. But none of the rest fits.' His manner was dispassionate, professional, brooding, and Nikolai answered in the same tone. 'There could very well be a confusion. Gorin is a common name, and one lazy official, or one lazy morning indulged in by an active man, could substitute your Gorin for my Gorin on the records for ever. Do what one can, such things will happen.'

'Mm,' agreed Chubinov, reflectively, and again they were policemen. ('Sergeant, there's a pane here that's been taken out and put back recently.' 'Yes, but not last night. There's three kids in the house, see if one of them hasn't sent a ball through the window a week or so ago.') Chubinov went on, 'I'd better tell you about my Gorin, the one who quite certainly wrote to me about my article. He's no older than I am. He was born in Lyskovo in the Grodensko province. I've never known him to be ill till recently, and I doubt if even now he's gone to a sanatorium. He's a man of nondescript but pleasing appearance, so indeterminate that I don't know why it pleases. He is,' he said hesitantly, 'a wonderful man. Tell me, didn't any of your men who spied on the students at Karlsruhe, didn't any of them tell you that Gorin was a wonderful man?'

'They reported his height, the colour of his hair and beard and his eyes, and his treachery and blasphemies,' said Nikolai. 'Nothing else would be in their line of business. We are not composing fairy-tales like you lot.'

'Well, Gorin, my Gorin, is a wonderful man. An old professor at Karlsruhe, who was a German but who was on our side, said to me, "It's a pity that future generations will know nothing of your friend. He can have no future for he's spending himself on the present. Nobody can meet him without becoming a better man, without being purged of all trivial or base thoughts, all crude instincts. He can never achieve a great historical act or a scientific discovery or a work of art, because all his force is expended on his elevated personal life. Be happy," he told me, "for your friend is bestowing on you what would have enabled him to write another *Hamlet* or add a third part of *Faust*." '

'German professors gush like young ladies but are not so pretty,' said Nikolai.

'The years have not made this praise of my friend seem anything but literally true. Not that Gorin ever gives any proof of outstanding intellectual gift. Of course he knows where he is with the philosophic fathers of our Party, with Kant and Hegel. He's against Marx and for Mikhailovsky, he's always ready to demonstrate lucidly and without heat that the existence of our movement refutes Marxist dogma, for it's born of the intelligentsia and of the people, and couldn't be termed a class movement. He's warned us often that we must listen to Nietzsche's call for a transvaluation of values but must close our eyes to his hatred of the state.'

'You speak of names that will be forgotten in twenty years time,' said Nikolai. 'Except, of course, Kant and Hegel. But you have misread them. They prove our case, not yours.'

'Yes, they can be read both ways,' said Chubinov drily, and again changed his pair of spectacles for the other. 'But one way is wrong and one is right. Ours is the right way. But all that isn't really Gorin's field. He's never been attached to the theoretical branch of the Party. He was an organiser of our practical activities.'

'You mean he's a damned murderer,' said Nikolai.

'I was about to say that his field was friendship. One would be sitting in the dark in some wretched lodging in a strange town, afraid to light the lamp because some comrade had been arrested, some plan aborted, and there would be footsteps on the rickety stairs, one's heart would sink, there would be the five reassuring taps on the door, the handle would turn, the unknown would enter and annul the blackness with the spark of a match, would bring out a little dark-lantern – and through the half-light there would show the face of Gorin, smiling. And then, with so little demand for thanks, he would set down on the table a loaf and some sausage and a bottle of vodka and perhaps a precious revolutionary book, and it would be as if there were no such thing as despair.'

'The only one of you who had the sense to think that you might need a dark-lantern, the only one who knew where and how and when to buy bread and sausage and vodka,' said Nikolai. 'There was no reason, was there, why you shouldn't have all these things by you? It is an extraordinary thing that suddenly village idiots have become enormously prolific, and their spawn has all joined the intelligentsia. Well, while the men and women who truly love the people were training as schoolteachers and building hospitals and going to schools of agriculture, you were sitting in garrets either before you had done mischief or after having done it, sustained by your infernal Gorin who might have added a third part to *Faust*, though even the second was too many, all feeling like little lambs.'

'Oh, Gorin was certainly no lamb,' said Chubinov. 'He was a wolf. He has in his time slain many. And always, from the beginning, with your help.'

Nikolai looked at him with hooded eyes.

'Did you never wonder how one of our members presented himself at the Ministry of the Interior in the guise of the aide-de-camp of the Grand Duke Serge, and was shown straight into the presence of General Sipyagin? It was because Sipyagin had received a letter that very morning, forged in your hand-writing, on your private notepaper, sealed with your seal, and making an allusion to a funny story he had told you when he had dined with you at your house a week before. The letter told Sipyagin that the Grand Duke Serge was sending him a newly-appointed aide-de-camp who would not know the routine and should be shown straight into the Ministerial office. Gorin arranged all that for us.'

'I've only your word for it,' said Nikolai.

'Better take it,' said Chubinov. 'For that story, and for much else. A railway worker and a schoolteacher both went one day to see the Governor of Ufa. Neither had had any opportunity to learn his habits. But they climbed over a wall and went straight to a secluded corner in the cathedral garden where he went every day to sit and recite the day's prayers. And he had told you this was his custom in a letter you had received a fortnight before. So Gorin had told us.'

Nikolai covered his mouth with a trembling hand.

'And that letter displeased you, for the Governor was a worldly man, and you suspected that when he did this at noon he was trying to curry favour with you and your devout kind. That was what you wrote in your diary. Gorin read it.'

'God forgive me for my lack of charity,' said Nikolai. 'You do not hurt me as much as you hope by telling me that I am betrayed. I am a Christian and I know it must be so. Judas exists for all of us. That he touched Christ with his foul hand means that he touches every member of the human race with his eternally polluted finger, at all moments in time, in the past, in the present, in the future.'

'If I pester you for the name which Judas has assumed for you and for me at this particular moment of time,' said Chubinov, 'it must be your showing by the will of God that I should pester you.'

'Leave me alone,' said Nikolai, 'give me a moment that I may pray for forgiveness for my lack of charity towards that poor man who was slaughtered by your assassins as he sat with God in a book upon his knee —'

'Grandfather, Grandfather,' said Laura, 'what are you saying? Do you mean that these people killed the Governor?'

'Yes, indeed, and Sipyagin also was shot through the heart,' said Nikolai. 'But my lack of charity, how unseeing, how insolent it was. If a man is brought to God by hopes of advancement – and the Governor of Ufa was a man with few social advantages and must have been tempted that way – nevertheless he is brought to God, and is sacred.'

Her spine stiffened, she sat up and stared at Chubinov with the total fury of a cat. She said to him. 'You're mixed up with all these murders?'

'They were not murders but surgical operations designed to cure the cancer which devours our Russia,' he answered. She hissed with hatred. She could not bear to think of a man with such meagre hair, such weak eyes, being responsible for the stopping of life. But he ignored her, asking Nikolai, 'Don't you really want to know the identity of the man who has made use of you to remove those objects of your loyalty, Dubassoff, Plehve, the Grand Duke Serge —'

'Oh, God,' exclaimed Nikolai, 'were you, the son of my friend, a party to all those crimes?'

'Why, so were you,' said Chubinov.

The old man winced. She put her arms about him. 'Why do we have to bother with this awful man?' she asked. He said, 'Leave me alone, Sofia, Tania, Laura. I have to find out whether I have been negligent.' She had not the slightest idea what to do. This was possibly because she was only half-Russian. She had an idea that her grandmother or her mother would have found some means, which would perhaps have been a gesture rather than anything said, of persuading Nikolai to stop talking to this horrible man who owned that he was as wicked as Jack the Ripper or Charles Peace. Perhaps they would have thrown themselves kneeling at his feet. But if she had done that she would simply have looked silly. It was open to her of course to go along the corridor and get the attendant to put Chubinov out of the carriage, but she did not dare leave him alone with her grandfather, for he probably had a revolver on him. Perhaps she could get the Frenchwomen to watch for that while she went and got the attendant, they looked as if they might have a talent for screaming. She turned to them and was checked by the repugnance on their faces. She remembered that nannies and schoolmistresses were always saying that people who behaved oddly made themselves unpopular. The truth seemed to be sharper than that. Also, if she got the attendant, her grandfather would probably say he wanted to go on talking to Chubinov, that he was a friend. She kept her arms ineffectually on the great mass of his body while he and Chubinov talked about people with Russian names in the policemanly way.

'Yes,' said Nikolai, thoughtfully. 'I did know someone called Pravdine. And, yes, I have a vague impression that he had some connection with the Ministry of Justice. I can even remember what he looked like. He was a small man, a very small man; and now I speak of him I can see him quite distinctly, holding his little daughter by the hand, a little girl who looked like a doll, who had golden curls and blue eyes and cheeks like painted wax. There was a toy trumpet swinging from her little hand. But I had hardly anything to do with him. He can't have told your Gorin anything about me of importance.'

'I'm of that opinion also,' said Chubinov. 'I think Gorin lied when he said his informant was Pravdine. There. I have said it. I think Gorin lied.'

'Yes,' Nikolai went on, 'now I see Pravdine very clearly. He's standing in the entrance of his apartment with this little girl by his side, this child who looked like a French doll. She was wearing a fine muslin dress which spread out like the lampshades ladies have in their boudoirs, and she carried this toy trumpet. Behind him was an open door, opening on a gaslit room, and I can just see the tips of the branches of a Christmas tree, and I hear the sounds of children's voices. I can't imagine why I should have been present on such an occasion at this man's home, for he was a person of no importance. Ah, yes, now it comes back to me, Pravdine was the man we used to call "the fifth cow" in the Ministry of Justice. But you wouldn't understand that.'

'Indeed I do,' said Chubinov. 'I've known the story ever since I was a child. When your father inherited your grandfather's St Petersburg palace he invited my grandfather to go over it with him, and they found five cows kept in stalls on the roof, with a serf from the estate living with his wife and children in a hut beside them. That was usual enough, of course;

but only four of the cows belonged to the family, the fifth was an intruder whose milk was sold in the street by a Kalmuk who was living in another hut on the roof and could give no account of how he came to be there. The serf had found him there when he was sent up from the estate. And always at my home, as I think at yours, we spoke of the unidentifiable person, the guest at the party whom nobody knows, the speaker at the conference whose name is not on the agenda, as "the fifth cow".'

'Oh, Vassili Iulievitch,' breathed Nikolai, 'how pleasant it is to talk of what there was between your father and me, your family and mine. You smiled like an innocent man when you told me that story. For a minute it seemed as if nothing had gone wrong, with any of us, with Russia. Ah, well, the fifth cow. The fifth cow. But of course I know why we called Pravdine that. He had a room in the short corridor leading from the main one to my office —'

'Then Gorin's story might be true?' Chubinov asked eagerly.

'Not possibly. The room was very small. At one time the cleaners had kept their pails and brooms there, and it was no place for any official, but we had to find somewhere to put poor Pravdine, who kept office hours but had almost nothing to do. You see, this was a case of impulsive royal generosity. The Empress Mother had visited some town in the provinces and had been touched by the plight of the widow of an official who had been struck by lightning in a storm which struck the city at the moment of her arrival. The official was of quite a humble rank and his family were left with no means, and therefore the Empress arranged for the woman's son, who was Pravdine, to be appointed to a post in the Ministry of Justice which she herself had just insisted on being created because she had formed an erroneous impression that there was no school for the staff's children in a prison she had inspected on the Polish border, and had concluded, as erroneously, that there were no schools for the children of prison staffs anywhere in Russia. The whole story was consonant with the Empress Mother's unique personality.'

'You know what the Tsar and Tsarina call her in private?' asked Chubinov, smiling. '*L'Irascible.*'

'You know that too,' said Nikolai. 'Your lot know more than I like. Well, there lived Pravdine in his little cupboard, sometimes ordering a blackboard or some exercise-books. But I never spoke to him except once, when I went to his Christmas party at his apartment, because his wife's sister had married a priest of whom my wife thought well. I don't see how the poor man could possibly have told you anything about me, even if he had wanted to, and I don't believe he would want to.'

'I'm sure that's so,' said Chubinov. 'This is, as you say, a case of A. bringing valid information about B. and saying falsely that it comes from C. Now let's get on to the next stage of the story. For years we accepted that Pravdine was our informant on you. Then when you went for your trip to Paris – which we knew long before you did was to be your permanent exile – we were distressed. We were, you see, specially anxious to go on studying the serial story of the Tsar's perfidy which you were writing in your diary without knowing it. Also, we wanted to know whether you and your associates went on being baffled by the mystery of who it was in your entourage who had betrayed you over the attack on the two grand dukes at Kiev and the one on the Tsar at Reval.

'Then, also, and perhaps most important for those of us who bear the responsibility for the terrorist branch of the revolutionary movement, there was another mystery which had to be solved. I'll talk of that later. But, for the meantime, you'll see the situation. It was important that we should find someone to spy on you in Paris as Pravdine had spied on you in St Petersburg. Yes, yes, I realise now Pravdine wasn't the man, but we then thought that he was. But we never imagined we'd find anybody who could get his foot inside your door in Paris for weeks, or months, or even years. Just think how difficult it was bound to be, with the Russian secret police having its own office in Paris to deal with expatriates.'

'Well, those fellows don't do much,' said Nikolai. 'They all get corrupted by the West. The ideal would be for all Russians to live and die in Russia, seeing only their own kind and maintaining their own system. It's only you accursed expatriates which make us break our rule in the case of the police.'

'Oh, those fellows keep their claws. You're wrong if you

think they give our people much rope. Well, it seemed to us a remarkable example of Gorin's efficiency that almost at once he found someone in Paris who would be able to report to us just as regularly as we thought Pravdine had done. But that's what's so wonderful about Gorin. He seems so gentle and, as it were, so bemused, turning from one object of kindness to another, not knowing whom to comfort first, and then there's a specific task to be done, and all of a sudden he changes into somebody else – he might be one of those great industrialists, those railway magnates, those capitalist monsters whom Count Witte is always trying to let loose on our country for the exploitation of our wretched people. Well, Gorin sprang into action now. In no time he found us a man who could tell us from moment to moment what you are doing. A man named Porfirio Ilyitch Berr.' He repeated the name softly. 'Porfirio Ilyitch Berr.'

'You ought to be in a lunatic asylum,' said Nikolai Nikolaievitch. 'You and all your friends. First my diaries are being read and my most intimate secrets revealed by a man named Pravdine who in fact sat in a housemaid's cupboard all day ordering blackboards and spoke with me, so far as I can remember, once in my life and then to wish me a happy Christmas, and never set foot in my office. Now I'm having my soul put under the Röntgen Rays by a man I've never seen or heard of. Porfirio Ilyitch Berr. You're all mad.'

'You're wrong when you say you don't know Berr,' said Chubinov, looking for the first time rather disagreeable, sly and harsh. 'It's the world you live in that makes you think you don't. That world where everything good and noble and enduring is annulled by the system, the monstrous, murderous system that subordinates everything to the aim of putting the few over the many. You know Berr. You even derive, because not all your heart is calloused by power, the most exquisite pleasure from his company.'

'Mad,' said Nikolai, 'raving mad, the lot of you.'

'But all that I'll explain later. First, before I can make that explanation, I must express to you that we are two halves of a whole. We're in the same plight as you. We have our Judas.'

'Oh, I know who he is,' said Nikolai.

123

'You know?' cried Chubinov. 'Then tell me, tell me!'

'Berr,' said Nikolai. 'Old Berr,' and chuckled into his beard.

'You're impossible. For God's sake do not be light-minded, as all you reactionaries always are, and answer me one question seriously. The names of Vesnin, Patopenko and Komissaroff mean to you what they mean to me. They mean a man who was shot, and two men who are slowly dying in the most northerly penal settlement of Siberia. Oh, the cruelty of Tsarist authority, which sends the political idealist into the Arctic cold. How did you come to arrest these three men?'

'That's an official secret,' said Nikolai, 'so I'll not discuss it.'

'You must tell me if you want to live.'

'I wouldn't buy my life by the betrayal of any official secret.'

'Imbecile old man,' shouted Chubinov, 'will you risk your personal safety to keep the secrets of the Tsar, when he has treated you far worse than my grandfather or yours would have treated one of their serfs?'

'The answer is, yes. I will do nothing to help the enemies of the Tsar, even to save my life, or the life of any one of my family. There are men who are called to serve God by conformity and I'm one of them. I've always known that. At certain times in my life I've greatly longed to drink and to gamble, I've been hungry for the enormous pleasure in the loss of my senses and in gaining or in losing large sums for no reason. But I've always foreseen that these things would give me no lasting happiness, that my part was to be a pillar and that a pillar must never even sway. Go on telling your story if you like. But I can't believe it'll mean anything to me. You and I were created in different dreams of God.'

'There you're mistaken. We're the children of the same dream. Listen. We revolutionaries have, as you know, had many successes in the last few years, but many failures also. We've inflicted the sentence of death on a far greater number of social criminals than have ever been brought to justice before in the same period, but at the same time we've lost more and more of our men to your forces of reaction. Of these Vesnin, Patopenko, and Komissaroff were the most important. They'd all the qualities that would have made them leaders of our organisation, particularly Vesnin. But there were many others, and we find the circumstances in which you arrested them incomprehensible. There was always a great knowledge of the workings of our organisation behind all these arrests, but they weren't the arrests one would have expected any man who had that knowledge to make. Before each of our great achievements —'

'You mean assassinations.'

'Of course. Before each of them, and after them, the police became very active and rounded up a number of terrorists, but never the men and women really engaged in the current conspiracy. Vesnin, however, was arrested just after he had killed the Commandant of St Petersburg —' Laura drew in her breath with a hiss again – 'and Patopenko and Komissaroff when they were just about to execute another important plan, but they were exceptions. Most of the arrested revolutionaries had either struck their last blows some time before or were subordinates not yet ripe for terrorist action. Now, Nikolai Nikolaievitch, what would you make of that?'

'Why, what you do, I expect,' answered Nikolai slowly. 'That on our side we weren't receiving the information which we'd really have liked, which would have enabled us to uproot the terrorist organisation here and now. We were being given just enough to let us cripple the revolutionary movement and prevent it from realising its full potential. Awkward for us. Awkward for you, too. You lost your leaders of five or ten years ahead, and the survivors were left in a state of mutual distrust, without the old hands to steady them.'

They grumbled on. They talked about a lot of people: in Russian conversation there always seemed to be a crowd of faceless personalities doing violent things. It seemed that many of them lived very uncomfortable lives. Men were told to go from St Petersburg to Kharkov and choose their own day and their own route and keep the choice a secret. That, apparently, was insisted on by this man Gorin. Then the traveller arrived at noon and sat about in a dark corner of the station with the story of a further journey ready on his lips if he were questioned, and waited till the afternoon to go into the town, because by then the police were less vigilant. Then he'd be crossing the station square and as he went by the line of droshkys two of the lean horses would paw the ground and jangle their harness, fretted by the two men standing in wait between them, two policemen, who stepped forward with the right interrogations, the proper incredulities.

In some room at the headquarters of the Secret Police a voice had said, 'Don't try to take him at the station, inside or at the exits. Many of the workers are on his side and they'll warn every solitary traveller if you're about. But you'll find him making his way across the square at about four o'clock in the afternoon.' Yet the traveller had never said to himself, 'At four o'clock I'll go across the square into the town.' He'd just gone there when he felt like it. Some of them had been able to tell the organisation that afterwards.

Nikolai said, 'Someone knew that if one sits on a station bench from noon one's back feels as if it were breaking just about four o'clock, and stretching one's legs doesn't do any good. Just as someone on your side knows that when my lot have to raid a café where your miserable pack meet to plan their villainies, it's nervous work, as your lot have their revolvers and their bombs and no mercy in their hearts; and the inspector's nerve will break at a particular hour and he'll hustle out his men to get the thing over. And when they get to the café they find no soul there who isn't a blessed saint.'

Chubinov said, 'But it remains to be learned how they know the day.'

'Yes. Or the place.'

Both sighed. Then they talked of more men with Russian names that had to be heard several times before they could be clearly grasped. How could Nikolai be content to absorb his attention in this ugly male world when his women called for his interest, his pity! Only a little time ago, when Sofia lifted her small, strong, ringed hands to pat a hunter's neck and rub his muzzle it had been on a parity of health; and at night she had stood upright within her satin gowns, unbowed by the weight of her jewels; while now she was a shrunken mummy, dead, except for her courage which was kept alive by her fear. And Tania, she needed pity too. When she used to stand by the window of her bedroom, her elbows supported on the sash and her cheek pressed against the glass, scanning the gardens to see if the double peonies with the heavy scent were open, the corner house, to see if the South African diamond people who had bought it had moved in yet, the summerhouse to see if the old Colonel who lived next door and had been so ill was sitting there with his nurse, she had the air of an inquisitive child happily dispelling the boredom of the nursery; now she looked as if she were hanging face backwards on a cross, as if you would only have had to turn her round to see tears on her cheeks, bitten lips. How could Nikolai free himself from the thought of these two women who needed his help, and listen to this chit-chat about murderers who should only be hanged!

Chubinov was saying, in the unctuous tones of a medical missionary lecturing to the Upper Fifth: 'In order that the secret should be kept we didn't disperse at the end of the meeting, we stayed in the café until there was time for them to have executed the plan and got away. That was Gorin's idea. "Just so that there can be no Judas-work," he said. He and I sat down together and played a game of chess. I can see him now, pausing in play and putting down his queen, to say to me in his gentle way that we must avoid all bitterness in thinking of the traitor amongst us, for it might be that he was one of the older members of the Party and had perhaps been deranged by many years of imprisonment. And then I tried to go on with the game, but kept on making the stupidest mistakes. And Gorin laughed and said, "You're like me, all the Party members are as your own children and when they are in danger it is as if one had sent into battle the real fruit of one's loins." But then Lydia Sture came into the café, weaving her way among the tables like a drunken woman, and she bent over our chessboard and whispered that Patopenko and Komissaroff had been arrested even as they left their lodgings with their bombs. For a long time we three were silent and stared at the chessmen as if the way the game was set out would give us a clue to the mystery which was engulfing us.'

'Very touching,' said Nikolai. 'Particularly as Patopenko and Komissaroff's arrest meant that they weren't able to murder the Chief Military Prosecutor. I can't cry over your story, Vassili Iulievitch.'

'And you won't tell me how those three arrests were made?

127

Then I'll have to tell you how it is our paths have crossed again.'

'The most talkative man I ever heard of was Goethe,' answered Nikolai. 'Dear God, why should I be called upon to be another Eckerman? Particularly as you're no Goethe so far as quality rather than quantity is concerned.'

The train was slowing down, and the two Frenchwomen were collecting their bags. 'Where are we?' asked Chubinov, staring about him. 'I forget what line we are on.'

'It's Amiens,' said Laura.

'A town I've never liked,' said Nikolai. 'A blasphemy is committed here. In the Cathedral there is a Byzantine Christ which should not be in a heretical place of worship. But one can't do anything about it. I once tried. The bishop was most unreasonable.'

Chubinov politely helped the Frenchwomen get their luggage out into the corridor and got them a porter by gesticulating from the window. Then they sat in silence while the hubbub of the station boiled around them. But as soon as the train started again Chubinov said, 'It's the *Rurik*.'

'The *Rurik*, the cruiser we're having built in Glasgow? Do you mean to say that your infamous company of assassins have got to work there too?'

'As you probably know the ship is so far advanced that the skeleton crew has been sent over to get their hand in so that when the full crew comes to take her to the Baltic they can be taught quickly the ways of the new ship. Among the skeleton crew are several members of our Party. More of us will come out with the full crew.'

'Everywhere, everywhere,' muttered Nikolai. 'When I told them so they wouldn't believe me. They said it was only students and the intelligentsia, but I knew better. Plague doesn't select its victims.'

'These sailors and some of the Admiralty staff have informed our Committee that all arrangements have been made for a ceremonial review by the Tsar on the ship's arrival at a Baltic port. These sailors and officials were eager to use the opportunity to assassinate the tyrant.'

'This appetite for death, it's amazing,' said Nikolai. 'The

whole of our social structure is being liberalised, people are being taught to read and write as never before, they are less hungry, they've less reason for social vengeance than ever before, and all they think of is killing.'

'But they thought it unwise that one of their own number should be made responsible for the dead, for it was certain that some agents of the secret police had been planted among the crew, and would keep a continuous watch on the men who had shown signs of revolutionary sympathies as the time of the naval review drew near.'

He said this, Laura thought, as if he regarded this police action as unsporting, like shooting a fox.

'Therefore the sailors begged our Committee to send to Glasgow some of our members who were properly trained in terrorist methods, so that arrangements could be made to smuggle aboard one or two activists at the proper time, who could be kept in some safe corner until the North Sea was crossed on the homeward journey.' His eyes became glazed and he went into an account of the plans the Committee had made to prevent detection. It was as boring as a card-game. '. . . So we've been sending small groups to Glasgow, never less than two or more than four, to travel on false passports to Paris or Berlin or Brussels, where our local branches gave them a new set of false passports, made out in names they had invented, till then unknown even to the travellers themselves, and instructions from the Glasgow sailors as to the place and time of the meetings, couched in a code unknown to the French or German or Belgian members who transmitted them, though it had been imparted to all the delegates before they left Russia. There was also a lapse of time left between the delegates' departure, first from Russia and then from whatever Western centres they used, and their arrival in Glasgow, so that nobody knew exactly till the last moment when they would get there —'

'Such an ingenious plan that I'll give you a hundred to one that there's a member of yours sitting at this very moment in a bathing-machine at Ostend wondering how he got there and what he should do next,' said Nikolai, 'and I'll lay another bet that you get a lot of your delegates cutting off with the travelling expenses.' He laughed hugely, vulgarly, with his mouth open, like a peasant. ' "Ah, poor Ivan Ivanovitch, he must have been arrested by the wicked police!" And where Ivan Ivanovitch really is, I wouldn't like to say in front of my granddaughter.'

'Nothing of that sort has ever happened,' snapped Chubinov. 'At least, only once or twice.'

'Forgive me, Vassili Iulievitch,' said Nikolai. 'For what you've spent your life doing, you're a sensitive man.' But Chubinov was bitter as he said, 'What has gone wrong is quite different, and it went wrong in your apartment in the Avenue Kléber.'

6

'I'VE TOLD YOU,' said Chubinov, 'that Gorin has been ill of late years, though it's not true that he's ever been in a sanatorium. I was one of the first to realise that at last his vitality had snapped under the strain of constant warfare for the rights of the people, austerity, and rough travelling. About eighteen months ago, while you were still in office, the police suddenly threw a dragnet over the larger towns and made innumerable arrests. At once our organisation warned its members to leave their homes and lodgings, till the storm was over, to sleep here and there in hotels not ordinarily used by the Movement, to keep away from friends and write no letters, and to give up frequenting our usual cafés. I myself took refuge in a cottage on a sympathiser's estate thirty miles out in the country, but I was called back to the city to dismantle one of our printing-presses, as the police had been making some enquiries about a man with the same name as the landlord of the little workshop where it had been set up. I went to that workshop, packed the parts of the press under the floorboards, brushed shavings all over them and saw to all the other little precautions one has to take in such circumstances, locked up, and went into the street, and the first thing I saw was Gorin, the head of our Battle Organisation, driving by in an open cab, wearing that little air of peace which he carries about with him as his own private angelic world. I couldn't believe my eyes.

'He didn't see me. But as soon as the bad time was passed and we revolutionaries could safely meet again, he sent for me and without knowing it, provided an explanation for this curious event. He told me that he'd had a most disquieting experience. For several days and nights he'd worked without cease, getting this suspected man out to Scandinavia on the Finland route, getting that unsuspected woman home to her family in the Urals because she was a chatterbox, snatching an hour's sleep when he could, and forgetting all about food and drink. Suddenly he had a brainstorm. He'd no recollection of what he did or where he was for a period of about twenty-four hours, and suddenly he found himself sitting in a night-club in the Nova Derevnia, with two police agents at the next table staring at him. When he got out into the street he nearly fainted. "What am I to do?" he asked, smiling that very sweet smile I knew very well, which meant that he wanted to soothe me but at the same time warn me of a danger, "If I become a peril to you all?"

'When I told him that I'd seen him driving through the streets of St Petersburg in an open cab during that terrible period, he was shocked. He hadn't the slightest recollection of doing any such thing. Then he admitted to me that for some time past he'd been hiding from us that he was not well. He'd been suffering from attacks of dizziness, lapses of memory, and headaches. At once he consented to go to a doctor. I don't think he would have done this for his own sake, but he realised he'd become a danger to his comrades. Well, there were some visits to a couple of specialists, and the verdict came that he must live – at any rate for a time – in a milder climate. The doctors recommended the Isle of Capri, but Gorin insisted on going to Lausanne, though it was not nearly so suitable for his condition, because there he could establish relations with the Swiss Universities and also carry on collaboration with our French and Italian members.

'We haven't had to say good-bye to him. Every now and then, when he feels better, he returns to us and though there's now another head of the Battle Organisation – I expect you know all about him, yes, I mean "Hilarion" – he always defers to Gorin, and we accept his advice and the admirable material he brings us. About a month ago he was with us again in St Petersburg, and he arranged that I should go to England, to take some manuscripts of pamphlets to be printed at a Russian press we have working in a district of London called Camden Town. There's an English wine-merchant who's enthusiastic for our cause and not only gives us money but lets us use his name and his warehouse as a cover for our work. I tell you we are going to win, we are going to take over the world. Well, to my delight Gorin told me that he wished me to break my journey to England by detour to Lausanne, so that I could stay with him and receive some last instructions. I went there ten days ago, and stayed for five days.

'I haven't had such a happy time for many years. Gorin doesn't live in Lausanne, nor even very near it, but in a pretty lakeside village on the outskirts of Montreux, where there's an italianate villa on a little island in the middle of a harbour, so that one has the illusion of living on a stage set for an opera. Gorin's lodgings are in a pension with a fine view of the lake and the harbour, and it's more than comfortable, it's even luxurious. His sitting-room is really beautiful, it opens on a marble balcony covered with wisteria. I was filled with nostalgia, it was so like the places I used to go to with my parents when I was a boy and even until I was a young man, before I had seen the light and taken to the way of suffering. For though my father was not rich like yours, Nikolai Nikolaievitch, who owned a villa in Corfu, I seem to remember – and there was one at Nice, wasn't there, but we had our holidays abroad at beautiful hotels, at the Schweizerhof in Lucerne, at the Grand in Rome, at Danieli's in Venice. It was surprising to find Gorin in such quarters, for he came from a poor family, he hadn't the habit of going to such places, and he's never taken a moment's thought for his own comfort. Of course there was an explanation. Though the proprietress looked precisely like any other proprietress of an expensive pension, a stout woman with a military expression and pompous yet obsequious manners, she was a sympathiser and she gave Gorin special terms. I was very pleased to hear this, for it removed the scruples I would otherwise have felt at returning to a way of life I had promised myself to abandon for ever.

'What filled my happiness to the brim was the arrival, the day after my own, of three comrades from Moscow, Korolenko, Primar, and Damatov. They're all younger than I am, much younger; and of each I'd thought at one time or another, "How I wish there was more leisure in my life, so that I could make this young man my friend". Korolenko had just graduated as a doctor, and I remember that when I heard that I reflected happily, "how fortunate, if there is any young wife among my kin who is going to have a child, any old man who is finding it difficult to leave the world, here's someone who will be the rock they can cling to", though of course I now have no kin, they will have nothing to do with me. Primar was the son of a timber merchant who had renounced a rich inheritance and never thought of it again, plunging himself into poverty and danger as into a carnival ball. He had a wave of fair hair which curled forward across his head, like the crest of a macaw, which somehow aroused one's tenderness. And Damatov was the most charming of them all. He was one of those who are born to make a mock of our aristocracy; for he looked like a prince, he might have been Hamlet, but he was the son of a rich fishmonger in a town two hundred miles north of Kharkov on the River Selm. You know how such people used to pile up the roubles before there were railways, when they fetched the fish up in ice from the Sea of Asov. It happened that his father was one of those whom the tours of the Moscow Theatre Company make stage-struck, and he'd bred his son to be the same. So Damatov had come up to St Petersburg to work at the State Theatre, and had soon become a stage-designer, and then a dramatist. But simply to be with him was to attend a better play than he would ever write, indeed it was like crossing the footlights and changing into a character in a drama written by Shakespeare or by Schiller.

'Now I had leisure to know them, and to know them well, better than it might seem I could in such a short time. You can't think what Gorin adds to any meeting by the quality of his friendship. He turns his face from one friend to another, and his smile says, "Not one person here but is wonderful". This is not empty benevolence, not the unfocused beam which shines from the bland faces of so many holy personages in pictures, for he opens his friends' minds like jewel-boxes and brings the enclosed treasures out into the light. It turned out Korolenko could play the piano like a master, that Primar's supple mind had a talent for mathematics, and when he talked of a problem it was like watching the faultless tumbling of a child acrobat at a fair. Damatov made up poetry, not the elegant odes and tragic laments one would have expected, but funny little poems, about such things as a fat lady taking a fat little pug-dog a walk by the lakeside, not at all vulgar, not at all cruel, indeed kind and good-natured. What added to our happiness was that all this talk and laughter and music never seemed too much for Gorin. He had evidently recovered from his illness to a degree quite wonderful in a middle-aged man who had suffered years of privation and strain. He even insisted on going a long walk with us up in the mountains, and though he did things we knew his doctors wouldn't have allowed he really seemed afterwards to have done himself no damage. He actually took a swim in a lake up in the mountains.

'The three young men left in the afternoon of the fourth day, and I wasn't invited to go with Gorin to the station to see them off. I found this natural enough. It had crossed my mind that this must be another team on its way to a *Rurik* conference in Glasgow, and it would have been contrary to our security plans for anyone to see what train they'd boarded. When Gorin came back he asked me to go for a stroll by the harbour, and we got there just at the time when one by one the lamps went up on the mastheads of the little lake-going craft, and the windows of the italianate villa on the island began to glow a beautiful rose-colour – they must have had red curtains. I can never see lights coming on in summer twilight without emotion. When I was a little boy the sight always made me cry – not because I wasn't happy, for I was a happy child, as you know ours was a happy home – but because I used to feel that my happiness would not last. My mother would be trailing her long flounced skirt round the croquet-lawn, still playing though it was too dark to see the balls except when they rolled into the bright panels cast on the grass by the lit rooms in the house, simply because her nature, which was like a child's, couldn't bear to admit that the little pleasure of the game was coming to an end; and then I used to weep because though I really was a child and she wasn't, I was so much less childish that I could see further than she did, to a day when she'd be unable to finish the game, not because the twilight had fallen but because she would be neither in the dark garden nor in any of the rooms, lit or unlit, of the house. My throat would swell with love for this precious figure which would not always be there; and I felt a return of that emotion when I walked by the little harbour with my dear friend in the dusk. This made me think of you, Nikolai Nikolaievitch. Such recollections always make me think of you, you were such a commanding figure in my childhood. To cover my emotion, I said to Gorin, "What of the Diakonov situation?" and he answered, "Well, you have seen the material I've been forwarding. Valuable as it is, it's very painful reading, and it's not easy to collect either, for Berr is nothing like so amenable and comradely as Pravdine."

'Yes, yes, I know, it is not necessary for you to protest, Nikolai Nikolaievitch, I am just telling you what Gorin said. He went on to tell me that this man, Porfirio Ilyitch Berr, had been employed at the Ministry of Justice, but in middle life had inherited some money and had come to France with his wife to live with a niece, who had married the proprietor of a small restaurant near Les Halles in Paris. Berr was apparently an unamiable character, so unamiable that Gorin expressed surprise that you, Nikolai Nikolaievitch, should have engaged him to act as a sort of clerk and account-keeper to come to your house every day for an hour or two. But Gorin supposed it had something to do with his qualifications as a book-keeper, which were high. It wasn't so, then? Well, that tells us nothing about Gorin's honesty. For he explained that he was only vaguely informed regarding Berr, whom he had dealt with always through an intermediary, who said that Berr must never be approached by anybody but himself, because his niece's husband was fiercely opposed to his political views and might even denounce Berr to the police if he had any idea of Berr's role as a member of the revolutionary movement. Gorin said that at any rate he believed the stories of Berr's unamiability, for an agent of his had once followed Berr from your house, and found him most unprepossessing. We then talked of you, Nikolai

Nikolaievitch, with great respect and a sense of shame. We both wished we were not obliged to set spies on you, we wished we were not obliged to eavesdrop on the Tsar's attempts to degrade you. But we have assumed responsibility for the future of Russia, and that involves us in much guilt which we must accept for the sake of the people. We were so unhappy about it that we fell silent, and simply sat together, watching the strange whitish radiance which the night casts on the waters, and the sparkling lights in the towns on the other side of the lake. I felt that if I could have given my life for you I would have offered it up gladly. When we rose to go home Gorin laid his hand on my shoulder and said, "I know well that much that is best in you comes from Nikolai Nikolaievitch."

'I left Montreux the next morning, and after a day at our centre in Lille I got to London the next evening and was met at Victoria by two English comrades. I was still so happy at having been with Gorin that I had walked the whole length of the platform before I realised that they were utterly overcome by misery. They laid their fingers across their lips to tell me that the cause of their distress could be safely discussed only in some private place, and they took me in a cab to a room in a dark and dingy place called Pimlico, very Gothic, which was no surprise to me, for I knew my Dickens. Locking the door, they asked me if I had known that Primar, Korolenko, and Damatov had been intending to come to London. I stared at them in embarrassment. I hadn't known it, but I'd guessed it, and I was very sure that there were very good reasons why they shouldn't be told. However, they informed me that that morning a woman named Nadya Sarin had arrived from Paris with a story that these three comrades had been arrested there on the eve of their departure for London. They themselves had known that a team was to arrive on its way to Glasgow, but they hadn't known how many men were coming, or who they were, or when they would come, and they were not certain that she was not mistaken or, perhaps, a lying police agent.

'When I cast my mind back I remembered that an actress called Nadya had been Damatov's mistress at one time, and that they had parted because she had a brother much younger than herself who was still at the gymnasium, and several incidents had suggested that her love-affair was leading the authorities to regard the boy with suspicion. I remembered also hearing that as her French was unusually good she had joined a Parisian company of players then in St Petersburg and had returned with them to France. So I told the English comrades that in all probability the woman was who she said she was and that her story was true, and I asked them to take me to her at once. We then got into another cab, and went to another part of London called Notting Hill. She had been taken in by one of our members who ran a lodging-house and we found her lying in bed, surrounded by comrades, in a room which looked across a wide railway-cutting, a positive chasm, with many tracks running along the bottom. The aspect was not unpicturesque for on the opposite cliff of the chasm stood a line of tall houses, neo-classical in design, which were reflecting an orange sunset from their stucco façades. London is very exotic. All these places like Camden Town and Pimlico and Notting Hill have a wild majesty.

'But it was a pity the poor woman hadn't been found other quarters, for every time a train ran through the cutting she buried her head in the pillows, and screamed. Also the room was too full of people who seemed to be taking pleasure in witnessing her agitation, and even going to some pains to outdo it. There was one person I marked with special disapproval, a tall young man with straight yellow hair and broad shoulders, who was striding up and down with a glass in his hand, making exaggerated gestures of despair. In consternation I asked the comrades who had brought me to this place what sort of story we were all going to tell if the police broke in, but they assured me that this was most unlikely. It filled me with joy that an admittedly great power should be so much more liberal than Russia, but I also saw that it must be difficult to run a revolutionary movement if one cannot tell the comrades that if they make too much noise they may attract the attention of the police. It was some time before I could make myself heard and really get down to questioning the actress, who was of a refined and elevated type, pale and slender, with an oval face and long black hair. She could have sat to an artist for a picture called "Melancholy" or "Autumn".

'She told me that she and Damatov had never ceased to be sincerely devoted, and that she had been overjoyed when he had called her at her lodgings in Paris, which was somewhere near the Bridge of Passy, about one o'clock two days before. He had told her that he had come to acquire the rights of a new French play which our State Theatres wished to perform, and that he had two friends with him, named Primar and Korolenko, who could call for him later. The other two came about five, and as it was a very fine evening they decided to go for a walk. The actress went with them, though she had to leave them before long, as she was acting that night. When they were outside on the pavement, Korolenko, who knew Paris better than his friends, said, "Here, this way", and they made their way up the Avenue Kléber. They went the whole length of the Avenue, right up to the Etoile, and there the actress said good-bye to them, and took a cab to her theatre. She had imagined that she would be seeing Damatov before very long, for he had promised to be at her lodgings when she returned from her performance, and to stay with her till he had to go to the station in the morning.

'She stayed awake all night but Damatov never came to her. In this London room, she beat the people away from her bed-side with a gesture so that she could whisper in my ear, and she told me that as the hours had passed she had grown terri-fied, she found herself praying that he might have changed since their separation into the sort of man capable of insulting a woman. In the morning she was at a loss to know what to do. Though he had told her he would have to leave Paris that morning, he hadn't said where he was going, so she couldn't go to any station and see whether he was leaving. But she hadn't believed for one moment his story about buying the rights of a play, she had known he hadn't expected her to believe it, that he was telling it as part of his terrorist drill. So in the end she went to consult a Russian medical student living in an hotel not far from hers, and when he heard what had happened he took her to an old revolutionary who was having a late breakfast in a nearby café. He had known Korolenko, he was sure too that there would be a terrorist reason for the presence of these par-ticular three young men in Paris; and, thinking it over, he thought it probable that if Korolenko had taken his party up the Avenue Kléber it was with the intention of ending up at the Café Viborg in the Avenue de la Grande Armée, which is much frequented by our people. They hailed a taxi and went straight there, and had to go no further. The proprietor told them that Korolenko and two young men unknown to him had come into the café early on the previous evening, and a quarter of an hour later half a dozen police agents had driven up in a van and taken them away.

'On hearing this the actress assumed that her friend was doomed either to death or to many years of imprisonment, and, as you know, Nikolai Nikolaievitch, she would be right. The older man took her back to her lodgings, and then went to see somebody, but she didn't know who it was. He came back after an hour and helped her pack her baggage and put her in the afternoon train for London, giving her the address of some London members, and telling her that he would telegraph them and they would meet her at Victoria. He said she was not to mind leaving Paris so suddenly and embarrassing her employers, for she must be removed from the sphere of the French police and the Russian Secret Police operating in Paris. She said that as for that, she didn't care, she only wanted to die. But then she was told that the three young men might have been going to London, and that their interception might mean danger to members of our movement there, and the brave woman had consented to make the journey. So there she was, in this London room, full of chattering and gesticulating people who seemed far more theatrical than she was, and she looked up at me and said that she had accomplished her mission, and she lived now only to find out whether Damatov was alive or dead. She said it very quietly. One would not have thought that an actress could speak with such little resonance. It was as if her voice had been taken out of her throat and beaten and put back. I did not doubt what she thought she would do if she found out that he was dead.

'I had to do my duty, I had to enquire into all the circumstances as if I were a police officer. She had fallen back on the pillows and I made them give her some brandy, and then I asked her if she had had any impression during her walk through Paris with the three young men that they had been watched. No. Not exactly. But there had been one little incident which she had noticed with distaste and could not forget, though she had thought it impossible that it could have any bearing on what had happened. As they were drawing near the end of their walk and the Arc de Triomphe was well in sight, Korolenko's cigarette went out, and Primar stopped to give him a light but found his matchbox empty and called out to Damatov, who turned back and gave them his. While the three men were halted, the actress strolled slowly on, came to a stop, and stood smiling around her at nothing, as she put it, because it was all so delightful. Suddenly she realised that she had been smiling at something, or rather at someone. She had come to a standstill a few yards away from the doorway of one of the larger houses on the Avenue, which was wide open, showing the vaulted entry to the courtyard. Unconsciously she had been smiling into the shadows of the entry, just where a man was standing. She couldn't see him very well. There was a blank space of wall between the left-hand leaf of the door, which had been folded back, and the entrance to the concierge's lodge; and this man was in the thickest of the shadow. He wore spectacles, and he was holding a pair of gloves in front of his mouth and chin. She wouldn't venture to say he was doing that to hide his face. It was something people did when they were sunk in thought. She could really see nothing of him except that he was of medium size, and she could not have sworn to anything about him. Yet she had a nagging impression that when she first caught sight of him he had already been staring out at her with the intensest interest.

'For an instant she was terrified, and thought of running back to the three young men and saying to them, "There's a man here watching us." But then the man in the shadows made a gesture of unmistakable meaning. It was as if he said to her, "Just wait for a minute, my dear, you're exactly what I fancy, I'm coming out, or will you come in?" She forgot everything in her indignation, and just then Damatov and the others caught up with her. The man in the entry shrugged his shoulders and spread out his hands in a pantomime of dismay, spun around on his heel, and withdrew into the courtyard. Damatov

140

just saw the tail-end of the movement, and said, with not very great anger, "What's this going on? If I'd the time I'd stop and give that Don Juan a black eye." That was how it had seemed to him, and how it had seemed to her, and she had some experience, for since she had come to Paris many men had spoken to her on the street. She still thought that might have been all that happened, for the gesture of invitation had been so truly vulgar, so deeply nasty in its lecherous *bourgeois* way, that it couldn't have been feigned, except by a really great character actor. Yet she had to admit that when she first saw the man he seemed to be watching her with an intensity beyond that, and a selective intensity, which would not have been satisfied by the sight of anybody but herself and her companions.

'When I heard this I couldn't speak. I was sure that the man in the entry had been our scourge, our Judas, our false brother, the traitor who could betray the secrets he had never been told, because his experience was our experience, his past our past, his present our present. Of course he hadn't had to follow his quarry. The actress had told us with some wonder how the old revolutionary had known from the mere fact that Korolenko had led the party up the Avenue Kléber that he meant to take them to the Café Viborg, but I had drawn the very same conclusion myself. "Ah," I'd said to myself, "he was going to take them up to see old Alaner at the Café Viborg. No doubt our traitor had told Korolenko to take them there. Then he'd only to stand in a doorway at the Avenue Kléber, which was right on the route they were bound to take, to make sure that his victims were on the way to the place where, as soon as he had time to make the necessary telephone call, the police would pick them up. Our traitor had the knowledge for that, and also the abominable intelligence to throw off the scent a woman whose sensitiveness had detected him, by an insulting trick which depended on her being virtuous.

'I asked the actress, "Can you give us any idea of the whereabouts of the house? Was it on the right or the left of the Avenue? Was it as far up as the Rue Dumont-d'Urville just off the Rue des Portugais?" But she interrupted me by saying, "I can do better than that. I remember the number." It seemed that as she turned away in disgust from the door the small enamel number-plate on the wall had caught her eye, and she had noted the figures because they were three more than the year of the century in which she had been born. Perhaps because I was so tired by my long journey, and because I was overcome with grief over the capture of these three young men, with whom I had been so recently, I passed at this moment into a state of lightmindedness. I didn't listen to the number as she said it. I sat there, smiling, almost openly laughing, because it struck me as so ridiculously characteristic of an actress to remember a number because it was three more than the year in which she was born. Any of us might say, "Why, '68 or '69, or whatever it might be, that's the year I was born", but to say, " '71, that's three more than the year I was born", that takes the theatrical temperament, the innocent egotism of the player.

'Then I suddenly heard the young man with the straight yellow hair, of whom I've already spoken, exclaim, "Why, that's the number of the house where the Minister of Justice who was disgraced, the Count Diakonov, has an apartment. And it explains the whole thing. For there's a Tsarist spy working in that household." I asked stupidly, "How should you, an Englishman, know that?" He answered, "What do you mean? I'm not English, I'm Russian. You should know that, aren't we talking Russian now? Very few Englishmen know any Russian and when they speak it you'd take it for Double Dutch. I'm a student at Oxford. I'm in the West because my father's one of the secretaries at our Embassy in Paris. It's from my father's papers that I know there's a Tsarist spy working in Diakonov's household." I thought he was talking nonsense. A revolutionary spy, but not a Tsarist spy. What an extraordinary idea, I told myself, and wondered how the confusion could have arisen; and I said coldly, "What grounds can you have for saying that?" as I have often said before, when we older ones have had occasion to keep our younger comrades from spreading false rumours.

'The young man said, with what I realised afterwards was great good nature, considering my tone: "I go home for my holidays to stay with my father in Paris. He knows nothing of

142

my revolutionary sympathies and I see what I can see for the good of the cause. I can tell you for certain that there is a Tsarist spy in Diakonov's household who sends to our Embassy in Paris the fullest reports of all his doings, and who photographs all his diaries and his letters. His diaries are pitiful, and show the Tsar in the worst light, and as they are all sent back to St Petersburg the old man is in great danger. The Tsar is eagerly looking for some excuse to recall him to Russia and lay some trumped-up charge against him, and then discredit him thoroughly by never bringing him to trial and abandoning the proceedings on the pretence of showing him mercy. It's easy to see that my father, who is an honourable though unenlightened man, hates the whole business, which is indeed repulsive. There was one letter from Baron Roller, written from Vichy, in which he refused to come and see old Diakonov, though they'd been friends since childhood, because the Tsar had forbidden it; and that disgusted my father so much that when he read it he tore the copy across, and it had to go on its way to the Tsar, with a note from the secretary saying there'd been an accident. My father's often quite bitter these days, and I'm sure it's about this."

'I sat there, asking the actress questions which I knew didn't matter, while it sank in: the knowledge that the Tsarist authorities were receiving precisely the same documents which were being regularly transmitted to us by our agent, Porfirio Ilyitch Berr. But when I tried to visualise a Tsarist spy and a revolutionary spy working side by side in your department I couldn't believe it. We know, of course, how many rooms there are in your apartment and how many servants you have. You've greatly reduced your household, it could be said that you live more like a French or an English aristocrat than a Russian one. It seems most unlikely that in your comparatively modest household there should be two men, both having access to your papers and both taking advantage of their opportunities to remove those papers and photograph them surreptitiously, who didn't sooner or later become aware of each other. But I knew Berr's reports by heart, and I was sure he'd never expressed any suspicion that there was a police spy working beside him in your study. I could draw only one conclusion. There were not two spies in your household, but one. The spy who was working for us was also working for the police. It was he who had stood in the entry and looked out at Korolenko and Primar and Damatov; and if he knew enough to betray them then he was the Judas who had long persecuted us. I remembered too the unpleasant impression Berr had made on the few people who had seen him. I said to the diplomat's son, "Have you no idea who supplies your father with Diakonov's papers?" and he answered, "I don't know the man's name, he's always referred to by a number, which I've forgotten. But he's an agent who has worked for the police over a number of years, and again and again he has given them most valuable information." '

'Laura,' said Nikolai.

'Grandfather?'

'You're biting your nails,' he said icily. 'It's an ill-bred trick. You have the good fortune to inherit the long, narrow hands of our family, do not spoil them.'

'Yes, Grandfather,' she said, tears standing in her eyes. He should not have said that in front of a stranger.

'As I've said,' continued Chubinov, 'there was no further doubt in my mind. I was sure that at last we'd uncovered the trail of our Judas, and that we knew his name. I had to keep my thoughts to myself. There might be some traitors in that very room. I stood up and said that I could do nothing. I must return to Paris and confer with the head of the organisation there, to the end of finding out what charges the police had brought against Primar and Korolenko and Damatov, and of warning our other centres that a traitor was at work. I also told them that I would try to get in touch with Gorin, and the mention of his name instantly tranquillised everybody. I bent over the actress and kissed her hand, and she looked up at me with her great eyes and told me that if Damatov were to die she would not wait a single day before following him into the Absolute. She said this with perfect sincerity, but also in perfect style, with that same utterly heart-breaking lack of resonance, and I knew that she would not fulfil this prediction, but would live to enjoy much happiness and success. There was nothing unpleasant about this realisation, on the contrary, it was as agreeable as looking forward to spring in the middle of winter. I smiled down at her and kissed her hand again, and then asked the comrades who had met me at the station to take me somewhere where I could send a telegram, and said my good-byes.

'We had to walk quite a long way, and then take a bus, and then go a journey by underground railway, to the General Post Office, which was the only place from which I could send a telegram at that hour. It was dark now, and the city was fascinating and terrifying in its exoticism. The streets round the General Post Office were empty, except for a large number of cats. It all might have been a fantasy drawn by Gustave Doré. I sent a telegram to the deputy head of our Battle Organisation in Paris, whom I can now dare to name to you as a man called Stankovitch, who would, I was certain, know all that was to be known about the investigation of Berr, asking him to meet me at the station when I arrived in Paris the next afternoon. Then, finding that it was not so very late, I asked my companions to take me to look at St Paul's Cathedral, as I remembered from a passage in the correspondence of either Herzen or Marx that it was not far away. The two Englishmen seemed surprised by the request but agreed. I stood with them in the street looking up at the dark mass of the superb building against the starlit sky, but when I turned to them to compliment them on their national possession and asked them if they didn't consider it wonderful that Wren had never seen a dome until he built one for himself, I found they were not looking at the cathedral but at me. One of them said, "You know a lot about all this, don't you?" I said that I knew no more than he and his friends. They said, "Well, when we asked you if you had known that Primar and Korolenko and Damatov were coming to London, you said you hadn't, but it seemed to us you weren't entirely surprised to hear that they'd meant to. And why are you smiling? You smiled twice when that woman was telling her story. What's funny about all this?" I could not tell them that I had smiled at the actress remembering a number because it was three more than the year she was born, or because I thought that she would not take poison if Damatov were to die. They were good men, but they wouldn't have understood. They took me back to my room in Pimlico, and arrived next morning to take me to Victoria as if they were police agents seeing a criminal out of town. I found myself resenting this for reasons which made me ashamed. It is hard to overcome the disadvantages of one's birth. I was angry because one of the men who doubted me was an old soldier from the ranks, the other a tailor.

'When I arrived at the Gare du Nord Stankovitch was waiting for me. We went to a bar, and ordered a meal, and I left him in order to telephone to Gorin at the pension near Montreux. But he wasn't there. The proprietress answered me and told me that he'd gone to Paris to see his doctor. This disquieted me and I asked anxiously about his health, but she answered with such indifference that, remembering she was a sympathiser, I concluded that she was probably repeating an untruth which Gorin had told her to give strangers. I rang off and tried to find him at the hotel he always stayed at in Paris, the Hôtel de Guipuzcoa et de Racine, it's a little place between the Hôtel de Ville and the Tour St Jacques. But he wasn't there either. My heart sank. I then went back to Stankovitch and the meal we had ordered, and while we ate I spoke of the disappearance of the three young men and found that he knew all about that and the dispatch of Nadya Sarin to London, so I went on to question him about Berr. He answered reticently. Gorin, he said, had always impressed on him that Berr was to be handled with kid gloves, he might at any moment throw up his job as an informer. "Is he really so disagreeable?" I asked. "I don't know that first-hand, I've never spoken to him; but Gorin's had him thoroughly investigated, and all the reports say so. Apparently he strides along with the most arrogant expression on his face, and he's unkind to his wife, leaves her trotting after him, hardly able to catch up, and never seems to speak to her. But it's not merely a question of his disposition. What's to be feared is that he may get into difficulties with his niece's husband, who's a reactionary, and who, if he found any of us hanging about, might denounce him and us." I found myself wondering if Gorin had not, since his illness, lost something of his genius. Surely this tale that no revolutionary must speak to an informer on account of his family was the very yarn which would be spun by a police spy who didn't want his master to know that he was doing business with both sides.

' "So you're quite satisfied," I asked, "that Berr is loyal to us?" "Yes, quite satisfied," he said. "He's a very isolated man. He makes no contacts at all except with the Diakonov household, and nobody goes there now except the blind and the halt and the lame who are pensioners of the Countess's charity." "There's nobody else at all," he said, "except a man named Kamensky, who worked for Diakonov when he was Minister of Justice and is of no importance at all. Gorin was interested in him at first, and three times set a comrade outside the Diakonov apartment to see if perhaps he was someone we'd known in Russia under a different name, and twice he didn't turn up, but the third time he did. I forgot who saw him, but anyway he was nobody; and Gorin put me to search Kamensky's room at his hotel, the San Marino, near the Hôtel de Ville, and that told us everything we needed to learn. It's a funny thing, he's an engineer, and apparently quite a good one, and one would expect him to be enlightened, but he ought to have been a monk, there were several icons and shelves of religious books and a very full diary, full of pious vapourings. He's evidently a thorough nincompoop and he spends much of his time toadying to the Countess Diakonova, who is a bigoted and reactionary woman." I must beg your pardon for that, Nikolai Nikolaievitch. "Anyway," Stankovitch went on, "Berr keeps us fully posted about all Kamensky's doings, and they add up to exactly nothing. But don't worry about Berr. He's completely reliable. We've tested him again and again."

'It was on the tip of my tongue to tell him what I had heard from the diplomat's son in London. But then it suddenly struck me that if Stankovitch spoke so well of Berr he was probably a traitor himself. It struck me that my world was terribly uncertain. I had been seen off from Victoria by men who thought I was a traitor, though I was loyal, and here I had landed at the Gare du Nord to be met by a man whom I had thought was loyal but who was probably a traitor. And I could not get in touch with Gorin. "Where does Berr live?" I asked, quite without subtlety. I try to follow no technique but I am apt to get flustered. That is one of the reasons why I admire Gorin, who is never at fault. "There's no harm in my telling you that," said Stankovitch, "for strangely enough he's in the telephone book. He lives in a block of flats in one of the newer working-class suburbs to the north-east of Paris, one of those places built on the English model, with gardens around them. He really must be a very disagreeable man. Apparently his wife runs about like mad all day, working for him, but Gorin says that in fine weather he's apt to spend the whole day idling in a queer sort of hut, a summer-house affair, in a patch of his own he has in the vegetable patches which are part of the estate. I'll tell you something. I think Gorin has kept a pretty close watch on this man Berr, in case we have to take disciplinary action against him some day."

'When Stankovitch said that, I saw my duty clear before me. I'd been wrong to doubt Gorin's efficiency. He'd long suspected what I had just found out. Had he been available I'd have asked him what the next step should be, but he wasn't and I didn't think he would be for some time. He wasn't in Lausanne and he wasn't in Paris, and I suspected that either he had gone back to Russia on one of his periodic trips or had gone to London or Glasgow to look into the *Rurik* situation. So there was no help for it. I myself would have to kill Berr. This wasn't easy for me. Not in any sense. I love humanity, therefore I can't wish to shed human blood. I also have insufficient preparation for the performance of such a deed. It isn't that I can't shoot; you know I can. But as I've told you, though I'm associated with the terrorist group within our organisation, it's only as a theoretician and an archivist. I don't know how to set about such things.

'But I hadn't the slightest doubt that that was my duty. Berr was a traitor to our movement, who had just betrayed Korolenko, Primar and Damatov, and God knows how many of our comrades before that. As for the future, I didn't believe that Berr could yet know of our plan to take over the *Rurik* and use is as a stage for the supremely desirable purge, the extirpation of the Tsar, but in view of his known resourcefulness I was afraid that once he had the three young men's papers in his hands, he might report to his superiors some deductions which would lead them fairly near to the truth. I also wished, for once, to take some of the guilt from the shoulders of my beloved friend Gorin. Not that I thought the guilt of eliminating Berr was heavy, if, indeed, it existed at all. I would probably pay for Berr's life with my own. I believe in Kant's Law of Nature and it follows that I have a right to kill only if I am willing to give my own life in expiation. I am aware that there are philosophical difficulties in this position, but I think I could justify it, though perhaps this is not the most suitable time and place for such a discussion.

'Also I was drawn to this deed, because it centred round you, Nikolai Nikolaievitch. For many years I've had dreams which I always felt were important, though I didn't know what they meant and they were inherently absurd. In these dreams I see something familiar, something rooted in my infancy and my childhood, mixed up with things quite unrelated to them. You remember that little lake in front of my father's country house? It wasn't a lake, really, just a large pond. In the middle of it was an island covered with birch-trees, and coarse yellow grasses, an island which is round, quite round, as if it were drawn with compasses. Well, I dream that someone has set down on that little island a merry-go-round, the kind you see at fairs, with swing-boats like dragons painted scarlet and gold, or I dream of our conservatory, and it's got a printing-press set down among all the delicate stove-plants my mother loved to cultivate and, that's funny too, the press is rose-pink. Now I'm having a waking dream of that kind. There you are, whom I've known all my life, my father's dearest friend, who far more than my father was the image of the man I hoped to be, for you were stronger than he was. You taught me to shoot, game-birds, and red deer and the wild boar, because you were a better shot than my father, and though you are not a patient man you were more patient with my sickliness, too. I can still shoot, you know. Every now and then I take out my revolver again and go to a range and practice, because – that's what I pretend to myself – it's the most useful small arm for our movement. But it's also because you always said that good revolver shots were very rare, and I was one of them. Now I'm going to use my revolver to protect you, the giant. I'm protecting you from your Judas. I know that it's absurd to think of me protecting you, but that's what I'm doing.'

'For God's sake,' said Nikolai, wiping the sweat from his brow, 'did you kill this poor devil Berr?'

'Wait, wait,' said Chubinov.

'Or did another of you hyenas get him? But probably not. Since so far as I can remember the man never existed.'

'You'll wish that it were so. I had to take the train to get to Berr's home, and I found myself in one of those very ugly suburbs of Paris where the Town suddenly stops, leaving a raw selvedge which isn't Paris and isn't countryside. There's a jumble of factories and small houses and tenements along the high road, and then a large new factory. Just beyond it a track leaves the high road and runs a couple of hundred yards up a hill to two blocks of tenements, which, I learned at the station, had been put up for the workers in the new factory. They're the kind of hideous buildings which capitalists think fit for the dispossessed. I realise how unpleasant a character Berr must have, for he must be a materialist, or he would not be a Tsarist spy; yet he is indifferent to material beauty, or he would not live in such a drab place. I followed the track, which ends in a big square pavement, with some flower beds set into it, extending all round the two blocks. I identified the block in which Berr lived, according to the address in the telephone book. The track started again on the other side of the square and led up a slope covered with vegetable gardens divided into allotments. There were several benches on this paved square, and I sat down on one facing the door from which Berr must come out.

'I opened a newspaper and pretended to read it, but I had no real need to keep up this pretence, for there was nobody about except some children playing together in a sandpit on the edge of the square, near an open wash-house where their mothers were working. So I was able to look about me, and I soon saw the hut in which I would have to confront the traitor Berr. There were many bits of home-made carpentering standing among the vegetable plots, but they were all simply tool-sheds. This one alone looked as if it had been made by a builder and planned as a summerhouse, with a wide casement-window. I recognised the peculiar character of Berr in the perversity with which the window had been set on the side which had no view but looked back at the two hideous tenements. It was troublesome that it was not far away from them, but I counted on being able to induce him to take a walk with me, and I had a silencer on my revolver.

'I wondered how long I'd have to wait. But the morning, which had been cloudy, suddenly cleared, and as soon as the sun was shining the Berrs came out of the block opposite me and made their way to the hut. They answered exactly to the descriptions I had been given. Berr had an arrogant appearance which was peculiarly objectionable because he was so mediocre that he should have felt obliged to be humble. His pride was generalised, it even made him walk stiffly and slowly, but it had not given him the geniality which sometimes accompanies self-satisfaction. His expression was like barbed wire. As for his wife, she was the very prototype of the bullied wife. She was a stout, short woman with a round face and flat nose, like millions of our Russian peasant women, and she had about her a goodness that can often be remarked in her kind. She had to hurry, hurry, hurry, to keep up with her striding, scowling husband. When they came to the iron gate into the vegetable gardens she ran ahead and opened the heavy catch for him with a willingness which could only be described as pretty. But he stood back and let her do it, without a flicker of gratitude on his pompous face. She was talking all the time and he did not answer, and this was very touching, for it was clear that she was talking sensibly, she wasn't babbling, and she was speaking playfully and kindly. I could imagine she was using all those endearing diminutives in which our language is so rich. I thought Berr must have a heart of stone to remain mute and unsmiling.

'I watched them go up the slope, keeping to a strip of grass that ran beside the vegetable plots. Her arm had been in his but as might have been expected he soon disengaged it and fell a pace behind her. For that coldness, however, he showed some remorse, for he put out his hand and rested his finger-tips on her shoulder, in a way which would have seemed in-expressive enough in an ordinary person, but which no doubt counted almost as a caress from him. When they got to the hut he stood aside while she opened the door, flung wide the windows, and shook some cushions out into the sunlight. He did not offer to help her, but when she had finished he went in and sat down. She made as if she were at once going to return to the tenements, but before she'd gone a few steps she looked down on the ground, halted, dropped awkwardly on her knees, picked a sprig of some plant, held it to her nose, then struggled to her feet again, flapping her arms like a hen, and went back to the hut and handed the sprig to him. My heart began to beat very fast. I wished I was not under the necessity of bringing pain to this excellent creature.

'There was now no reason why I shouldn't carry out my plan. But my legs refused to raise me from the bench, and I began to wonder whether my whole life was not a pretence and an evasion, whether I had not adopted intellectual pursuits simply to cover up an inaptitude for action. But I turned my mind back to Kant and Hegel and received their benediction. Fitting my hand round the revolver in my pocket, I went through the iron gate. I found myself walking more and more slowly as I drew nearer the hut. I decided I wouldn't try to get Berr to take a walk with me, I would satisfy myself of his guilt in the hut and shoot him down there, and take my chance of being caught. If fate was against me, so much better for the Law of Nature. But when I came to the hut and looked through the window I did not see the man I had come to find. True, there was a man in there, sitting in a cushioned chair and holding a sprig of green leaves to his nostrils, but he looked as humble and patient as a saint on an icon. And he took no more notice of me than if he were a saint on an icon. Though I had come as close to the hut as I could without treading on the flowers growing round the walls, and though I was darkening his window, he did not raise his head.

'I gripped the window-sill and leaned right into the room. Immediately the man's expression changed, and he assumed again his air of arrogance. He lifted his head and asked, in French, "Is someone there?" He was looking straight at me, but not at my face, at a point somewhere below my collarbone. I remained quite still, and after some seconds his proud mask melted, he again appeared gentle and abstracted, though he continued to stare in my direction. I was incredulous and leaned further into the hut. I took my revolver out of my pocket and then, without releasing the safety-catch, I pointed it straight at him. Knitting his brow, doubtfully, summoning back part of his insolence, he asked again. "Is someone there?" And then I knew that he was not our spy, he was not a Tsarist spy, and that if a million men told me so, they would all be perjurers. For he was blind.

'I put my revolver back into my pocket, and I answered, speaking French as he did, "Yes, I'm here."

'He then demanded pompously, "And who are you?"

'I gave him my right name. I was astonished that I did so, I had not meant to. "I am Vassili Iulievitch Chubinov," I said, and I couldn't go on.

' "What, a Russian!" he exclaimed, breaking into our language. "I'm a Russian too, I'm Porfirio Ilyitch Berr. What brings you here, friend?"

'I spoke quite strangely to him. "I'm in trouble, in great trouble."

' "That makes you like a whole lot of other people," he answered, smiling. "We're all in trouble, all the sons of men are in trouble. But what sort of trouble are you in?"

'To my own amazement I burst into tears. I wished I could tell him the whole story, but of course it was impossible. I found myself blurting out, just as I had blurted out my real name, "I've lost a friend."

' "What do you mean, lost a friend?" asked Berr. "Has he died, or has he done something wicked to you?"

'I didn't know how to carry on this conversation, for I couldn't be honest, and I hated to deceive this man, partly because he was blind, and partly because he was so pleasant, so unexpectedly pleasant. I'd have liked to turn round and rush away, but I knew it was my duty to my comrades to clear up this mystery which, during the last few minutes, had become so much more obscure and menacing. Also I wanted to stay with him. I can't tell you how enjoyable it was, just being there with him. But all the same I didn't know what to say next, for of course I hadn't lost a friend, the words had just come into my head. So I determined to speak about you, Nikolai Nikolaievitch, who are at the core of this mystery, and

153

who are a fixed point in my life. I said, "Well, my trouble's a long story, and I won't burden you with it now, but my friend, he isn't dead, and he hasn't done anything wicked" – this of course is not true, as a minister of the Tsar you are sunk in wickedness – "but I've lost him, I can't get at him, and I believe you know where he is, and as he's the one person in the world who can help me, I wish you'd tell me how to find him, for I believe you know him. I speak of Nikolai Nikolaievitch Diakonov."

'He threw out his arms, he laughed, he shouted your address aloud, as if he were cheering at a game. "That's where he is! You're lucky to have such a friend. Unlucky to have thought you'd lost him! Go and find him. It's no distance from the Arc de Triomphe, it won't even cost you much to get there. You've come to the right place to get news of him. For my wife, did you see her a minute ago, you should have met her on the way up, my little Emilia, we owe all we have to Nikolai Nikolaievitch and his wife, Sofia Andreievna, who though she is still alive may be counted among the saints, and we visit their home at least once a week. For, listen, some years ago the Evil One afflicted my wife and me with the most unimaginable stream of misfortunes. I used to be janitor in the Law Courts at Moscow, but a rich grain merchant who had noticed me when he was bringing a case asked me and my wife to come and be caretakers in his apartment house here in Paris, and as I wanted to see the world and as our niece, whom we brought up as our own, had married a Frenchman who had a little restaurant here by Les Halles, I took the job. Well, the grain merchant died one day from a heart-attack and his heirs sold the house without ever leaving Russia, and just at that moment I . . ." he paused, and his face became sullen and aggressive, as it had been when I first saw him ". . . just at that moment I lost my sight. You can't think, my friend, what it was like for me to become blind and helpless, because, though I am nobody I was a little bit of a somebody in my way, I was not only head of the janitors' corps at the Law Courts, I was the best billiards player among our sort of people in St Petersburg; and as for family responsibilities I'd always been the one who was leaned on, not the one who leaned. And my niece's husband had made a terrible mess of his little restaurant, and there were three children by then, he would have helped, but I couldn't let him. I thought we'd come down to begging in the streets, if somebody at the Russian church hadn't told the Countess Diakonova about us, and ever since then she and her husband have been our mother and our father. They got my niece's husband a job in the canteen in the big new factory down the road, which belongs to the family of the Count's sister-in-law, and they put us into this flat, where we all live together and are very happy, and they never tire of thinking of this and that which make this horrible affliction easier for me."

' "Just look," he said, "at this hut. They sent men to build it, facing south, so that I can sit here with the sun on my skin. They've put a telephone in the flat, so that my wife can call help if I fall, as I sometimes do, and everybody else is out. Oh, go to them quickly, they'll give you the blood out of their hearts." He went on to tell me that when he and his wife went to your apartment they were always graciously received by Sofia Andreievna, and were given a meal of good Russian food in a little room, either by themselves or with some other Russians who'd been unfortunate, and afterwards they were taken back into Sofia Andreievna's drawing-room where she'd be sitting with some friends and a priest or two from the church in the Rue Darou, and they would have edifying conversation, but it was not too pious, they would laugh a lot. There was an intimate of the house whom they liked very much, who turned out to be the Monsieur Kamensky of whom I had been hearing the day before. Stankovitch seemed to have got a very accurate idea of him from searching his room, for Berr said that he talked with the priests and the Countess as piously as if he were a priest too, though he was an engineer, told them funny stories which made him and his wife laugh but were at the same time suitable for the nobility to hear, and gave them Russian newspapers and magazines, always of an improving kind, to which his wife read to him in the evenings. "He's a good fellow," Berr said, "but he's not a fountain like the Count or the Countess." "Who else is in the house?" I asked, but Berr, frowning, said, "How should I know? But you're wondering if they've got too many poor souls round them, there'll

155

be no room for you? Oh, never worry about that." I could not go on questioning him.

'I felt I must go back to Paris and talk all this out with Gorin at once. The error he had made about Berr was monstrous. It was true that anybody might have been deceived by seeing Berr and his wife walking through the streets; the defence his pride had built up to conceal his affliction was convincing. But Gorin should have told the investigating comrades to do much more than merely follow Berr from his tenement in the suburbs to the Avenue Kléber, he should have insisted on them collecting material from his neighbours. Because of this gross technical blunder the spy who had passed himself off as Berr had used the confusion he had created as cover for the betrayal of comrade after comrade, and I, who was of value to the cause, had nearly risked my life by murdering a man whose death would have done us no good whatsoever. Also I had the most terrible feeling that, if I had killed the man who sat facing me so brightly, smiling out of his darkness, I would have been vile beyond simple vileness, the earth and the sea would have rejected my spirit, I would have fallen off the world through the atmosphere into the nothingness of space, rejected, rejected, rejected, not by your God, but by me. By me. I did not want to talk to Gorin. I wanted to try him.

'I went into the hut and kissed Berr on both cheeks and said, "Good-bye, my brother, I must be on my way." He would not let me go, he held me close to him, and said soberly, "But, for the love of God, don't go back to Paris yet. I'm blind but I feel things. You're rigid with suffering, you're like a poor soldier that's lain wounded all night on a frozen battlefield. You're not fit yet even for the short journey back to Paris." I was in agony as he spoke. I was afraid he would feel the revolver which I had slipped into the pocket of my overcoat. When I freed myself and moved away, he followed me, though he plainly felt afraid of moving when his wife wasn't there, and his steps were short and hesitant. But he risked falling because he was so anxious about me. "Stay and sit here in the hut and get the good of the sun. It's free," he told me, smiling. "Or go up to our flat, it's number 36, that's always been my lucky number, and tell my wife that I've sent you and she's to make you some good Russian tea. For that's something which Sofia Andreievna always gives us, and the little fellow Kamensky too, he sometimes gives us special tea he gets from a cousin who's out in Samarkand." I could only stammer, "Porfirio Ilyitch, I'm not worth all this." He said, "You're talking nonsense, for I can feel you're a good man, wasted by abstinences. You smell only of soap and smoke, and what's a cigarette? Stay with us, you can sleep on a mattress on the floor, and perhaps tomorrow it'll seem to you that what you've done hasn't been so serious." I was relieved that he hadn't understood what I had told him, for of course I had done nothing. Unaccountably I found myself weeping, and I was just able to stammer out, "I'm very grateful, but I can't stay and I can't explain why, it's just that I have to hurry away for the sake of many people." Even then I couldn't bring myself to go. I crossed the threshold and then turned round and stood still, looking back at him. That puzzled him, he knitted his brows and I could see he was listening intensely. He muttered to himself, "I suppose I can't hear him walking over the grass," and he shouted past me down the slope, "Don't think you're lost, I thought I was and all my dear family with me, and we were all saved." I crept off, and from a safe distance I called back a wordless greeting.'

7

NIKOLAI SAID, 'POOR Berr. The poor blind one without an evil thought in his head, who gave so much to beggars when he was a janitor at the Law Courts, that it grew troublesome, they hung about the place. You nearly killed him. And if you had, the lie your friend so vilely told about him, the lie you so fatuously believed, would have lived after him. A most honourable man would have been remembered as a traitor and a spy. I've often cursed my police agents as thick-witted blunderers. Compared to you clever ones, they don't look so bad.'

'How deeply privilege corrupts,' said Chubinov. 'You are a

kind man. You have been kind to Berr. But because you are an aristocrat your kindness towards Berr has lacked a heart. You have never troubled to learn his name.'

'I don't see why, simply because I've raised up one of the afflicted, I should be put under the obligation of knowing his name,' said Nikolai. 'God must know the name of every human being created from the beginning of time to its end, for He takes their whole experience in His bosom. But what difference does it make whether I remember or forget anybody's name? I've given this man a hut where he can sit in the sun. It doesn't make the sunlight less warm because I didn't take a note of his name and it certainly won't make it any warmer that now you've used his name so often in your infernal maunderings I shall never be able to forget it. This is western emotionalism. Your father never thought you would come to anything, and he was right. I'm not moved by your story, you know. You seem to be patting yourself on the back because you've found yourself respecting a good man. But your father and mother, my wife and I, and all the people on our side have always respected such men. If you hadn't gone off gipsying with all these professional criminals and atheists you never would have thought of doing anything else. Have you anything more to say that I would think better worth listening to?'

'Can't you have patience with me, Nikolai Nikolaievitch? Isn't it clear to you yet that I've a story to tell which is immensely important to you? Listen. I beg you to listen. I caught the train back to Paris, and I found myself in a strange state of mind. I had, as you will realise, many things to worry me – yes, yes, I know that it is I who have got myself into this mess, but am I in any worse mess than you are? I tell you, listen. My journey was in a sense very happy. Whenever I thought of Berr my heart glowed with joy. But at the same time I was appalled by the corruption I had discovered within the movement to which I had given my life, a corruption which seemed not less than that which had repelled me in the Tsardom. My mind kept on turning back to this filthy mystery I had uncovered, and I was anguished. When I got to the Gare du Nord I rang up Gorin's hotel, the Hôtel de Guipuzcoa et de Racine, but they told me he was still not there; and when I rang up the

Pension at Montreux the proprietress told me that he had not returned there either, and though I tried to gain her confidence, knowing that she was a sympathiser, she repeated that she knew nothing of his plans. Her tone was indeed so impatient that the thought struck me, if Gorin was so wrong about Berr, was he wrong about this woman also, was he perpetually betraying the movement by a foolish credulity, previously quite foreign to him, perhaps the result of his recent ill-health?

'I found myself standing outside the station in a state of bewilderment. This was so large a business, who could I take it to but Gorin? Just as a child who is hurt will run to its mother's room, even if he knows that she has gone out, I found myself walking across Paris to the Hôtel de Ville until I came to Gorin's hotel. I persuaded myself that I meant to go in and make enquiries to see if the concierge hadn't made a mistake and he was really there all the time, but I hadn't the smallest reason for supposing this, so I didn't go in, but sat down at a table outside a café on the opposite side of the narrow street, and drank one cup of coffee after another. At first I was the only person there, and I sat with my face turned to the traffic and talked to myself. Then noon came, and the place filled up, and I had to behave normally. I found this a great effort, and I marvelled that anybody as unstable as I am had for so long been able to carry the burden of belonging to a secret society without betraying it; and I began to fear I might have done so. All my thoughts brought me back to the idea of betrayal, which seemed to pervade the air, so that everyone alike was tainted with it. I felt so guilty, though of what treachery I couldn't define, that when the waiter brought me an omelette I had ordered, I eyed him as if he might be going to arrest me. But I found peace in thinking of Berr. I fell into a sort of happy trance, which lasted until I saw Gorin walking down the opposite side of the street towards his hotel. At the sight of the neat, small figure, walking so lightly yet so soberly, everything that I had been thinking and feeling seemed absurd, and everything that had happened to me that morning seemed trivial. I had nearly killed an innocent man, I had discovered that I was enslaved by a faceless iniquity, but all that seemed unimportant. I would have liked to push away my plate and bury my head on my folded arms and go to sleep, and let what was happening happen. But before Gorin turned in at the door of his hotel, he paused and surveyed the people on the *terrasse* of the café opposite, a routine glance, such as any of us would give when entering our lodgings, in case we were watched. His eyes passed quickly and without impertinence from face to face, and paused for one moment at mine. My heart stopped. I felt sinful and untidy. Of course I did not greet him. We never did that in the street. But a look crossed his face that I knew was a command, an intimation that he wanted to speak to me as soon as possible, and he turned and went into the hotel.

'As soon as I had paid my bill I followed him, and the concierge told me that he'd left word that I was to be sent up to his room. As I went up the stairs to the fourth floor I felt as sick as if I were going to consult a doctor about the health of someone I loved and feared was about to die; and I also felt bewildered by this misplaced emotion. For I had simply to tell Gorin I thought he had made a mistake, and the worst that could happen was that I might have to defend my point of view to the Committee of the Battle Organisation, a duty which I believed Gorin would make as easy for me as possible, since he was the fairest and least self-regarding person I'd ever known. Why then did I feel as if I were going to hear the words, "Yes, your mother has cancer"? And when I entered Gorin's room I suffered another irrational change of mood. It seemed as if I had no good reason for coming to see him, and that as soon as I had said what was in my mind my own words would prove I'd made a fuss about nothing.

'He was standing by the window, looking down on the street below, and he made no move to meet me. From this and a certain withdrawal of himself in his greeting, I could see that he was as nearly annoyed as his nature permitted. "Vassili Iulievitch, you've forgotten the first duty of a revolutionary. Come over here and look what's happening on the *terrasse*." True, a waiter was standing in front of the table where I had sat, and with shrugs and gesticulations was showing another waiter the dish of eggs which I had paid for but not eaten. He began to make ridiculous mouthings and to wave his hands, and I recognised he was imitating the way I had behaved when I believed myself unobserved. I stepped back from the window in miserable embarrassment.

'"The first duty of a revolutionary is never to attract attention," said Gorin, not unkindly. I could only mutter some disconnected words, and he said quickly, "Why, what's the matter with you? You look as if you'd had some sort of shock."

'I said, "You think that the spy in the Diakonov household is Berr. It isn't Berr." And it was just as I had feared. Now I had told him of my discovery it seemed absurd. My voice sounded thin, it felt as I might at a party when I was young if I had started a funny story and nobody had laughed, and it had suddenly come to me that the story was not funny at all, but I had to finish it.

'Gorin repeated, "It isn't Berr? It isn't Berr?" and was silent for a moment, stroking his chin. "But this is interesting. It really is. Because for some time I myself have suspected that there's something wrong there, something not quite as we had been led to believe. But all the same —" and he spoke sharply, as if bidding himself not to be a fool, not to be seduced by idle talk – "It must be Berr."

'"It can't be Berr," I said, still feeling as though I were wasting his time as thoroughly as if I were telling him how many varieties of butterflies there are in Peru, or how many racehorses are owned by the Rothschilds. He asked quizzically, "And what makes you so very sure it isn't Berr?" My eyelids were heavy, suddenly I would have given anything to lie down and go to sleep.

'I answered, yawning, "Because he's blind."

'Gorin turned away and softly closed the window. "Why do you do that?" I asked him. "It's already too warm in here." He answered, "I want to shut out the noise of the traffic. You're speaking so faintly that I can hardly hear what you're saying. And I wanted to be certain I understood you. Were you really telling me that Berr is blind? Blind? What's your reason for thinking that? It seems very unlikely to me." I answered him, "I know it. I've met him and spoken to him, and he's blind."

' "When did this meeting occur?" asked Gorin, almost languidly. "A lot depends on that, for if it was a long time ago and you've just realised it, he may have been cured, and if you've just met him he may only recently have gone blind. But he can't have been blind, surely, all the time, it's just not possible."

' "I met him this morning," I said, "but he's been blind for some time." "You met him this morning?" asked Gorin. "But why?" Then he corrected himself, "I don't mean why, for I suppose you met him by accident. You surely wouldn't have tried to contact an agent without my permission. But how did it happen?" "In the strangest way," I said, "But please let me sit down." "My poor Vassili, certainly you shall sit down, you aren't at all yourself today," he murmured, and he pushed me into the wicker arm-chair which was the only comfortable seat in his poor room. I leaned back and closed my eyes and told him, "I went up to see him at his home, and I found he is blind."

'Gorin came and stood over me and asked, with some amusement in his voice, "But Vassili, don't you simply mean that when he met you he behaved as if he were blind? For from all I have heard he's very cunning, as such an experienced agent would have to be, and he's more reason than most to be cunning, for he's terrified that one of his family, who's a reactionary, will find out that he's one of us and denounce him. It's probable that unless you were introduced to him by a comrade in whom he had confidence he'd pretend to have lost his sight, just in order to throw you off the scent." The idea of Berr pretending to be anything that he was not made me laugh aloud, though I kept my eyes closed. "No, he quite simply can't see." "How can you be so sure?" said Gorin, speaking in a more sarcastic tone than I had ever heard him use before. "Because," I said, feeling as if I were stepping off a cliff, "I looked at him through a window and pointed a revolver at him, and he did not flinch."

'There was a silence and when Gorin spoke again it was very gently, with not a trace of anger or derision. 'Vassili, Vassili, what's this you're telling me? How did it come about that you pointed a revolver at a comrade, with whom anyway you shouldn't have had anything to do? You're only an associate of the Battle Organisation, we've never accepted you for terrorist work. You'd no right to take such a responsibility upon yourself, particularly when you're treading on such delicate ground. For though I think you're wrong, and I think Berr is not blind, but a very active agent, and a very loyal one, I must admit there are certain complications concerning the surveillance of the Diakonov household, which are very strange, very strange indeed. But now you must tell me your story, for you haven't yet given me the slightest clue as to how and why you've been behaving in such a very odd way, by your own showing." His tenderness overcame me. I covered my face with my hands, I felt the most urgent need to cleanse my breast by confession, though I didn't know of what sin I felt guilty. But I was quite ready to acknowledge that I had been utterly unworthy of the cause, and had endangered it by my rashness and frivolity. But Gorin sighed, "And so grotesque that all this should happen round Berr! Poor old Berr!"

'The sound of Berr's name brought his image to my mind, I saw the man I had been talking to only two or three hours before, the man who sat in his hut holding a sprig to his nostrils, patient like a saint on an icon, the man whose only fault had been that he seemed arrogant though he was not, the man who had spoken of receiving charity not abjectly nor ungratefully, but with pure joyousness, as if the giving and receiving of alms was a dance. But I didn't think as you might expect, "How guilty I am for having tried to kill this innocent man". I thought simply, "That is an innocent man", and I became fixed in contemplation of him, like a compass pointing to the North. It was as if what he was, the pure substance of him, wiped out my offence against him. I understood for the first time what is meant by the forgiveness of sins.

'"But your story," said Gorin, standing in front of me, "let's have your story." He had a right to hear it, so I told him everything, beginning with my arrival in London and the scene in the actress's lodging and what the yellow-haired boy had told me, and ending with my meeting with Berr in his summerhouse, though of that I did not speak fully. I did not tell him what Berr had said to me in the way of pity. I had great difficulty in getting it all out, because my real inclination was simply to go on thinking about Berr. When I was forced to turn my mind away from him, or share my knowledge of him with Gorin, I was overcome by drowsiness, my lips felt thick, my limbs were heavy. I told my story in a demented way, for sometimes I spoke in terms of self-abasement and sometimes aggressively, and these changes occurred without relation to what I was saying at the moment. I would have given anything to go to sleep, and when I'd come to the end of the story I actually rolled over on my side in the chair and fell into a doze. Gorin passed a cool hand over my forehead, and said in the tones of a doctor dealing with a delirious patient, "Rest as long as you like, there's no reason why we should be in a hurry to discuss such a very complicated affair." But after a few minutes I felt better, I sat up and saw that he had opened the window and was sitting on the ledge, with his face buried in his hands. I said to him, "You see why I had to hasten to you. All this has to be put before the Committee as soon as possible, because of course the man who told you that Berr is the spy in the Diakonov household is the same traitor who handed over Primar, Korolenko, Damatov and God knows how many of our comrades to the police."

'I was astounded by the effect of these words on Gorin. He always spoke very softly in a moment of crisis. Now he asked in a shrill voice, "Why did you say that?" Though his face remained smooth – it always did – he was rocking as if he had been struck, he had to put out his hands to steady himself on his narrow seat. "I've too much responsibility to bear as it is!" he went on in the same shrill voice, which he lowered to a harsh, grating whisper, just as uncharacteristic. "I can't cope with all these fanciful stories. You've told me that a certain unknown man looked at our poor friends out of the Diakonovs' doorway in the Avenue Kléber, you've told me that in your opinion a certain unknown man has been lying when he represented that Berr was the spy working for the Diakonov household. But the Diakonovs' apartment is probably crammed with Tsarist spies and you have no proof at all that these two actions are the work of one and the same —" I interrupted him to say, "No proof is required, that I can see. It's self-evident." A gust of fury swept through me, I had pains to stay civil as I added, "and you need not whisper."

'"Yes," agreed Gorin mildly, "it's absurd of me to whisper. But I've so much on my mind, and this I find the last straw." He stood up, folded his arms and looked down at his feet, as he often did when he had to solve a difficult problem. "You see, I can't follow you at all in this theory, I can't see why you say these two actions must have been committed by the same man."

'I was aghast. I had come to bring home to this man a failure in efficiency, committed in a dangerous field, of which I had hardly been able to believe he could be guilty. But by his incapacity to grasp the obvious point I'd put before him, he seemed to be showing that he was capable of quite gross stupidity. Yet again and again when I'd seen him fall into just this attitude, leaning against some ledge or balustrade, folding his arms so that his cuffs, which were always very white and clean, projected from his sleeves, and staring down at his small, shining black shoes, calling on his resources to solve some snare set for our cause by its cleverest enemies, and always there had issued from his lips the subtlest cunning and the most loving and lovable wisdom. I said to him, "You can't have heard what I said." He raised his eyebrows in mild mockery, and I went on, unable to bear this change in him, "Listen, when the man looked out and saw that the actress had noticed him, he waved his hand to her in a way that made her think he was a vulgar *bourgeois* in need of a street-walker; and as she is a pure woman she gave him a proud and disgusted look and passed on, forgetting her first suspicion that he was a police agent interested in her companions. He exploited her chastity. And the man who has told you that Berr is the spy in the Diakonov household has made use of certain meritorious circumstances in the life of the Diakonovs and the Berrs to induce you to believe a lie. He's exploited the Diakonovs' generosity which makes them befriend the Berrs, and he's exploited the arrogant air which poor Berr assumes rather than cringe under his affliction. God forgive him, he's exploited Berr's blindness itself. Don't you see, that in both cases someone clever and not at all well-bred, not at all *nice*, as the English say, picks out something creditable in a person and ruthlessly turns it to her or his disadvantage? We can take it, surely, that the person responsible for each of these rules had some connection with the Diakonov household? Surely you go on and take a further step and admit that it's as unlikely that two people frequenting the same house should possess the same complex sort of character which would permit them to be at once able, perceptive, *louche* and treacherous, as it is that they should both be of extraordinary appearance and exactly alike?"

'My words appeared to me, and still appear, perfectly reasonable. So I was again astounded when Gorin repdied: "But what you're saying doesn't seem to me to mean anything at all. Surely any sensible man with an ordinary amount of ingenuity would think of waving his hand in the manner you describe if he wanted to put a respectable woman off the scent, and surely any such man, with the same not so uncommon qualities, would have chosen Berr if he wanted a scapegoat for the spying in the Diakonov household, for the very reasons you've given, that he was a blind pensioner of the family. There's no trace of idiosyncracy about that. My God, Vassili, just look twice at this matter of blindness! Supposing that you were being chased by the police through the streets and you saw a woman giving money to a beggar with a certain air of unction, wouldn't you knock against her, explain that you were blind and wanted to cross the road, on the off-chance that when the policemen came up with you they wouldn't recognise their quarry in a blind man who was being led by a woman?"

'I shook my head. "What, you wouldn't?" asked Gorin. "No," I said, "no." Gorin shook his head. "I hope," he said kindly but reproachfully, "that this isn't because you have forgotten that we must forget our private scruples when the good of the cause is at stake." "No," I said, "it's just that it wouldn't enter my head to do any such thing." "That only shows," said Gorin shortly, "that you have no experience of terrorist work." I answered, "I'm sorry, I am still of the opinion that these two actions must have been committed by the same man, and I believe that man to be the unknown traitor in our ranks who has handed over to the police comrade after comrade ending with Primar, Korolenko, and Damatov." Gorin turned away from me, shrugging his shoulders, and to strengthen my appeal I added, "the same man who not so long ago also destroyed Vesnin, Patopenko, and Kommisaroff." For the third time in this conversation I was astounded by the effect of my words on Gorin, and felt that I had never really known the man. He spun round, tweaked my sleeve, put his face close to mine, and spoke as if he were trying to rouse a drunkard whom he was trying to induce to leave a burning house. "Vassili, Vassili, what's the matter with you? What in the world is there to lead you to suppose that these two actions, performed here in Paris, can have any relation to a whole series of quite different actions performed in St Petersburg, Moscow, Kharkov, Odessa, Kiev, Warsaw, Helsingfors, and Stockholm? For God's sake give me any evidence if you have it, but if you haven't, stop tormenting me with this nonsense." I answered, "It's hard for me to think of evidence, for I'm absolutely sure already that these two tactical exercises in treachery and the grand strategy behind them are the work of one and the same man."

'Gorin bent low over me and cried in exasperation: "But who do you suppose this someone to be?" Shutting my eyes again, that I might the better think of Berr, I found myself murmuring, "I believe it's Kamensky." "Kamensky!" exclaimed Gorin. He put his hands on my shoulders and began to shake me. "Vassili, what are you talking about! What maggot has got into your head? Kamensky, that nincompoop, that mediocrity! Why, we searched his rooms and found nothing but icons and pitiful maundering tracts and a diary such as a little girl of twelve might have kept! How could this idiot, who is just able to be Sofia Andreievna's lap-dog, how could he be this wonderful spy who has tricked us all, this mixture of Machiavelli and Judas? Or do you, Vassili, know something about Kamensky that the rest of us don't?" I found myself spreading out my hands in a gesture of despair and saying, "When Pilate asked, 'What is truth?' he got no answer except from his own heart." As when I had said, "I believe it is Kamensky," I hadn't known what I was saying till after I had said it. And indeed I believed that only because there was a sort of silence about the name of Kamensky: the silence at the heart of the storm.

'He went on bending over me saying nothing but suddenly straightened up. There were voices in the corridor outside. Gently and pleasantly he asked, "Have you told anybody to meet you here?" I exclaimed, "Ask anybody to meet me here, in your room, without first getting your permission? Of course not, Gorin!" Though he smiled and nodded and pressed my hand, he did not speak again until there came the sound of a door opening and shutting further down the corridor and we heard the voices no more. "Well," he continued, "what is it you know about Kamensky?" "Why, nothing more than I have told you," I said. "Then you're guessing," he said. "You should never do that. One mustn't guess if one is a revolutionary, one must draw logical conclusions from observed facts, for revolution is a science and revolutionaries must work by scientific method." He went slowly to his bed and sat down on it. After some minutes he said in a low tone, "I must put an end to the whole thing." Then he gave a little laugh and said, "No, I don't mean that." I was surprised he hadn't meant that, for obviously he ought to put an end as quickly as possible to the state of affairs in the Diakonov household. "I mean we must have a thorough investigation, before the Committee, of how matters stand in relation to Berr and Kamensky. You must understand, Vassili, that although I've been tearing your story to shreds it's only been to make you defend it as fully as you can. For though the situation in the Diakonovs' apartment isn't quite as you see it, there is, as I told you earlier, something wrong there." He went over and stood looking out of the window, then turned and spoke to me with an air of abrupt good sense. "I only regret that I can't tell you all the details, but that I can't do till I've put it up to the Committee. You see, our real contact there is, and always has been, back in Russia as well as here, the Count's footman, Pyotr. He's a very sound fellow who's been with us from his early youth, and he's been of the greatest service to us, because his apparent simplicity led his employer to trust him absolutely. For example, he was always allowed to go in and out of the Ministry, to take down special dishes if the Count was going to give visitors luncheon at his office, or to deliver notes which had arrived at his private house during the day and seemed to demand his attention.

That's how he was able to act as our intermediary with Pravdine. Well, shortly after the Diakonovs made their desolate Hegira to Paris, Pyotr informed us that he'd found a new sympathiser to keep his master under surveillance, and this was Berr. And I think you're wrong about Berr, but I have to own that you may be right. There are other suspicious factors. I wish I knew. Perhaps you saw the wrong Berr? Just think, Vassili, I've continually been going to that house in the Avenue Kléber myself. I'll trust you with the secrets we've had to keep next our hearts – the apartment above the Diakonovs is empty, and Pyotr has possessed himself of the key, and he's put in a kitchen-chair, on which I've spent many a most uncomfortable hour waiting for him to find a chance to slip away and bring me papers which had been collected, so we thought, by Berr. But . . . but . . . Well, I can't tell you of the things that have come up during the last few weeks. Still, you're shrewd, you're undoubtedly shrewd.

'"I wonder," he said, as if speaking to himself, "whether Berr has not become someone very different from what he was a year or two ago." He fell into a brown study, and I went back into my trance, astonished that Berr, who seemed to be as unambiguous as a tree, should be spoken of as if he were a warlock who could change his form. If I hadn't met Berr that morning, I might have made some sense of the hinting half-sentences that Gorin was dropping, but as it was he might as well have tipped a basketful of mice on the floor. There was activity of a sort going on, but it did not matter to me, it was just faintly, but not alarmingly, repulsive.

'At length Gorin came over to me and said, "I must ask you a question," and my blood ran cold in my veins. I thought, "If only he doesn't ask me whether I've told anybody else about this. That he mustn't ask me." But he did. I answered as truthfully as if I had been Berr. Then he proceeded to give me just those instructions I had guessed he would, once he had heard that I had spoken of my discoveries to him and to him alone. It seemed the Committee was meeting the next day, to discuss this very matter, and I could help him greatly. It seemed that two people in touch with the Diakonov household were leaving messages with two of our comrades that afternoon, and he would be much obliged if I would collect them and bring them to him. "We must have only the most reliable members concerned with this," he said, knitting his brows. From habit I felt pleased because he was taking me into his confidence.

'He explained to me who the comrades were and where I was to find them. One was a comrade of whom I'd never heard, a Russian who was accustomed to pay a visit every afternoon to his brother-in-law, a Frenchman who kept a pharmacy in the Rue St Phillipe de Roule, near the Rond Point, for the purpose of picking up material left by various agents. I was to be there at three; and to leave, if the comrade hadn't arrived by four, and go on to the other comrade, who was someone I knew quite well and had some reason to dislike, a doctor who lived on the other side of the river in the Rue de L'Université. I was to wait for Pyotr's message there until seven but no later, for I had to go back to Gorin's hotel and then, he said, gravely, I might yet have another mission to perform. "That is," said Gorin, laying his hands affectionately on my shoulders, "if you really feel fit for all this running about. You've taken all this terribly to heart, haven't you? I don't blame you."

'I said to him, "What have I ever minded doing for the Cause and for you?" My own words sent my mind running back through the years, and I reproached myself for the irrational love I had suddenly conceived for Berr, the stranger of whom I knew so little, while the proper object of my love stood beside me, the friend who had been for so long my brother but without the awkwardness that comes of kinship. All real brothers are Siamese twins, and inconvenience each other when they want to turn over. The association of separates, friendship, that is the real blessing. I held out my arms to him. But to my astonishment he backed away, his mouth open, as if to call for help, his hands thrust out. He feared I was about to attack him. For a minute we stood staring at each other then he relaxed, murmured, "My noble comrade," and kissed me on both cheeks. But the moment didn't really come to an end.

'Yesterday, you remember, was a hot day. The Hôtel de Ville isn't too close to the Rond Point, and I was quite glad that on my arrival at the pharmacy in the Rue St Philippe de Roule my man wasn't there, and I could sit down and rest for an hour. It was a pleasant place, set in one of those districts embedded in Haussmannite Paris, which obstinately remain villages and are hardly modified by the metropolitan Paris all around them, and it was just such a pharmacy as you might find in Nevers or Yvetôt, with polished wooden counters, shining brass scales, porcelain jars with gold letters on them, and scrubbed floorboards, all in a style banished from the boulevards for many years. So far as this shop was concerned there might be no Art Nouveau today. The pharmacist, a stout middle-aged Gascon, gave me a handsome welcome, regretted that his wife had gone out and wasn't there to entertain me, and said that his brother-in-law wasn't expected, but might come in, and that I could wait for him either in the shop or in the sitting-room at the back. I chose the shop. There was a plump black cat sleeping in a circle on the counter, and a small mongrel dog, far too fat, trotting in and out, both testimonies to the good nature of the family. One customer went out as another came in, and always the pharmacist gave a kindly greeting, took trouble, sent salutations with his good-bye; and when the shop was empty for a minute or two he asked me civil questions through my dream, and offered me in turn coffee, snuff, and a free sample of throat pastilles. Searching for one customer's requirements, he moved a panel behind the goods in his window, and a shaft of light shone into a dark part of the shop. The motes of dust were dancing in it, which I thought looked beautiful and reminded me of Lucretius. But the pharmacist was distressed. He said he was glad his wife wasn't there to see it, she worked so hard to keep the place clean; but in Paris, struggle as one might, one had to live in dust.

'The brother-in-law didn't come. I hadn't thought he would. Many of our women comrades keep good homes, but they would not keep on talking about the dust, it isn't the sort of thing that really distresses them. Also there was no trace of the anxiety which is the hall-mark of our kind. I was sorry to leave the pharmacy and go on to the Rue de l'Université, for both the doctor who lived there and his wife belonged to the one class of comrade which I cannot endure. He was the son of the station-master in a small town near Riga, and as a child he had shown such unusual intelligence that the local landowner had put him through school to the University. But he was without charm, and the landowner dropped him as soon as he'd got the boy qualified. You know what the Baltic nobility are like, they lack even the superficial virtues which we Russians of the same class possess, and probably this landowner showed his disenchantment brutally. It was always my impression that the doctor had joined the revolutionary movement not out of true selfless love for the people, but out of a desire to revenge on the landowning class the disappointment he'd felt at the withdrawal of this landowner's patronage. Yet he was embarrassingly pleased when the movement brought him into contact with people like myself who are of aristocratic birth. So I never felt comfortable with either the doctor or his wife, who was of the same type, the daughter of a German shopkeeper in another small Baltic town; and I was aware that this uneasiness was noticed by both of them and that they suspected me of despising them for their birth and, by implication, of not being a sincere revolutionary. This made my manner towards them quite unnatural, for I wanted to show them that they were mistaken in thinking that I despised them, though in fact I did.

'But when I got to their apartment I was most cordially received. The doctor was out and no message had been left, but his wife warmly invited me to come in and wait, and she took me into her salon and gave me tea and cakes. Though Gorin had said he would not telephone her and I must take my chance, the vulgarly furnished room was extremely tidy, as if she had expected visitors. It was as if I were a little boy again and my father had taken me to call on some shopkeeper or functionary in one of the towns on our estate. My simple heart used to swell at the kindness with which these people laid their best before us, though as I grew older I saw that the relationship between our family and these people was tainted through and through by the poison of our inequality and that what I had accepted as a heartfelt welcome was nothing but an attempt of servility to buy its own ends. My hostess pressed food and drink on me, and she made small talk, but the thought of Berr was strong in my mind. The flowers growing round his hut, which I had trodden on when I looked in at him through the window, were of a clear bright blue, which hadn't interested me at all at the time, but now it delighted me to recall their colour, and when I forced myself to attend to what the woman was saying, it was just as it had been when I had tried to listen to Gorin, I became sleepy, I stammered, I even yawned.

'My drowsiness lay so heavy on me that she couldn't help but notice it, and she asked me if I wouldn't like to lie down on the sofa. I said I'd be glad to, as I'd been travelling and was tired out. When I'd lain down she brought me a pillow and a rug and assured me that I could rest with an easy mind, for she'd be sitting in the next room, which was divided from the salon only by an arch hung by portières, and nobody could come in without her knowledge.

'I contemplated the character of Berr, which I saw as erect and suffused with lights, and which changed as sleep fell on me into the likeness of a tree, a poplar, receiving and storing the sunshine in its leaves. But I was dragged back to wakefulness. A clock was chiming. I stirred and sat up immediately the portières – which were of a material which imitated brocade and looked worthless even to me – jerked apart, and the doctor's wife looked down at me with a panic-stricken expression, replaced without delay by a smile which showed her gums. She told me that it was only half past five and begged me to sleep on, since I was so tired, assuring me that she'd wake me the minute her husband got back. I sighed as if I were still weary, and indeed I was, but for some time after she had gone I couldn't sleep, remembering the look on her face when she had first parted the portières. She had been asked to detain me for some hours. Why had Gorin done that? He wanted time. Time for what? Time to set in motion some hostile plot against me. Why should he want to prepare such an act? Because my discovery that Berr wasn't the spy in the Diakonov household and that Kamensky probably was might be supremely inconvenient to him. I didn't let myself ask any more questions. I clung to the image of Berr. I slept and dreamed deliciously.

'But again I was dragged back to the surface, this time by a memory. I saw Gorin as he had been when he had considered my reasons for my belief that the Tsarist and the revolutionary

173

spy were one spy. I saw him with his arms folded, leaning against the window-ledge, and looking down on his small feet in their shining and well-fitting black shoes. I smiled at the remembrance of Gorin's shoes, they had always amused me, they were smooth and bright as a seal's fins, they might have been part of his body. Then it struck me that my father had worn shoes like that, shoes which reflect the light and closely follow the line of the foot, and that I'd worn such shoes too, in the days when I was an idle and parasitic young man. But the shoes I wore now were not at all like that. I had taken them off before I lay down on the sofa, and now I bent down and picked them up and looked at their scaled and greyish surface, the deep creases in them, the worn heels. They didn't often get a proper cleaning and they cost very little to begin with. It came into my head that I'd only Gorin's word for it that the proprietress of the pension in Montreux was a sympathiser and gave him his luxurious rooms at a reduced rate.

'Again I brought my mind to a stop and fell asleep, but not for long. I had to go on admitting to myself what I knew. If Gorin had wanted to keep me out of the way for some hours in order that he might prepare a plot against me, he had sent me to the two best places I could imagine. Nearly all our members in Paris knew and respected me, and if Gorin had asked them to detain me, their astonishment would have been so great that he would have had to invent an explanation which would bear subsequent discussion before our Committee. But if the pharmacist's brother-in-law had nothing whatsoever to do with our movement and was simply a Russian living in Paris for business reasons, who had run into Gorin casually, perhaps at a café, my visit to the shop in the Rue St Philippe de Roule would simply mean that one Russian had another Russian to see him, in our gregarious way. As for the doctor, anything he could do against me would count as an instalment of his revenge against the Baltic landowner. I wondered if I might not be doing the best for myself if I got up and went at once. But I decided to get a little more sleep. It was odd how I could command it.

'I woke with a start and found the doctor's wife holding apart the portières with an expression which indicated no anxiety but much relief. In the room behind her the clock was striking half past six, but this time she didn't urge me to go on resting. I rose and thanked her for her hospitality, at which she smiled to herself, in a way which would have been unworthy, no matter how well-justified she might have been in acting as a decoy. Her baseness shamed me as much as if I myself were guilty of it, and I became conscious of my crumpled clothes and my uncombed hair. I went up to a long mirror on the wall and tried to improve my appearance, smoothing my hair with my hands, and she came and stood beside me. Our eyes met in the mirror, and we were both embarrassed, as if our relationship were pushed to a further degree of indelicacy by the presence of our reflections side by side within the mirror-frame. I turned away, appalled because I should have become involved in a situation which obliged me to think badly of Gorin when I was in the company of this despicable woman. I still honoured him too highly for that to be tolerable. With a burst of foolish, apologetic laughter, which she echoed, I took my leave.

'When I got into the street, I automatically looked around to see if any spy was waiting for me, according to our routine, and indeed there was a tall young man, very pale, lounging in a doorway opposite, whom I had seen before. On my way from the Rue St Philippe de Roule to the Rue de l'Université, I'd crossed the Seine by the Pont Alexandre Trois, that bridge which the French, who certainly love liberty, have so strangely chosen to name after one of our Russian tyrants. Half-way over it, I stopped to take off my hat and let the river breeze play about my head and rest my eyes by looking down on the water. This same tall young man had been leaning against the parapet ten yards away, his body taut as if he were an archer bending his bow. I'd seen him then. I was seeing him now. I was going to see him later. I went along the Rue Jacob to the Boul' Mich' and while I was ordering a cup of coffee the tall young man brushed past me, his face averted, and sat down at the table behind me.

'After a few minutes I put a cigarette between my lips, pretended to search my pockets, stood up, looked round, and bent over him, asking for a light in the peculiar manner of the

French. You must have noticed how oddly they do it. Though they're a ceremonious people, and commonly apologise when they have to accost strangers, they simply lean towards the man who has a lit cigarette, say tersely *"Du feu"*, and when the cigarette is alight, turn away without a smile or a word of thanks. It's solemn, as if the rite of some forgotten religion had fused with the mechanism by which a contemporary need is satisfied. *"Du feu,"* I said to the boy who was staring up at me. The whites of his eyes were bluish, as they are in people who are very young and have never abused their youth by dissipation. He drew back his head and his nostrils dilated. He had the noble look of a young stag. His dark eyes wide open, he took his cigarette out of his mouth, and held it out to me, supporting his elbow on the table. I steadied my fingers against his and his hands recoiled just as his head had done, but he forced himself to endure the loathed contact. His whole body was trembling with the force of his pure aversion, his exalted reaction to some lie he had believed out of sanctity. As I breathed the light from his cigarette into mine, I knew quite well that he wasn't a police agent, he was one of our marvellous incorruptible young men. I was being spied on by my own party.

'I sat down again and drank my coffee and stared at the passing crowds. I knew that I must not go back to see Gorin. Something would happen which would convince other people of something about me which was not true. I heard again Gorin's voice as he asked me whether I had told anybody else of my discovery about Berr. I heard, which was worse, his murmured remark, "I must put an end to all this," and the nervous little laugh which had followed when he realised he'd spoken aloud. I tried to guess the exact form in which Gorin would put an end to "all this", which meant me. Possibly a crime had already been committed for which I could be handed over to the police but I didn't think so. The police couldn't be trusted to deal with me finally. I had an idea that some time during the night, in one of the darker streets, I'd find myself confronted by this young man who'd just given me a light, and he'd have a revolver in his hand. His burning purity would be at the command of anybody who spoke to him in the name of the people, even if obedience meant his own destruction, and it would. He'd never get away, and he'd die for killing a friend of the people at the command of an enemy of the people, and that was why I felt sure it would be he who'd do it. He'd something one might almost call beautiful about him, though that's a strange word to apply to a man, something which I've learned to recognise in the course of my years in the revolutionary movement. It's the moral counterpart of the consumptive's flush, it's the sign of those whose sacrifices are going to be premature, fevered, and useless.

'I couldn't think anything about my own death beyond the fact that it was probable. I was preoccupied by my anger at the abuse of Berr's innocence, and by the anger that flamed up in me every time I remembered what the diplomat's yellow-haired son had said in the actress's bedroom in London: "The Tsar's eagerly looking for some excuse to recall Nikolai Niko-laievitch to Russia and lay some trumped-up charge against him, and then discredit him thoroughly by never bringing him to trial and abandoning the proceedings on the pretence of showing him mercy." I couldn't bear that to happen to you, and I couldn't bear the Tsar to have the satisfaction of a victory which was so peculiarly to his disgusting taste. I couldn't let this happen, if I couldn't prevent it then I'd been defeated by the universe as I wouldn't be defeated by my own death. I walked out of the café, meaning to take a cab up to the Avenue Kléber, and then I realised that Gorin, who knew everything, would know that I would sooner or later want to go to you and offer you what I could give in the way of a son's protection. Hadn't he laid his arm across my shoulders, as we stood by the little harbour on Lake Geneva, and said, "I know well that much that is best in you comes from Nikolai Niko-laievitch"? He hadn't cared where the best of me came from or the worst. He'd said it simply because he knew I loved you like a father. Therefore there'd already be someone stationed outside your door, another idealistic boy, waiting for me. But I didn't see how he could stop me from telephoning your apartment, and I went back in the café and did that very thing.

'I'd difficulty in finding your number, because I didn't know how you transliterated your name. How utterly we

Russians are not at home in the Western world! But at last I got it, I was put through, I repossessed my own life, I did something which Gorin couldn't have foreseen. No, nobody in your home would have reported it to you. I didn't dare to give my name to the lady who answered me, because of your spy, so I said I was the youngest of the Volkoff brothers, who was passing through Paris on his way to the family palace in Venice, and wanted to pay you his respects if only by speaking a few words to you. She said, "I'm Tania," and I had realised that already for we had, of course, known that she was staying with you. "How are you?" she went on. "How pleasant that you're ringing us up." But though she was scrupulously polite she sounded distraught in her indifference, it was as if nothing mattered to her any more, and when she told me that her mother was ill her voice flooded with grief strong as a child's. That was so like you, Nikolai Nikolaievitch, your own indifference, which seems arctic, yet melts in a moment. "I want," I told her, "to speak with your father," and I hinted that I'd something to say of special interest to you. Wearily she told me that you were asleep, and whatever it was I had to say had better be said to a nice little man, Monsieur Kamensky, who'd worked with you long ago as a civil servant and now acted as a confidential secretary whenever he was in Paris. "You could speak to him in half an hour," she promised me. "He's dining with us."

'I couldn't face that. Not yet. I said I must go to a dinner engagement, but would speak to him tomorrow, and she answered, that that would be impossible. "The good Kamensky is spending all his day helping us one way and another. Tomorrow morning early he's taking my father to the station to see him off to Mûres-sur-mer, where he's going to stay with Aunt Florence – you'll remember her – and later on he will be with me at the clinic where my mother's going for her treatment." I held my breath. Now I had Gorin in the palm of my hand. I told your daughter that I had to leave Paris the next day, and sent you my salutations, and said that I wished I could bear her troubles. Out of the black earpiece your daughter's sweet and fatigued voice said, "All you Volkoffs are so nice. You're charming and gay, but you have hearts as well.

There should be more Volkoffs in the world." I wished I hadn't been forced to deceive her.

'Then I rang up Gorin. I said to him, "Gorin, it's I, Vassili Iulievitch. I'm not coming to see you tonight. I can't." After a pause he gently enquired why I was not carrying out the orders he'd given me. "You don't understand," I told him, "I've made a great discovery. Somebody else besides me knows all about Berr." There was silence at the other end of the line. I went on, "Yes, suddenly, about ten minutes ago, I remembered something, which I can't tell you over the telephone, and I rang up a certain comrade and asked some discreet questions, and got some very indiscreet answers. I find he knows everything. Yes, what I know, and much more besides, and he says the full truth will astonish me when I hear it." "Who is this comrade?" asked Gorin. "He's thoroughly reliable," I said, "and that's all that's safe to say over the telephone." "Do I know him?" asked Gorin. "We both know him well," I answered, "but don't ask me any more questions. You'll have an opportunity to talk to him yourself if you come to the Café Viborg tomorrow morning, for he's going to meet me there. I didn't tell him you were coming, in case it put him off. But I'm sure he'll talk freely to you, he talked freely enough to me. Though I can't quite see where all his information leads. But that, as I say, he'll tell you and me tomorrow morning."

' "When are you meeting him?" asked Gorin. "At ten minutes to ten," I answered. I heard Gorin click his tongue against the roof of his mouth in annoyance, but he said, "I'll be there." "And don't be late," I said, "for he may be able to stay with us only a very short time. And by the way, there's another thing. I'm being followed by a police spy. A tall, dark young man, with blue eyes, and a deep cleft in his chin." "Oh, my dear friend, be careful, be very careful," said Gorin, with tears in his voice. "What worries me," I said, "is that if he continues to follow me I'll have to tell the comrade not to come to the Café Viborg tomorrow, and I won't come myself. We can't take unnecessary risks." "No, you can't," he said. "That would," I pressed him, "be the right thing to do, wouldn't it? If the police spy goes on following me, I should call the meeting off, shouldn't I?" "Yes," said Gorin, "yes, that would be the correct procedure." "Well, good-bye," I said, "till tomorrow, I hope." "If I may use the language of our childhood," Gorin said, "let me say, God be with you."

'I went back to my seat on the *terrasse*, just in front of the young man who was spying on me. I wasn't going to leave until I'd seen him get his message to go home. Then I meant to slip into another café, which has two exits, and from there, when it was quite dark, scuttle off to one of those hotels near Les Halles, where they take in farmers and carriers coming to the markets without luggage, and are too busy to be curious, so that I could make my way to the Gare du Nord this morning and board this train: and that's in fact what I did. I found it almost unendurable to wait the half-hour that passed before the young man was handed a note by a child. I was afraid that Gorin mightn't have believed me and would have told the boy to put an end to me as I sat there. In order to preserve my calm, I set myself to watch the crowds that were passing, as methodically as if I had been asked to report on them by our Committee. They were gay crowds, as Paris crowds are on summer evenings, and there were many lovers among them. It's often been remarked that every human activity, whether it be love, philosophy, art or revolution, is carried on with a special intensity in Paris. A Polish professor has found an explanation in the presence in the subsoil of the city of certain earths heavily charged with electricity. It is wonderful how science is solving all mysteries. It seemed to me that the proportion of men and women quite evidently in love was higher than would have been the case in Berlin or Zürich or St Petersburg, but also that they were exhibiting their state more candidly than they would have done in these other capitals. They walked arm in arm, their eyes shining, and they chattered and laughed.

'As one is bound to do when one observes a large number of people sharing an experience, I recalled my own journey along that same road. I never felt such an exaggerated and carefree emotion as was inscribed on these people's faces, and it's many years since I've felt a fervent attachment to anything but the Cause. Nevertheless I had much to remember. In my youth I was greatly attracted by the young daughter of some neighbours of ours, and I falsely imagined she was much attracted to me, until I realised that she was moved by nothing more than an ambition to marry the son of the wealthiest man in the district. But I had also the beautiful memory that later I was bound by the closest and most honourable ties to a fellow-member of our organisation, a woman doctor of powerful intellect and the most exalted ideals and that, strangely enough, she never wearied of me and we were together when she died. I wondered how I had survived her loss, and the answer came to me at once. I had had a friend, a devoted and selfless comforter, I had had Gorin. Oh, believe me, my friendship for him was not an illusion like my passion for little Tamara Pallicer, it was on the same plane as my long union with my noble companion. I'd be a Judas myself if I forgot this.

'But as I sat there on the *terrasse*, it became quite, quite clear to me who was my Judas. I'd received absolute proof when I told Gorin about the two actions which showed the same sort of perfidy: the gesture which exploited the actress's knowledge of her beauty and her chastity, and the use of Berr's blindness and innocent pride to foist on him the guilt of treachery. Gorin failed to recognise these actions as having any similarity, or as the results of a deliberate and nasty choice; they seemed to him automatic responses to the pressure of necessity, and therefore neutral in quality. Now, what class of actions always appear to us as automatic and neutral, inevitable and therefore exempt from censure? Our own. We always believe that what we did we had to do. Other men have free will, we ourselves live in a determinist universe. And though we may know everything about our actions, how they are carried out and what results followed, we cannot know them for what they are, as we know that a rose is red and is scented, a plate of soup brown and hot and made of beans. Each man is a mystery to himself; and the two men, the man who waved his hand to the actress from the doorway, and the other man who lied about Berr, they were both mysteries to Gorin. Therefore I think that they were one and the same man; and that man was Gorin.

'I was a coward when I told you a little while ago that I

couldn't tell you the name of the spy in your household. I knew it well, as soon as Gorin clicked his tongue in annoyance because I told him he must come to the Café Viborg at ten to ten. I knew it past all doubt when you came to the Gare du Nord this morning, with your grand-daughter and your footman, and nobody else. I was standing by the bookstall and you strode right past me. You can't think how extraordinary you looked. You're so abnormally tall, Nikolai Nikolaievitch – like certain types of primitive man, who've become extinct in the course of evolution, and though it must have been right that they should disappear, for evolution can't make a mistake, it's impossible not to admire your strength; and your air of wealth seems something that you've fairly earned by being so strong, though of course that's quite an immoral idea. And this grand-daughter of yours with her golden hair, which is by nature the colour so many unfortunate victims of capitalism dye theirs, and her high cheekbones that are so Russian and her hard air that's so English, and her general appearance of being a barbarian princess, she's a form of inalienable wealth. If we took everything away from you, Nikolai Nikolaievitch, somehow you'd still have more than is ethically permissible. Yet you and I are beggars together. For Kamensky is Gorin. Gorin is Kamensky.'

8

IF KAMENSKY WAS Gorin, Laura thought, it was terrible that he had used the same forks and spoons, eaten off the same plates and drunk out of the same glasses as the Diakonov family, sat at the table as it had been furnished by their dead. The silver equipage had been given to an ancestor by Catherine the Great: a string of silver elephants trod a narrow silver track on the shining white cloth, round a larger elephant on a column, like the one in the square in Rome. The forks and spoons were different from the Georgian ones which they used at home in Radnage Square, they were French. Another ancestor had taken his bride to Paris just before Louis XV had issued his decree requisitioning his subjects' silver to pay for his wars, and they had taken back to Russia two great chests of it. The glasses had come from Prague, from another honeymoon, and they had survived a hundred years, only because they were always washed in a basin lined with several layers of flannel. People had forgotten what the plates were, and there were so many services, nobody bothered whether they were Meissen or Sèvres. Some were Chelsea but were painted with Japanese landscapes. They had the childish look that belongs to a picture of a place by someone who has never been there. All were so beautiful that she looked at them at every meal. Now, if Nikolai went into the dining-room and said, 'Take all these things away for ever, they are spoiled,' he would be right. It would be no use just washing them. At home in Radnage Square they would pretend there was no problem, everyone would eat off the polluted ware, and it would be a sort of poisoning. There was some good in being Russian. But perhaps Kamensky was not Gorin.

Nikolai and Chubinov were talking languidly, two tired men, about the origins of Kamensky and Gorin. Chubinov was saying that Gorin was forty-three years old and was born at Lyskovo in the Grodnensko province, and had studied at the university of St Petersburg until the police began to harry them, then at Karlsruhe, and later at Darmstadt, where he had taken his diploma in engineering. Nikolai was saying that Kamensky was forty-one, was born at Kharkov and had taken his degrees in engineering at Moscow and Berlin. That was certain. The Ministry had checked. 'And Darmstadt too,' said Chubinov, 'we checked that.' They were silent.

'What does Gorin look like?' Laura asked.

'He is dark. His eyes and hair are dark, and his face is unlined, considering his age.'

'Kamensky is dark, dark and short, pleasing but not distinguished,' said Nikolai.

'Gorin is not short,' said Chubinov, 'he is not much shorter than I am.'

'But you are short.'

'For you who are abnormally tall, it's difficult to get a conception of normal height.'

183

'But what's Gorin like?' asked Laura. 'What would you tell somebody to look out for, if they had to meet him at a railway-station?'

'Well, he's a Russian. It isn't only that his cheekbones are high, he's got the Slav signature on his face. If you met him anywhere you'd say, "Ah, here's one of us." I really can't think of anything else. I've often thought it strange that such a remarkable man should have such an ordinary appearance, for to tell the truth hundreds of thousands look exactly as he does.'

'Millions of Russians look exactly like Kamensky, provided they're not of noble birth,' said Nikolai. 'But God forbid we should hang a man because he looks so like a great many other Russians that maybe he might be another man who also looks like a great many other Russians.' He spoke with a hint of cunning.

'Gorin also looks as if he wasn't noble,' meditated Chubinov. 'I should think his father was probably a minor functionary in a not very large town, or perhaps a merchant, but in a small way of business. But he had, now I come to think of it, one physical trait as outstanding as his mental endowments. He has the eyes of an eagle. I've never known a man in middle life with such sight. Walking on the hills above Zürich, I've known him tell the time by the clock on a tower in the heart of the city, though not the youngest among us could see anything but the round dial.'

'Then Gorin's not Kamensky,' said Nikolai in calm and dis-agreeable triumph. 'Kamensky's almost blind. I've never seen him without his spectacles. He's helpless without them.'

'No, Grandfather,' Laura said, 'he isn't.'

He looked at her out of the corner of his eyes as if they were both Orientals and should not be speaking so directly.

'Don't you remember that the other day I tried on Monsieur Kamensky's spectacles?'

His glance did not soften.

'I tried to tell you, but you were angry with me. What I wanted to say was that Monsieur Kamensky's spectacles are glass, plain glass. He can see as well as anybody.'

Without a pause Nikolai answered, 'Thousands of our minor functionaries do that. Wear spectacles which are plain glass.

I've come across the practice again and again among those not well born. It's a sign of distinction among the undistinguished. A claim that one's not coarsely perfect, like one's cousin the peasant. That my friend Kamensky, of whom I know nothing ill, wears such spectacles is no proof that he's Chubinov's friend Gorin, who seems to be all one might expect of his pack of enlightened scoundrels.'

Chubinov said gently, 'So you're determined not to ask, just to die. I can't do so. I feel it's my duty to live until I've discovered the truth and proclaimed it.'

'There's no need for anyone but God to know the truth,' said Nikolai. 'The part of man is to obey, and for obedience one does not have to know the truth. One has only to pay attention to the command.'

'Please, Monsieur Chubinov,' said Laura. 'Does Gorin put anything on his hands? Monsieur Kamensky uses an ointment which his grandmother made for him when he got chilblains, with a herb in it which has a very strong smell.' She stopped, astonished, even after all that had happened, by the horror on his face.

'In winter-time his room reeks with the stuff.'

'People of that class always smell to high heaven from October to April, with the salves and messes made up for them by their old women,' said Nikolai. 'It is no proof of anything.'

'Gorin's salve,' said Chubinov, 'is made from a herb we call *pizhina* in Russia.'

'We call it tansy. It's very green and it doesn't grow very high but it isn't flat on the ground either. Would that be *pizhina*?'

'I've never seen it,' said Chubinov. 'For me it's a puff of steam from a bathroom door. When I was a little boy my mother and my aunts used to put *pizhina* leaves in their baths and my German tutor used to sniff and say, "*Ach, der gute Rainfarn,*" and I recognised the smell again in Gorin's room.'

'*Rainfarn.* I don't know that word. In French it's *la barbotine*, that's what Mummie calls it.'

'We're lost unless a cook comes into the carriage, or someone carrying a German-French dictionary,' said Nikolai. 'This is an absurd conversation, belittling to us all. If one's stabbed, one doesn't spend one's last breath guessing what tradesman sold the dagger.'

'But of course Kamensky's Gorin,' said Laura, and shook with fury. 'There's something that makes it certain. Grandfather, don't you remember? The way he got free this morning when he was bringing us down to the station. He cheated in the same mean way as the man who waved at the actress, as the man who lied about Berr. Monsieur Chubinov, my grandfather has a little footman, he's just a boy, you must have seen him with us at the station, he's really too young to be a footman. He's very nice. He's devoted to Monsieur Kamensky, he says he's been very kind to him. When we were all getting into the carriage outside my grandfather's apartment, Monsieur Kamensky pretended that the little footman had slammed the door on his hand and hurt him. The poor boy said he hadn't, but Kamensky pretended he was in great pain and went on humbugging and humbugging, shamming not only that he was hurt, but shamming too that he was making light of it, and that for the boy's sake. I wish this wasn't true.' She stopped for a minute and prayed. 'God, let all this not have happened.' But there was no answer. She went on, 'Finally he pretended he was in such pain he had to get out of the carriage and go to a pharmacy where he could get his hand bandaged. But of course he was going off to the Café Viborg. And the boy was terribly upset. Oh, certainly Kamensky's Gorin, and he ought to be killed.'

Nikolai was staring out of the windows at the fields. 'It's not so bright as it was,' he said. 'Every time the sun goes behind a cloud in France you see the country's damp as a sponge.' He shuddered, dropped his chin on his chest, closed his eyes, and softly asked a question.

'Oh, speak clearly!' groaned Chubinov. But it was not for him to complain. He had covered his ears as if he did not want to hear.

'I asked you,' said Nikolai, 'whether the name of Kaspar meant anything to you?'

'Nikolai Nikolaievitch, why did you not ask that question an hour ago?'

'For the same reason that you're not answering it now.'

They sat side by side in silence, looking out at the dull day. When the sun came out of the clouds they turned their faces away from the brightness.

'Well, here it is, the bitter morsel,' sighed Chubinov. 'Kaspar is the Party name of Gorin. Only those of us who know him intimately call him Gorin. To all others he is Kaspar. Since you've asked this question, I suppose that Kaspar is the name used by Kamensky when he acts as a police spy.' He broke the silence that followed by crying out quite loudly, 'Nikolai Nikolaievitch, this is all your fault. None of this would have happened if you had been true to your own class, to your own kind. How could you take a police spy into your home? Blind as you are with bigotry, infatuated with your imagined duty to defend reaction, how could you let a police spy sit on your chairs, breathe the same air, talk with you, eat with you, meet your women folk? Even if the jackal cleans the gutters outside your house, the jackal is a jackal.'

'But he wasn't a police spy like other police spies,' said Nikolai. 'Perhaps being with your kind corrupted him. He used not to be vile, he was a good, good man. He came to my notice first when I was at the Ministry of Ways and Communications. He was in charge of some important pumping operations which had to be done when they laid a railway-line over that marshland down by Vologda. Good God, he cannot be a villain, he simply can't. Up there we had an epidemic of typhus among the workers, and he behaved like a saint, he was fearless, he was a father to the sick, he caught the sickness himself, and all this when he might have got leave to come back to Moscow, for he was among the experts whom we could not afford to lose. When the doctors sent him to us to convalesce he wanted to return long before he was fit. I had to keep him with me by pretending I needed an extra secretary for the moment, and in a very short time I realised he was a subordinate beyond one's dreams. An excellent engineer, with much knowledge of the new work done in Germany and France, particularly in the field of hydraulics, and so good, so pious, so gracious. Charity bubbled up in him, the janitors and the cleaners and the old clerks all loved him, and if he came to me on day weeping, to tell me that he could give information

187

regarding the iniquitous proceedings in certain revolutionary circles, you, Vassili Iulievitch, you know quite well why that was, and that it was neither unnatural nor dishonourable. How can you have the impudence to transfer to him the shame that lies on you!'

'I've not the slightest idea what you're talking about,' said Chubinov.

'I'm talking about his brother,' said Nikolai, heavily.

'Gorin's brother? He hasn't got one.'

'Not now. But he had one.'

'No, never. Three sisters, yes. But I've heard him say several times that he had never had a brother. Indeed, when we were at Montreux he told me that it had always been his great desire to have a brother, and that he'd found a substitute in me.'

Trembling, Nikolai hissed, 'Kamensky had a brother. Younger than himself. He was enticed into joining your organisation, when he was a student at Kharkov. Suddenly the boy appeared in St Petersburg at Kamensky's lodgings and begged his older brother for his protection, saying that he'd been ordered by your Committee to shoot the Goveror of Kharkov, and that he'd suddenly realised he could not kill, he could not break the Law of God. So he refused. No actual threat was made by your Committee, but he'd become aware that he was going to be punished for his resistance to evil, and he feared the worst. Kamensky left the boy in his lodgings, went to the house of a friend who had a telephone, and tried to ring me up to ask for an appointment next day, but I was out. When he returned to his lodgings the boy was gone. Vassili Iulievitch, have you so many crimes on your conscience that you do not remember this one?'

'I don't remember it because it never happened. It couldn't have happened. For some reason which I can't bring to mind at the moment, we've never contemplated murdering the Governor of Kharkov.'

'An odd omission. You must try to recall the reason, and tell me about it some time. But either you are lying, or you know nothing about the workings of your organisation. Your father was quite right in all he said about you. For there was such a boy. We found him. When Kamensky, in a frenzy of grief, so far beyond himself that he ventured to come to my house in the middle of the night, a great liberty for a man in his position, we alerted the police both in St Petersburg and back in Kharkov. After four days a peasant reported to the police that at a time which was a few hours after Kamensky's brother had disappeared, he had seen three men carrying a young man, whom he supposed to be drunk, into a villa on the Peterhof Road. A couple of nights later he passed the villa and it was in darkness, and a neighbour told him that the family was away on a long visit to the Crimea. That puzzled him, and he told the police, who went in and found the body of Kamensky's brother in the kitchen. A noose had been thrown round his neck and the rope had been slung on to a meat hook in the ceiling. The wretched boy had been slowly strangled. Be careful how you speak of this. I went with Kamensky. I saw the boy's tongue lolling from his mouth. I am a soldier. But I had not seen any such thing before.'

Chubinov stammered, 'What was the name of the villa?'

'What a thing to ask. I don't remember. It was ten miles out on the Peterhof Road.'

'Ten miles out on the Peterhof Road. A corpse hung from a meat-hook in the ceiling. The tongue. Nikolai Nikolaievitch, that wasn't Kamensky's brother. It was a student named Valentine. A traitor. A shameful traitor. He had led the police straight to one of our printing-presses. It was no mistake. Gorin took his papers off the body.'

'The police found papers on the body which showed he was Kamensky's brother.' Nikolai's voice fell to a whisper. 'If you had seen how Kamensky wept.'

The train stopped at a station and the two men did not speak again until the guard's trumpet sent it pushing on.

'This is the end of my life,' said Chubinov.

'If I say that it has no meaning, simply because it is true,' said Nikolai Nikolaievitch. 'But in any case I do not feel what you convey when you say that. It keeps on running through my head that the messengers came to Job and told him that fire had come down from heaven and burned up his servants. I do not feel that my servant Kamensky has done anything. I feel something has been done to him.'

Presently they began to talk like policemen again. 'I have to admit,' said Chubinov hesitantly, 'that there was always something mysterious about the case. We never actually knew who had performed the deed of vengeance, and it was premature. The Committee was in the course of examining the proofs of Valentine's treachery, but it had not come near to the stage of giving orders for his punishment. Then Gorin found an unsigned note at his lodging telling that three of our members could wait no longer and had trodden the viper under their heel, and it gave the address of the villa on the Peterhof Road. Gorin picked me up at my home and we went there at once. It was a terrible scene. Gorin is exquisitely sensitive. I've often heard him say that while he would dare to commit any murder in order that the tyrants who are strangling Russia should pay for their crimes, he can never reconcile himself to the harsh necessity that to make a murder, a sentient being has to be murdered.'

'I see that's awkward for him,' said Nikolai Nikolaievitch. 'But don't worry. He showed himself quite robust that night. For if he took Valentine off the meat-hook for you, he must have put him back on it for me.'

'I had forgotten, I had forgotten. But you don't mend anything by your mockery,' said Chubinov.

'From our side,' said the other, 'there was something odd. We found Valentine's baptismal certificate in the Kharkov church records, and his school registration, but he had never attended Kharkov University. It turned out that Kamensky had never seen him there or had any proof that he was enrolled there. You see, I am like you, I slip back into thinking that he was honest. Well, the tale Kamensky then told us was that he supposed that the boy's revolutionary friends had seduced him into consenting to spend his days on some illegal activity before the term started, so he never went there at all.'

'You should have known what could have been behind that,' said Chubinov. 'Some boy called Kamensky died after leaving high school and before getting to the University, and our people stole his identity for one of our workers.'

'Yes, that ghoulish trick I should have recognised by this time. But to get back to our loved one. He came into my office the next day, grief-stricken, enraged, alone, helpless, weeping – weeping again – and with a peculiarly touching quality about his tears. He asked if he might join your organisation and report on its doings, so that he could expiate the guilt which lay on him for not having protected his young brother from your devilry. Well, as I said before, this reaction seemed neither unnatural nor dishonourable. I was then given to understand, and until you came into this compartment it was never suggested to me that I should doubt it, that he presented himself to your organisation, pretended that he believed his brother's disappearance was due to the secret police, gained your confidence, and thus enabled us to punish many criminals and avert many crimes. In my personal relations with him I experienced a curious pleasure. Now I know all about him, or more about him, the only virtue I can credit him with is courage, but he seemed to have all the virtues, and one more than is named, a kind of gaiety. And when I was disgraced he did not waver. I have come to love him. And I am not such a fool as you think,' he suddenly roared, 'for he was on our side. Assuredly he was on our side. He must have been on our side, he gave us your Vesnin, Patopenko, and Komissaroff. Yes, and many others of your abominable breed.'

'He was on our side,' said Chubinov, changing his glasses. 'He in his own person planned the executions of Dubassoff and Sipyagin and Plehve – yes, it was he who coached the cab-driver in getting his horse to move on slowly while he seemed to be trying to restrain it, so that Sazonoff could use it as cover up to the very last moment, when he ran out and threw the bomb which freed us from the butcher of Kishinev, the past master of pogroms. Without him the Grand Duke Serge would be alive today —'

'Do not speak to me of that death,' Nikolai begged him, with sudden gentleness. 'Every time I hear of it I sin. I loathed the Grand Duke Serge, he was the incarnation of that evil which must not be blamed, since it arises out of stupidity, and is thus, God help us all to understand, plainly God's will. When there is any mention of his assassination I fall straight into sin, I blaspheme, before I know what I'm doing. I thank God he is dead. Again and again I've done penance for this, and again and again I offend. This too is part of the trouble you've made for all of us, you accursed murderers.'

'But it's you, not we, who are the murderers. We are the instruments of justice. No guilt rests on us. There is blood on our hands, but it is turned to glory by the rectitude of our cause. How strange it is that one of us two should have lived a life which is like a noble poem and the other a life which is that poem's ignoble parody.'

'One day you'll learn which side it was that produced the parody,' Nikolai promised. 'From the lips of the Lord himself,' he added spitefully. He called to an attendant who was going down the corridor. 'What's the next station we stop at? Grissaint? It is a big station? With frequent trains back to Paris? Good.' His eyes went back to Chubinov. 'Forgive me, I shouldn't mock a dead man. And you're a dead man, Vassili Iulievitch.'

'No,' said Chubinov. 'Not yet.'

'I think you will be very soon. I'm going to die quite soon. Not at once, but quite soon. My grand-daughter and I will get out at the next station, this Grissaint, or whatever it's called, and take the next train back to Paris. My duty dictates that step, because there's no more direct route I know of between Northern France and St Petersburg, and that's where I must go. If the Tsar wishes me to return to Russia in order to humiliate me and accuse me of a crime I have not committed, and insult me by pardoning my innocence, then to Russia I must go.'

'No,' said Laura. 'No. Can't you think for one single moment of Grandmother?'

'I've spent my whole life telling my inferiors that the Tsar's will is sacred, even when it ordered their destruction. There's no reason that I can see why I should alter my attitude when it is myself whom he wants to destroy. So I must return to Russia and there I will die, either in prison or out of it, from rage. But it will take some time to wear me down to that. But you, Vassili Iulievitch, you will be dead quite soon.'

'You under-rate me and the party. I will get out at Grissaint too. Which is quite a large place. We have some members there. Some sympathisers, I should say. I will take the first train to Paris which is not an express, which stops at all stations. I'll get out at the last but one stop before the Gare du Nord, or perhaps the last but two. Then I'll walk and take a bus, walk and pick up a cab, and so on till I get to my hotel near Les Halles. I'll have to keep in mind, of course, that at any moment Gorin may try to kill me, and dodge him while I get a telegraph in code sent off to my committee in St Petersburg, acquainting them with his treachery, and I'll embody the same information in an express letter to the Paris representative. Oh, God, oh, God, do you know what I was thinking then? I was thinking that I must get Gorin to help me, he's so good at drafting messages. But when I've done all this I'll be able to take the train to Berlin, and on to St Petersburg, without fear. We're really very, very highly organised,' he said, taking off his spectacles and beaming through his tears, 'and a man who has lodged an accusation against a fellow-member in the proper form will never be molested on his way to headquarters. It would make it look too bad for the accused person.'

'Imbecile of all imbeciles, you'll never be granted the immunity which is ceded to a member who is lodging an accusation against a fellow-member of your organisation, because already, as you sit in this compartment, you are a member of your organisation who has had a charge lodged against him by a fellow-member, that trinity of evil who is Kamensky who is Gorin who is Kaspar. Let me draw your maimed mind to some aspects of your situation which don't seem to have occurred to you. Do you suppose that a police spy like Kaspar – well-paid, and what is more, in a peculiarly happy position, thanks to my folly – do you imagine for a moment that however disloyal he was, he could wish success for a plan to assassinate the Tsar at a naval review – or anywhere else; but particularly at a naval review, where a small number of conspirators would have had to be admitted to a restricted area comparatively easy to supervise? A police spy who let that happen would not only lose his job, he'd find himself in prison, possibly in Siberia for life. Of course Kaspar had to upset the *Rurik* plans as soon as you idiots had begun to carry them out.

And of course he had to make it seem as if he hadn't done the upsetting and someone else had, and that someone else is you.'

'Yes, I suppose that is the only reason why I had those beautiful days by the Lake of Geneva, with those marvellous young men,' said Chubinov indistinctly.

'With those blood-stained Benjamins. Yes. You can take it too that for the same reason you were sent off to London to fiddle about with your infernal printing-presses, churning out rubbishy lies under the shelter of a criminal democracy, and that for the same reason the actress was dispatched to London to tell the faithful there that the three conspirators had been arrested. And what a stroke of luck that was for Kamensky, for Gorin, for Kaspar, that she looked into the courtyard and saw him and was able to tell that story in front of idiots of your own kind, while you gave yourself away with that fatuous face of yours, so honest that it's past a joke, that it makes one vomit even if one's on the side of honesty. All your expression gave away was that you had guessed the three young men were *Rurik* conspirators. But Kamensky, Gorin, Kaspar, had made certain that these English simpletons thought that what you were giving away was that you had arranged for their arrest. And they became so suspicious of you that you recognised it, even you who if you had been in Moscow when Rostopchin burned it wouldn't have noticed that anything unusual was going on for at least twenty-four hours. By the way, how funny to think of you of all men being got into trouble by an actress!'

He guffawed, and Chubinov tried to laugh too.

'But you can't go back to Russia, Grandmother's too ill,' Laura went on saying, but neither of them heard her.

'Already, at this moment, you can be sure,' Nikolai went on, 'the startling news of your treachery has reached your fellow-members, not only in Paris, where by your own account they're all loading their revolvers to take a pot-shot at you, but in St Petersburg and in Moscow and everywhere else where your pestilential co-conspirators poison the air with their stench. By this time you've no more chance of defending yourself than Judas if he came before a Church Synod. You lamentable ass, you're already dead. In a few days some dupe no brighter than yourself or me will be taken to some villa which has been burgled by Kamensky, and he'll be shown your body hanging from a meat-hook in the kitchen ceiling, and listen gaping to some tale about how you handed over three innocent boys to the cheka, long live the Revolution.'

'You put it odiously, but you are right,' breathed Chubinov. 'But how well it has all been planned. It has, hasn't it, in a sort of abhorrent way?'

'No, it hasn't,' said Laura. 'If you do something so awful that nobody could imagine you doing it, then nobody's going to work out ways of stopping you.' But again neither of them heard her. They were sitting in a fog of solemnity; though surely what they had found out should have made them angry instead of impressing them. Were men perhaps too good? Even when things were still going well at home, she had suspected that though her mother loved her father she did not feel an all-out respect for him. Often Tania talked of her husband and her father as if they were magnificent horses, probably marred – though she was not yet certain – by some incurable fault, like a tendency to take off too soon before a fence. As for her grandmother, conflicting ideas about men were always passing through her head. Her manner to Nikolai was submissive, it proclaimed her readiness to obey him in all circumstances, but hardly concealed her lack of conviction that this would serve any useful purpose. One could see even more clearly how odd her feelings were when she was dealing with the men servants and was more detached. She ordered them about imperiously, but always with a reservation, as if admitting that though here on earth she had the upper hand, there was another world of immaterial values, where superiority would be accorded to them simply because they were male. Nevertheless when she spoke to them her mouth was vigilant. She checked whether they had carried out her orders; she always entrusted any task demanding conscientiousness and reticence to her women servants, and not to the men servants; but she liked to have men servants about her, standing about the place, as if they brought good luck. She did not approve of that other world which accorded men a supreme value, but evidently she thought it might exist.

Nikolai and Chubinov were behaving as women never would dare to behave. Laura could not imagine any woman saying that she and her friends had never contemplated murdering the Governor of somewhere, and searching the distance for the cause of this exceptional abstinence, with a gentle, misted eye, as if speculating on the whereabouts of a lost umbrella. It would have been funny if the missing object had not been a murder; and what was infuriating was that the two were now suffering agonies of self-pity because it had not paid to treat murders as of no more consequence than umbrellas. What was the point of all these corpses, even leaving out that they were horrible? They could just as well have hung a dummy from that meat-hook in the kitchen of the villa on the Peterhof Road, and agreed that one side would say it was Valentine, and the other that it was Kamensky's brother. They never need have started this stupid game, and they could have stopped it at any moment they chose.

She was vexed at that moment, quite unaccountably, by a memory of Susie Staunton, standing before the tall cheval-glass in the visitors' room, her narrow body narrowed by her narrow dressing-gown, her extravagant fortune of pale-golden hair falling broad about her shoulders, and that look of hopeless hungering after plenty making a shadow triangle of her face. It had all been nonsense, it turned out afterwards. Someone who came to luncheon, a man from the Foreign Office who had never been made an Ambassador because there was something funny about him, had known her family well, and he had dropped the information that she was quite rich; and that not even at second-hand, but in her own right. A cousin of her father, who drew the ground rents from acres in an industrial Midland town, had died, after her two sons, her only children and unmarried, had been killed in the Boer War; and a mention of Susie in her will as a residuary legatee, intended as a mere expression of good will, had brought her a great inheritance. Mr Staunton was in the Caribbean not to eke out a livelihood but to develop a property which looked like a staggering long-term investment. Few people had yet heard of her new wealth, her friend had said, for she carried it without ostentation.

But that was silly. For Susie was ostentation itself in her pretence that she had no money at all. She always drew her gloves on and off with humble, smiling carefulness, as if, though she would never utter a word of complaint, they were the last pair she would be able to afford for a long time. What was the point of that perpetual fraud? What did she gain by it, why did she not settle down to spending her huge income joyously? And it was as strange that she always looked as if she must ache with pain, would have to go away, would perhaps die, if someone did not say certain kind words to her, enfold her against a winter which seemed to continue all the year round for her, even when it was summer. But people liked her, and surely she could have got happiness as other people did out of family and friends? Perhaps she secretly did. For the spectacle of bruised fragility which she presented did not cause any of the distress which normally comes from contact with pain, which had made it so heartrending to be with Tania for the last year or so. Nobody ever looked less like a man than Susie; yet she was like a man. She could have stopped playing whatever game it was she was playing any moment she chose.

Was it strange that she should think of Susie at this moment, when such horrors were being discussed? No, Susie fitted in here.

But Chubinov was saying, with an air of astonishment: 'But there's something you don't see. I'm forced, absolutely forced, to commit, alone and without the approval of a single human being, the act I've always dreaded. I've been in the Movement so long without having to do it. I hoped I'd escape the necessity for ever, but hope is the angel without wings. I'll have to do it. I'm in for it.'

'What does he mean? Grandfather, what does he mean?'

'I won't trouble to ask. What is it that he and his friends do, instead of reading Greek and Latin in their libraries, managing their estates or following their professions, raising godfearing and solvent children, attending church or shooting boar? He will be doing that other thing, we can be sure. Let's avert our minds from the spectacle. And the train is stopping. Let us get out of this accursed carriage, this moving Golgotha, this

197

rolling-stock abode of skulls.' He rose and stood rocking on his feet.

'Please, please,' said Laura. 'Let's stay in the train and go on to Aunt Florence's. Think, you can't rush off to St Petersburg when Grandmamma's just gone into a clinic.'

A wordless roar came out of Nikolai's throat. He lurched towards the door into the corridor and stretched out his arms towards the handle, but his body had suddenly suffered a stony change. He could not bend his elbows, he was beating out with his hands as if he could not move his fingers, and he continued to rock from one side to another, as if he were a statue propped up, though the train was slowing down. His face looked as if he would never break silence again. He was simply a huge oblong inflexible shape within his flexible clothes. Laura thought that they were saved, he would not be able to open the door into the compartment, they would have to stay in the train till they got to Mûres-sur-mer and the strength of Pyotr. But a number of passengers had gathered in the corridors, their baggage in their hands, ready to get out at the station, and one of these, a spectacled elderly woman, turned a kind face towards the compartment window, saw the old man flailing his arms and hastened to open the door, with a smile of such good will that Laura had to smile back through her anguish. Out in the corridor they were surrounded by up-turned apprehensive faces, fearful lest the staggering old man, a head taller than any of them, should fall this way or that. She looked over her shoulder and saw that Chubinov was still in the compartment. She called, 'Come quickly, help me with Grandfather.'

He joined her and, with unexpected competence, slid an arm under Nikolai's shoulder and braced him firmly.

'Why has my grandfather changed so suddenly?' she asked, not expecting an answer. 'Look at him!'

The train had slid under the glazed roof of the station and come to a stop. They drew the old man back against the compartment door, to let the able-bodied hurry by.

When the last passenger had gone Nikolai lurched back into the corridor and rolled along it, falling first against one side and then ricocheting on to the other, like one of those

Russian dolls with weights in their base which always swing upright. 'God forgive me, I had forgotten how old he is,' said Chubinov, staring after him, 'it's terrible he should have had this shock.'

'Go and help him then, you gave him the shock,' she said, and went back into the compartment to pick up her trinket-box and his case. The other two were at the top of the steps when she reached them, and the attendant was saying, 'But we'll never get him down to the platform,' and Chubinov was explaining, 'But I'm stronger than you might think. I worked hard at gymnastics in my youth because of this same old man. I must tell you —'

'He doesn't want to know,' said Laura. 'Tell me later. Get down on the platform.' People were waiting at the bottom of the steps to get on the train, and she looked down on a circle of upturned and exasperated faces, some of them old and tired. She said loudly to them, 'You must forgive us,' and added, 'my grandfather has been taken ill on the train.' But that was not what she had meant at first. She had felt ashamed. If these two men had not spent their lives playing this cruel and stupid game they would not be getting in the way of people without half the advantages they had had. She pulled down Chubinov after her to the platform, and put down the two cases and they both stood with their arms spread out ready to catch Nikolai. The attendant shoved him down on them, and he heeled over on top of them, his weight covering them like a thick cloak. They reeled under it and just managed to keep their balance while he got his, the people pushing past them and blinding them with their haste. When the three of them were standing clear, Nikolai stood sawing the air with his arms and uttering an angry cry. For an instant she lost her Russian and asked stupidly, 'What's he want? What's he want?'

'His case,' said Chubinov. 'Just hold it up and show it to him. He seems not able to see it. Considering the world he's lived in it's not unnatural that he should have developed an excessive attachment to material possessions. Now we can start. You take one arm, I'll take the other, and I can manage his case. We'll look for a bench and make him comfortable, and then I'll enquire about the trains to Paris, a slow train for me, an express for you. I think he'll be able to get on the train. This business has been a great shock to both of us. Try to behave so that nobody will notice us. That's an important part of our revolutionary technique. People do not remember one afterwards.'

Poor creature, what nonsense he talked. It was quite a big station. There was no barrier, they had come in at the main platform and passengers leaving the train gave up their tickets when they left the station; and everybody was staring at them. They must have looked very odd indeed: a huge old man with disordered white and gold hair and elegant clothes, staggering along between a silly-looking man wearing in midsummer a winter overcoat like a lunatic's dressing-gown, and a young girl with hair of the colour which made people gape anyway. 'Oh, we'll be remembered all right. Chubinov is a funny too,' she thought, shaking her hat straight, as her grandfather had knocked it askew with a windmill gesture. But Chubinov was more efficient than she had expected. He found a bench for them against the sooty wall between the entrances to the ticket-office and the waiting-room, and after lowering Nikolai down into a huddled and twisted sort of comfort, he went away, making a gesture which frightened her. He might have been bidding her good-bye. She was surprised to find how much she would prefer that he came back. She wet her lips and tried to laugh. Awful people in England said they were going to see a man about a dog when they wanted to have a drink. She supposed Chubinov's friends would say in like circumstances that they had gone to see a man about a bomb. How odd that this whole episode wasn't a joke, like the executions in *The Rose and the Ring*, like the Queen of Hearts's 'Off with their heads!' in *Alice in Wonderland*. How odd it was that this man really had killed, not with his own hands, but, worse still, by planning the killing. She should not be wishing that he would come back.

But he was leaning kindly over her, and had brought a porter with him. 'I'm sorry, Miss Laura, my slow train leaves before your express, indeed it's starting quite soon. But this man will take you and the case to the Paris express when it comes in at half past two, and he'll bring another man with him, a strong man, to get Nikolai Nikolaievitch into the carriage. I've chosen him,' he explained, raising a didactic forefinger, 'because he has silver hair and grey eyes and a bronze skin. It would be interesting to know what stock he comes from. I hope you will read the anthropological works of the brothers Reclus some day, they are anarchists and therefore politically futile, but their scientific ideas have a bearing on the new society. Because he has silver hair and grey eyes and a bronze skin, you will be able to pick him out from the other porters. If you are looking for someone, and he's also looking for you, and you memorise his characteristics, you can join up with him and excite only the minimum interest during your search. Keep that in mind. You must do everything to prevent people from remembering you.' With a vaguely conspiratorial gesture he dismissed the porter, who had been so interested in the queer group of foreigners that he walked away backwards, unable to take his eyes off them.

Chubinov bent over Nikolai and sighed. 'He's fallen asleep. Let's not disturb him. If one had come on Oedipus sleeping in the grove at Colonus one would have let him sleep.' Straightening himself, he went on. 'If one had been a pious Greek one might have insulted Oedipus and tortured him to death as an outcast condemned by the gods, and if one had been a rationalist Greek one might have insulted him and abandoned him for his surrender to gross superstition, but whichever side one had been on, one couldn't have been cruel enough to waken him out of his sleep. What a dreadful thought! The one mercy we feel we must show our fellow-men is to allow them such moments of unconsciousness as they attain. That can mean only one thing, that we live in a state of despair. Yet, of course, one despairs of life only because one lives under a tyranny. But perhaps I'm feeling specially acute despair now because I have lost Gorin. Ah, Gorin, Gorin. Also there is this repugnant action I have to perform, this duty I must fulfil regarding you. Miss Laura,' he said, suddenly recovering his air of sense, 'have you really got plenty of money?' She gave him all the francs Tania had put in her handbag, and he left her, again with this gesture which might have been farewell. That puzzled her, frightened her. She called him back. 'Why do you look at me and half wave your hand, as if you were going off for good?'

'Well, anything might happen now,' he said vaguely.

It was just one of his ideas. There would be nothing in it. She wished that her grandfather had not fallen asleep, his closed eyes were so like the eyes of a statue. But as she looked at him, anxious lest this change in him should mean more than itself, he opened his eyes and lifted his clouded topaz gaze to the great clock hanging above the platform. It seemed to give his mind a place to rest. Now and then his pale lips parted in his white and yellow beard when the minute hand swung, and closed when it swung again. It was as if he had asked a question and the clock had answered it. There was no use worrying him. The clock was nursing him. Laura let herself be distracted by a natural comedian, a woman with a foolish round face surmounted by a pork-pie hat, an unfortunate figure, narrow above the waist and broad below, and pulled to left and right by the weight of the two heavy holdalls swinging from either arm. She went circling below the clock in little steps and casting anxious glances up at it until she reached the spot exactly beneath it. There she became serene and dumped down the holdalls. 'How lovely,' thought Laura, 'somebody has promised to meet her under the clock, so she has to see to it that she really is under the clock, right under the clock. She must be a nice funny.'

Chubinov was beside her again. 'Look,' he said, 'in his envelope are your tickets back to Paris, and the right amount of money for the two porters' tips here, and for the other two you'll need at the Gare du Nord. And here's the rest of the money. An astonishing amount. It is surprising, it is even shocking, that your parents should have given you so much for the journey. Force yourself, I beg, to think sometimes of the sufferings of the poor.'

'I hear of the sufferings of the poor from morning till night,' said Laura. 'You can't know my grandmother very well if you don't know that she worries about the poor all the time, and my father's people are Irish Low Church, and they're nervously charitable, because of being the ascendancy, and ashamed of it. Indeed, if you're reckoning up the sufferings of

202

the poor, you might take into account that they must be sick of the sight of our family. It's a funny thing, Monsieur Chubinov, but you never, never say anything that isn't wide of the mark.' It was the first time that she had ever been rude without restraint to a grown-up person. She found great pleasure in it, but was instantly ashamed. She said, 'I'm sorry, I got nervous because I was afraid you weren't coming back. I'm really most grateful to you. You're a murderer, but you're very kind.'

'I am not yet a murderer,' he said pedantically, 'and I am not specially kind,' and sat down beside her, lifting the tails of his overcoat, evidently obeying an injunction given him long ago regarding some other garment, for this one would have looked no better uncrumpled. 'I perhaps don't have an accurate impression of your circumstances,' he said, 'because I am dealing with you as I would deal with my two sisters, who are the only girls of your age I've ever known, and they would certainly have felt utterly lost in your situation. I suppose you're more or less in the same case. I don't suppose you go out by yourself in London.'

'There you're wrong,' she said. 'I took myself to school all the last year before I left, and now I take classes, and I go to them alone if Mummie doesn't want to come too. But she nearly always does. She says it keeps her mind off things, learning new subjects.' She looked up at him defensively. 'Off things,' she explained, 'like housekeeping worries, you know. We're very modern. My father's elder sister was one of the first women to go to Girton.' She was hardly thinking of what she was telling him. The way things had gone wrong at the house in Radnage Square was a smart behind her eyes, a lump in her throat.

He was as abstracted. 'I'm glad to hear it. Only by education will the world be saved,' he murmured absently, and then snapped out in his distress: 'I'm not thinking of what I'm saying. I'm failing my moment. I'm not getting to the point. This journey has been a horrible shock to me. Not that I haven't been on a number of railway journeys which were the very reverse of agreeable, but those were also glorious. You see, I often accompanied my wife when she was carrying dynamite to groups in other cities who had not the facilities for manufacturing it, and it can never be pleasant to transport dynamite. It has to be carried under one's clothing, in case one's baggage is searched, and when it's warm it gives off exhalations which are quite unwholesome, causing sickness and headache. And if the train's not heated, then, of course, one's on tenterhooks, for when the surface gets chilled and is then brought into the warmth, well, then, chemical changes occur, and there's a risk of an explosion. But none of these inconveniences troubled us, for we were doing what was right, we were obeying the demands of idealism, and there could be no taint of wrong in it, for we were running the risk of sacrificing our own lives. So we could bear anything.

'But now I'm suffering. As I've never suffered before. I realise that I'm a weak man, for it makes a great difference that I'm now alone, I haven't my dear wife with me. I even find myself thinking on a deplorably low level, a personal level. I find myself imagining that the worst crime of Gorin is not his betrayal of the sacred idea of revolution and the slaughter or imprisonment of many of our most splendid comrades, but the frustration of my sainted wife's unremitting labours, which were what killed her. The doctors said she had contracted the tuberculosis of which she died because she worked so hard, and often in insanitary improvised laboratories, but I think what made her succumb to it was her many disappointments. For some of her most earnest efforts came to nothing.'

'You mean nobody got killed?'

'Nobody. Not on the occasions I am thinking of. On others, yes. But not on these. And now I know why. Gorin. We always worked with him. I find myself thinking so bitterly of that, to the exclusion of other and more fundamental issues. That shows what a weak man I am, and now I can't escape the obligation to act as if I were strong. I've every conceivable handicap. I'm weak, I'm unpractical, I'm unobservant, and though I've taught myself to observe certain routines I'm apt to become abstracted at the wrong moment. But all the same, I've got to kill Gorin.'

'To kill Gorin? To kill Kamensky?' she repeated incredulously. She felt sick. 'Oh, you can't mean it! Not another murder, on top of all the rest? You're mad, I tell you, you're completely mad.'

She turned in her seat and looked him full in the face, to bully him the better. But he was such a poor thing that she was silenced. The veins in his hollow temples recalled to her some straggling violets in a hand-shaped vase of translucent white china Tania had once put on the drawing-room window-ledge one winter's day. Beyond the glass there had been a grey sky, bare trees, ridges of discoloured snow on the lawn, and birds hopping avidly on the stone flags of the terrace, pecking the tea-time crumbs out of the cracks. His beard was so scanty, his eyebrows so scruffy: feathers on a small ailing bird. 'You mustn't keep pets,' a nameless voice said, out of some other occasion of the past, 'if you aren't prepared to look after them.' It was a pity nobody had ever said that to God. She wanted to tell Chubinov what could not possibly be said: 'You mustn't commit murder. You'll be hanged. You're not good-looking enough, people simply won't care. They're brutes.'

For the sake of saying something, and because the birds had put it into her mind, she asked, 'Aren't you hungry? Go and get something to eat before you start. Those biscuits I gave you in the train were all I had.' He put a hand into the pocket of the awful overcoat and took out a biscuit of his own. 'Oh, you can't eat that,' she said, 'it's got thread all over it.'

He murmured absently, 'I'll rub it off,' did so ineffectually with his dirty gloves, and lifted the biscuit to his lips again.

'Oh, please,' she begged, 'go to the buffet, get something solid, you really need it, and my grandfather's sound asleep, we'll be all right till you come back.'

He shook his head. 'Please don't worry about me. I've two or three biscuits in my pocket. It's enough.'

He had nothing, nothing, least of all good luck. He wouldn't get away. For one thing, that overcoat would make him a sitting duck. 'That overcoat!' she muttered wretchedly.

'My overcoat?' he asked, smiling. 'Then you have noticed my overcoat?'

She had not known she had said the words aloud. She brazened it out. 'I wondered if it came from Russia.'

'No,' he said, his eyes brightening. 'It is, as you have noticed, something special, but it didn't come from Russia, it was made by the wife of a comrade in Switzerland. An excellent woman. She trained as a dentist in Germany, hoping to use her skill among our peasants, but was chased out of Russia by your grandfather's police. So now she has set up a tailoring business in Vevey.'

A dentist. How Tania would laugh at that. The woman obviously made the clothes with forceps and a drill, and put her customers under gas as soon as they got into the shop, and clad them in her monstrosities and took the money out of their wallets while they were still unconscious. Chubinov was now on his second biscuit, which looked worse than the first. She said, smiling, with tears in her eyes, 'Please, Monsieur Chubinov, don't think any more about killing Gorin. Don't go back to Paris. Take a train in the other direction, get on a Channel steamer and hide in London.'

'Why, you brave, kind Russian girl,' he said smiling, 'I really think you mind what happens to me. But there's something you haven't realised. I'm rather surprised that you haven't, but then an English upbringing is not suitable preparation for all this. Don't you see that I have to kill Gorin for your sake? Don't you understand that, without meaning to, I've put you in a position of the gravest danger? I didn't know you'd be travelling with your grandfather. Your mother didn't say so on the telephone, and I didn't consider it possible. I'd so many things to think of, and my heart was broken by what I'd just found out about Gorin, and it never even crossed my mind that a young lady like you would be allowed to go a long railway journey alone with an old man. I tell you, I took it for granted you'd be as helpless as my sisters were at your age. Then when I saw you with Nikolai Nikolaievitch at the Gare du Nord I couldn't stop what I was doing. I'd gone too far, and I was sick and dizzy, because there was no Kamensky and that meant that he was Gorin. And anyway never for one moment did I think that Nikolai Nikoliaevitch would insist on leaving the train here and going back to Paris. I thought he'd continue his journey to Mûres-sur-mer and deal with the issues we'd raised from there, in something like safety. You do

206

see, don't you, that nothing, absolutely nothing, has happened as I expected? But reproach me as much as you like. For there it is, it happened. Gorin must have taken the precaution of posting a watch at the Gare du Nord. It would be inevitable, according to our technique. So now he knows that I travelled with both of you, and he cannot fail to guess what we talked about.'

'Well?' Then a sword struck at her. 'You mean,' she said, 'that Kamensky will want to kill my grandfather and me because we know he's Gorin?' At his nod she learned how mistaken she had been when, from time to time in the past, she had believed that she was frightened. Fear was what she knew now, and she never felt it before. It was chiefly a sliding of her bowels and a blackness before her yes. Unseeing, she turned towards her grandfather and laid her hand on his knee, and wondered at the thinness of the layer of flesh above the bone, and wondered again because through the scant flesh there flowed a slight movement, as slight as movement can be. She raised her hand and put it into the gap in his overcoat over his chest, and pressed her fingers against the fine linen of his shirt, under his beard. It was the steady rhythm of a sleeper's breath that made his chest rise and sink, but also there was running through him this delicate tremor, more pervasive and wayward than a pulse, a signal made by some excitement of the body, never likely to be expressed in the grossness of words or gesture. She said, 'But my grandfather too?'

'Yes. He too. But his time is nearly come. It's you that must not be killed.'

Long ago, in some house curtained against the heat of a summer afternoon, she had woken in a darkened bedroom beside a bed where a figure lay swaddled in sleep, she had dropped from the sheer height of the bed, reached up to the door-handle, gone out on the landing and peered between the banisters down on a silent hall, with its doors ajar on silent rooms. A Red Admiral was fluttering and alighting and soaring through the shafts of sunlight and the alcoves of shadow, out of the silent hall into the silent rooms and back again, the one small fragile living thing. Life was like that, very fragile.

Yet she found herself saying to Chubinov, almost with laughter, 'I'll get out of this.'

'My brave Russian girl,' said Chubinov, sadly. 'We'll work together. As I told you, I'll get out of the train at a suburban station outside Paris and then I'll make my way to my hotel near Les Halles. I'll stay in my room for thirty-six hours so that they'll think I'm not in Paris. I think they'll rely on my being very helpless without Gorin. I'll spend the time piecing together what I know of Gorin's habits so that I can make plans for waylaying him. Then I'll go out and shoot him. That will be easy. Your grandfather really made a fine revolver shot out of me. Then I'll try to get away. That won't be so easy. I really will be helpless without Gorin then. And I will not take too much trouble to save myself. My life-long friend will kill me after I've killed him, and I won't care, for I love him too much to want to live after I have been his executioner.'

'It's disgusting of you to kill him, but it's just as disgusting for you to love him after you know how horrible he is.'

He paid no attention. 'Now as for you. You should hurry back to London, of course. Or take your grandfather to rest at a hotel in the town. But he had made up his mind to return to Paris, and that's what you'll find yourself doing. He's got more will than is usually possessed by individuals, he moves as irresistibly as a species, as the wild geese flying south in autumn or the deer on the tundras seeking the summer pastures. It will be the same even if he is quite ill and his mind is affected. His will never had much to do with his mind. So you'll find yourself rashly, dangerously back at the Avenue Kléber. Now listen to what you must do.'

He put his arm round her and drew her close so that he could speak softly. Little pellets of advice were thrown at her, another and another. She was to tell her mother everything the moment she saw her. No matter how worried Tania Nikolaievna was about Sofia Andreievna, she must learn everything, everything, about Kamensky. Of course her grandfather must be stopped from starting for Russia. He would not get to Berlin alive, perhaps not even to the station. Nobody must go out of the apartment, nobody must be allowed in. 'You see,' he whispered, sounding like a ghost telephoning from the grave, 'one can never tell for certain who anybody is.' Then if everything went well, they would hear of Kamensky's death; either it would be in the newspapers or they would get a letter from him saying he had done it. Then they need worry no more. 'But if Kamensky does not die, if I die, and if you have heard nothing at the end of three days, then your mother must ring up the British Embassy and ask for protection.' She need not fear they would disbelieve her story, for though their Secret Service was elementary they would know enough. But even after the British Embassy had sent round their men, the whole family must go on staying indoors and not letting anybody into the apartment, even if they were friends. Meanwhile her mother must get her father to come over from London, to make arrangements to take them all back to London under armed guard. 'You could telegraph to your father from here, asking him to go to your mother at once —' But the whisper stopped. She was glad, her ear was tickling. Hesitantly the whisper began again: 'Ah, but you'd have to explain to your father, wouldn't you, that there was something extraordinary going on, if you were to be sure he would come? There's – there's a difficulty, isn't there?'

'A difficulty! What sort of difficulty?' she cried.

She had recoiled from him, but his face followed hers and was still close. Through his thick spectacles his magnified eyes seemed vague wet stumps, like sea anemones. 'Why, a difficulty. About your father,' he sighed.

She jerked her head away. 'I can't understand what you're saying! There's no difficulty about my father. I don't know what it could mean, "a difficulty about my father".'

'Forgive me,' said Chubinov meekly. 'I must have misunderstood something I heard.'

'Something you heard from Gorin, I suppose.' Somewhere in the station an engine was letting off steam, and hatred hissed out of her like the steam. 'Go away. Go away at once. You're planning a murder, a common murder, you're like Jack the Ripper and Charles Peace. What have my grandfather and I to do with that? We're the sort of people who'd rather be murdered than be saved by a murder.'

A porter drove his hand-truck into a suitcase which had

been left standing on the ground, its owner ran up and there was shouting. Till it died down Chubinov could not hear her, and he kept his hand spread out round his ear, his mouth open, till she repeated what she had said, and then he appeared hurt and astonished.

'Miss Laura, do not be foolish. I won't reproach you because you can't help having been brought up in capitalist hypocrisy. But your grandfather and you have no real objection to murder. Your grandfather has sent many victims to the gallows. Your father, being in the House of Commons, ranges himself on the same side as the English hangman.'

'That's different. If you're going to try Kamensky in a proper law-court, well and good.'

'But, dear Miss Laura, in our present society, there are no proper law-courts. They exist simply to protect the exploitation of the many by the few, and now you've strayed into a domain where there are no law-courts at all.'

'I'll get out of that domain, just you see if I don't,' she told him, her face blazing. 'And whose fault is it I ever got into it? Yes, I know you didn't grasp I was on the train. But you knew my grandfather was. You must have realised you'd drag him into trouble, and what did you get on that train for, anyway? Simply because you wanted to know if Gorin was Kamensky. But we Diakonovs didn't particularly want to know if Kamensky was Gorin. What harm was he really doing us, when you come to think of it, what harm could he do to people who are so old and will soon be out of it, twaddling pious nonsense to them while he's reading all their letters like a scoundrelly butler. And does it make it so much worse, if you have a scoundrelly butler, that he's being someone else's scoundrelly butler at the same time? But you would butt in, and now here my grandfather and I have got to dodge your horrible friends who want to throw bombs at us and shoot us, and to crown everything you have the impudence to put the responsibility for another murder on us. What a nuisance you are, what a nuisance!'

What would it be like to be blown to pieces, to be suddenly hurled to the ground by a bullet as pheasants are hurled out of the air? She had to cover her mouth to stop a scream.

'You utterly fail to allow for the ideal,' said Chubinov miserably.

'You and my grandfather, with your ideals,' she muttered through her fingers.

'Ah, you're very sad, Miss Laura,' he said. 'But you must try to understand that neither your grandfather nor I have ever been able to choose what we did. You see, he and I are embedded in Russia, up to our necks, we can't move. The river has broken its dams and it's made mud of all our land. Your grandfather and I and all Russians have to stay where the flood waters have cast us, where we were sucked down into the marsh, we can't free ourselves, we've just go to wait there. I can't help feeling that a clever girl like you should realise how it is with us, how it would have been with you if you'd been born in Russia. You too, as we say, "would have had to take sides", though what we really mean is that you'd have had to realise at what point in the Russian marshland you'd got stuck. You're a truly Russian girl, you're full of ideals, you would have made an excellent revolutionary. You truly want me to save my life, don't you, and to save me from the guilt of murder? Yet I don't suppose you like me. I haven't got sufficiently positive characteristics to be likeable. I don't know how it was that my wife felt the affection for me which she undoubtedly did. And I am always surprised that Gorin liked me —' his pale face grew paler – 'But I forgot. All these years he has not liked me at all.'

'But lots of other people do.' She looked at Nikolai and made sure that he was still asleep, and said with a confidence which she would have lacked if he had been awake, 'I'm sure my grandfather's very fond of you. I know he's awful to you, but that only shows how much he bothers about you. And I like you very much.' She was startled to find that this was true. 'Forgive me if I was rude to you on the train. The fact is, I couldn't tell you the meaning of the thing I called you in English, for the reason I don't know it myself. It's just something I heard a cabby call our coachman once.'

'All the world over it's like that,' laughed Chubinov. 'Cab-drivers swear terribly at coachmen, and always the children hear and remember. Their lessons they forget, and the good

211

counsel given them by their elders, but what the cab-drivers call the coachmen, that lingers on and on —'

His laughter was unbearable, it was so tender, pleasant and well-bred, thin and defenceless. It was drowned by the noise of the train which was puffing in to the shadow of the station from the outer track, slowing down to a standstill just in front of them on the main platform. It must be the slow train to Paris. She shouted into his ear, 'Please, please, go to England. To London. Then see my father. He'll help you. Tell him everything. He looks as if he'd mind but he won't. He always calls the Home Rule members Fenian assassins, but he's great friends with some of them. The best ones come to dinner. I won't give you our address, you won't remember it, but you can get him at the House of Commons.'

His eyes crinkled with amusement. He took another of the dreadful biscuits out of his pocket, but it broke and fell in crumbs on the lapel of his coat. It must have been very stale. He took out a fourth, but it crumbled at once and fell in pieces on the stone flags at his feet. 'What a waste,' he said. 'There are no birds here. But what could I do in England?'

'Why, you could teach in a school. Your French is beautiful. And nobody could murder you if you were teaching in a school.'

'Why not?'

'It just wouldn't happen. Not in a school. If a man came into a school and tried to murder you the headmaster or headmistress would send for the police and they'd come and arrest him. Your friends are awful but they wouldn't stand a chance. You've got to go to England. Now, from this station. Now! From this station.'

'Oh, Miss Laura, you are like my wife. She also was a dove and an eagle. But do not distress yourself about me. I would rather not murder Gorin. But I must do so, in order to protect you, your grandfather, and the revolutionary movement. And I will be sustained by certain considerations. I am justified in my action by my masters Kant and Hegel.' The didactic forefinger was up again. 'The supreme end of reason is the complete subordination of nature to the prescripts of morality, and if I use my freedom to renounce my life, my unique place in nature, to perform an act I think moral, then I am in a morally unassailable position. Almost certainly I will die for the murder of Gorin, either at the hands of his dupes or of the capitalist government of France. So I am in a sense happy; because, broken as I am, robbed of my life work and my major friendship, I am in a sense happy, because I am going to perform a moral act, the murder of Gorin, and – you do see don't you – absolve myself from all blame by dying myself. So I am in a state of complete integration with the Absolute. I can't be subject to the slightest reproach whatsoever, don't you see, because I'm a proven instrument of the supreme good. Also I think Berr will know that I am doing right.'

'The blind man!' exclaimed Laura. 'You think he'll feel you were right?'

'He would find some difficulty in understanding the problem,' said Chubinov, 'he has the advantage of living in an extremely simple world, where ethical considerations rarely come into conflict with one another. My world, on the contrary, has been thrown into extreme ethical confusion by my ineluctable connection with the crimes of Tsardom, forced on me by my birth into a family belonging to the minor nobility. It's my duty to stamp out the crimes of Tsardom, as it is the duty of every man to renounce his own sins. This can only be done by punitive acts directed against the criminal Tsar and his criminal officials. I'm obliged to become a criminal myself, and the execution of Gorin, whom I know now to be one of those criminal officials, is one of the crimes I am thus compelled to commit. I doubt if Berr could understand this predicament, but if he could understand it, he would give me his approval. So I move towards my horrible duty of killing Gorin safeguarded by Berr's intense goodness. He is, to use his own way of putting things, giving me his blessing.'

'He isn't doing anything of the sort,' said Laura. 'Nobody, practically nobody, gives people their blessing for going about killing people. The idea's absurd. It's funny. If death can be funny, and if course it can be. There's that song the servants sing at home when Papa and Mamma have gone out.' It was lovely to speak English for a little.

'Oh, a Norrible Tale I have to tell
Of sad disasters that befell
A family that once resided
Just in the same thoroughfare that I did.'

How does it go?

'First the father into the garden did walk
And cut his throat with a lump of chalk,
Then the mother an end to herself did put
By hanging herself in the water-butt,
Then her sister went down on her bended knees
And smothered herself with toasted cheese.'

'What is that? Repeat it, please, I did not follow. Sometimes when I am tired my English quite deserts me. Perhaps you'd kindly translate it into Russian.'

'No, no. I really can't. It's untranslatable.'

'Ah, yes, like much of your English poetry, and most of ours. Pushkin. But to return to Berr. He will recognise that I am acting as an instrument of the supreme good, not by use of his intellect – which is quite undeveloped – but in his simple way, by intuition. I am sacrificing myself, and already he admires self-sacrifice in the saints and martyrs, and in his God, and his Christ. Therefore he is certain to give me his sympathy.'

'Really, you're incredibly silly,' exclaimed Laura. 'Berr may be simple, but he can't be so simple that he couldn't pick out a number of differences between you and Christ. People in the Old Testament are as silly as you, but absolutely nobody in the Newt Testament. Of course you can't help being silly, but what I can't stand is something you could help, and that is that you're such a humbug. You haven't spent your life in all this plotting and blowing up people because of the supreme good, but because you like doing it, just as my father and my brothers like playing cricket, and they don't pretend they're saints and martyrs. Oh,' she wailed, 'try and have some sense and stop blithering and think what you really want to do. Do

214

you want to go to Paris and kill Kamensky and get killed, or won't you be sensible and go to England?'

'It is perhaps not the time or the place to discuss that now. And you are upset.'

'It is the time and the place. Don't you see that that's the train you said you'd take to Paris? The one in front of us. Look at the boards on it. If you don't want to take it, well and good. But if you do, there it is. It'll leave in a minute. It's crowded. I don't want you to go to Paris and be killed, but if you've made up your mind to it you may as well have a seat on the way.'

'You're quite right. But now I wish I hadn't to go. You are rude, you're very rude indeed, but you are a good girl. Truly, there's something about all your family, something.' He rose and stood for a second looking down on Nikolai Nikolaievitch, who stirred, as if the glance pierced through his sleep. 'Goodbye, my friend,' said Chubinov. 'How mild and beneficent he looks, as if it had been his office to sentence people not to death but to eternal life. How well one can believe, at the sight of him, in the legend that our Tsar Alexander the First had a corpse from a hospital buried under his name and lived for many years another life as the holy hermit Kuzma.'

'You haven't time to tell me that now, you must go,' said Laura. 'Don't you see, the train's starting.'

But he was writing, with exasperating slowness, on a piece of paper. 'Here, don't lose this. That's the name of the hotel near Les Halles, where I will be staying under the name of Baraton, and the telephone number. If I can be of any use to you during the next few days ring me up or send me a telegram, and please remember I had no idea, no idea at all, that you would be with your grandfather.'

'I tell you it doesn't matter. But,' she said, suddenly moved by the weedy height of him as he leaned over her, the shabbiness of the cuff above the tobacco-stained hand he held out to her, the biscuit crumbs on his lapel, the weak pure beam of friendship filtering through his thick spectacles, 'how kind you are. Everything about you is all wrong, everything you believe and do, but you're awfully kind. I don't want you to commit that murder but I quite see that you're doing it partly for my grandfather and me, and anyway you keep on worrying about me, as I wouldn't worry about anyone if I had to commit a crime and might get found out. But now you must go, you really must, and try to get something decent to eat when you can.' She put the piece of paper into her bag out of politeness, she would never use it.

Now he was looking through rather than at her, and when he spoke it was with the imitation of briskness which meant that he was following his revolutionary technique. He asked, 'Tell me, has Gorin any fixed time for visiting your family? The day after tomorrow, now, when would he be likely to come to your grandfather's apartment?'

She knew what he was at. 'He's no fixed time for coming. And if he had I wouldn't tell you. My grandfather and I will get out of this in our way, not yours. But hurry, hurry, or you'll lose that train.'

It was on the move when he reached it. Some soldiers leaning from a corridor window burst into laughter at the sight of him as he loped across the platform with his overcoat flapping round his thin legs, and they opened the door and pulled him aboard in the nick of time, with an air of acquiring an amusing mascot. He waved to her from the window, and so did the laughing boys round him, when they saw who it was he was waving to, and as the train puffed off she heard them raise a roar, *Auprès de ma Blonde*. She was glad her grandfather was asleep, he would have been angry. But she waved back, laughed back. The boys meant no harm and had they known what was happening they would have been on her side. That seemed the only important thing now. She waved till she could see them no longer, and the train had jerked its way out of the station and into the open brightness beyond. Clouds of yellowish smoke were blown backwards from the engine and hovered under the glass roofs, slowly wasting to traceries of mist and then to nothingness. The crowds had thinned. There was nobody in the full agony of travel, trudging under the weight of luggage or dragging children by the hand, only some people sitting on the bench. It could not be said there was silence, but the space of the station was not quite filled by its noise, there was an emptiness high under the roof.

It was there that her fear seemed to be, not within herself. Up under the sallow glass and blackened iron was her recognition that she might be hurt and die. To avoid it she looked away. On her right the roof came to an end not far off, and she had an oblique view of a high embankment of dark bricks, stained dirty tawny by the sunshine, and topped by a row of street-lamps. One could just see the roofs and upper storeys of the line of mean little houses that they lit. She would rather live out the span of her life simply looking at this one hideous scene, than be dead and see nothing; and the thought brought her fear out of the air into herself. Even if she got out of this, and of course she would, she would never be quite alive again.

She heard her grandfather say her name. His voice had changed. There was water in its wine. She would not let them do anything more to him. She slipped her hand into his and held it to her lips.

'Laura,' he said, 'did you not hear the trumpet?'

Perhaps she had lost her Russian again. What trumpet? But of course a trumpet had sounded when the Paris train left. The tinny little trumpet which did the work in France that the guard's flag and whistle did in England. 'Yes, I heard it.'

The blanched voice went on. 'It was the little girl. The little girl who looks like a doll has put the trumpet to her lips.'

There was not only murder, there was not only death and the fear of death, there was this also.

'Oh, hush, hush,' she said, 'there's no little girl here.'

'But Pravdine's little girl is here,' he told her, 'the little girl at the Christmas party. She looks like a doll and is wearing that dress of fine muslin, like a lampshade. I told you they had given her a trumpet. She has put it to her lips. It had to happen some time, and now it has happened.'

'Nothing has happened,' she assured him. 'You've been asleep, you're still dreaming. What you heard was the trumpet they blow to send out the train.'

'She has blown her trumpet,' persisted Nikolai, 'and all has come to an end.' He raised his eyes to the great clock which hung above the platform. 'The hands are not moving.'

'They are, indeed they are,' said Laura. 'Look, the minute hand is swinging forward now.'

'No, no, the clock has stopped,' said Nikolai. His hand on hers was shaking.

'Grandfather. Nothing is happening that isn't ordinary. You just can't see the hands.'

'The clock has stopped,' groaned Nikolai, and he rose from the bench. 'God have mercy on our souls.'

He began to rock on his feet, as he had done in the train. Then his unbending body slanted slowly towards the ground, like a falling tree. His hat dropped off and his cane clattered on the stone flags and rolled away; and still the slanting mass of him continued to keel over. Laura cried out, and a porter, passing by with a hand-trolley, halted it beside them and waited with bent knees to catch the lethargically-moving weight that was as hard to deal with as if it had been crashing down quickly, because it was so huge; and the porter's own movements were slowed down by wonder. He was very young, and she saw his lips pout as he recognised the prodigiousness of Nikolai, like a child who goes to the Zoo and sees a rhinoceros for the first time. He was just able to keep the old man from falling to the ground and to break his fall on to the trolley. Only his head and torso rested on it; his legs stuck out stiffly to the ground. His eyes were closed, his skin was the colour of white silk long laid by in a drawer.

Everything seemed to be happening somewhere else or behind a wall of glass. The station had seemed empty, but at once a crowd was round the prostrate body. In the past, when Nikolai went about London or Paris, people had found it embarrassing to look at him except by stealing narrowed glances at him and then frowning into the distance as if they had not seen him at all. But now he was performing in public the private act of dying they were not ashamed to stare at him with wide eyes. Most of the men took off their hats. Several men and women crossed themselves, there were mumblings of prayer, and a slight devout stir started up like a breeze.

Someone said, 'He must have been a magnificent man', and someone else said, 'His hair, that's very strange', and indeed his thick white locks, streaked with bright gold, looked very unnatural now they were spread wildly round a still face. He might have been a saint whose halo had been broken over his head by a persecutor. Laura said to herself, 'It is not possible this should be happening. It's only two minutes since Chubinov went off and left me alone, simply so that he could commit another murder. How awfully like him. But one shouldn't blame him, he didn't know.'

The porter had already called to another porter, telling him to fetch the stationmaster, and she knelt by her grandfather and spoke to his pale face, though it was like speaking to the sky or a shoulder of the downs. For his sake she was glad that he was dead. If she had had to struggle with Kamensky for their lives, if she had had to take a revolver out of his hand, her grandfather would have been humiliated because he had lost the strength to kill, and because the man he should have killed was the man he had loved. 'God,' she prayed, 'thank you for sparing him all that.' But this was humbug. She was relieved because now she had only herself to think of she would have a better chance of escaping from Kamensky. In shame she cried, 'God, don't let him be dead', and kissed his hands. But there was a touch on her arm, and she found that there were two men standing beside her. One was the stationmaster in his uniform, the other was a silver-haired man with a small trim beard and bright grey eyes, neat clothes, and an air of command.

She asked herself, 'Who can this be? A friend of Gorin's?' and her heart stopped. But he had the red ribbon of the Legion of Honour in his button-hole, and the stationmaster was explaining that she was fortunate, there was a medical school in the town, and this was Professor Saint-Gratien, the head of the surgical faculty. He had come in on the same train from Paris as herself and had been lunching in the station restaurant with a friend before going home. It sounded all right, so she turned to him in trust. He asked her questions and she answered them, regardless of the listening strangers round them. They might have been meeting in a wood, with people as trees. Yes, her grandfather had just fallen down. No, she had never seen him have such an attack before. He lived in Paris, and they were on their way to Mûres-sur-mer, but had got out of the train, because – she had to sob here, till she could think of a reason she cared to give – because he had got worried over something and had wanted to go home, partly, she thought, out of concern for his wife, who was very ill.

It was vulgar to tell people who one was for the sake of impressing them. But now she was in danger she felt she had to use everything at her disposal to grapple the two men to her. She told them her grandfather was Count Diakonov and had been Minister of Justice in Russia, and that her uncle had been Russian Ambassador in Paris. The stationmaster inclined his head several times to show his respect, and the doctor intimated that he had not needed to be informed of the social importance of her and her grandfather, he had divined it at sight. From his manner she realised that he was not overawed at meeting grand people, though he was pleased that to the number of grand people he knew pure chance had added two more. She thought no worse of him for that. There were many such people in Kensington, where she would have liked to be. She went on to exploit this vein by confiding that she had been travelling alone with her grandfather only because the Diakonov household was disorganised by her grandmother's illness and that she was quite at a loss.

'But what relatives have you in Paris who could come immediately?' asked the stationmaster, taking out a notebook. 'You see, the body of your poor grandfather the Count must be left here till a policeman has viewed it, and I've already sent for one, and then it has to be removed to a mortuary attached to the hospital, where, since it is also a convent, they'll take you in till your relatives come to make arrangements, and come they must, for —'

'But the young lady's grandfather isn't dead,' said the doctor. 'Not dead!' exclaimed the stationmaster, and a woman standing by said quite sharply that all she knew was that her husband had looked just like the old gentleman when he had fallen down in his shop, and he had been dead all right.

'Well, I can't claim to see as many dead people as some members of my profession,' said the doctor. 'A certain number of my patients recover. But my experience, such as it is, inclines me to believe that that old gentleman is for the moment alive, not so much alive as some of us but more alive than others.'

A hush fell. The crowd was losing sympathy. It was even with coldness that they watched him as he bent down and put his fingers on the old man's wrist. He straightened himself and mocked them with a smile, just slightly more elegant than a clown's grin.

'A disappointment for you all,' he said, 'he's got a pulse.' But he turned to Laura and murmured, 'That'll get rid of them. But he's very ill. He has a pulse, but it's only a pulse of sorts. The stationmaster's quite right. You must send for your relatives. But what's this? It's formidable.'

Nikolai had groaned, stirred, and turned his head from side to side, and now he was sitting up. A deep part of Laura silently exclaimed, 'Oh, God, he is alive, I won't be able to get away.' Now she knew for certain that she had been relieved when she thought he was dead because she had a better chance of escaping Kamensky if she were alone. Nothing in the day had been so bitter as this revelation that she was a coward. She sat down on the trolley beside her grandfather and wrapped him in her arms and told him again and again how glad she was he was better, how frightened she had been, while her heart said, 'I am a coward, I am that for ever. I can't rub it out.'

Above her the doctor wondered, 'Why is he staring up at the clock?'

The old man said in this new diluted voice which had gone half-way back to a childish pipe, 'Little Laura, you were right. The hands are moving.'

'I told you,' she said, 'nothing has happened, everything is as usual.'

'I should have known it,' he said, shaking his great head. 'I should have known it to be unlikely that time would come to an end because a child had blown a trumpet, a child of no importance, Pravdine's daughter. There are archangels and angels, cherubim and seraphim, it will be their appointed task. Ah well, I must wait a little longer.'

Laura's arms were still about him, and she felt a tensing of his muscles which she took for strength. But it was only effort. He could not get on to his feet. He lost hope and softened into a heap of clothes. Most of the crowd had dispersed, but a few people still watched him as they might have watched a cab-horse fallen in the street, with maudlin smiles of pity confused with gratification at their own pity and a cold expectation of further calamity. The stationmaster, without troubling to lower his voice, said, 'We must do something. I don't know why that policeman doesn't come. The Paris express is due in twenty minutes. We must have the platform cleared by then.'

Nikolai gave himself the face of an unstricken man and said, 'The Paris express is the train I and my grand-daughter must catch.' A great part of him had gone, spilled out, but some was left. He would not catch that train, but when the train came in he might be obstinately sitting there, in everybody's way.

The doctor said coldly, 'You can't catch any train.' He said it as if he were throwing a stone at him. Then he threw another. 'You're very ill.' He threw a third. 'You're going to a hospital.'

Nikolai threw them all back. 'I must catch that train. I am never ill. I will not go to a hospital.'

The doctor answered, 'Good. You're not ill, and it is an absurd idea for you to go into hospital. See where your hat and cane are lying. Since you are not ill, pick them up.'

Nikolai looked at them with the sad gaze of an old dog. They were not four feet away from him. He made no reply.

'Since you can't do it,' said the doctor, 'I'll do it for you.' He stooped and recovered them with ostentatious suppleness and dexterity. 'How dirty they are,' he commented, 'what a pity you had to let them fall when you had a seizure.' He dusted the hat with his handkerchief, shook out its folds fasti-diously, murmured, 'Excuse me, Count,' and set it on Nikolai's head.

Nikolai meekly inclined his head in thanks. 'Ah, ah,' said the doctor, 'that nearly sent your hat spinning again, didn't it? Now we'll get on to the hospital. These two porters will help you to my carriage, and we'll drop you at the hospital.'

'You are very courteous, sir,' said Nikolai. 'But not to a hospital. Not to a hospital. It would be a Catholic hospital, wouldn't it? I'd be looked after by nuns, wouldn't I?'

'Yes,' said the doctor.

'Then no,' said Nikolai, and turned away like a sulking child.

The doctor said loudly and blithely to Laura, 'Oh, you are Liberal exiles? Well, you needn't fear any lack of sympathy. The Voltairean spirit isn't dead among Frenchmen yet.'

'Oh, hush, hush! My grandfather thinks Voltaire worse than nuns. He's a very devout member of the Orthodox Church and they all hate Catholics.'

'The Catholic Church disbelieves the doctrine of the Procession of the Holy Ghost and whoever rejects that doctrine does not know how divinity is placed in relation to itself, and therefore cannot know where he himself is placed in relation to the universe,' said Nikolai. 'Also, what evil has the Roman Church not wrought on our poor Byzantium? Who can forget the Fourth Crusade?'

'Alas, your Excellency, I can and do,' said the surgeon. In an undertone he asked Laura, 'Your grandfather isn't like this ordinarily? He's delirious, isn't it?'

'I wouldn't say so. It's true that he's had a lot of trouble lately and since then he's talked more like a preacher than he used to, but what he's saying isn't so mad as you might think. In fact it isn't mad at all. He's just talking about the things Russians go on and on about, just as you French go on and on about Napoleon.' She went on slowly. 'You see, we met a Russian in the train . . .' But it was no use. If she told him the truth this man would not believe her, and she might lose his kindness. She simply stood there, her mouth a little open.

'And this Russian frightened you and your grandfather?'

'Oh, no. No.'

'Odd. For a moment you looked very frightened indeed.' He remained silent and questioning till he saw she was not going to speak. 'Well, then, let's not bother about that. I see you're very fond of your grandfather, which is to his credit.' He turned to Nikolai and said, quite gently now, 'Since you don't like my hospital I'll find you a room in a hotel and you can go to a bed there, and I'll put in a nurse.'

'Not a nun?'

The surgeon smiled brilliantly. 'No, not a nun.'

The two porters closed in on Nikolai and gently heaved him upright, and the three joined figures staggered off. Laura started to follow them, but the doctor held her back. 'They know where my carriage is and they'll take some time getting him there. We'd better settle about sending for your relatives now. The stationmaster can send a telegram from here more quickly than any post-office in the town would do it. What's your family's address?'

She stared at him blankly. Nobody at the apartment in the Avenue Kléber must know where she and Nikolai were till she had a chance to tell them about Chubinov. Otherwise they might tell Monsieur Kamensky. 'Please, please believe me. It's no use telegraphing to Paris. It would be cruel to do it. My mother's almost out of her mind with worry about my grandmother, she's so ill, she's gone to a clinic today.' She stopped and thought what she should say next; and in the midst of the clang and bustle which the arrival of the Paris express was starting off, she received some intimation that though the silvery little man standing in front of her would not understand what it meant that Gorin was Kamensky, his experience had taught him nearly everything else. She said gravely, 'And my mother's very unhappy, specially unhappy even for that situation,' and paused. 'But my father and mother live in London, and my father's there. Just let's send a telegram to the people at Mûres-sur-mer we were going to stay with, so that they don't fuss. But it's my father I want. Only my father. We'll have to send two telegrams. One to 80, Radnage Square, the other to the House of Commons. Then he'll be sure to come at once.'

'It shall be done. We will send for your father. And how beautiful you are when you look happy.'

It was odd. He meant to be kind. She knew he would do anything for her that he could. Yet he understood so little what she was like that he did not realise how she hated people to say that sort of thing. It was really very odd that people wanted to be kind to one when they had absolutely no sense of what one was.

9

FOR QUITE SOME time Laura sat with Nikolai in the carriage outside the hotel, his hand clutching hers, loosening, falling to his lap, then clutching hers again. The hotel was the one large and solid building in a square of tall old houses, themselves crooked, with pale shutters hanging slightly crooked on their crookedness. In the gravelled centre of the square a market bubbled and boiled, the crowd here and there divided by strings of cattle being led away, past stalls hooded by tarpaulins, shaking and bellying, in a high wind which was making the white linen caps of the women rock on their heads like little ships on a rough sea. She hoped the Channel would be smooth for her father's crossing. Presently Professor Saint-Gratien put his head into the carriage and explained that he had had to keep them waiting because he had forgotten something: that the most important ball of the year was held in this hotel on this very night, and the place was upside down. All the same, he had got rooms for them, and what was more, two men strong enough to help her grandfather up the staircase, which was, it appeared, for a staircase, quite a staircase. This hotel had been a nobleman's palace in the time of Louis Quinze, and it had its grandeurs, which were sometimes inconvenient, but these two men could handle anything; and when they came that seemed plausible enough. One was an ostler in a leather jerkin and breeches, the other a blacksmith smelling of metallic toast and wearing a tawny apron as long as a woman's dress, and both had to bend their knees before they could look in at the carriage window. They offered soft, gruff exclamations at what they saw. 'They're surprised,' said the doctor to Laura in halting English, 'to find that one of their size can be old and helpless. Human beings are very amusing.'

The vestibule was so splendid that the ordinary people and the servants who were standing about made both the splendour and themselves seem not quite real. This might have been a rehearsal on a stage by players who had not yet been given their costumes, though the stage was set; and the landlord bowed and greeted her with the sincerity and over-emphasis of a bad actor. He said that until Monsieur le Comte could be found a room in the hospital he would be the hotel's honoured guest, but that he himself had a thousand things to do, the mayor's secretary was there at that actual moment to talk about the night's festivity, he would have to go to him at once, but it was a pity, such a pity. In his effort to make his excuses he conveyed the impression that to attend on Nikolai, ill as he was, would be a gay and carnivalesque diversion, and that the Ball on the contrary was, in his eyes, sad as a funeral. That was the sort of thing, Laura reflected, that her brothers called flannel. But the landlord kept it up well when it appeared that the staircase, which was indeed magnificent, presented a difficulty.

It rose in merciless elegance, climbing first in a diminishing semi-circle, then dividing into two flights curved like soaring wings; its wrought-iron balustrades were mineral lace, not to be clung to, and the blond wooden steps shone like ice. Before this lovely peril the two giants halted, and Nikolai, drooping between them, uttered faint sounds of command which every-one disregarded. The landlord, in tones suggesting that it was all merely a matter of academic interest, asked the porter if the back-stairs would be better, but no, they weren't broad enough for three abreast. The landlord lifted up his voice and called for Rose and Marthe, they hurried in, they hurried out, they came hurrying back, they knelt before the ostler and the black-smith and wrapped dusters round their boots. The two men took care not to let go of Nikolai while they were working on their feet, they managed to keep him propped up, swaying and continuing to issue orders which became less and less audible, while they struggled to keep their balance. A cen-sorious and contented male voice came clearly to Laura's ear, 'The old man shouldn't have been allowed to travel in this state,' and another voice, belonging to a woman, agreed, 'Yes, it can't be good for him, and it's causing so much trouble.' What made it worse was that the words were spoken sweetly, with no sense of what they meant, out of a desire to make agreeable small-talk. The two giants swung Nikolai up the stairs between them, but his feet were blind and wilful animals off on their own. The doctor called the men to halt and said to Laura, 'Go ahead of them up to the landing. Have a look at our assembly room there. It's very pretty, if life were what it should be you'd have come to Grissaint to dance there.'

The wide door was just ajar. She did not open it any further, she could see without being seen. She wanted to hide, for she felt dirty from the train, dirty from disaster, and this place was so clean that it abashed her. The assembly room was white and was flooded with light from tall windows on one side, and it was being preened to further brightness for the evening's festivity. There were four chandeliers, three of them in full glitter, and under the fourth was a step-ladder, with a man in a green-baize apron standing half-way up and cautiously freeing the lustres from a holland bag. At work on a low stage at the end of the room other men in green-baize aprons were setting up music-stands, and two were on their knees beside a harp, which was rocking slowly, like a sensitive animal recoiling from the human touch. Behind the stage, in high relief, a plaster Apollo in a semi-circle of plaster nymphs struck a gilded lyre, and in alcoves on each side of the stage stood statues of slender young men, one with a bow and arrow, one carrying a fawn. On the polished floor two women in blue-grey cotton gowns knelt among patches of sunshine, devoutly leaning forward as they pried at the parquet with little tools, while two others, erect but with heads bowed, pushed forward mops and their own reflections across the gleaming wood. There was a high step-ladder by one of the tall windows, and on the topmost rung stood a graceful girl, seeming to greet a friend up in the clouds, for she was rubbing a duster round and round on the pane of glass above her head; and at the foot of the ladder a blond and spectacled young man, with his back to her, held a sheet of music at arm's length and sang, with widely open mouth, but silently. All these people were so grave that they might have been preparing for some religious or philanthropic meeting rather than a ball, but the light from the wind-scavenged sky, shining through the high windows down on the bright brown floor, the sugar-white gods, the chandeliers, the white-and-gold walls, lit up a formal but extreme gaiety built into the place. They must have been using beeswax on the parquet, there was a smell of honey. But behind her came the panting and stumbling sounds of the people it was her duty to be with, and she had to turn round and follow the knot of bodies along the corridor, up another staircase, along another corridor, and into a salon which gave out the ruined sweetness of an old scent-bottle.

Nikolai groaned, 'To the sofa, to the sofa.'

The blacksmith said, 'But it's too short for you. You'd never be able to lie down.'

'I don't want to lie down on it,' said Nikolai, 'I want to sit on it.'

'What a ridiculous idea,' said the doctor. 'You're not going to lie down or sit up or do anything else in this room. Your place is not in the salon, it's in that bedroom behind those folding doors.'

Nikolai drew back his head like a scolded child. '*Da, da*,' he mumbled, and the ostler and the blacksmith exchanged kindly glances and nodded and said, 'Yes, *da, da*.' Laura exclaimed angrily, 'He's saying, "yes", in Russian.'

Nikolai said in a neutral tone, as if he were telling her the time, 'You need not trouble. My dignity does not matter any more.' Then he said in French, 'I'm quite willing to go to bed, if it's ready.'

'It ought to be by now,' said the doctor, and opened the folding doors. A chambermaid blinked at the sudden entrance; a big stout woman in her forties, with faded fair hair parted in the middle, and the convex profile of a cow. She was standing beside a curtained bed, edging the plumpness of a pillow into its slip. When her protruding blue eyes fell on Nikolai's face she could hardly finish her task, her fingers stiffened. It might have been thought that she recognised him, and Laura wondered in panic if all these people were really Russians in disguise; but the next minute she saw that all the woman had recognised was his state. She might as well have said aloud, 'Is this the gentleman who's ill? Well, ill he is, and no mistake.'

Nikolai lurched over to the bed and stroked the coverlet.

'How strange. When I got up this morning I didn't know this bed existed.'

'Oh, beds ambush us all our lives long,' said the doctor, 'they're the great conspirators.'

Nikolai sat down heavily on the bed and looked at the ostler and the blacksmith, as attentively as the chambermaid had looked at him. He asked the doctor, 'Do you have a special regiment in the French Army where you draft men like this?'

'Not since the time of Napoleon, I think,' the doctor answered. 'But if there was one I don't think that the blacksmith would have obeyed the call. He's a different sort of soldier. He's a great preacher for the Salvation Army, aren't you?'

The blacksmith's eyes flashed and he nodded shyly, his long black hair shaking about his ears. 'That's a good thing,' said Nikolai. 'We men who are very strong need to be controlled by religion. We must be ringed like bulls, and only God can do that. May I go to bed now?'

'This very moment,' said the doctor. 'Where's that case? I brought it up myself. Would you open it please, Mademoiselle? He may have something useful in it. Yes, his sponge-bag and his nightdress, and isn't that what you call an icon? What a strange thing. It's barbaric workmanship, isn't it, Byzantine, one would say?'

'Give it to me,' said Nikolai. 'It is my most precious possession. No. It is now my only possession.'

'You'll feel better tomorrow,' said the doctor. 'Now, Mademoiselle, go into the room. These two men will help me to undress him and get him into bed. The maid here will bring you up some sort of cold meal, and mind you eat it. You've got to hold the fort until your father comes.' His manner was to real cheerfulness as false teeth are to teeth.

Nikolai quavered after her, 'When these two men go, give them a lot of money. Not only for what they have done but for what they are. Specially subject, like myself, to the delusion of strength.'

The salon was an odd room to find in a hotel, even this hotel with its past. It had an air of being part of a small private house, occupied by someone old and tedious and averse to change. It had been furnished in the Empire style, in the distant day, long before Laura was born, when it was not yet considered ugly. Laurel wreaths and bees lay against the dark and light stripes of the green wallpaper, the round table was upheld by twined dolphins, a clock on the mantelpiece rested on the haunches of two metal sphinxes, there was an ormolu-encrusted desk. The laurel wreaths and the bees should have been golden, they were dust-coloured; the dolphins had lost some wooden scales, the clock had stopped, some of the ormolu mounts were missing, but there were signs of recent occupation. On a shelf above the desk was a line of ledgers in marbled covers, the later ones quite new and unfaded, and in a corner was a man's travelling hatbox, the brown leather crumbling to an unexpected red fundament, but labelled as if it had been taken on a journey not so long ago. But what was strange about the salon was what had struck her grandfather about the bed in the other room. When she had got up that morning she had not known this room existed, and there she was, shut in it with her fear, perhaps endangered simply by being there. 'Can this be a trap?' she wondered. 'Is that doctor really a doctor? He seems to be thinking something about me all the time which he never says, and he's always making fun of something, but I don't know what. Did Kamensky arrange for us to be brought here?'

But this room belonged to someone French, wine-drinking and sensible. People had never stayed up here all night making tea and exchanging wild guesses about salvation, as Russians would, whether they were honest or deceivers, whether they wanted to murder her and her grandfather or protect them. It could never have been stuffy in here, not really stuffy, as people like it who have been warmed since childhood in the winter months by great porcelain stoves in rooms with double windows. She had no reason to be frightened here. When the ostler and the blacksmith came out of the bedroom they were plainly not parties to a plot. They were muted by thoughts of sickness and death, and nothing else was on their minds.

Uneasily they looked at the money she held out to them, as if they were taking it from a dead man and therefore, supposing he had not wished them to have so much, were robbing his ghost. She said to the ostler, 'He wanted you to have it because you are tall like him', and to the blacksmith, since he was a preacher, she repeated what her grandfather had said about the delusion of strength. He looked disconcerted, as if he were more accustomed to say such things than to have them said to him, and preferred it to be so. But both gave her gentle smiles and went out, shutting the door softly.

'There's nothing to be afraid of here,' she told herself, and went to the window and cooled her forehead against the glass panes. Outside was a broken landscape of roofs, of red and orange and tawny tiles, sloping this way and that, surmounted with chimneys giving out spirals of blue wood-smoke; and below was a line of shuttered windows; and two storeys under that, a wide paved street of little shops. The one directly facing her was a pork-butcher's; long and thick and shining sausages, white and black and red, hung from hooks in the open window, and at the doorway stood the pork-butcher himself, wearing a high white cap. At his feet a mongrel dog, with a lot of pug in it, played with a bone. The pork-butcher stooped down and rubbed a forefinger along its fat neck, smoothing out the creases. That brick embankment outside the station, with the street lamps at the top of it, this dull man stroking his dog outside his horrid shop, she would choose to spend years and years looking at them and nothing else, rather than be dead and not see anything at all. What was beauty, what was ugliness? Only existence mattered.

The doctor came out of the bedroom, closing the doors very softly. 'Well, he's settled in bed and he's asleep. The examination, though it wasn't thorough, has tired him out. For the moment he's not too bad, you needn't be anxious. I've told them to send you up some boiled water and some boiled milk, you can give it to him when he wakes. I wish I hadn't to leave you alone with him, but I must go and get your grandfather some proper medical help. For I'm not a doctor, you know.'

He was owning that he was not a doctor: that he was playing a part. She held her breath and waited.

'I'm a surgeon,' he explained. 'But why have you gone so white? You're shaking. Sit down. You must be very much attached to your grandfather, but just think, he's old, you can't expect him to live for ever, and he isn't suffering much pain that I can see or even discomfort. And as for the responsibility, your father should get here late tonight if he catches the early afternoon train from Victoria.' He looked at her inquisitively, disregarding her murmurs of thanks, with a tiresome smile, as if he thought she might be in genuine distress but only for a reason that was foolish, born of her youth and inexperience. There was a knock on the door and the fair stout chambermaid came in, carrying a tray. 'Good girl,' he said to her, 'chicken and salad and cheese, it couldn't be better. But not the red wine. She won't like red wine. Get her some still champagne.'

'I don't drink any wine at all,' she said, and added, to be strictly truthful, 'except at Christmas.'

'Well, there are times when the only sensible thing to do is to pretend it's Christmas,' said the doctor. 'Isn't it so?' he asked the chambermaid, and then broke off, and scrutinised her through narrowed eyes. 'Why, I know you, I've operated on you twice, but so long ago that if there's any trace of the scar I ought to be ashamed of myself. Yes, I remember, your name's Marcot, your father worked for my uncle.'

'Catherine Marcot,' she said, with a melting, hero-worshipping smile.

'Yes, Catherine Marcot, and I've operated on you twice. Well, well, you've put on weight since then. If I have to set about you for a third time there'll be much more to cut through than there was on the first two occasions. But you're looking well.' With a conscious exercise of charm, he asked, 'You'll keep an eye on this young lady, won't you?'

'I'll do what I can, but we're very busy with that Ball. It's a shame. It's a shame. The young lady should,' she said firmly, as if forced into taking a liberty, 'have her own people with her at such a time. She's very young, doctor.'

'Ah, yes,' sighed the doctor, 'how young she is! Youth! Youth!' Catherine made a faint sound of impatience. It was evident that she and the doctor had not been talking of quite the same thing. She joined her hands as if prepared to wait till he would get past this stage of comment and say something useful. 'You're quite right,' he said hastily, 'Mademoiselle, haven't you anybody nearer than your father? Is it quite impossible to send for your mother?' She shook her head. 'And there's nobody, nobody else? What about the relatives you were on your way to stay with?'

She shook with sudden terror. If they wired to Aunt Florence she might send them Pyotr, and Pyotr had come into Chubinov's story. She put her hands to her head and tried to recall exactly what part he was supposed to have played. Surely Kamensky had told Chubinov at some point that Pyotr was the agent who reported to him on what went on in the flat at the Avenue Kléber. But that would certainly be a lie, if Kamensky said it. Yet she could take no risks. 'No. There's absolutely nobody there either. It's my grand-aunt we were going to, she's quite old, and so are her servants. And she's American, and so are the servants. They don't speak French. They wouldn't look after me, I'd have to look after them.'

'You're going white again,' said the doctor, curiously. 'That'll be all now, Catherine. Come and see Mademoiselle the princess again before too long.' As the door closed he put his head on one side, stroked his neat beard with his probing forefinger, and let her have the full brilliance of his grey eyes. 'It seems to be that you've more on your mind than a sick grandfather. If you've a trouble which seems to you terribly secret, forget that it is a secret and confide it to me. Surgeons and doctors, you can't astonish them, you couldn't if you were Judas himself.'

She forced a smile. But it seemed an odd coincidence that he should speak of Judas.

'Not a very good smile,' he said. 'Far from your best, far from the smile you would have given us all if your visit to Grissaint had been something quite different, and you'd come to dance at the Ball in our lovely assembly room downstairs.'

As pianists run their hands over the keys when they have no notion what to play, her mind went back to her view through the door, to the slender girl on the step-ladder polishing the high pane with her round stretched arm waving to her lover in the clouds; to the women in their sober clothes, devoutly working on the floor; to the smell of honey in the air.

'That's a better smile,' said the surgeon. 'Have you been to your first ball?'

'Not yet,' she said.

'Delicious. Well, eat your chicken and drink your champagne. That's very important. It'll really do you good. Don't worry about your grandfather. I'm off to find the right doctor for him.'

But as soon as he had gone she went into the bedroom and pushed a chair up to the bedside. Nikolai's face was luminous and yellow as if he were lying under strong light filtering through citron-coloured stained glass or curtains. But the shutters were not fully open, the room was half-dark, and the hangings of the bed were greyish with a cornflower sprig between blue stripes. The glow on his face came from within. In awe she said, 'I'm sorry you're ill. I love you very much.'

He spoke to her in his own full voice again. His strength was evidently something apart from his health. 'You are a good girl. You listen to your blood, which is my blood, that's why you love me. I have only my blood to stand by me now. My wife loves me, my sons and daughters love me, though they have often been tiresome to the point that I have been obliged, much against my will, to chastise them; they have learned to love me for my wise severity. You love me. But that's not enough. Like all men, I'm not content to be loved by people only of my own blood, which is a kind of compulsion, leaving them no free choice. I would like comrades who simply elected to laugh when I laughed and weep when I wept, for no other reason than that they shared my opinion of what it's right to laugh at and weep over. I thought I'd such a comrade in Kamensky. He was completely alien from me, he was low as I was high, but I laughed when he laughed and I wept when he wept, simply because I chose to, and I never doubted that he'd made the same choice. I'm not asking now why he betrayed me, I'm asking why he didn't love me.'

'Well, he was more interested in you than in anyone else. I suppose that's love.'

'It was not enough for me,' he said, and lay quite still, knitting his brows and mumbling from time to time. She felt some irritation, surely he might have spent a little time to worry about what Kamensky might do to her, she was as he said of his blood. To get rid of the resentful thought she went into the

234

other room and got the plate of chicken, reminding herself that he was ill. But when she got back he was worse. She put down the plate, her hunger gone. He was ill in a way she had thought he would not be again.

'All mysteries will be made clear quite soon. For I was right about the trumpet. It was blown by Pravdine's daughter, the child of an insignificant official, the fifth cow, to prove that the last shall be first. She was given the privilege of announcing that all was over. She, not you, Laura. I know that must be hard for you.'

'No, I wouldn't mind her doing it, not a bit. But, honestly, Grandfather, she didn't blow a trumpet, and nothing's over. It's all just as it's always been. When you're well we'll go back to Paris, and life will go on in the apartment just the same. That trumpet you heard in the station was simply the tinny thing they sound when it's time for the train to start.'

'You're wrong and I am right,' said Nikolai. 'I will admit I was wrong over the clock. It didn't stop. It doesn't stop, not all at once. It goes slower and slower, minutes are like hours, like days, like weeks, like months, like years, like the whole of time. Once when I was young I made a journey from St Petersburg to Persia, it was many years before we'd finished making the roads. I rode on horseback all the way from the frontier to Teheran. The ride didn't take as long as it took me to mount the staircase up to this room between those two peasants who should have been in the Army if this were not a poisoned democracy. And now go away until I call you. I won't sleep well, sound sleep takes vigour, like riding, shooting, fencing. But in my short sleep I shall dream hundreds of dreams, as many dreams as I did in the ten years of my youth.'

He turned away from her, nuzzling into his pillow. She took the plate of chicken back to the *salon,* and found that while she had been in the other room a carafe of yellow wine had been left on the table. This she supposed to be the still champagne which the doctor said would do her good. As if it were medicine, she poured it into her glass, cheating a little by scanting the quantity, and drank it without hope of enjoyment. Of course it was horrid. She recalled regretfully the clusters of decanters on the sideboard at home, which she and her brothers were forbidden to touch by the pleasantest of prohibitions, for they got some credit for obedience from their elders, and all disliked the taste of wine. Reluctantly they swallowed some drops on Christmas Day, only because there was a silly tradition that when the plum-pudding had gone out and the Chinese ginger and the crystallised fruits from Nice and the Carlsbad plums and the muscatels and almonds had been set out on the table, the Rowan family drank a toast to the memory of its least distinguished member, Grand-Uncle Lionel. 'Having thus concluded his army career, not a moment too soon if the sun were never to set on the Union Jack, he devoted his talents to public affairs. For twelve years he represented the Borough of Damer, Suffolk, in the House of Commons. During that period he caught the Speaker's eye four times. But he made his mark, for on three occasions the House was counted out.' That was true. But a different aunt or uncle or cousin had to propose the toast every year, and some of them drew the long bow. That story about the tiger-hunt and the third edition of the *Encyclopaedia Britannica* could not have happened. Though Uncle Desmond was a bishop, he must have made that one up. But it was queer how last Christmas the toast had not been any fun. Nothing was any fun that holiday. Even Lionel, who hated Eton, had said he was glad when he had to go back.

A quarter of the dose of champagne was left. She took the glass and a sliver of chicken over to the window. The wind was still blowing high over the red tiles, and blue smoke was curling out of the chimneys, like ribbons blown off their spools. But the paved street below was sheltered, and the afternoon sun was shining straight down its length. The townspeople must be taking an afternoon rest. Nobody was in the bright channel except two old women, who were dawdling past the shops, pausing sometimes to turn to each other in an ecstasy of gossip, their foreheads butting the air between them, their white linen caps, gilded by the sunlight, sawing backward and forward in time to their recital. Then a little girl came out and hoisted herself and a big book up into a chair outside the pork-butcher's shop. Open, the book was wider than her lap. She sucked on a finger and stared down at the page, her head turning from left to right and going back to left as she went on to the next line. Later the pork-butcher came out and bent over her and tickled her and then grew serious and pointed at something in the book. He was making her read to him, but it ended in him reading to her. When a customer came, a waddling woman with a great basket, the child was angry, and he had to free himself from her arms to go back into the shop. She wriggled on her chair, beating the air with her little fists, and almost let the book fall to the ground. But of course her father came back when he could, he hurried to her and made his peace with kisses, and pointed at the page again, and tried to make her read, but read to her himself.

Laura wished she would not have to wait so long for her father. She shut her eyes and thought how it would be when he came. He hated admitting strangers into his world, so he would thank the person who brought him into this room as if there were nothing happening of any urgency, speaking casually and smiling faintly. Then when they were alone he would strip the gloves from his fine hands, take off his overcoat, put his arms round her and kiss her quickly and coolly, pull up a chair and question her as if they were together settling some official business. 'What has happened? Don't get excited. Tell me the whole story, without hurrying, and begin at the beginning.' She would not be doing anything that called for such sharp demands for restraint, but he always made them when she or her brothers had to tell him anything, and it was all to the good – like the way that the groom who was teaching one to jump shouted, 'Hands down,' long after one had learned always to keep them down, which seemed stupid but meant that one went on keeping them down even if one lost one's head. Anyway, when he heard of her danger he would not coldly receive, he would warm, he would blaze. She was sure of that.

Once at Torquay, when she was quite little, she was allowed to bathe though the sea was rough and a big wave had knocked her down; and then when it had broken the screeching shingle had dragged her back from shore, and the surf had hissed over her blind face, and suddenly she was swung up to the light by a grasp stronger than the sea. Then she found herself standing on dry stones, while her father knelt before her, his face level with hers, and explained in his clear metallic voice, sometimes stopping and going back on a phrase and simplifying it so that she was sure to understand, how unforgivably stupid he had been in letting her bathe on such a day, and how unforgivably careless he had been in taking his eyes off her for a single moment once she was in the sea. 'Why, it's all right,' she had said. 'It's really all right,' but he had broken off, uttered a dry sound not quite like a cough and pressed his face against her bare shoulder. She would have thought that he was crying, but his eyes were dry against her skin. That was the last splendid touch, the dryness of his eyes.

If he felt like that about her when she was simply in danger, and not perhaps in any real danger (for there were boats about) of drowning, what would he feel like when he heard that someone wanted to murder her? She heard herself telling him, 'Well, he might shoot me, or, of course, throw a bomb at me. His lot do.' She could imagine her father's impassioned silence. Kamensky would be wholly frustrated, Edward Rowan would not let him kill her, and instead of inflicting on her the greatest conceivable harm the traitor would give her what she most wanted. She hesitated to call that thing by name. It was not that he would give her back her father, for she had not lost him. She never had. Her mother might have, for married people sometimes tired of each other, everybody knew that, but people could not stop loving their children any more than their children could stop loving them. She frowned down at the glass of champagne, wondering if it had made her drunk, for what she saw as being restored to her was the house in Radnage Square. For the last year or two it had been as if they were living in its ghost: as if nothing remained of it but a diagram drawn in the air, as if there were no walls, only spectral uprights, enclosing transparent stairs, and floors and furniture, no solidity to make being inside it as different from being outside it as any one thing can differ from another. Smiling at the thought of how much was to be restored to her so soon, she drank the last drops of the champagne, and went back to sit beside her grandfather, feeling triumphant and powerful.

It was quite a long time before he brought his face out of the pillow and put out his hand to hers. 'It is quite agreeable, being here with you. Your mother has seen to it that, like all the women of our family, you know how to be a pleasant companion. But I'll be glad to get back to Paris. Sofia Andreievna will understand how it is with me, that I'm not really ill, that I need only a night or so of rest and proper food to be able to start on my journey to Russia.'

'Yes,' said Laura. 'She'll know exactly what to do. She's very clever.'

'No, what she has is not cleverness,' said Nikolai. 'It's a womanly quality. Ah, how troublesome it is that she's not here. She could tell me at once something I need to know. When I was ill in Russia I always went down to Datchina as soon as possible, and there they used to give me some strengthening soup which put me on my feet very quickly. I wonder if they could make it in this hotel. It seems quite a large place, and the French are always boasting about their food.'

'I'll ask them,' said Laura, 'if you'll tell me what the soup was made of.'

'Nothing simpler. It was made from the carcasses of the eight most ordinary kinds of game-birds.'

'But, Grandfather, this is the summer, and I shouldn't think they have eight kinds of game-birds in France, not common ones. But they'll probably make you a soup which is just as good —'

He was already thinking of something else. 'How I hunger for religious consolation. I am humiliated by the treachery of a friend to whom I have condescended over and over again for many years. I am humiliated by the desertion of my body, which is leaving me, rather than being left by me, for I am here as much as I have ever been, but my body will soon decline and rot and have to be buried. I ache to have the Office of Holy Unction said over me.'

'Well, perhaps there's an Orthodox priest in Grissaint,' said Laura.

'One is not enough,' said Nikolai. 'Seven priests are necessary. Absolutely necessary. Each one has to play his part.' His eyelids drooped. But they lifted, and he tried to sit up in bed.

239

'How is it that you don't know that it requires seven priests to perform the Office of Holy Unction? Does your mother, do her children, not receive Holy Unction when they are ill?'

'We're never ill,' said Laura.

'Never?' asked Nikolai suspiciously.

'Never. Mummie's as strong as a horse, like you and Grandmother. We all are. Really and truly, if any of us had needed Holy Unction, we'd have had it. I promise you. Like a shot. But Mummie couldn't bother eight priests —'

'Seven.'

'Oh yes, eight was for the soup. Well, Mummie couldn't bother seven priests just because we had mumps or measles.'

'In a way what you tell me makes me happy,' said Nikolai. 'I'm glad that you and your mother have inherited the wonderful health which has been one of God's greatest gifts to me. But I'm sorry that you've had no opportunity to see this rite, for it's very beautiful. As I say, seven priests are necessary. They prepare a small table, and set on it a vessel containing wheat and a lamp such as one sees before an icon, but it isn't burning. It would not be appropriate that it should burn, for on this occasion light and heat are not being poured out by the Creator, this is an hour when He is dispensing darkness and cold.'

'What, does He ever do that?' asked Laura.

After a pause Nikolai said through his teeth, 'Constantly, constantly.' He continued, less pettishly, 'Round the lamp is set out a vessel containing wheat, and seven wands wrapped in fine linen are thrust into the wheat. One for each priest. Also on the table there lies the Book of the Holy Gospels —'

What was needed here was not seven priests but her father. It was not only his bravery she wanted. What she needed was his gift for stopping a fuss, as he had used it when the Welsh cook got drunk and was furious when the butler refused to believe she was a witch and threw all the pots and pans at him, even the ones that had soup and vegetables cooking in them, while the other servants hid under the kitchen table or locked themselves into the pantry. Once her father had gone down into the basement, how quickly the sounds of clanging ironmongery had died away, how quickly the cab had come to remove the cook and her luggage. There was the huge ugly black mongrel, unmuzzled in spite of Mr Walter Long's law, which had got into the Square gardens and coralled the children and the nannies into a shivering group against the railings; her father had gone out and called it to heel and brought it straight back to the terrace where it had lain till the police came. Papa had worked the miracle easily, telling the cook over and over again in icy tones, 'If you do not leave the house immediately, I shall report you to the Lord Mayor of Cardiff and the Bishop of Llandaff'; and he had gone out to the dog armed with a beef-bone snatched from the larder. The recollections were to the point. Her grandfather's conversation with Chubinov, his long story about Gorin, was of a dark and confused and hostile state, like drunkenness, and the death which was attacking her grandfather from inside, herself from outside. 'Come soon,' she said aloud to her father, and leaning over her grandfather, stroked his hand in an effort to be more concerned about his death than her own.

He was going on and on about oil. Why must he talk so much about oil? It was a symbol of God, it seemed, for it can heal like His mercy and sear like His anger, and is itself colourless and cold, yet has all colour and heat within it; as God, who has no human attributes, is the source of all human attributes. Oil had many loving names conferred on it by the Church. It is called the holy oil, the oil of gladness, the oil of sanctification, a royal robe, the seal of safety, the delight of the heart, an eternal joy, the oil of salvation.

'What sort of oil?' asked Laura. 'Just olive oil?' Not the thing that came in bottles from the grocer at the corner of Queen's Gate Terrace, the thing that went into salad dressings and mayonnaise?

'Yes. Olive oil that has been blessed according to the forms of the Church.' She did not like that. She thought of witch-doctors and Voodoo rites. But it sounded quite civilised as he went on. 'We don't produce very much olive oil in Russia, the earth is too cold. That's why we use sunflower seed oil so much, which is not oil at all in the holy sense. It has not been called to serve God. How strange it is that wine and oil, two substances which have been made sacred by our religion and which make us sacred, are found chiefly in the Latin countries where they are inevitably used by schismatics for their profane purposes!

'The Latin countries, where the food of the children is given to the dogs. Latins wallow among the full plenty of the Mediterranean and defile it. We Russians stand in the south only up to our ankles down by the Black Sea. But we do well with it. There we too make wine. Leon Galitzin has great vineyards on the stony coast between Yalta and Theodosia. His cellars run far out under the sea. I have been happy in our South, and so would you be, Laura. We Russians are pulled two ways, we are a northern people, but a southern people too. Our culture comes from Byzantium, we are the real Greeks, we are pre-Greek, part of the mystery which hung over Greece, since the beginning of time. Ask where that first blood that was in Mycenae came from and went back to, if not us. Their huge crimes are ours, their huge unequal contests with the gods. All vineyards should be ours too, all olive terraces. It is beautiful to look down on the sea, shining blue between olive trees, their trunks dark, their branches loaded with the silver of their leaves. The Bible and the classical writers, not that one can believe a word that pagans say, tell us that once there was a race of giants. I've sometimes thought when I looked at the sea through olive terraces I saw it as the giants did. The leaves on the branches might be an old giant's silver eyebrows, bristling over his eyes, the dark trunks would be like his great eyelashes. And beyond would be the blue sea. Such a giant would not smooth back his eyebrows, he would not open his eyes wide, he would want his sight shaded, because in those days the sea must have been brighter than it is today. There were few men then. Millions of men have lived since to pollute the waters with their filth. Human beings have produced nothing more persistently and in greater quantities than excrement. If only I could look once on the dazzling water the giants saw. But that is just what I am doing. The sea is before me at this moment far brighter than it is. Staring at a bright object induces sleep. That's called hypnosis. A useless parlour trick, like reading poetry aloud, which on me has always had the same effect.'

A few minutes later he woke with a start. 'Did you ever hear a story that sailors on a ship among the Greek islands heard a voice crying, "Pan is dead, great Pan is dead"?'

'Yes.'

'Who was the first to hear it?'

'The captain, I think. Then everybody did.'

'I wonder if the man who first heard it died soon afterwards.'

'That wasn't in the story I read.'

'No. Nor in the one I read. But in those days when they didn't know much about the sea any man who was a sailor must have been a brave man. Brave and skilled. Well, if a man who was, you know, someone, who wasn't a mere nothing, if he heard a voice on the waters saying, "Pan is dead, great Pan is dead", it might be a prophecy that he was going to die.'

This time Nikolai slept longer. Then he began to talk about oil again. 'The oil of regeneration makes all those anointed by it terrible to their adversaries. Some of the promises held out to us are useless. This is one of them. I do not wish to be terrible to the adversary who is the spearhead of all my adversaries. I do not want to be terrible to Kamensky.'

'Wait a moment,' Laura interrupted, 'somebody's knocking on the door.'

'That is mere imagination,' said Nikolai, 'I hear it all the time. I will tell you a strange thing. Kamensky is a middle-aged man, but I see him always as a young animal, a setter learning to work with the guns, a tame fox-cub reared by a gamekeeper. How unreasonable. How inexplicable.' There was another knock on the door, 'Come in, Alexander Gregorievitch. Come in, Sasha.'

Outside stood Catherine, too much awed to find the voice to do more than murmur. 'It's Professor Barrault.'

It was unfortunate that he was as full of character as Professor Saint-Gratien. She wished help could be brought to her by somebody as impersonal as an old nannie, or if men were never like that, by an automaton like the mechanical chess player one kept on reading about in the newspapers. This man's hair and beard flowed in thick curling chestnut waves, his head recalled one of the nobler and newer plaster casts in an art school, and his pince-nez trembled perpetually like the organ of a highly discriminating sixth sense. He held a black bag as if its contents were magical. Retaining her hand too long, and looking at her with unnecessary intensity, he explained that he had been unable to obey his colleague's summons earlier because of circumstances which he left vague, but not so vague that it could not be suspected of being unimpressive, while vague enough to prevent him being accused of boastfulness. But he dropped her hand when he looked past her and saw Nikolai, who indeed looked almost as much out of place in the coquettishly curtained bed as if he had been a horse or a bull. He was sitting up, almost the whole of his torso free of the bedclothes, and he was saying angrily, 'If I were anointed with the holy oil I might know what I really feel about Kamensky. As it is, I can't be sure. I can't understand how God can do this thing to me, to bring me here where there is no oil, no possibility of Holy Unction.'

'What is he saying?' asked the Professor. 'My colleague Professor Saint-Gratien tells me that you are Russian. Of modern languages I speak a tolerable English, German, Italian, some Flemish, and even a little Syrian.' He spoke with an air of humility which would have been appropriate if he had been admitting that he could just read and write. 'But Russian, no. Is he delirious?'

'Who is not delirious?' asked Nikolai, in French. 'I was, however, saying something entirely reasonable at that moment. I was saying I wished to have something like your rite of Extreme Unction, only this is for people not dying, but simply like myself, temporarily not in perfect health.'

'Perhaps we can arrange that you need not go without this fortification of the spirit,' said the Professor. 'The town of Grissaint has more resources than the passing stranger might guess. We must make an effort,' he said, turning to Laura, 'for it's sound medical practice to put the patient's mind to rest before we start on correcting his body.'

'I think you'd better get on with his body,' said Laura. 'The ceremony he wants takes seven priests, and they all have to have special wands, and there has to be some wheat, and I

244

think that has to be special too. And the ceremony must be immensely long.'

'The rites of the Church and the State cannot possibly be too long,' said Nikolai, still in French, 'for one could not spend time in a better way. Your mother should have made such a fundamental principle quite clear to you.'

'She has, really she has,' said Laura. 'My brothers and I find the Trooping of the Colour awfully long, and she's always told us that we shouldn't mind. But this gentleman is a doctor, Grandfather, if we don't talk about your illness he won't get on to his other patients.'

'Go to those other patients at once, my dear Doctor,' said Nikolai. 'Don't trouble about me. Not that I'm ungrateful for your visit. I've a great admiration for French doctors. I've known several, and my mother when old and my wife when young were treated by your admirable Dr Jean Pehan. But I myself am in no need of your services, all I want is some rest before I make the long journey back to Russia. My grand-daughter is unnecessarily alarmed about me, young girls are often hysterical. It is iron, I seem to remember, that excitable young girls require. Prescribe her some iron. And tell her that I'll be fit to travel to Paris tomorrow.'

'But how can I tell Mademoiselle any such thing until I have examined you?' asked the Professor, with an air of cunning, looking at Laura to be sure she had observed the ruse and was admiring it.

'I have been caught up in something,' sighed Nikolai. 'Do what you want with me. I feel as if I had let myself in for be-ing fitted for a lot of clothes I shall never wear. Make haste. I want to think.'

When Laura got back to the salon Catherine had taken away the tray with the chicken on it, but had left the bottle of still champagne and a glass. 'How funny she should think I would want to drink more of that stuff,' she thought, 'but then lots of people like it. Next time she comes I'll get her to bring me something really nice, like Evian or Vichy or orangeade.' The emptiness of the room now seemed a threat that she had come to a place, or a time, where there was nothing. She would have liked to take down a ledger from the shelf over the desk, or to open the decaying hatbox, just to assure herself that objects existed and actions were performed, that people kept accounts and made hats, wore hats, travelled with hats; but her fastidiousness disliked touching other people's belongings. She went to the window and knelt beside it. Now only one side of the paved street below was gilded by the sun, and the town was awake again, customers were going in and out of the shops, coming out brightly-coloured from the doorways, crossing the pavements and entering the shadows and turning grey. The child and her book, and the mongrel at her feet, were on the sunlit side and shone in the strong oblique rays, their shadows lying long on the pavement, parallel with the shop-front. The little girl was not moving, she was simply waiting for her father.

10

THE DOCTOR TOUCHED Laura on the shoulder. She had fallen asleep while she was praying for a miracle which would bring her father to her at once, faster than the railway could do it. Looking up at the doctor, she asked, 'How ill is my grandfather?'

'It's not easy to say.' He had lost all his affectation. His fine head was less like a plaster cast, he was blinking and polishing his pince-nez. The gesture sent a shudder running through her. The lenses might be clear glass. He might be on the other side, one of Kamensky's men. True, his eyes, which were singularly beautiful, violet-blue and set far apart, had grown soft with concern for her grandfather, and even seemed to be a little moist as they met hers. That meant nothing: Kamensky would choose his lieutenants from people who could look like that when they did not mean it. But her suspicions left her, for he began to speak with a bewilderment which could not be pretence. It had the prick of hurt pride, and deceivers, she had noticed at school, were always proud of themselves.

He was saying that he could not understand her grand-father's case. The Count ought to be very ill, to go by his pulse, his blood-pressure, his respiration. 'Yet he's fully conscious. He's talking vigorously, and he grasped my hand a minute or two ago – thinking we were saying good-bye, though of course I'll be looking in every couple of hours or so – quite firmly. Indeed, quite painfully. I understand he had a shock?'

'A shock?'

'Yes, I understand there was a man on the train —'

'How could he know that? He must be one of them.'

'A Russian, wasn't it?' She could not speak. 'Did I make a mistake, then? Didn't Professor Saint-Gratien tell me that you and your grandfather had been bothered by some Russian on the train?'

'Oh, that. Yes, of course. There was a tiresome Russian on the train. I'd forgotten that. But it was nothing.'

'Odd, I understood from my colleague that he thought you'd been quite upset over it.'

'No. Not really. To tell the truth, I didn't quite understand what was going on, but it was nothing my grandfather couldn't have dealt with ordinarily, in spite of his age. They're wonderful people, his family,' she told him, her voice shrill, as she were lodging a complaint. 'I can say it without being conceited, for I'm half-English. What they are is diluted in me. But the whole strength, it's something tremendous. And for the family he's not very old. My mother says most of their relatives live to be far older. Oh, you don't know what the Slavs are like. Why, my grandmother's got Polish blood in her, and one of her ancestresses rode at the head of her serfs to defend her property against an army led by a general who was her own great-grandson. They're not like us, those people at the other end of Europe.' At the thought of the power of some of them, and how it might be exercised, she went over to a chair at the other side of the room and sat down with her head in her hands. 'They're not Europeans at all.'

The professor murmured, 'Yes, everybody knows that the Russians are formidable, formidable. But all the same,' he objected sadly, 'even Russians don't live for ever.'

'No,' she agreed bleakly. 'We don't live for ever. We haven't the prescription for that.'

'Nor even for long, with such a pulse, such blood-pressure,

such respiration rate. No, really, that he can't do. Whoever he is. And is it really impossible, as Professor Saint-Gratien says you feel it is, for your mother to come from Paris? You're quite sure?'

As she shook her head she thought, 'Will they never leave me alone?' It appeared the only sensible. thing that she would have to tell them the truth, but that was impossible. 'No, I'm sorry, if my mother was told she might tell a man who would come and kill my grandfather and me. Who is he? Well, he's two people. Gorin and Kamensky.' But it sounded sheer madness.

'I'm sorry to hear it. For this is going to be a very harrowing sick-bed. Your grandfather, he's in a highly emotional state. He cried out to me that he must go back to Russia, and that at once. I've never heard anything like the passion behind his cries. I avoid dishonesty in dealing with my patients, what happens to them is the will of the good God and it is my duty to acquaint them with it, but I felt obliged to assure him that he would be able to start on the journey after a few days' rest, may God pardon me for the falsehood.'

His eyes lay on her with a certain fixity. It might have been that he was racking his brains to think of a way to help her, it might have been that he did not believe her. But in any case he was not being annoyed with her for being in a difficult position, making him feel he ought to do something about it. Tania had always taught her and her brothers to stop when they met beggars in the street and give them money, telling them that this was the only way they could guard against the sin, prevalent among happy people, of disliking the unhappy. Laura never knew whether her brothers did it. She could not possible have asked. They had never asked her. This man was free of that sin, and so was Professor Saint-Gratien; and in that they were like Chubinov, of whom she thought with love. Smiling gratefully, she said, 'But don't worry about me. My father's coming. He'll start from London the very moment he can. I'll be all right.'

'But have you heard definitely that he's on his way? I understood from my colleague that —'

'No. But he'll come.'

'I wish you had heard from him. A telegram or a telephone message. I know from experience how difficult it can be to get in touch with relatives in cases of emergency. There seems to be a malignant fate at work —'

'But it'll be easy to find my father. He'll be either at home or at the House of Commons. There's nowhere else he could be. He's sure to come.'

'All the same,' sighed the professor, 'I wish you'd had an answer.' There was a knock at the door and he grew calmer. 'This may be some message. Come in, come in.'

Something had gone wrong. The chambermaid Catherine came in slowly, her mouth a little open, her pale eyes wide, plainly the bearer of news so bad, and yet not so very bad, that it was enjoyable. 'Professor,' she said, 'Monsieur Saint-Gratien has sent along Madame Verrier to nurse the Duke.'

'Madame Verrier!' repeated the professor. 'Not Madame —' his voice cracked – 'Verrier?'

A little woman with clear-cut features pushed past Catherine, dark and pale and slight, wearing a severe coat and skirt and hat, like a man's, and carrying a black bag. Lowering her head as if about to butt, she said, 'I am a qualified nurse as well as a midwife. And there's someone ill here, isn't there? So why are you surprised to see me, Monsieur the Professor?'

'My grandfather is your patient,' said Laura, going into an impersonation of her mother, and holding out her hand. 'I'm so glad you have come. I am Laura Rowan. How do you do?'

The woman made a truce with the world just long enough to return the greeting, then said, 'Now perhaps I might be taken to the patient, Professor.' They went into the bedroom and Laura was left with Catherine, who was still breathing heavily. 'You know Madame Verrier?' asked Laura. 'Why are you surprised to see her? Doesn't she nurse as a regular thing?'

'Oh, yes, she's a regular nurse. But it's not suitable,' said Catherine. 'It's funny of Professor Saint-Gratien to have sent her. That's all.'

'Isn't she a good nurse?'

'Oh, yes,' said Catherine, looking this way and that in embarrassment. 'She's a good nurse all right. She never has an accident. Not like the others. But it's not suitable.'

249

'Lots of things that aren't suitable are happening today,' said Laura. Then she caught her breath. 'Madame Verrier isn't connected with Russia, in any way, is she?'

'With Russia? No. Whatever made you think that? We've no Russians here in Grissaint except some students at the medical college, and a doctor or two, and she's nothing to do with them. She's the daughter of Brunois the watchmaker down by the Prefecture.'

'She isn't mixed up with politics? She isn't a revolutionary, you know what I mean, a nihilist, someone who would throw bombs?'

'Heavens, no. I never heard her worst enemies say that about her. She's not a Catholic, of course, that she couldn't be, doing what she does. That's why Professor Barrault doesn't like her. He's a very good Catholic. He's the President of all our Catholic societies.'

'But what is that this Madame Verrier does, then?' asked Laura. 'Could she hurt my grandfather?' Catherine clapped her hand over her mouth to hide her laughter, and Laura shook with sudden rage. 'Please go and get me some Evian or Vichy water.'

'Yes, mademoiselle,' said Catherine, trying to smoothe out the amusement on her face, and she turned at the door to say timidly. 'I didn't mean any harm, but it's not suitable, not at all.'

The professor hardly spoke when he left. He simply kissed Laura's hand and said, 'I'll be back before long, and in the meantime you will find Madame Verrier —' he almost moaned it – 'very competent.' She did not dare ask him what it was that Madame Verrier did which showed her to be a bad Catholic, and the mystery became greater when the nurse came back into the salon. It seemed impossible she should have been a bad anything, and she even might have been uncomfortably good. She had clear grey eyes which probed and might easily accuse. She had taken off her coat and had discovered some speck adhering to the cuff of her very clean, slightly starched, white blouse, and she scratched at it constantly with her exquisitely kept hands, frowning deeply. She was thin, not merely slender, but thin, as if she ate too frugally. At first she spoke in an argumentative tone, but this was evidently habit, her voice softened as she told Laura that her grandfather was sleeping and that she would call her when he woke.

It was not long before she did. Through the shadows of the bedroom the old man was weakly complaining: 'I long to receive Holy Unction, not only for the sake of the anointment, but for the sake of hearing the priests chant the hymns of the rite, which are of a special beauty. I hunger and thirst to hear them, and not a word will come back to me. Some of the prayers, yes, they are with me. "Oh Holy Father, Physician of Souls and Bodies, who didst send Thy only Begotten Son, our Lord Jesus Christ, which healeth every infirmity and delivereth from death." Yet is that right? It seems to me I'm making some mistake, but what? At any rate, the hymns are much dearer to me, they would give me back my lost power over myself, and of them I've forgotten every phrase.'

'Please, dear, dear Grandfather,' said Laura, 'you're forgetting the hymns simply because you're tired. Rest and in the morning you will remember them.'

'It isn't entirely because I'm tired that I can't remember the hymns,' said Nikolai. 'It's partly because my mind is in an impure state. I keep on thinking about Kamensky and wondering why he did not love me. Also the real reason I'm tired is because I can't remember the hymns, not the other way round. Each of the services the Church appoints for an ordeal common to mankind is appropriate to that particular ordeal, to it and no other, and it alone can make that ordeal tolerable. Oh, God, give me back my memory of those dear hymns and take away my fatigue. Which is enormous. I feel as if I were about to fall through the mattress.'

'When I can't remember poetry at school,' said Laura, 'I shut my eyes and don't think of anything at all, and sometimes it comes back to me.'

'I'll try that,' said Nikolai, 'but I am afraid I will think of Kamensky.'

'No, you don't think of anything if you do something funny with the front part of your head.'

'Why, I knew that trick also when I was very young.' He grew still, so still that she sat back in her chair so that the bed-curtain was between her and the sight of his stony whiteness, which could not have been more like stone, or whiter, unless he died.

His cry was happy. 'I've remembered one hymn! How the words comfort me as they flow on to my tongue. Where are you, Laura? Listen, listen! This is the hymn to the Mother of God. "Like drops of rain dried up by the summer sun, my days which are evil and few, gently vanish into nothingness. O Lady, save me . . ." But, Laura, my memory hasn't come back. Not altogether. For this is beautiful, but it is not quite right. Ah, but now I remember. "Through thy tenderness of heart and the many bounties of thy nature, O Lady, intervene for me in this dread hour, O Invincible Helper." Strange, it's not right. "Great terror imprisoneth my soul, trembling unutterable and grievous, because it must go forth from the body." It must go forth from my body. It must go forth from my body. Ah, now I understand.'

He lifted up his voice in a shout which became a weak howl. The nurse opened the folding doors and stood at the end of the bed, looking down at him with bent head and scrutinising brows.

'My memory is perfect. Of course it is perfect. We Diakonovs never lose our memories. My memory has simply more common sense than my foolish heart, which makes me desire the consolation of Holy Unction, which is no longer for me. The prayer and the hymns which are coming into my mind are those appropriate to my state. They come from the Office for the Parting of the Soul from the Body.'

Laura cried out, 'No!' The idea that he was dying shocked her as if it had never occurred to her before, as if she had not thought him dead at the station, as if she had not discussed his death first with Chubinov and then with the doctors. Until this moment some part of her had not believed that anybody could really die. 'You're ill,' she argued, 'very ill, but you're not dying.'

'Allow your elders to know their own business best. I am on the point of death.' He began to pray again. '"O our Lady, Holy Birthgiver, O Conqueror and Tormentor of the Fierce Prince of the Air, O Guardian of the Dread Path, help thou me to pass over unhindered, as I depart from earth. Lo, terror is come to meet me, O Lady, and I fear it." '

She sat quite still, covering her eyes, while the wild prayers flew about the room like bats.

' "Vouchsafe that I may escape the hordes of bodiless barbarians and rise through the abysses of the air, and enter into heaven, and I will glorify thee forever, O Holy Birthgiver of God. O Thou who dids't bear the Lord God Almighty, banish thou far from me in my dying hours the Chieftain of Bitter Torments who ruleth the Universe, and I will glorify thee forever." ' The nurse was standing at the end of the bed, crushing a tablet with a spoon in a glassful of water. 'Who is she?' asked Nikolai. 'But that I don't really want to know. How vast is the number of people who exist, who even serve one, and whom one doesn't want to know about. But I would like to know who the man was who told us that long story in the train. A senior police official, I suppose. Trust no one of his occupation. Do not trust me. Do not trust any of us – from the greatest man of state to the last lowest simpleton – who aid our Tsar in the sacred task of taking on the guilt of power in order that the common man may remain innocent. All, all of us are saved and tainted. But this man knew his business. You didn't happen to hear his name?'

'He was Vassili Iulievitch Chubinov.'

'Really? I'm surprised at that. I knew him as a boy. He never showed any promise of being as good as that. All one could say in his favour was that he was a good revolver shot, and there are not many of them. Someone must have worked hard to raise him to what he is now. I wonder who it was.' He lay staring through the wall beyond the end of his bed. The nurse held the glass to his lips and he drank the water without looking at her. 'If only I had a secretary who could take down my thoughts as I dictated them. If only Kamensky was here.'

'You shouldn't think of doing anything tiring like that,' said Laura. 'Try and go to sleep and tomorrow you can do everything you want.'

'You don't understand the obligations inherent in this event, my death, I mean. It actually is written in the rite, "Arise, O my soul! Oh my soul, why sleepest thou? The end draweth near and thou must speak." Go into the other room, dear child, while I think what words they are that I ought to speak. It's not easy. For one thing, I should speak of my own sins, and though I know I'm a very sinful man, I've never been able to see what my sins are. They don't seem comparable to the sins which have been committed against me. But I understand that before I die I must really convince myself that I also have been in the wrong. I will have to work hard on this during my last hours, I will have to concentrate, for up till now it seems quite obvious that I have always been in the right. Also, little one, if I rave of the deceptions and injustices which have been practised on me, you might feel that the world was too horrible for you to bear, not realising that though these afflictions should by logic be unbearable, God gives you strength to bear them. I have really been enjoying myself all the time. But my agonies also have been stupendous, and my groans over them might mislead you, so go away, my dear little girl, my dear little Tania's dear little daughter. It is not because I don't love you that I wish you to leave me, it is because I do.'

She leaned over him to give him a kiss, and he said, 'Tell the lace-makers not to sing so loud. I approve of them singing hymns while they work, but they are disturbing me.'

She went back to the salon and found that Catherine had brought in a bottle of Vichy water, which was standing in a bowl of ice. She filled a glass and went back to the window. The street was busier now. More customers than before were going in and out of the lit shops and stopping to gossip with the women and old men who were sitting on cane chairs beside the doorways, while the younger men leaned against the walls. Nearly all the women were sewing or knitting as they sat, and some of the old ones were bending their white linen caps over the little pillows on which their lace was pinned, but their real occupation was the talk, which by jerked hands, shrugged shoulders, hands flung out palm upwards, wove the French fairy-tale about other people having shown an extraordinary lack of common sense. In the middle of the paved causeway children in blue overalls played gentle games. If a wrangle turned rough, parents started forward in their chairs and shot out jets of scolding, but the mellowness set in again at once. As

254

the street darkened the sky grew brighter. The red roofs glowed terracotta, and in one of them, some distance off, a high sky-light blazed scarlet and diamond. There must be a magnificent sunset. Red sky at morning the shepherd's warning, red sky at night the shepherd's delight. The Channel would be smooth for her father.

When it was nearly night all the children ran to one end of the street and escorted back a boy and girl of eleven or nine or so, dressed in party clothes, carrying toys and leading between them a little girl, not more than five, golden-haired and dressed in a white frock with a blue sash low on her hips, who was clasping in her arms a doll dressed in white like herself. They all bore themselves like celebrities, and the occasion from which they had returned had evidently been recognised by everybody in the neighbourhood as quite out of the ordinary. As they went along the causeway, bright figures at the head of their blue-clad companions, the people sitting outside the houses eagerly called on them to stop, questioned them, examined their toys, admired their clothes, rubbing the hems of the little girls' dresses between finger and thumb, kissed them all, and waved then on with congratulating gestures. After they had gone, the other children lost interest in their play and by twos and threes went indoors. Now the roofs were darkening to brown, and the sky-light might just have been a hole, the glass gave back no light. Above, across a crystal blue-green sky pricked with the first stars, there raced black clouds, sometimes mounting up into great cliffs fissured with gulfs and staying so, sometimes marching like armies, substanceless but full of purpose. Up towards this aerial confusion the smoke rose from the chimney-pots in tight blue spirals and swallows descended from the higher air to the eaves and up again in flight as quick as cries. Her fear was like a dark arch over the lit stage where these things happened. She drank the cool water and put her forehead against the cool glass and prayed that her father would come soon.

Madame Verrier came out and said, 'Your grandfather wants you. That sedative hardly worked at all. But the professor will be coming back.'

Though the nurse had lit the gas and the bedroom was not

dark, Nikolai asked Laura 'Who are you?' and said to himself, 'Yes, it's her voice. And her slight accent. You would know she was not born in Russia.' Then he told her, without tenderness, as if giving instructions to a clerk, 'Well, now I know what it was all about, and you must listen.'

'And what was it all about?'

'Why, nothing at all. When I say, nothing at all, I mean that that Kamensky business was of no importance.'

'What, you mean that what Chubinov said wasn't true, was nonsense?'

'No, nothing he said was nonsense. He was one of us. He was one of the Russian nobility. Not a great family, but noble. If our sort talked nonsense, it was only because the occasion made it useless to talk sense. There have been many such occasions in Russian history. This was not one of them. The story Chubinov told us about Kamensky was perfectly true. But it meant nothing. Had no significance. Neither had the story of which it was a part, including my disgrace. That had no significance either. All that has happened is simply a consequence of the law that if opposites exist and meet, they must destroy each other. To me the Tsar's power is the point at which historical being meets the will of God. But it seems to Kamensky and his imbeciles that the Tsar debauched history and that there is no God. If we could have remained separate, Kamensky and I, we might have done each other no harm. But we were drawn together by the existence of the Tsar, by the existence of God. They forced us two to confront each other. So all that was he rushed out to destroy me, so all that was I rushed out to destroy him. It is an accident, that is all, like a collision between two railway trains.'

'But you aren't destroyed.'

'In an earthly sense, I am. Utterly destroyed. First my honour, then my life. I would have lived years longer if I had not learned this morning that little Sasha was my Judas. I felt the sword coming out at the other side of my thick body. And Kamensky will die too. Chubinov will kill him.'

She breathed, 'You're sure of that?'

'Quite sure. To begin with, Chubinov is not such a fool as he looks. And consider his education. I took quite a lot of pains to

256

make him a good revolver shot. My reason was that it was the sort of thing his father thought he would not be able to do, and he despised him for it. But whether I went to all this trouble out of Christian charity, because I was sorry for poor young Vassili, or because I wanted to keep his father in his place as inferior to me, I really cannot say. Well, there was I training him to kill Kamensky, without knowing it, and on the other side there was Kamensky training him to kill Kamensky, without knowing it either, by rubbing into him through the years the tactics and strategy of assassination. But, Laura, I hope you understand that you must do everything you can to prevent Chubinov killing Kamensky?'

'Of course, Grandfather.'

'Don't say "of course". It is your Christian duty, but nobody can say "of course" with any appositeness about a Christian duty, which is always forced and extravagant and the last thing any sensible person would choose to undertake. I feel more certain that it is your duty to attempt to stop Chubinov killing Kamensky because it is so very unlikely that a young girl will be able to avert this crime. Oh, Laura, my little Laura, I grieve for you. Kamensky is very low. I had to raise him up to a great height before we could speak together and form a mutual affection, from what I believed to be a mutual affection. But through his lowness a great force travelled. Oh, my little one, dear child of my dear child, it may destroy you, it must certainly alter your world. The universe is full of great forces which manifest themselves in disgusting ways through our fallen humanity. O Lord, when I am dead, explain to me the folly of Thy creation, for the wisdom Thou Thyself hast given me faints with bewilderment.'

Professor Barrault and Madame Verrier had stolen in quietly through the folding doors. 'What are those two shuffling about for? Do they think I cannot see and hear? Till the last moment of my life my senses will be sharper than theirs have ever been. Ask the woman to leave. The man can stay, but not the woman. Yes, I know she is a nurse, but she affects me disagreeably, like the women students in our Russian universities. Thank you, my dear. Now give the man a chair. I am sure he knows his business so well that he will notice when I give signs of actually dying and will come forward and do what is necessary. Convey to him my respect for his skill and my gratitude that I should be the object of it. Now let me get on with what I must tell you, Laura. It's fortunate for you that you have inherited the Diakonov intelligence and will understand at least part of my story. You see, I have discovered what my sins are, or rather what my great sin is. What is extraordinary is that, though nobody could call me a vain man, it proceeds from vanity. Some time ago you left the room – what did you do?'

'I sat at a window and looked down at the street.'

'What did you see?'

'Old people sitting at the doors, people going in and out of the shops, children playing, three children coming back from a party. It was quite pretty.'

'It may have been pretty but it can't have been of the slightest importance. Whatever you did when you left the room can't have meant anything at all. You see, when you went away I tried to imagine what it will be like when I am dead and come into the presence of God, and it wasn't very hard, for I am no longer with you in my entirety. Half of me has already left my body and this world. So I could see how it will be when I meet God. And it will be a meeting between two beings who are different, more different than a man from a woman, more different than a white man from a Negro, totally different. It was like that —' he could still snap his fingers —'I saw the difference between God and man running through the universe as a flash of lightning runs through the sky. I say that because that difference is a thing in itself. Other differences are comparisons. Not this, which is unique.'

He wept and impatiently dried his eyes with the sheet. Laura wiped away his tears with her own handkerchief and called him softly the tender names her Nannie used to call her when she was ill, knowing that he would not understand them and could not blast them away with his scorn. He could not argue offhand that he was not a cocker-nonny. Choking, he went on: 'I've been wrong all the time. O my God, when I have done my best to serve Thee, why didst Thou not inform my ignorance and keep me from this sin? When we are face to face explain to me the mystery of Thy lack of candour. Almost before Thou dost anything else. Well, I have always known that God is good and the maker of all things good, the sower who broadcasts good seed and reaps the good harvest, and I have known too that man is not good, he is a chaos in which evil mingles with good and is always preferred by its host, he is the bad land in which the good seed can grow but poorly, and then only by grace. But I thought man was a lesser member of God's family, even as I have relatives who are drunkards and adulterers and many things that I am not. I saw God as a man divinely free of man's evil, with no human qualities save when he clothes himself with Jesus, and I saw man as a God with the divinity extracted and the human qualities grossly proliferating into perpetual sin. On the contrary, God is God and man is man, and there is no bridge between them but grace; and that does not change man into God, it simply saves him from damnation. In the same way, I could not make Kamensky my kinsman simply by making him my friend.'

'Well, then, that's settled, you're not God, you're man,' said Laura. 'But we all loved you as a man. Of course God will forgive you. Now lie back and rest, dear, dear Grandfather.'

He sobbed a little longer and said as soon as he could, 'I would be glad if you would see that Kamensky and Chubinov are each given some little possession of mine as a souvenir. An object of some value but with no family associations. Neither is related to me.'

'Yes, Grandfather,' said Laura. She turned aside and muttered into her wet handkerchief, 'I'll see them damned first.'

Professor Barrault said, 'But this must stop. He is exhausting himself. Another tablet, I think, Mademoiselle ——'

'He's being quite happy in his way,' said Laura.

'You grasp the appalling consequences of my mistake. Since I didn't understand that God and His son are unique, I didn't grasp that His suffering was unique and unlike that of any human being. Therefore I was led into the blasphemy of supposing that because His suffering has meaning, so has mine. Pretentious idiot that I was! I thought that in suffering I was buying something at a great price, carrying out a costly sacrifice which in time would be hailed in heaven and on earth as

259

glorious. So I have lived in anguish. I've been tormented by the itch to enquire into the mechanism of my disgrace, for a martyr can't help, I imagine, but have some curiosity about the details of his martyrdom. Sebastian must have wondered why all those pagan arrows did not harm him, though later the pagan rods beat him to death. Without dignity I panted like a thirsty dog, waiting for the day when my persecutors would be routed and my martyrdom acclaimed by men and angels. So I howled and caterwauled and made the lives of those around me a misery because I impudently expected my agony to be a sacrament, to be the symbol in this material world of an event in the spiritual world. I've been no better than a peasant who goes mad and believes himself heir to an immense fortune, to an estate in the Crimea and mines in the Urals, so that he refuses to work and lets his wife and children and old parents starve. I have wasted my life because I have not seen that my pains are of no more significance than my pleasures, and they have none, and that my only worth lies in my love of God, and that all that I did and was on earth is without meaning, because I am a man.'

He was in agony. She said, 'This isn't true. I love you, my mother loves you, my grandmother loves you, many people love you, for all sorts of reasons which matter. Oh, for one thing, you were so brave when you were hounded down.'

In a small voice he said, 'Above the window.'

She turned about and looked.

'That blotch on the wall, running towards the corner of the room. The rain's seeped in from a gutter on the outside. A workman's scamped his work. My suffering means only that. I am evil because I am human, my evil heritage called to those cursed by the same heritage, and together we laid out our portion so that it increased. I am repenting. God will forgive me. But that doesn't make my sufferings any more interesting. If you remember my misfortunes and your kind heart and your family loyalty make you pity me, remember that blotch on the wall. My whole life is as important as that blotch, no less and no more.'

Laura prayed aloud, 'Oh, God, don't let him think anything so awful. Do some sort of miracle.'

Nikolai said, 'Ah, I've broken your heart. But I had to tell you, and it's of no importance that anybody's heart is broken. Conquer your pride and your respect for the emotions, which should be despised with all you can muster of contempt, which I hope is not much, since you are a woman, and remember what I say. "Man is not God, God is not man", and repeat it often to yourself. You will have children, all women in our family marry, they never lack great attractions, and you must repeat it to those children of yours also. You may think it isn't necessary, for the difference between the human and the divine is stated in every book of the Bible and in every office of our Liturgy. But there's a treacherous paradox here. There's no better guide than custom, but on all that's customary there settles the thick dust of material time, so that the mind turns away from it in distaste. For me that message of the Scriptures and the Church was dimmed with many readings and many hearings, so only in this last bitter hour did I learn what they had been trying to tell me. What a mistake, what frustration, but it does not matter, I know now I am a man.'

She prayed silently, 'God, let him die now, God, let him die now.' Surely God could see the foam on his lips.

'I hope you go back to Russia, Laura. Oh, God, grant me this, since I am penitent; send my little Laura back to Russia. Our Russian society is the society which is precious to Thee, all the others are chance coagulations of pagan mobs. Russian society alone serves God, but not strenuously enough. It prays but it does not fast. At present it simply tells each of its members to spare himself the trouble of deciding what he shall be and do here on earth, since the Tsar makes all such decisions for him and takes on himself the guilt of earthly power. How beautiful, how very beautiful is our system. As time goes on it will be admired as the most merciful and fatherly form of government the world has ever known. Yet it has its faults. It is insufficiently rigid. There are occasions when it permits a man to use his own will. Even I, who have given my utter loyalty to the system, can look back to moments when I have made my own choice, God forgive me.'

Her eyes and mouth opened wide. Was he really unaware that from his birth he had done exactly as he pleased?

'At many moments our Russian state turns to water. It does not stand four-square often. These weaker moments are speciously attractive. My own doctor is the son of one of my father's serfs, and in my folly I have rejoiced in this as admirable. But now I see I was wrong, for such liberty leads straight to the sin I have committed. If a man can change his place in the world and the condition of the world, he must construct for himself some philosophical belief which will teach him what changes to make, and since he is vain he will attach great importance to this belief, since it is the work of his own mind. Then he is bound to sin with me and forget that God is God and man is man. He will become a rival to God and pretend that he understands life as well as God does and can control the direction of history. Then he must become a miserable and grieving rebel against God, and he will insist that his suffering has a meaning, though the whole of existence will prove to him that it has not; and he will waste his life in useless lamentations as I have wasted mine, or in murderous conspiracies like my poor little Sasha and that idiot Vassili Iulievitch. A small man has come into the room, my eyes are failing, I can see that he is small. How curious it must be to be small. I am glad I was spared that humiliation. Who is he?'

'He's the doctor who was so kind to us at the station.'

'Tell him he may stay if he does not interrupt. Oh, Laura, we Russians have been too lax. Let Russians build up a citadel of goodness, where nobody places a vain value on his individuality, where everybody realises that his highest destiny, his only respectable destiny is to obey. Let each Russian offer up the dear wayward son of his soul, his will, as God the Father offered up His dear obedient Son, Christ. For the sake of the world we must surrender our souls to God and our bodies to His servant the ruler of Russia. This is not even very much to ask of ourselves, for it is not a sacrifice which need be made for ever. When Holy Russia has been anointed for centuries by the blessed oil of its children's abnegated will, all Russians will be born committed to innocence. The state is only an instrument of man's moral struggle, so then, all men being moral, there will be no need for the state. It will wither away. Grace will replace the law. The kingdom of heaven will be established on earth. Laura, go back to Russia and await that day.'

He threw himself back in his bed and closed his eyes violently, as if to kill his sight. Professor Barrault came forward and put his fingers on his wrist and said to the nurse, 'Quick, the syringe.' But Nikolai flung off his hand and said, 'Remember, Laura, to give my love to my dear wife and all my family, the women as well. I realise how much I must have tried their patience by my preoccupation with my griefs. But I suppose I made it up to them in quite a number of ways.'

'Nurse,' said Professor Barrault, 'let's try again. He really ought to have the injection.'

'I shouldn't bother,' said Professor Saint-Gratien.

Nikolai heaved himself up in bed again. Shuddering, he said, 'In the desert place I may see a giant hand or foot. I must try to keep my self-command though I will be dead and remember that it's an illusion of the devil. Why has nobody lit the gas? I saw a gas jet when I came into the room.'

'The gas is alight,' said Professor Barrault.

'Then get candles,' said Nikolai, turning his face about so that everybody present got the full force of his displeasure. 'Must we talk in the dark like gipsies?'

It was as if he himself were a candle: a lit candle which was then blown out.

When the doctors sent Laura out of the bedroom, she went back to the window and looked out through the lenses of her tears. The shops were still bright and had some customers, but there were no children in the causeway, except a few who were leaning against the walls and eating sandwiches or supping out of bowls, with an air of discontent and abandonment. All the chairs had been taken in from the doorways. Most of the upper rooms were lit and it was there life was being carried on now: dark figures moved backwards and forwards against the wavering glow of lamplight. The hours were passing, it could not be so long before her father would be with her. She did not know how she could bear this sharp pain without him. For as she had found earlier that fear is an affliction of the body, gliding about in the bowels, so she was now finding out that grief was a wound in the chest. Presently the doctors came in and drew up two chairs beside her. Now that she had seen a dead person the living seemed more strange. How did one move and feel? While she listened to the doctor she surreptitiously looked down at her hand, spread out the fingers, brought them together again, and wondered at the miracle.

It seemed that she must not go back to the bedroom for a time, the nurse had various things to do to Nikolai. She nodded, accepting that there were yet more mysteries, and told them that it was important his icon must be put on his breast. The doctors went on to say that her grandfather must have been a very great man. A man of state, said Professor Barrault, drawing himself up, broadening his shoulders, impersonating unassailability. She wanted to deny it, to disclose that Nikolai had been oppressed and deceived and persecuted and pitiful, but was not sure that he would have liked them to know it. Then Professor Barrault asked if she would care to spend the night at his house, Professor Saint-Gratien breaking in to explain that he could not make such an offer, since his was a bachelor establishment. Professor Barrault hastily mentioned, as if to clear a colleague from a suspicion of lightmindedness, that Professor Saint-Gratien had the misfortune to be a widower. He himself enjoyed the happiness of having a wife and three daughters, and his eldest girl would be glad to give up her room to Laura. True, he and his family would be out all evening, for they were going to the Ball which was to be held downstairs – so heartless, he added, was circumstance. But his servants would give her supper and help her to retire early.

She was shocked. They should not think her capable of leaving her grandfather alone. While she was talking to them she was also talking to him, in her mind, assuring him again and again that the giant hand or foot would be an illusion of the devil, and letting her own left hand hang over the arm of her chair so that his spirit hand could grasp it if he wanted. As soon as the nurse had finished whatever it was she was doing, she would go and pray beside him. But it turned out that Professor Saint-Gratien and Madame Verrier had known that she would want to keep Nikolai company during his first night of death, for they had already arranged for a camp-bed to be put in the salon, and Madame Verrier was to stay with her till the morning. Then the two doctors said good-bye, promising to come in later, when they were at the Ball, and Laura said she would be glad, but that her father would be here soon, and would want to meet them. When the door had closed she knelt by the window and again put her forehead against the glass and let the tears run down her face, and repeated all the prayers she could remember from the Orthodox Liturgy, sometimes speaking to Nikolai. Now there was true night above the roofs, and the street was empty. Most of the shops were shuttered, though the windows above still glowed with lamplight and were crossed by silhouettes. Down below the Ball had begun. She could hear the band.

Madame Verrier came out of the bedroom and stood beside her at the window, patted her shoulder, and gave her a clean handkerchief. Two dogs chased a cat down the causeway, a door opened, the cat shot in, the dogs yapped and sauntered on. The half-hour struck on a distant clock. Then a woman, her cloak drawn high about her head, ran in a soft helter-skelter along the causeway.

'Madame Gallet,' said the nurse. 'I'd know her anywhere, wrap up as she likes.'

'Is she one of your patients?'

'She's been to me twice.'

The woman down in the causeway came to a halt, let the cloak fall on her shoulders, smoothed her hair, shook out her skirts, and went at a sober pace into a house.

'Thoughtless girl,' said Madame Verrier. 'I wonder where she's gone. But she's no worse than thoughtless. Life's very hard.' Staring out into the darkness, she raised her small clean hand and beat out the rhythm of the quadrille which was bumpety-bumping through the walls and floor. 'Your grandfather,' she said, with hostility, 'must have been a very handsome man.' But then, as if an extenuatung circumstance had crossed her mind, she exclaimed, 'The poor old gentleman. It's hard on a man when he comes to die. Harder than it is for women. For many dying men, it's the first time that anything's gone against them; the first time they find their bodies not doing just what they're told. Women are used to that, which of us would choose what happens to us every month?

That's an idiotic business. And as for children, it's the women who want them who don't have them, and the poor women who don't want them. God help them – nobody else does – who get them. In either case it's a great injustice, indeed one might call it the great injustice. But men, everything goes as they want it till the last moment and then they aren't able to credit it that their luck's turning. One can't,' she said in an unforgiving tone, 'help feeling sorry for them.'

11

THE TROUBLE WAS to stay awake till her father came. She wanted him to find her self-possessed and in control and as elegant as if she had been grown-up for a long time; and she asked if she might have a bath. But the night was out of hand. The gaslight simmered and wavered on the walls, keeping time with the singing in her ears, while the thudding rhythm of the band downstairs hammered on the exact place in her head where, she suspected, it was decided whether she slept or woke; and she was not sure which she was doing. The music itself confused her, for it seemed strange that a ball should be taking place in a room which was for her still occupied by white light, space, a man on a ladder removing a holland cover from a chandelier as reverently as if it were a vast inverted pyx, women in distance-coloured cotton gowns kneeling on the floor and tending it like put-upon lay sisters at work in a chapel built on the bones of saints. When Catherine came to tell them the bath was ready, Madame Verrier took Laura out into the corridor on her arm, but she staggered. Out here the music was different and stranger. The violins and clarinets which could not pierce the walls and floor of the salon came up the staircase shrill and sharp and unashamed, and so did the laughter and applause which burst out when the playing lurched to its close. She was again confused, seeing in her mind's eye the dancers going off the dance-floor in a flushed, chattering and vulgarly excited crowd, backing dangerously against the ladder by the window on which the slender girl, raising her arm and pressing her duster round and round the upper pane, still signalled piously to the clouds, though the night had fallen. Laura knew it was not so; but yet it was so, inside her head.

Madame Verrier tenderly asked her what was the matter, calling her *tu* as if she were a little child, warned her that the water would be getting cold, and drew her on along the corridor with her compact, featherweight-boxer strength. In a linen-room walled with cupboards painted greyish-blue, a pendant gas-jet reflected as a primrose-yellow highlight on each cupboard door, Catherine was bending over a hip-bath, pouring in now hot water and now cold, stooping so low that she had the stance of a four-footed animal, the gravity of a cow on her face, as she tested the heat with her finger. She might have been one of the beasts round the manger at the Nativity. When she left them Madame Verrier knelt down at Laura's feet and took off her shoes and peeled off her stockings, rose and swiftly stripped her to her skin, and turned aside to feel the bath-water, leaving her standing naked. Laura felt surprise at having no clothes on, with someone else there, which had not happened since she was grown-up. Amused, she said to herself, 'I might be a statue in the British Museum', but statues were men and women, gods and goddesses, involved in business which meant nothing to her. It was like a pillar that she felt. Madame Verrier's voice came to her through darkness, 'Hurry up now, I want to get you into bed', and she realised that for an instant she had been asleep on her feet.

Madame Verrier steadied her as she stepped into the bath, saying, 'You have a beautiful figure,' without admiration, even with grimness. She might have been warning her of a defect bound to cause trouble later. Solemnly and scrupulously, she washed Laura's body with a soaped pad of cotton wool, let her lie back in the warm water and close her eyes, stood her up and dried her as swiftly as she had stripped her, and pulled a fine lawn nightdress over her head and down to her feet, remarking, with the same air of not liking what she saw in the crystal ball, 'A beautiful figure.'

Laura said drowsily, 'This is a lovely nightdress. It's like the ones my mother wears. I'm only allowed plain crêpe de

Chine. And this peignoir too, it's very nice.' A wonder struck her. 'Where do they come from?'

Madame Verrier told her tersely that when Professor Saint-Gratien had arranged for her to come to look after the old gentleman he had instructed her to buy soap, a hairbrush, and some night apparel on her way to the hotel, as the Russian young lady had no baggage. Her fingers wavered as she was tying a bow on the peignoir, she smiled, began a sentence, checked it, and interrupted Laura's thanks to finish it. 'He was as grave about it as if he were telling me I was to buy some food for someone starving.' The amusement in her voice nearly rose to laughter. Her arm round Laura's waist, she led her out into the corridor, into the harsh bumping music, halting at the top of the stairs to say, in the tone mothers use when they are dissimulating their pride in their children, 'But the Professor's like that.'

In the salon Catherine, half-way through making up the campbed, was taking from a page-boy a parcel wrapped up in lilac tissue paper and a letter addressed to Laura. 'But nobody knows I'm here,' she said, and then caught her breath. Since her grandfather had died she had hardly thought of Kamensky. 'Put it down on the table. Please put it down on the table.' Her fear had split into several images at the back of her mind, like paintings hanging on a wall. One was a dark cloud bursting into the opposite of a thunderstorm, a single flash of darkness more blinding than any lightning, followed by silence, rolling on and on for ever. Then her fear became practical. She spent a full minute staring at the parcel on the table, pitying the two women because they were looking at her with pity. They knew so much more than she did; but what she knew that they did not was so much worse. Slowly she put out her hand and felt the parcel, but it was not a bomb, it was quite soft. It did not interest her to open it after that, but under the women's puzzled eyes she had to read the letter. 'It's from Professor Barrault,' she told them. 'He's sending me a nightdress belonging to his daughter Elodie. How kind everybody is,' she murmured, forcing her eyelids to keep up.

'So they should be. Young girls,' said Madame Verrier, 'should be protected. Usually they are, if they are rich, but emergencies like this do happen. Well, you've been very brave. Look, they've sent up a tray. It's all stuff from the Ball supper. Lamb cutlets, salmon, strawberry mousse. You'd have liked something plainer, but try to eat a little.'

'I think I should be fasting,' said Laura.

'Fasting? Ah, because of your grandfather's death. Ah. Tomorrow. Start fasting tomorrow. Tomorrow's a good day for fasting, the best.'

Laura was bewildered. Tomorrow would be Wednesday. Why was that a good day for fasting? If it had been Friday there would have been some sense in that. But Wednesday? 'Also, I'd like to pray beside my grandfather before I go to sleep.'

Madame Verrier bit back a short word, 'It's quite unnecessary. God and His angels,' she remarked, with an air of handing a baby a rattle, 'have him in their care.'

'It's not like that with us Russians. Us Orthodox.' But she did not feel equal to explaining that Nikolai was now traversing a desert, confused by the loss of his body and assailed by the fierce Prince of the Air. 'He hasn't,' she said vaguely, 'got there yet. We don't. Not at once.' She thought of the giant head and foot. 'I really must go and pray beside him.'

He was dead. His face was quite dead. But his great yellowish hands were clasping the icon to his breast as a strong man still feeling pity might hold a small wounded bird close to give it warmth. She knelt and muttered encouragement, telling him that his strength would take him through the desert and that God could not help loving his strength. Something brushed her face. It was the counterpane hanging down from his bed. She was huddled on the floor, and Madame Verrier was lifting her up by gripping her under the armpits. Laura explained that she had not really fallen asleep, and Madame Verrier said that she quite realised this, but feared that she might have come near to falling asleep, and then might have been startled if she woke from a doze and found her poor grandfather as he was. She might cry out, and that, Madame Verrier suggested with patent insincerity, might disturb her grandfather's soul. Pursing up her clear-cut lips before she could force out the pietistic phrase, evidently as repugnant to her as oaths, she assured Laura, 'The poor gentleman is at rest.'

Laura agreed to have some supper, and settled down in an armchair, and the far-off clock sounded another hour. Time was passing. Grissaint was so near the coast, it should not have taken so long to come from London. She told her grandfather, 'I am in a desert too.' She ate a cutlet and said, yes, she would try to eat another if Madame Verrier thought she should, and smiled to think how amused Tania would be when she heard of this good Samaritan unbeliever, forcing herself to engage in the improprieties of belief. Tania was always ready to be amused, or had been so. Laura remembered an afternoon, before things went wrong, when she had gone into her mother's bedroom and found her rosy and golden with that pleasure which came round regularly twice a year. She had been to her milliners in Bond Street the day before and had chosen a dozen hats or so, to be sent home on approval, and there they were, all over the floor, in the great round hatboxes made of pale buckram looking like tenor drums assembled for a peculiar concert. Of course Tania had asked Susie Staunton to share the treat, but Laura had not seen her when she first entered the room, for Susie, always self-effacing, had found a seat in the background, out of the way of the afternoon's ritual. Tania was sitting at her dressing-table in her chemise, her shoulders bare except for the narrow ribbon straps, but her hair as carefully done as if she were about to start for a grand party; and half a dozen ostrich-feather boas were hanging over the back of her chair, black, white, sea-green, sea-blue, beige and emerald. Hélène, the lady's maid, was opening each hat-box in turn, tilting its lid against it, withdrawing a hat in its nest of tissue paper, disengaging it, and carrying it with an acolyte's deliberation over to the dressing-table, where she pinned it to the golden whorl of Tania's hair. Then she went to the wardrobe and took out the dress which Tania was most likely to wear with that particular hat, and stood behind her, passing her hands between her mistress's arms and sides and holding the dress up in front of her. If the verdict was not immediately yes or no, Hélène made Tania get up and stand in front of the cheval-glass in the corner, sometimes festooning her with one of the feather boas.

It should have been a tedious ceremony, but Tania laughed when a hat suited her, as though she and it together were going to play an impudent fraud on the world, and when it did not suit her she laughed even more, as if she had been caught cheating, but in any case had been doubtful of getting away with it; and she kept on turning away from the glass and calling over her shoulder to Susie, inviting her to join in this ridicule of her own beauty or crying out some scrap of gossip she had just remembered, or propounding one of the theories which kept on bubbling up in the champagne of her mind. At that moment she was expressing her belief that Englishmen did not really like playing cricket – who could? – but had it forced on them in their schools and universities by a secret and subversive society like the Freemasons. To all this Susie, from her seat beside Tania's broad bed, responded by her timid kind of laughter and by sounds of agreement uttered in the soft tone and with the strict rhythm of a cooing dove. Every now and then she put out a vague, hovering finger to trace the design of the creamy Venice-point counterpane, or looked up at the canopy of faded Persian brocade which fell from the crown of crystal plumes fixed high on the wall, with her air of admiring things she could never hope to possess herself. When Susie was looking up like that, one could see how long her throat was, and how curious her mouth, so indeterminate, so hard to describe or remember. The blackness of sleep was before Laura, she flung herself into it.

She woke to wonder why there was a cutlet frill on her lap, where the dance-music was coming from, why she was in this faded room which smelt like an old scent-bottle, and who was whispering. Madame Verrier had been facing her at the table, but now she was sitting across the room on the sofa beside Professor Saint-Gratien, who looked very elegant in evening clothes. They were enmeshed in silent laughter, and they were struggling. He was holding close to his face the parcel Professor Barrault had sent Laura, and peering between the folds of the lilac tissue paper, while Madame Verrier tried to wrest it from him.

'Let me see what's inside,' he was whispering, 'you can easily say it was our little beauty who opened it, before she'd read the note.'

'No, no, paws down!' laughed Madame Verrier.

'How well they know each other,' thought Laura, 'and what fun they're having, for people of their age.'

'But I absolutely must open it,' chuckled the Professor. 'I must know what the unfortunate Mademoiselle Elodie wears in her virginal couch. It's impossible for me, in spite of all my experience of the human frame and human underwear, gained professionally and otherwise, to guess. This evening I've been watching her going round and round the ballroom looking like a giraffe. Well, what does a well-brought up young giraffe wear at night? You can't tell me, I don't know, I've the information in my hands, you won't let me avail myself of it. Ah, now I can see, now I realise what it is, and it's not a nightdress, it's a tent, a bell-tent —'

'You'll tear the paper,' gasped Madame Verrier through her laughter.

'A tent, and how much rather I'd bivouac under the stars, in quite another terrain —'

'How horrible you are,' said Madame Verrier, suddenly ceasing to laugh, suddenly flushing with anger, 'making fun of a poor ugly girl of whom you know nothing except that she's ugly, rejecting her when she's never offered herself to you. How impossible it is to imagine an ugly young man having such humiliations poured on him —'

'How you hate men,' said Professor Saint-Gratien, rocking backwards and forwards in amusement, pressing the parcel against her face and taking it away again. 'How you hate men, except at the moments when you like them, when you extravagantly like them, when you like them even more than most women like them, I can assure you of that —'

'But where's my father?' asked Laura. Everything had come back to her. Her grandfather was dead, she might die. 'My father. He should be here by now, shouldn't he?'

The couple on the sofa were still as marble. Then Madame Verrier turned to Monsieur Saint-Gratien and exclaimed, as if she were going to cry, 'We woke her!'

'Please don't mind about that,' said Laura. 'It's not of the slightest importance. But my father. Hasn't he come?'

'Not yet,' said Saint-Gratien. 'I'm sorry. Not yet.'

'But perhaps I'm being stupid,' said Laura. 'I don't know the time. I forgot to unpin my watch from my dress. Probably it's too early for my father to have got here.'

'Well, he could have done it,' said Saint-Gratien, smiling at her as if they were speaking about something of great moment, 'but he hasn't, and there's sure to be some very good reason for that.' He went on telling her, in his sharper way, what Barrault had already told her, that messages sent to the relatives of the sick and dying took far longer than exchanges between the hale and the hearty. 'It's as if,' he explained, still inappropriately smiling, 'the patient's malady slowed down the pulse of the telegraph wires and set up inflammation in the telephone exchanges, so I was quite prepared, when I came up here after having made my bows down in the ballroom, to find that your father wasn't here, and indeed my only aim was to see how you were getting on, and perhaps to give a fillip to Madame Verrier's genius for nursing by bringing her some champagne. I'm not sure how that's worked out, but as for you, I'm very pleased. You've done what people of your age can do, you've had new life put into you by just a couple of hours sound sleep.' He was not smiling now, his tone of voice did not match his words, he was watching her. He knew quite well that more than grief was the matter with her.

Madame Verrier crossed the room and knelt beside her, and in a hard, pressing voice, but with some endearments, reminded her that her father could do nothing to the point if he were there, her grandfather was dead and nobody could do anything for the dead. But was there nothing they could do for her, was she worried about anything? Her eyes were tender, vigilant, fierce, detective. Certainly these people were not on Kamensky's side. Laura felt like saying, 'You're quite right, I'm frightened,' and telling them the whole story. But she remembered how Kamensky, that day at the stamp-market in the Champs Elysées, had guided her away from the Russian dealers, and how she had asked, 'But are the terrorists here too? In France?' and how he had answered in his sweet, sad

273

voice, so softly that she could hardly hear him, 'They are everywhere'. Well, he should know. Catherine had said that there were Russians at the medical college here. Though the surgeon and the nurse were all right, they might go for help to people who were not. She put her hand to her bewildered head, and the scalloped cuff of her peignoir caught her eye. For an instant that too amazed her. She was wearing something that was not hers. Then she remembered how that came about, and she said, 'Professor Saint-Gratien, it was so nice of you to ask Madame Verrier to do all this shopping for me. I must own that though it's all been so terrible, my grandfather dying, and my father not coming, I like wearing these lovely things.'

The tautness of their stares relaxed. They still knew that she was keeping something back. But they were not annoyed. They were resigned. They were not going to pester her. The Professor had said of the hotel staircase that for a staircase it was a staircase. Now he and Madame Verrier were thinking that for a trouble, her trouble was a trouble; and though they were still watching over her, they were going to leave her undisturbed, as a sick patient for whom little could be done till her malady took a more definite course. 'I'm glad you like what Madame Verrier bought,' said the Professor, putting his head on one side, narrowing his bright grey eyes, 'but I was wondering, I was just wondering, if Madame Verrier's taste hadn't been a thought too severe. Isn't that peignoir on the plain side?'

'Oh, for heaven's sake,' said Madame Verrier, giving a comedienne's impersonation of impatience, 'Mademoiselle, think of it, the great surgeon's mad about frills.'

'Yes, indeed I'm mad about frills,' he said, acting too. 'Nor do I see why I shouldn't be and why everybody else isn't. Why, frills are delicious. Be truthful, Mademoiselle, don't be intimidated by this gorgon, wouldn't you have preferred a peignoir all foaming, all sparkling, all bubbling with rows and rows of little frills?'

'I'm sorry, I couldn't have borne it. Frills are awful, perfectly awful.' All three of them were laughing now, out of pity, out of gratitude for pity, out of a desire to get the unspoken truth about the occasion out of the way, not to admit that it was there.

'You see, Professor Saint-Gratien,' said Madame Verrier, pretending to regain the self-control she had never lost, 'you just haven't got taste.'

'You're wrong. My taste is all right, but my luck is not. I adore frills, but the women I adore always detest them. Well now, it's getting late. Try,' he said, his eyes sensitive while he said these dreamy, unsensitive mechanical things, 'to cultivate a little sympathy for me in your hard young heart before we meet tomorrow morning, and let Madame Verrier give you a sleeping-draught.' But there came a knock on the door. He dropped her hand and exclaimed, 'Ah, after all.'

But it was Professor Barrault who entered, searching the room with his vague violet gaze while he saluted Laura. Seeing two other people in the room he sent a social smile in their direction, put on his pince-nez, saw who they were, drew back his bearded chin, and greeted them coolly. Then, after knitting his brows he greeted them all over again, warmly. Saint-Gratien guffawed; he liked taking a holiday from his own delicacy every now and then by laughing hugely. But Madame Verrier raised her head, thrust forward her fine small chin, and looked blindly past Barrault, who all at once became the only truly piteous person in the room. Madame Verrier took the steel out of her face and said, 'There's no news yet, Professor,' and Saint-Gratien said, 'The young lady's still sad. I've brought up some champagne to cheer her, and perhaps you'll take a glass to show her what we really call drinking in Grissaint, Professor,' and Laura said, 'If you're going to have some, Professor Barrault, I will.'

They raised their glasses to each other in gaiety which was false yet true; it was a container for their kindness to her. Professor Barrault, who was moving and speaking more slowly than in the afternoon, put down his empty glass and murmured, 'It's impossible to do all one wants, impossible to prevent things going wrong,' and helped himself to a plate of strawberry mousse. 'This appeared to be plentiful downstairs,' he said sadly, 'but that was an illusion. All over the place I saw people eating it, but when I tried to get some, there was none.

Strange.' It was remarkable, the way he raised the spoonful of pink foam to the orifice in the regular waves of his chestnut beard and never missed.

When she thanked him for having sent her his daughter's nightdress he waved his spoon at her and replied, as if he had been waiting for the cue: 'Not at all, it was a privilege for my daughter Elodie, who is a good girl but of mortal stock, to offer a garment for the use of a stranger who seems to come from another world. I think of the words that Odysseus used to the princess Nausicaa when he met her on the Phaeacian shore. "Art thou a goddess, who came from a home in the infinite heaven? If thou art divine it must be Artemis I see, the daughter of Zeus the All-Powerful, for both in thy form and stature and beauty thou art cast in her mould. Or art thou a daughter of man, who dwells on earth as a mortal? Happy then I deem, yes, thrice happy, thy mother and father —"'

'You bad old man,' said Saint-Gratien, 'I remember that passage perfectly well, and Odysseus didn't believe a word he was saying, he knew perfectly well she wasn't a goddess, he rather despised her as a provincial lady, but he wanted to get something out of her. Credit from her father's tailor, I think it was, as he'd been washed ashore as he was born. Why, Barrault, when you've got an authentic goddess here, do you greet her with that humbug?'

'My friend is irreverent,' Professor Barrault told Laura, 'but he has an excellent heart. An excellent heart,' he repeated, as if to keep up his courage, but vaguely, muzzily; he was only remotely distressed. 'So he'll be the first to understand how glad I am to have a moment's leisure to talk of what's so dear to me, the antique world, in the company of a young lady who might have walked on Aegean shores in the Golden Age. I regret it often that I never devoted my life to the study of the classics, but I had no choice, science revealed itself to me as my true master —'

'But medicine's no science,' jeered Saint-Gratien, 'it's a guessing game played by the more backward and brutal among University students on the steps of the laboratory buildings, always the least aesthetically satisfying parts of our Universities, and it's a condition of the game that once one starts playing it one has to play it till the end of one's life.'

'We may be as ridiculous as you say, but nevertheless, on our lucky days, we heal,' said Professor Barrault meekly. 'But anyway, here I am in a profession associated with science, which constantly confronts me with events arousing in me thoughts and emotions impossible to express within the limits of the scientific vocabulary. It's then that I thank God for the hours we spent at school studying the classics, for if it were not for the voice given me by the writers of the antique world, I should be mute, mute, and strangled by my mutism.'

'Oh, never that, my dear friend,' laughed Saint-Gratien.

'You also,' said Professor Barrault, blinking his wonderful eyes like an owl in daylight. 'My wife says I talk too much, and you evidently agree with her, but it never seems to me that I do. Which is it, I wonder, do I talk too much or does it merely seem to people that I talk too much? And which of those alternatives is the more disagreeable? Well, never mind. I haven't, of course, much to say that's worth saying when the grave things happen. But then neither has Professor Saint-Gratien. When he and I lose a patient, we feel a great deal, and we can find nothing to say that's to the point. When your grandfather died this afternoon, neither of us had anything to say, not of our own invention, which might not just as well have remained unspoken. But what we felt was said long ago in our dear Latin tongue. *Musa, mihi causas memora, quo numine laeso Quidve dolens regina deum tot volvere casus Insignem pietate virum, tot adire labores Impulerit. Tantaene animis caelestibus irae.* "Explain to me, O Muse, the reason for this thing: what injury to her godhead, what angry pain, made the Queen of Heaven drive a man so manifestly good to brave so many perils and endure such trials. Can heavenly spirits conceive such rage?"'

'An appropriate epitaph for Mademoiselle's grandfather,' said Professor Saint-Gratien. He started to say something else, checked himself, had a sip of champagne, put it down, and let the suppressed remark hiss out of him. 'And it would serve as well for Captain Dreyfus.'

Madame Verrier clicked her tongue in annoyance. Professor

Barrault went on eating strawberry mousse as if he had not heard, but presently he pushed his plate away. 'I was only trying to be pleasant,' he said. 'The Count died. He wanted to go back to Russia, his longing for his fatherland was terrible to witness; and this poor young lady was compelled to be present, though the proper setting for her is the rose-garden of Bagatelle, or the Bay of Naples, or the Parthenon; and all the plans we've made for fetching her natural protectors seem to have gone astray. Quite a catalogue of disasters. But at least Virgil said what we all felt about the old gentleman's death. I thought it might do the young lady good, do us all good, to hear those lines. But you, Saint-Gratien, you found it necessary to be sharp, sharp as one of your own scalpels.'

He held out his glass to Madame Verrier, who with a cluck of tenderness filled it to the brim. She put down the bottle with a bang and Laura saw her give Professor Saint-Gratien an angry nudge. It looked as if she had kicked him quite hard under the table. 'There must have been times and places in the antique world,' Professor Barrault went on, wiping his beard and moustache. A little of the strawberry mousse had gone astray. 'There must have been times and places in the antique world when life was lived much more agreeably than it is today. Oh, I know the antique world had its own coldness, how should it not, when it lacked the knowledge of Christ? – but it had its urbane moments when people met and were together, simply together, without pursuing their own ends or feeling anger, when they ate and drank and talked about things that had no cutting edge. Those moments must have been golden, like this champagne, this excellent champagne, which is so much better than the champagne that's going downstairs, though I drank a lot of that too. It's inevitable that the champagne you brought up here would be better, Saint-Gratien, you have always understood such things as I have not. But those golden moments of companionship, they're what I long for. I wake up in the night and wish I had been born in that time, when one could simply be together in a golden moment, when life would be like a golden sphere, perfectly rounded. And it was like that just now. I thought all our differences

278

were forgotten. And so they were, by me. But not by you. Not by you.'

'Oh, Barrault, Barrault! You should know what I am, by this time.'

'But that's just what I don't know, what I've never known. More brilliant than I am, but what else?'

'Why, I'm your devoted friend — But, ah, who's this?'

Laura had known it was not her father; he would not have knocked on the door quite like that. There came in the land-lord of the inn, who had struck Laura as possibly insincere, in the vestibule downstairs, by his insistence that it was tedious to attend to the Ball and he would have liked to have given himself up to the pleasure of devoting himself to her grand-father. She did not recognise him at first, for he was now in evening clothes, and his moustache, which had been a loose bush growing round his mouth, was waxed into tight upturn-ing points. But he bowed to her with the same humbugging air of desolation and after he had saluted the others he said, 'You must excuse this liberty, I wouldn't intrude on this sad occasion, for sad it must be in spite of all you gentlemen are doing out of the kindness of your hearts to comfort the young lady, but I've been sent by Madame Barrault to tell Monsieur the Professor that in five minutes' time Mademoiselle Elodie and Captain de Germain will be leading the quadrille, and Madame Barrault thought it would be agreeable if you and the General and his lady all sat together to watch the young people treading a measure. Not the last they're going to tread together, I understand,' he added, coyly.

'What are you saying?' mourned the Professor. He put on his pince-nez, having a little difficulty with the ribbon, and then got out his watch, having a little difficulty with the chain, and looked at it for a long time. 'That quadrille doesn't start for another twenty minutes. I made sure of that. Twenty minutes.' His eyes fell sadly on his plate, where there were still some pink castellations of strawberry mousse, and on his glass of champagne, which Saint-Gratien had just refilled. 'I'm sorry to leave you all,' he said. 'You're such superior people. The moment was golden. Ah, Saint-Gratien, in eternity all our differences will be reconciled, we shall achieve perfect understanding. But let us go a little way towards that now. Saint-Gratien, you might have understood I'm not quite a fool, how could you think I didn't know that Odysseus was simply flattering Nausicaa and never for a moment took her for a goddess? Of course I knew. But it's such a beautiful speech I've always wished that it had been spoken sincerely. I was simply pretending that that was so, and what's wrong with that? What's wrong with that?'

'Nothing, my dear, dear friend,' said Saint-Gratien. Someone called to Barrault from the corridor, his features contracted and he moved backward towards the door, as if the voice had been a hook which had caught in his clothes and was hauling him away.

'Ah, poor Professor Barrault,' said the landlord, 'it's like being in the army for him, always under orders, but married to his dear lady, whom we all respect, there's no fieldmarshal's baton in his knapsack, never a chance of a senior command.' He clapped his hand over his mouth. 'One must choose between being witty and keeping a hotel, particularly a hotel that caters for the quality. Surely it doesn't show cowardice and lack of principle to realise that if Voltaire himself had kept a hotel, he would have ceased to make jokes.'

'Good-night,' said Monsieur Saint-Gratien. 'No, we don't want anything more, landlord, nothing at all.' When he had gone a silence fell. Madame Verrier tapped her foot on the ground. Saint-Gratien refilled her glass and his with deliberate nonchalance, and said jauntily, 'Poor old Barrault. A shame he should be so hideously bullied by that woman. Sending for him like that.' Madame Verrier said nothing. He sipped his champagne, waited, and went on, 'And she'll be unjust. If poor old Barrault's had a drop too much, it's just a drop, but she'll take the hide off him, and by this time General de Germain will have drunk up the sea and all its fishes, but that'll be different.'

Madame Verrier's voice sprang out of her like a jack-in-the-box. 'Why did you have to say that?'

'To say what?'

'What you said about Captain Dreyfus?'

'Alas, I was wrong.' He lifted his hands above his head and

280

made the grimace of a penitent child, but she did not laugh. 'I was wrong,' he repeated. 'I won't defend myself.' But a cold, silvery fire flared up in him. 'Yet I will. Really, what he did was too gross. Wondering why the heavenly spirits conceived such a rage against a patient of consequence, a Russian count, a Minister of the Tsar, but refusing to put the same question about Dreyfus. And he's too intelligent not to have seen the truth. But how well,' he sneered, 'it's suited his book to limit his intelligence on this one matter. He's got a rich wife, they've got an ugly daughter, he's toed the line, he's come out against Dreyfus, the ugly daughter's leading a quadrille with the son of a general who's descended from Charlemagne – though who isn't, by this time. I don't like it. I can't like it.'

'And what does it matter? What can it matter what any of these imbeciles do? But what does matter is that you took the trouble to dig up Barrault's error when for the moment it was buried. He was at his best. He often is. You might attach some importance to the fact that he's a good doctor. You know that's all that matters really. But you have to say something that raised an issue on which he's at his worst. You do that to everybody. You like to feel this town of Grissaint round you like a hollow tooth. But what feels at home in a hollow tooth? Only the germ of decay.'

'How gently,' said Saint-Gratien, in a dry voice, 'you reproach me for my lack of gentleness.'

They sat in silence for a moment.

'Mademoiselle,' he said, summoning up a smile, 'it's time we left you to get to bed.'

'Yes,' agreed Madame Verrier, summoning up the same sort of smile.

'But I won't sleep,' murmured Laura, for she felt that they should not separate at this moment. But also she liked both of them being there. Fear was above her and below her and around her.

Madame Verrier put down her glass, took out her handkerchief, and blew her nose. 'Forgive me,' she said softly to Saint-Gratien, 'I'm so tired.'

'I know you are,' he answered as softly.

'And you,' her voice rising in self-reproach. 'You must be

dead tired. Those two days of hard work in Paris. The journey back this morning. And all you've done since. Forgive me. Forgive me, Professor,' she added, formally.

'I'm not so tired. But I'm on edge. While I was away, it seems, my son, he lunched with Barrault and the worst of the anti-Dreyfusard crowd of them. A kind friend told me at the hospital.'

'I heard it too,' she said, swallowing. 'Do forgive me, you know that when I'm tired I don't think, I bark like a little dog.'

'No, you spit like a little cat,' he said, and filled all three glasses again, and they all laughed and drank.

But the landlord was back with them. He shut the door behind him and leaned against it. 'I sent your learned colleague down to what was waiting for him,' he said, and shook his head sadly. 'You might say he's now in custody.' He came towards the table, and Laura thought that it was odd, it was summertime but he smelled of mince-pies. But of course it was brandy that made mince-pies smell as they do. He must have had too much to drink. Like some butlers, some cooks, and a wicked cousin of her father's.

'I'm so tired,' the landlord sighed, sinking into a chair. 'Thank you for asking me to sit down,' he said, though nobody had done so, 'and thank you for not asking me to have a drink. That's most understanding of you. I've been running here and there all day, seeing to the thousand-and-one things that have to be done on the very day of the Ball, no matter how hard one works beforehand, and I can do with a chair. But a glass of wine, no, indeed. Everywhere I turn someone offers me something, a cognac here, a port there, and the time comes when a wise man knows when to stop. Not another drop for me this evening.' But he made a long arm across the table to the glass of champagne Professor Barrault had been forced to abandon and brought it back to his lips. He looked over the rim at Laura's face and bowed. 'They're in luck, those ladies downstairs, that Mademoiselle isn't at the Ball. The flower of Grissaint, of all the Pas de Calais, but who would look at them if Mademoiselle was there?' His eyes went upwards as he lifted the glass of champagne to his lips, and before he drained it he paused for a moment to breathe, so softly that the others could just hear it, the words, 'The cows.' Refreshed by the draught, he continued: 'Oh, it's not right that Mademoiselle shouldn't be there, and for such a reason. Oh, that's most wrong of all. People keep on saying that death is no respecter of persons, but that's just what it should be, if there was justice. You couldn't run a hotel without being a respecter of persons, you'd never make it pay. It wouldn't have the right atmosphere. Well, the principle that's right for little things is right for big things. The great should live for ever. Napoleon should never have died. Long live Napoleon,' he cried, raising his glass, but lowering it to say, 'No offence to Mademoiselle. I had forgotten you were Russian, I know Napoleon burned St Petersburg.'

'Moscow,' said Saint-Gratien.

'Say Moscow if you like,' said the landlord, 'but how much rather the poor people in Moscow would have preferred it to be St Petersburg. You have to think of other people's points of view.' He drained the glass and said hopefully, 'No, not another.'

'No, not another,' agreed Monsieur Saint-Gratien.

'No, not another,' echoed the landlord, as if reading an epitaph. 'But what did I come here to say? Ah, yes, I'm so sorry not to have a bedroom for Mademoiselle, but this is a ball of the first importance. All our great families are here, it doesn't matter where they live, Arras and Boulogne, Roubaix and Poix, they're here tonight. Every room in the hotel is let, and that's had the frightful result that never have people with such luggage as yours, Mademoiselle, come to my hotel, and I am forced to treat them like vagabonds.'

'Ah, no,' said Laura, 'you're mixing us with some other people. We didn't bring our luggage, it went on to Mûres-sur-mer. We'd only my grandfather's small case.'

'But what a case,' said the landlord. 'What leather! I said to myself as it was brought in, "If that's their small luggage, what would I not give to see their big luggage, it must be magnificent", yet I couldn't give you a proper room. It's my Waterloo. Poor Napoleon. Marie-Louise was quite unworthy of the honour of being his wife.'

'Let's go downstairs,' Saint-Gratien said to the landlord, 'and see how things are getting on.'

'No, let me speak frankly of my failure,' said the landlord. 'You see how I was placed, don't you? There were only these two rooms in the hotel. And why were they vacant? Well, that worries me. Will there be articles in the newspapers about your esteemed grandfather's death? If so, I'll ask for your discretion, because strictly speaking, these rooms were not vacant. They're rented year in, year out, by a distinguished personage, the last representative of the family who owned this building before it was a hotel, whose palace it was. Oh, you should see the ballroom and the banquet-hall downstairs. On the mantelpiece of the banquet-hall there is carved the family escutcheon, in real marble from Italy. But what am I thinking of, Mademoiselle, such things seem nothing to you. If you saw it you would simply say to yourself, "Ah, just another escutcheon", and you would shrug your shoulders and turn away. That's what you would do. Shrug your shoulders and turn away.' He imitated the movement, was fascinated by it, went on and on making it.

'For heaven's sake,' giggled Madame Verrier through her handkerchief, 'send the idiot away.'

'In a minute, in a minute,' said Saint-Gratien. 'The little one's loving it, she's like me, she's got vulgar tastes.'

'What were we talking about?' the landlord enquired. 'Not surely just about escutcheons. A noble but not a fruitful subject. Ah, it's about these rooms. They're rented to the last gentleman who has a right to display that escutcheon we've been speaking of, who's now a brigadier in a colonial regiment. He's been my tenant ever since his father sold his house to the company of Grissaintois citizens which employs me, and in which my father held considerable shares, though what has happened to them I hardly know. This furniture you see around us came from the suite on the floor below which he occupied as a youth; chairs and tables, they all came upstairs, along with his hatbox and those ledgers, and his overcoat and his evening suit, which are in the wardrobe next door. I wish I liked him better, I wish I didn't feel so uneasy when he's staying here; it's his eyes, they follow one as if there was some question of owing him money. But it's not because I can't like him that I sometimes let this room, though strictly speaking it's let to him. But I have my reasons, in fairness to myself I must point out that I have my reasons.'

'What are they?' asked Saint-Gratien cynically.

The landlord looked blank. Then his face brightened. 'For one thing, there's Christianity. Or the religion of humanity. Call it what you like, which makes it impossible to turn away those in need of shelter, like Mademoiselle and her poor grandfather, the Archduke who is no longer with us. But it's not only that, it's my moral obligation to the Brigadier himself. He tells me not to let the rooms, but he's insane about them being kept clean, running his finger round the highest ledge, asking me if it's cleaned out regularly, with those dunning eyes of his. But, oh, if I didn't let the rooms from time to time when he's away, then he'd have something to grieve over! Just think, Professor, just think what would happen!'

'Well, what would happen?' asked Saint-Gratien, wickedly.

'What would happen?' He could not find an answer for a moment. 'Why,' he cried happily, 'no chambermaid will keep a room clean if it isn't going to be let, everybody who has ever run a hotel will tell you that. If I just locked up this suite, as he wants me to do, in no time you wouldn't be able to see out of the dirty windows, the curtains would be in rags, there'd be cobwebs everywhere, the carpets would be in holes, the furniture would lose all its polish, the castors would come off the chairs and, Heaven help us, I haven't thought of the worst catastrophe, there might be a fire. Why do you laugh? Easily, easily, there might be a fire, disaster might fall on the possessions of this last survivor of our greatest Grissaintois family, poor possessions but possessions, nevertheless, which he had entrusted to my care, under the roof, which allowing for alterations, quite extensive on this side of the establishment, may be said to have protected him when he still knew the affection of a father, yes, and of a mother, why should she be forgotten? No, that, that I couldn't do!'

Exultant, he made a long arm again, and took to himself Professor Saint-Gratien's glass. 'To your health, the friend of all Grissaint, the greatest of surgeons in France, in Europe, in the whole world,' he said, 'and let me drink to you also, Madame Verrier, so bold, so courageous, so heroic —'

'Yes, yes,' Saint-Gratien interrupted, 'let's drink to Madame Verrier rather than to myself, a toast to Madame Verrier, and then let's go downstairs, you and I.'

'But not without expressing our full gratitude to her,' said the landlord, his eyes growing moist, 'for if she withheld her aid' from those hapless girls who call her blessed, what would they face but death and despair followed by a life of shame —'

'It's time you and I left the ladies,' said Saint-Gratien, springing to his feet.

'But I can't go yet, I can't leave the ladies without making a certain matter to them clear,' protested the landlord, as Saint-Gratien laid a hand on his arm, 'and offer my apologies, for they're victims of my carelessness. For I've only one key to this room. There's another, but the Brigadier, with his foolish obsession about the room, his blindness to his true interests, he's laid hold of that. At this moment it'll be in Korea, in Seoul, to be exact. But I can't find my own key. Where can it be, I ask myself? Can I have let it fall into the hands of an unauthorised person? No, a thousand times no. If I have a fault, it's that my sense of duty is too strict. Well, anyway, whoever I gave it to, he left the room unlocked and didn't return the key, and probably for a reason with which we must all sympathise, for great happiness leaves us, as I'm sure the doctor will agree, in a state of confusion. Out of these rooms, out of the hotel, he went, whoever he was, feeling as if he had wings —'

'Let us go downstairs together and look for that key,' said Saint-Gratien, slipping his arm under the landlord's armpit, and getting him out of his chair and over to the door in a single quicksilver movement, his eyes bright with exasperation and amusement.

'Useless, we might as well stay here,' said the landlord, trying to sink back into his chair.

'Then we'll try and find some champagne instead,' said Saint-Gratien.

'But I never touch it,' said the landlord, 'except at some innocent child's first communion, or,' he turned his head to explain to Laura, 'the wedding of some young lady, the touching wedding of some young lady like yourself. Don't you, Professor, find something inexpressibly touching about the wedding of some young lady who is, if you understand me, Professor, such a bride as we are sure Mademoiselle will be?'

'Out, out,' said Saint-Gratien, 'and quickly.'

Laura laughed aloud. Those people in the *Arabian Nights* called calendars, who were always reaching out for the wine-cup again and again and accounting for their position by claiming that they had been turned into apes or a copper horse had bolted with them; they must have been like the landlord. But Madame Verrier gave only a twisted smile and got on at once with the business of finding cushions for her arm-chair and unfolding a blanket. She looked smaller than she had done. Laura offered to give up the camp-bed to her, as she had had two hours of sleep, but was refused, and she lay listening to the soft boom of the dance-music and looking at the stucco garlands on the ceiling, which shifted from high relief to low, as the gas-light wavered, while Madame Verrier padded about getting ready for the night. Once there was a flutter of movement and she remarked in a cold, resolute voice, 'When women are free, they will no longer wear corsets.' She was evidently getting back to her usual self. When she had turned down the gas to a small trembling source of twilight and settled in her chair, she yawned piteously, but Laura had to ask the question which was on her mind.

'Did all that nonsense the landlord talked mean that we can't lock the door?'

Madame Verrier's answer came like a shot from a gun. 'Exactly. But don't be frightened. I won't leave the room.'

It was disconcerting when older people showed themselves innocent. This woman had no idea that someone might come in the night so ruthless that it would not matter whether she stayed in the room. There lay like a bar across the darkness behind her eyelids the image of her grandfather, stretched on his bed in the other room, within a shell of discoloured light, which was his Asiatic part disengaging itself as all his human characteristics were disengaging himself from his body, which was finished, ended. When he totally abandoned his body perhaps his memory would go as well. The dead, she had heard from an Orthodox priest, could not forget the relatives whom God had chosen for them, but companions whom they had brought to themselves by their own will they might not remember except by God's special grace. If that were so, then her grandfather might have forgotten Kamensky, and only herself and Chubinov knew what Kamensky really was; and Chubinov was far away now, probably lost to her, up to the neck in the pit of some misadventure. She saw him lolloping down an alley, towards a full moon low over the roof-tops, in some town where he had not intended to be, pursued by people who thought he was someone else. She was alone in the universe with her understanding of Kamensky. But she should be glad that Madame Verrier would not need to know who or what Kamensky was to attack him if he came into the room. Laura wished that her grandfather had not been so horrid about Madame Verrier. True, he had spoken in Russian, but she must have been hurt when he sent her out of the room and let the doctors stay. It was a pity, for if he had recovered he would have given her a lavish present, forcing on her asceticism some indulgence she would have enjoyed, perhaps a fur coat. Both her grandfather and her grandmother liked making presents, as they liked food and drink, and so did Tania, who got high-coloured and flushed on it.

That afternoon, two summers ago, in Tania's bedroom, when the floor had been covered with the pale yellow buckram hatboxes, had ended in such drunkenness. One of the hats excited doubts in Hélène, the lady's maid, as soon as she took it out of its tissue paper. Her lower lip protruding, she brought it over to the dressing-table and Tania cried, 'Well, here we evidently haven't done well for ourselves, but don't look like that about it, when you stick out your lip like that anybody could see that you come from a rugged mountain district where they have avalanches. We have snow but no avalanches in Russia. She comes,' she explained over her shoulder to Susie, 'from Auvergne.' 'But never returns there,' said Hélène, 'not like this hat, which is going to return to its box, and return to the shop.' 'But let me look at myself for a minute,' said Tania. 'You can do that, but I won't trouble to pin it on,' said Hélène. Tania shouted with laughter at her reflection. 'Look what an awful face I really have! How is it people don't notice it? I look like the plain sister, the one that never got married, of one of those blonde cows Paris Bordone painted. How can I have chosen it?' 'Because you were alone,' said Hélène, 'the Duchess always took me with her.' 'Well, that I can't do, because I never know till the last moment when I'm going. But ah! ah!' Her voice soared into a sweet rowdiness. 'I know quite well why I chose it! I watched a woman on the other side of the room try it on, and she looked charming. And why? Because she had fine, fine, fine little bones, like you, Susie.' She whirled round on her chair, snatching the hat from her head. 'You'll look an angel in it! Come and try it on. I'll make you an un-birthday present of it.' She jumped to her feet and sprawled magnificently through space as painted goddesses sprawl across palace ceilings, holding out the hat as if it were a crown she had proffered to another goddess. It was all too much for Susie, who shrank into smiling, disconcerted waifdom. She did not rise at once, but gently cooed that, oh, no, such things were not for her, and went on pressing down one hand on Tania's broad soft bed, and pressing it down again, as a cat sometimes kneads a sofa or a comfortable chair.

Laura wished that afternoon had not come into her mind. She supposed it seemed repellent now because mean people would think that Tania had made a fool of herself giving Susie that hat, when Susie could have gone to Paris and bought a hundred hats from Caroline Reboux without feeling any poorer. Also, it had revived her suspicion about Susie, but there was no evidence for that, Laura told herself, she must forget it. She freed her right hand from the sheets, and let it lie on the coverlet, in case her grandfather wanted to hold it. The dance-music distressed her with its hobnailed boots; she saw Elodie and the Captain, Madame Barrault and the General, poor Professor Barrault and the General's wife, dancing awkwardly in the yellowness cast by the chandeliers, enemy of the whiteness which had been there this morning. It was strange that once a chandelier had been lit, though that was the very purpose for which it had been made, it lost its place among the magically pure things, swans, snow, icicles, moonbeams, Northern lights. But as she lay there the ballroom returned to what it had been, to what it always ought to be, flooded with undiluted light, save for the gods and nymphs, white like the icing on a wedding-cake, and the nun-like women tending the floor and the men with green-baize aprons gentling the harp and setting up the music-stands, all with a priestly lack of haste, so seriously that they were either serving other, darker gods, elsewhere or knew that these gods would have to change their substance before they were done. On the top of the ladder the girl still wrote great O's on the highest pane of the window with her yellow duster, O, I love you! O, I adore you! O, come soon and save me! The young man at the foot of the ladder holding a sheet of music covered with great O's, sang nothing but made more O's with his open mouth, O, I love you! O, I adore you! O, come soon and save me!

Suddenly Laura came out of sleep and found herself sitting up in bed. The music had stopped. Clear across the town came the lurching and panting of a starting train. Though the light was dim she saw that Madame Verrier was asleep. She was huddled in her chair as if she were never gallant, her hands lax in her lap, her head hanging defeated on one side. It was true, Laura thought, what Chubinov had said when he bent over Nikolai at the station, that it was a crime to waken any sleeper. Chubinov was not so silly, her grandfather had been right about him. She dropped back on the pillow; and mercifully the bed creaked, and Madame Verrier stirred and opened her eyes and said thickly, 'Mademoiselle?'

'I heard a train, could my father have come by that?'

Madame Verrier blinked at the window. 'No, it's still dark. That would be the late express from Paris.' She burrowed down into the chair and was asleep. The music started again. Laura pulled her sheet over her face and cried a little. The phosphorescent length of her grandfather stretched across the dark lining of her lids again. What had happened to him happened to everyone. That was harder to believe than any fairy tale. Shuddering, she slept, but not for long. There was a soft knock on the door, and another, and another. As she hurried to the door she hoped her father would not be too angry because she was barefoot.

12

OUTSIDE STOOD Monsieur Kamensky and Catherine, who was bright-eyed with happiness. She bobbed, said, 'We're all so glad this gentleman has come, after all we're only strangers,' bobbed again, and went off down the corridor, walking lightly, she was so pleased. Up the well of the staircase the music came in its completeness, gay with all its notes, the low ones and the high ones as well, which did not penetrate the walls of the room. The violins and the trombones fell silent, the clarinet ran a few steps up the scale, twirled about and ran down again, then the other instruments joined together in acclamation. Laura leaned against the doorpost. If she ran past him down the corridor he would realise that she knew he was Gorin, and would kill her. That would be the sensible thing for him to do; and he looked still sensible though wild, as if his sense had had to work on disturbing material. His face was as smooth as usual. But his clothes were rumpled, and the two straps of the small holdall he was carrying were not done up properly, the first strap was caught in the second buckle, the other strap was loose.

She asked, 'How did you know we were here?'

He did not hear the question. 'Is it true what they told me downstairs? Is he dead?'

She nodded. Kamensky set down his holdall, snatched off his spectacles and threw them on the floor. She stooped and picked them up, and put them back in his hand, saying, 'That's a gesture you can't afford.'

Again he did not seem to hear. He put his hands to his head and said softly, 'I feel like a masterless dog.'

Perhaps he was not Gorin after all. 'Tell me,' she asked, 'How did you know we were here? Why have you come?'

The sound of her voice simply did not seem to reach him.

'He was alive when I left Paris. I never thought he would be gone when I got here. This is a different tragedy.' A tremor ran through him, she thought he was going to fall. 'Can't I come in and sit down? There's a nurse with you, isn't there? They assured your mother there would be. It's quite proper for me to come in, isn't it, if there's someone with you? I am so tired.'

She softened to him because he was so tired, hardened again as it came on her what goings and comings had made him tired, reflected she might as well be shot inside a room as out-side, and felt neither soft nor hard but simply an exile, lifted suddenly to some place a long way away from anywhere she had ever been before. 'Come in,' she said, and settled him on a chair. She had to guide him, he was dazed and tremulous, and when her hand touched his arm he groaned. She went over to Madame Verrier, gently shook her, and told her that a friend had come from Paris: a special friend, she added, wondering why she troubled, for nobody's benefit, to be ironic. Would Madame mind if they talked? Madame Verrier muttered that nothing would keep her awake, reached out and found a swathe of cotton wool she had left on the table and plugged her ears, smiled with closed eyes, and said indistinctly, 'A pity it's not your father.'

Laura turned to Kamensky and said, 'We'll keep the gas low and talk quietly,' and stopped and choked. In the half-light Kamensky's spectacles hid his eyes as if they were black, and the two shining dark circles were levelled on her steadily, they might have been two gun-muzzles aimed at her face. She wanted to put up her hands but stood quite still. It came back to her that Dolly the housemaid had once told her that if a tramp attacked her out in the country she must kick him be-tween the legs. She supposed she could do that if she had to. It now struck her as idyllic, the world where, if a man attacked one, it would be a tramp.

Kamensky said as if in anguish, 'I used to think your mother was the most beautiful woman in the world. Now I think that of you.'

She exclaimed in bewilderment, 'What's that? What did you say?' Only an idiot could consider her more beautiful than

292

her mother, and anyway why should she be interested if he did?

And why would he bring that up at such a moment?

'I beg you to forgive me. You must think I'm rambling. But it suddenly struck me that if your grandfather had the worst possible fortune in some respects, he had the best in others. Such a daughter, such a grand-daughter.'

She pushed an arm-chair towards him and sat down in it, facing him. 'How does it happen that you're here?'

'It's quite a story. *A chapter of accidents*,' he said, in his un-pleasing English. 'Professor Barrault became distressed about you and telephoned to your mother in Paris.'

'Oh, yes, it would be he.' Not Saint-Gratien, not Madame Verrier.

'He knew that you and another doctor had communicated with your father, but he thought that the message to London might not be delivered at once. So he looked up your grand-father's address in the Paris Telephone Book, and rang the apartment, and was put through to the clinic, but your mother couldn't leave your grandmother, who is apparently feeling very unwell. I wasn't at the clinic, I'd had to go back on my undertaking to take them there. My hand, you remember.'

'Yes, I remember.'

'But I happened to call in at the apartment later, and, oh, Miss Laura, I knew that the dearest part of my life was over. It wasn't only that I learned that your grandfather was dying, I saw what his dying meant. What struck me sounds trivial, but it isn't, you see the apartment in the Avenue Kléber has al-ways been so orderly. Your grandfather kept his papers and his books so neatly, and all comings and goings were so formal that he might still have been a Minister of State with a secre-tariat working for him. That, of course, isn't entirely due to him. Your grandmother's very able. She saw to it, and please God will see to it again, that in her household there were no such muddles, no such inexplicable and annoying delays, no occasions for anger, such as there are in other homes. Early in the day each servant was given the appropriate orders and the machine ran without a hitch till nightfall. Oh, there was plenty of noise, you realise what our people are, but nothing went wrong. In Russia, you know, Sofia Andreievna managed her own stables, and other owners came miles to see them, even from Austria and Hungary, where they know what's what. Well, when I went to the apartment yesterday it was a den of confusion. The servants were all weeping, we seemed caught in a web of telephone calls and telegrams that were sent and never arrived, and even those, and I find this so horrible, that were to call me to my happy duty of serving you. For, you see, even after I'd had my hand attended to, I didn't go back to my hotel. This turned out to be one of the busiest days in my life.'

'It must have been.'

'For, though I'd have kept my promise to go to the clinic with your mother, I'd many other things to do. It happens that I've been asked – and how pleased your grandfather would have been, for he always took the most generous interest in my career – to take charge of a new construction. In South America. Under a French company. And it's this very day that I've had to settle this business, going from one tedious interview to another, so it was quite late before I got to the apartment, and telephoned your mother at the clinic, and got the whole dreadful story of how you and your grandfather had had to get off the train. Of course, I told her I'd start at once.'

'Of course.'

'But I couldn't keep that promise either. I hastened to the station, eager to be with your grandfather and pray with him his last prayers – and then, look!' He held out his left hand, which was now swathed in bandages.

She touched that white linen, and would not have been surprised had she felt underneath it the hardness of an artificial limb. She would not say she was sorry for him. Even though it meant that he must realise her disbelief, she said, 'Poor little Louison.'

But it went by him. 'Ah, poor little Louison,' he echoed, pausing to laugh tenderly. 'I'll have to keep it from him that he did rather more damage than we thought. Though my friend the chemist believed he'd settled everything by giving me a little laudanum, by evening my hand was hurting so intensely that I had to stop on my way to the station and go to a doctor to put a dressing on it.' Choking, he cried, 'But what's the use of talking about such stupid things! Nikolai's dead! I didn't think he'd ever die!' He covered his eyes with his handkerchief, then took it away to look at her directly and say, 'You're glad to see me?'

'Of course, of course. But your hand. It's so painful, shall we wake up the nurse and get her to look at it?'

'What, wake the poor toiler, worn out with her long day spent in works of mercy?' he answered, without a second's delay. 'And unfortunately,' he added, 'the dressing has to be left undisturbed for several days, or so the doctor said.' She laughed and was horrified by her lack of self-control, and wondered if in the half-light he had seen that she was mocking him. He went on, in a tone she could not understand, for it sounded as if it were he who were frightened and she who had no need to be, 'I caught the last train which could bring me here today. I got to the station in time to catch an earlier one. I couldn't force myself to climb into the carriage and take my seat. Think of that. The first time in my life I've ever done anything like that. So irresolute.'

Again his spectacles were trained on her like gun-barrels. She did not see how she could kick him between his legs if he went on sitting like that, bending forward. The advantage was to him. She smoothed her hair, and made sure that the ribbon bow at the neck of her peignoir was fastened. It seemed important that everything about her should be neat. She raised her chin and waited.

'Could you possibly give me something to drink?'

'There's some champagne on the table, not the fizzy kind. And there's lots of food.'

She had been watching lest he tried to get her to turn her back on him; but he turned his back on her, went over to the table, filled and emptied a glass, heaped a plate with food, ate only a mouthful, and then went back to his chair. He pulled it still closer to hers so that their faces were only three or four feet apart. 'Now, I must ask you something, Miss Laura,' he said, then groaned and put his hands to his forehead. He closed his eyes and rocked backwards and forwards. 'I don't feel well,' he muttered. She could not pretend that she cared. Opening his eyes, he stared at her, and again it was as if he were tracked down and panic-stricken. 'Tell me, did anything happen to you on the train?'

'Kind and sensible,' she thought, 'kind and sensible of Professor Barrault to telephone Paris. My mother would have done it, so would my father. And it means that I have to face Kamensky unarmed, with no lies properly arranged.' But it was not so bad. 'Yes,' she said, 'something quite odd happened to us on the train,' and felt braced, as if she had dived into a cold sea.

'What was that, Miss Laura?'

'After the train left Paris a man came into our compartment. Somebody Grandfather knew but hadn't seen for a long time.'

'What was his name?'

'Grandfather never told me. He didn't introduce us. They just said, "Can it really be you", and, "let's see, how many years is it since we met", and that sort of thing, and then the man said he had something private to tell my grandfather, and my grandfather shrugged his shoulder, you know the way he did when he was bored, like a sleepy mammoth. And he sent me off to sit in the next compartment. Then, just before we got to Grissaint, the man came and told me my grandfather was ill. He was in a great fuss. He said he hadn't meant to upset my grandfather, he'd only talked to him for his own good. I laughed, rather. My father says that phrase pairs with the raven as an ill omen. Then I saw my grandfather, and I couldn't laugh any more.'

'Was he ill already? How ill?'

'Very ill. He was quite yellow, and he was panting, and he couldn't walk or stand properly, and he was talking nonsense. When I got him out of the train at Grissaint and they blew that little trumpet they use here instead of a whistle, he thought it was a toy trumpet and that a little girl was blowing it at a Christmas party in St Petersburg. And he kept on staring at the big station clock and saying it had stopped, though it hadn't.'

Kamensky sighed as if to himself, 'They were there in the strange place. All alone.' He went back to the cross-examination. 'And the man, who had spoken to you on the train?'

'Oh, he helped us, he got us a porter, and then he went away.'

'Did he say where he was going?'

'Yes, and that was queer. For he said he was going straight back to Paris, but he didn't, for when the train we'd just got out of started again, I saw him standing in the corridor, and of course that was the Calais train. I don't think he liked me seeing him. He turned his head away.'

'I wonder who he was,' said Kamensky, thoughtfully.

He was not so clever after all. If he had not known the man was Chubinov he would have asked her to describe him. So that he would not remember the omission afterwards, she said, as if answering a question, 'Thin and middle-aged and shabby. He wore spectacles and he was mousey, no particular colour. But he might have been all right once. I mean, it wasn't surprising that they had known each other in Russia long ago.'

'What was it they had been talking about on the train?'

'Well, I don't know. I told you, I was in a different compartment, my grandfather sent me there.'

'But afterwards didn't he tell you anything about their conversation?'

'Afterwards? Monsieur Kamensky, you don't understand. When I say that my grandfather talked nonsense after he was taken ill on the train, I really mean it. He didn't talk about this man at all until we got here, and then he only spoke about him once, and then said that he'd told fairy-tales you'd tell children. There was something about a blind man being able to see the time on a clock miles and miles away.'

'Ah. And that was all?'

'All I heard, though of course he was rambling the whole of the afternoon and evening, and I may not have listened to every word; and I wasn't in his room all the time, I came in here. But most of what he said I got, and it had nothing to do with the present. It was all about things that happened when he was quite young, like going to Persia before the roads were finished, and of course he recited reams and reams of the Liturgy.'

'So that was all,' said Kamensky. He sighed, as if about to faint.

Then he rose and poured himself another glass of champagne and came back to his chair. She watched his fingers loosen and clench, loosen and clench round the stem of his wine-glass, and told herself that she must not grow careless and let down her guard too soon, simply because she saw that he was telling himself the same thing. 'Forgive me,' came the honeyed voice through the half-light, 'but I can't, I really can't hold back a question which comes from the sheerest selfishness on my part. I'm ashamed of wanting to ask it, even in the presence of death, which makes egotism look so petty a folly. I must know: did your grandfather speak of me in his last hours?'

She waited, like a chess player pondering the next move.

'Don't hesitate to answer, even if you think the truth may wound me. Remember that I'm a believer. If he remembered me with affection, that's good. But if he didn't, if his soul was alienated from mine at the hour of departure, and we know that such things happen under the terror of death, my prayers will bring me near to him again in the hereafter, we will be united by God's grace and in His presence.'

One should shut one's ears to this, as one should turn one's eyes away from the apes when they were doing odd things in the corner of the cage; but it was so interesting.

'Yet I must ask whether he spoke of me, because I'm weak, weak like a wife who attaches importance to her husband bringing her back a present from a visit abroad, even though his whole life is one long proof of his devotion to her. All the same I can't feel ashamed of my weakness, for it comes from my grief.'

She found herself saying, in an icy voice, 'Your grieving heart is like your bandaged hand.' That was suicide. Now he must realise she knew he was a traitor.

But he said, 'How sympathetic you are to remember my hand in the midst of your shock and sorrow! But how I wish my heart pained me only so much as my hand. Isn't it strange how any physical pain is more tolerable than mental pain?' With difficulty he reminded himself of his duty to make quite sure. 'All the same, I must ask you – it's really necessary for my peace of mind – did your grandfather speak of me, for good or for evil?'

'I don't like answering you,' she said, 'because all I have to report is such a little thing, considering all you'd done for him and his family. My grandfather only mentioned you once. He was talking about the time he was in Persia, and about making the roads, and he said, "I wish I had Kamensky here to take this down," and then he repeated your name twice. "Sasha, Sasha," he said. I'm sorry, but that's all there was. But he did sound fond of you when he repeated your name.'

'It is enough, till the hereafter,' said Kamensky, quietly. 'I am glad I was persistent in asking the question, for I like your answer. "Sasha, Sasha",' he repeated under his breath. He sipped his champagne, his face smooth again, his eyes wandering placidly round the room. He put down his glass with an exclamation of mild impatience, and went over to his holdall and tidied up the straps, putting each into its own buckle, then went back and settled into his chair, easy as a fed cat. That was comprehensible enough. When he left Paris he must have thought himself obliged to kill all the three people who knew he was Gorin; her grandfather, herself, and Chubinov, and three times run the risk of being caught and guillotined. Now her grandfather needed no killing: God had done that. As she had not heard what Chubinov told her grandfather – and she was sure Kamensky believed that now – there was no need to kill her. That left only one person to be murdered, and he might be an easy victim. As Chubinov ran for safety, his adoration would slow him down, it would spin him round so that those spaniel eyes could have a last look at the idol. Hatred of Kamensky flared up in her, she went over to the table and took the plate of food he had pushed away and set it in front of him. 'You're drinking, you might as well eat too,' she said, her mind rushing away from her into a savage childish fantasy that the food might turn into poison.

He thanked her so softly that she could not hear the quite long sentence. 'What? what?' she asked through her clenched teeth. 'You're moving about the room as your mother sometimes does,' the murmur came, 'with a certain impatience, but still with grace.' She went on straining her ears, but hardly got it. 'As if you were trying to make the world turn more quickly on its axis. And not only that. At this moment you want to break the world's orbit and send it circling to some other part of the universe, where there is no death. Ah, I know quite well how you're feeling. For what shall I do without Nikolai Niko-laievitch?'

'What indeed?' she grimly echoed. He was still eating, but his glass was empty and she opened the other bottle.

'He was the centre of my being,' said Kamensky. He had forgotten the sleeping nurse, and his voice was loud and of a piercing beauty.

'He must have been.' It was true. The apartment in the Avenue Kléber must have been to him what the House of Commons was to her father, what the Stock Exchange is to a stockbroker.

'He made me what I am,' Kamensky went on. She pointed to the sleeping nurse and he lowered his voice again. 'You don't seem surprised. You should be. It's very unlikely that a man like me, of no family, born in poverty, with serf blood, should have been made by a great noble, and when I say made, I mean mentally created, just as a son is mentally created by his father. Don't you want to know why he affected me so strongly? But I suppose,' he said, very faintly, 'that you feel no curiosity whatsoever about me.'

She was not safe for ever. She must remember that as soon as Kamensky discovered that Chubinov was not in London, and his spies would find that out, he would know that she had lied to him, and he would pursue her like an animal, a blood-hound sent after a convict. She had better learn all she could about the animal. 'No curiosity about you? You're wrong about that. I'd rather know all about you than about anyone else in the world.'

She watched him slowly raise the glass to his lips, his hands shaking, a shy smile brightening in his beard, everything about him tender and fluid. Even his glasses seemed to give back a melting light. 'So,' he said. 'So. I've just heard the most won-derful words that anyone has ever said to me.' He drank again. 'Oh, if I could tell you everything!'

'Why can't you?' She put the question, but she was amazed

that he wanted to go on talking. He had asked her if she knew what the man on the train had told Nikolai, she had lied to him, he had believed the lie. Why could he not be contented, and go away, and let her get to sleep.

'It's difficult. That something exists doesn't mean that it can be completely described. A grave disharmony. But I'll do my best. Miss Laura, this is an age full of temptation and confusion. I don't allude to the sins of the flesh. I've never wanted to commit the grosser faults. But intellectually, morally, it's so easy to go wrong today. Well, Nikolai Nikolaievitch lifted me right out of the bog where I might have splashed about until I drowned. He was a perfect example of the true Russian nature, as it's been formed by Orthodox Christianity, a traditionalist, a monarchist, an imperialist, a Pan-Slavist, though without any taint of rebellion, of attempts to claim the right of judgment in practical politics. He was more Russian than mere Russian human beings can be, he was like a tree in the Russian forest, its roots deep in the Russian soil, he was like the limitless Russian plain. He was matter not for history only, but for geography. Well, it was in a sense a waste, my friendship with him. True, I escaped pettiness in the service of his greatness, but who am I but Alexander Gregorievitch Kamensky, a simple engineer, who comes from nowhere, who knows very few people, who could not lay out to advantage the spiritual wealth he gave me. I'll give you a better idea of what his influence meant if I tell you about a friend of mine.' His voice became indistinct, he did not seem to want to finish his sentence. 'A more original man. He was to Nikolai Nikolaievitch as the anvil to the hammer. Because of what your grandfather gave him he performed an interesting feat, perhaps of importance to history.' The silence fell.

'You were telling me about your friend.'

'Wait a little,' he said. 'There's something else. More important.'

'What's that?'

'Your shadow on the wall. No, don't turn round. You're spoiling it. You'll have to let me describe it. It's just a shadow, a piece of wall darker than the rest. But it's such a particular shadow. The stupidest person in the world would see it wasn't cast by a man, that it's a woman's shadow. That it's a lady's shadow. It's a shadow cast by a beautiful young Russian lady. Of a certain sort. Well-bred and gentle. Above all, gentle.'

Now she knew that he was laughing at her. It could be that she had not deceived him, that he had recognised her rage against him. She would have to keep her head and not lose her temper while he made fun of her.

'Pictures which tell so much about their subjects are called masterpieces,' he went on. 'Your shadow is a masterpiece and a gentle one. Have you been to Venice? Ah, that's a great thing to have still before you. Well, in Venice, most of the pictures are too great, too splendid, right up on your grandfather's level; but in some of the churches, behind the altars, there are gentle masterpieces, like your shadow.'

For the time he simply sat there, holding his glass, but not drinking, not eating, not speaking, not moving. The persuasion came on her that he was very happy. Why should that be? Was he perhaps waiting for a signal to set in motion some plan which could not fail? Or was he just waiting, with time in hand, because everything was settled, and it would be done much later, somewhere else, when he was far away?

He said at last, 'The way the gas is trembling because it's turned so low. The way the light and the shadows are trembling on the walls.'

'Yes?'

'It's as if they were keeping time with something inside oneself. Not one's heartbeat. They're too slow for that. But something.'

She broke the long stillness by saying: 'Your friend, you were telling me about your friend. What was it that Nikolai Nikolaievitch caused him to do?'

As if he had not heard, he asked, 'Do you go to the opera in London? Do you go to Mozart's operas?'

'Yes, *Figaro* and *Don Giovanni*. We don't like Wagner.'

'I don't know much about music. I've not had the leisure for that. All my life I've been starved of time as the poor are starved of bread. But it always seems to me that the songs Mozart writes for women aren't just arias, they're, as you might say, receptacles for storing the essence of femininity.

302

When I hear them I think of the scent-makers down on the Riviera, distilling the scent of their jasmine and carnations and storing them in beautiful bottles. Such as I suppose your mother and you have on your dressing-tables. When the actresses sing those arias, it's as if the crystal stopper had been taken out of one of those bottles, and the fragrance floats into the air, at once intoxicating and sobering us, exhilarating us and making us unchangeably serene.'

She wondered how he dared talk such nonsense, with her grandfather lying in the next room, and his authority still harsh about them.

'To think of you sitting in an opera-house, in the grand tier, perhaps next to the Royal Box, wearing a white dress, wearing a pearl necklace — for diamonds are only for married ladies, aren't they? — when all the lights are turned down and only the stage is bright, and one of the world's great singers is standing before the footlights, pouring out her heart in one of these arias, and her voice rises above the dark auditorium and you're there in the darkness, so quiet and attentive — if I came into such a dark theatre, and I could not see anything at all, I'd wait till my eyes got accustomed to the darkness and I'd look about and finally I'd see the outline of a head turned towards the stage, just the outline, just the silhouette, and I would know it was you.'

But his spies would have told him the number of her seat.

'The femininity Mozart seeks to evoke is what your mother and you represent at its highest. Such beauty has great value as a philosophical concept.'

If he must talk nonsense, why such silly nonsense? Did he himself think it meant anything? 'What, you mean that just being beautiful like my mother has anything to do with philosophy?'

'Don't say "just being beautiful". Oh, it's such a thing, this beauty. And the philosophical concept I'm speaking of is most serious. It's called the doctrine of Sophia, of heavenly wisdom, and it holds that woman's beauty is the image on earth of the beauty in the cosmos, which is the wisdom of God as it is extended into the Universe. Becoming flesh and uniting the Creator and the Creation, with no breach between them. The

303

doctrine was formulated by a Russian thinker with whom I don't agree, but whose genius I can't deny; Vladimir Soloviev.'

'Your friend,' she reminded him. 'You said you'd tell me about your friend.'

'Ah, yes, my friend. It was he who brought me to Soloviev. Originally he couldn't tolerate him, but under the influence of your grandfather he came to revere him.' He got up, refilled his glass, and stretched a deliberative hand over the plates of food. 'Soloviev,' he murmured, and popped into his mouth a square of toast spread with prawns, which had garnished the salmon. He went back to his chair and sank deep into it, its rounded back framing him like a conch, his knees comfortably crossed between the two gilt dolphin's heads on the arm-ends, with a kind of contentment which suggested that he was sitting in warm water. 'An opera,' he said dreamily, 'an opera. A nightingale. It's not only the sound which matters, it's who listens to it. Who's in the darkened auditorium, who opens her casement on the moonlit garden.'

'Such queer twaddle,' she thought, and her attention wandered. How long would it take Kamensky to realise that Chubinov was not in London, that she had been lying, that she must be killed? And, what was more important at the moment, when would he stop talking and let her go to sleep? She found she was listening to the end of a sentence and had not heard its beginning.

'. . . and after my friend and I had spent two years together at the university, we felt like brothers.'

'Which university was that?' she jeered. It had been like a geography lesson in the train, when her grandfather and Chubinov had talked of the universities where Gorin and Kamensky had or had not studied: St Petersburg, Karlsruhe, Darmstadt, Moscow, Berlin.

Without noticing the gust of laughter which escaped her because he had to think for a minute, he answered, 'Berlin. We were there, yes, for more than two years. But it did not make us any less Russian. I can't imagine anybody more Russian than my friend. So inevitably he suffered.'

'What from?'

'That's a curious question. Why, what all of us young Russians suffered from. Do you know the poems of Pechorin? An insignificant man. He died a Roman, a Catholic, which is quite wrong for a Russian. We can belong to the Orthodox Church or become atheists, but only the most contemptible among us, the unbaked loaves, can adopt the Latin faith. Nevertheless, Pechorin wrote some wonderful lines. Listen. "How sweet it is to hate one's native land, and eagerly await its annihilation." Pechorin wrote that.'

'Well, I knew at once it wasn't by Rudyard Kipling.'

'Of course not. It couldn't be written by anybody but a Russian. Only a Russian could feel this, Miss Laura, and it is what all Russians who love Russia passionately must feel and do feel. So inevitably they must suffer, and my friend felt it more than most, so his sufferings were great indeed.'

'Uncomfortable for him.' She could not help yawning.

'You're not using the right word. It's rarely that I have to suggest that your Russian is anything but perfect. But you don't mean "uncomfortable" – you mean "tragic".'

'No, I don't. I meant uncomfortable. Your friend wasn't tragic. Not like Othello. Not like King Lear.'

'There's evidently a misunderstanding, but let us pass on. My friend is, in fact, very like Hamlet.' He brooded for a moment, then smiling complacently, took another prawn. 'Extremely like Hamlet. Well, he felt as I did, under the influence of Nikolai Nikolaievitch, being deeply impressed by the bravery with which he had faced the problem of Russia. Do you know what the problem of Russia is? I will tell you.' He wagged a forefinger at her. 'In our Russian society there is a minority of informed men and women with cultivated minds, who are ready to forgo all personal advantages and determine the course of history so that for ever morality is imposed upon the state. But the majority, the vast majority, of men and women, are passive as brute beasts. Their fates are determined by the blind flight of events, and therefore when they die they fall to dust, without having done anything to impart meaning to life and eliminate injustice and misery. It is the business of the intelligent minority to convert the unintelligent majority into a majority as enlightened as themselves.'

'Yes, yes.' The male world was deep, deep in the dust of

tedium. 'But people have that idea everywhere. If they didn't there wouldn't be schools all over the world.'

'That is a very English way of looking at the problem. We Russians look at it differently. With a Russian seriousness. And my friend was enormously impressed by Nikolai Nikolaievitch because, serious himself, he recognised a certain sort of seriousness in your grandfather. He was astonished because he himself was a Liberal. One of the few Liberals I have ever known. So he detested the Tsardom and thought that all men who worked for the Tsar were evil and stupid. But Nikolai Nikolaievitch was not evil or stupid, he saw the Russian problem clearly, your grandfather, as clearly as my friend. But he believed that the conversion of the majority from passive barbarism to activist intelligence could be brought about through the wise exercise of power by the privileged classes taking office under the Tsar and performing their duties ably and conscientiously. Many of his kind held the same faith; but there was, you know, Miss Laura, something wonderful about the way he held it. He was violent and his capacity for pleasure must have been immense – oh, what he must have been when he was a young man – but he had laid that faith in his duty to serve Russia as a yoke on his great shoulders. A little child looking up at a mammoth, that's how my friend felt when he met Nikolai Nikolaievitch, and so he became his disciple. He imitated him first by his devotion to his profession —'

'And what was that?' She wanted to sleep, to sleep.

'He was an engineer.' The pause had lasted only a hundredth of a second. 'A railway engineer. Most conscientious in the discharge of his duties. But your grandfather affected him not only as a servant of the state, but as a philosopher. My friend is of a very philosophical turn of mind. There your grandfather could not help him. He was a religious man, and the Orthodox Church has never been a friend to philosophy. Therefore my friend had to work out for himself certain aspects of the Russian problem and he was embarrassed by the obligation which all of us who love Russia recognise, the obligation to impose morality on the state. For what's morality?'

Now she was awake. The answer rushed out of her. 'Why, morality's not lying! Not cheating! Not murdering!'

Her wave of passion was so strong that he had to take notice of it, but it broke and scattered against his glazed calm and left it as it was. 'What's so wonderful about you, Miss Laura, is that you're at once so gentle and so fierce. So untamed. Are you a great rider, like your grandmother? I should like to see you on horseback. *Riding to hounds? Clearing a fence? Fox-hunting?*' he said in his horrid English. 'Yes, indeed. And what you say about morality charms, because it's so high-spirited. I can imagine your hair blowing backward as you *go into a gallop*. But it's not true save on the superficial plane. These things you abhor are sacrifices which have to be offered up on the altar of necessity. Think of your own army. *Your navy. Your red coats. Your Tommy Atkins. Your Jack Tars.* You wouldn't repudiate them, any more than I would repudiate our Cossacks of the Setch. But they spy. They kill.'

'That's why we English try to keep the peace. In peace one doesn't spy or kill.'

'You're right,' he exclaimed, his voice soaring and happy as if he were quite young and it were early in the night. 'But you don't know how right you are! Peace is what the heart desires. After the long pitting of force against force, after all the arguing, the scheming, the destruction, which even though it is necessary is still horrible —' he covered his eyes and shuddered – 'oh, it could be utterly, utterly horrible – after all that there comes the establishment of a perfect balance, of equilibrium, of the synthesis, of peace. And the joy of it's past believing. That's what my friend had found . . . oh, he's so happy. Mind you, he didn't know for a long time what he was seeking, and he never imagined how glorious it would be to reach the goal. He began simply by following a clue in Hegel.'

'Ah, yes, Hegel,' she said. Chubinov and Nikolai had talked of Hegel in the train. Both had found in his works the messages they wanted, though they must have been very different: and now Kamensky turned out to have found what he wanted in the same place, though he had nothing in common with the other two. She was reminded of her father's fast sister, Aunt Georgie, who had once been engaged to three men at the same time.

'You've heard of him? I'm glad. Some day in the future,

307

somewhere very far from here, we may read Hegel together. He is not only a writer: he is the writer. If all the rest of literature should be destroyed, and his works alone remained, humanity could still follow its path towards new being. He that seeks, in Hegel shall he find. My friend is a seeker. He is the human embodiment of the search. Well, Hegel held out his hand to him from immortality and brought him to his haven. Through the theory of the dialectic.'

'The dialectic,' echoed Laura. It was one of those words to which she never troubled to attach a precise meaning. Teleology, oolitic, proportional representation, symbiotic; what they stood for was part of the world, and might once have been bright like the world, but the dust which falls wherever there are males had buried them in its dingy drifts. But he had spoken of the theory of the dialectic before, on the first evening of her stay in Paris, with a special relish, as if dreamy enjoyment. She must listen: the hunted should learn all they can about the hunter.

'I shouldn't plague you with these serious matters. The opera, nightingales, rose-gardens, balconies overlooking Swiss lakes, marble landing-stages from which gondolas take off, the gondoliers singing. Your world should be made of such things only. But I talk like a schoolmaster because my friend is both a learner and a teacher, and as he was so very close to Nikolai Nikolaievitch, it relieves my sorrow to tell you about him.'

'Do anything you can which makes you better able to bear my grandfather's death.'

'You're so kind. Well, Hegel points out that every concept your mind can grasp leads it on to another. Why should it do that? Because all concepts are imperfect. Do you know why?'

'Because we are imperfect.' She added to herself, 'Imperfect, and can't do without our sleep.'

'That is not a satisfactory answer from the philosophic point of view. Rather would he say that it is because we can think about the universe only as we know it, and we can know only the small part of it which is within our experience, and that is always changing. Hence every concept we form is incomplete, or involves a contradiction or contradictions. We realise this, and so move on from the first concept to another, in the hope that it will complete the first or annul its contradictions.' He drank from his glass with an inappropriately pedagogic air, as if that were another way of wagging his forefinger. 'The most profitable type of second concept which we can choose is the exact opposite of the first, for it covers the same field. Thus we can very fruitfully compare them, and discard what is false in both the first concept and the second, and retain what is true in both, and lo! that gives us a third concept, which brings us a step nearer reality. Have you understood me so far?'

'Yes.' Her need for sleep was hunger, thirst, sickness.

'Excellent. Thus we saw that there are three stages in the dialectic process. We think of a concept, we summon up its opposite, we establish the truth which is common to both, and form it into a new concept. These three stages are called the thesis, the antithesis, and the synthesis. You should repeat these terms. They are very important.'

'Thesis, antithesis, synthesis. But what has that to do with my grandfather and your friend?'

'Everything. It explains the whole of life. In evolving this theory Hegel did something more wonderful than Columbus when he discovered America, and the theory has been further developed by a German named Marx, with whom I do not agree – for he is inferior to our own Russian thinkers, Lavrov and Mikhailovsky and Machajski – but whose genius I must admit. Because of Hegel and Marx we now all realise that ideas are not static but dynamic. Ideas live like us. And this, dear Miss Laura, raises the possibility, as my friend has seen, that perhaps we can live like ideas.' He looked at her with bright shy eyes, as simple people do when they are going to say, 'I've brought you a present.'

The dance-music thumped on the walls during his long silence, and in the street below a cat-fight spurted out jets of sound. It would be wonderful if Madame Verrier would wake and send Kamensky away, but even at the last tearing screech her tired eyes did not open, she merely frowned, shook her head, and pressed the cotton wool deeper into one ear.

Kamensky spoke again, as if he were now going to take off the silver paper and show the splendid present. 'Suddenly my friend thought to himself, and this is what was so wonderful, my friend thought, "why should we not apply the dialectic process to actions as well as to ideas? Why not follow one deed by its opposite? Why not go gloriously further, and serve one way of life and then its enemy?" Why not join one set of people who devoutly observe a system of morality, become truly one of them, not the loosest but the strictest adherent of their system, and pour one's whole being into the furtherance of their ends, achieving utter and final loyalty to it? And why not at the same time join another set of people who live as devoutly by another system of morality, if possible one that's totally opposed to the first, and pour one's whole being into that too? *Why not,*' he asked, in that detestable English, '*do first one thing and then the other?*'

'You mean,' she said slowly, her need for sleep gone again, 'Fight for both sides at the same time without either knowing one's working for the other? Be a Roundhead and a Cavalier at the same time? Fight for the French and the Germans in the Franco-Prussian War, for the Boers and the British in the South African War? Be a Liberal and a Conservative?'

'Just that,' he said and drank the last drops from his glass, and wiped his mouth.

'Why, everybody knows that's wrong,' she said. 'If you asked a child, quite a little child, or a navvy working on the road who couldn't read or write, they'd tell you that was wrong.'

'But we're superior to little children, and still more are we superior to men, who, debased by society, work on the road —'

'Oh, no, we're not,' she said, 'not if we do that sort of thing.'

'But you're so delightful,' he said, laughing and taking off his glasses to look at her tenderly with his head on one side. 'You're dismissing what my friend is doing in such an English way. You don't like it because it is *not fair play. Not playing the game. Not cricket.* Ah, but you don't understand that we're passing beyond that to a freer, happier, wiser day. Remember what I told you about the dialectic theory, about the thesis, the antithesis, the synthesis. You're standing at the point of the thesis. My friend's moved on, by throwing all his strength and ability into both of two organisations he's formed, quite opposite in their aims; he's attained the antithesis. Now will come the synthesis, both the organisations will destroy

310

each other, and a third will emerge which will be superior. Don't you now understand what my friend's doing, not just for those two organisations, but the whole world, for morality itself? If people practise at one and the same time what's considered bad conduct and what's considered good conduct, then they're bound to find themselves practising a new kind of conduct which shall be neither bad nor good but *lootshee – meilleur – besser – better* – more in accordance with reality, nearer the Absolute. Oh, Miss Laura, my friend is helping mankind on its journey as only the greatest teachers have done, as only the greatest teachers have done, he is with Christ, he is with Buddha —'

'What organisations are they that he joined and is destroying?' She was tired of all this deception. She did not care what happened if she forced him to show his hand, his murderous hand.

Smoothly he answered, 'Not very important ones. It is the principle which counts. Societies busying themselves with religious and educational activities in the oil provinces round Baku.'

She groaned because he was so clever. This time he had hardly paused at all before he found an answer; and her need for sleep was again a hunger, a thirst, an aching in the bones.

'Miss Laura, you must try to understand the greatness of my friend's achievements and their idealistic foundations. For he has grown this garden from seed given him by your grandfather. As I told you, my friend was a Liberal, and when he met your grandfather and saw that his ideas also had some value and that the situation was a theatre of the soul, a stage where history engendered its drama, he became a character in the drama and converted it into a masterpiece. Oh, won't you soften your heart towards my friend, who has given Nikolai Nikolaievitch true philosophic immortality?'

'My grandfather, my grandfather,' she groaned. She leant across and fingered Madame Verrier's skirt; to touch the hem of a garment worn by someone sane was as good as if it had been worn by somebody divine. She remembered that evening in Paris when her grandfather had slept in his chair for such a long time, so long that the white rose in the crystal vase on the table lost petal after petal, while the lights came on in the tall grey houses across the streets. He who had been so often afraid to sleep slept soundly then, because he had said to his friend, Kamensky, 'I am in torment because I think I am the victim of a conspiracy, and that may mean I am mad,' and Kamensky had spoken a sentence, sweet as a mouthful of whipped cream, 'You are not mad, for you are right in believing that you are the victim of a conspiracy.' The memory sent a shudder of hatred through her body, she said, 'The man who tormented my grandfather. He should be tormented in hell. For ever and ever.'

He did not seem to hear her. That was strange, he kept on not hearing what she said. There might have been a sheet of plate-glass between them. 'Don't you at all understand,' pleaded his innocent voice, 'what my friend's been trying to do?'

'How can I judge your friend's doings when I haven't heard how they worked out? When I don't know what he's doing now? When I can't think how it's all going to end?'

He hid in silence like a wild animal taking cover in a thicket, then murmured, as if the beast were venturing near the bushes on the fringe, 'Well, it's early yet to paint the whole picture. I told you, my friend's just come to the end of the antithesis, in a few days the negation will be completed, the two organisations will begin to perish in their own self-doubt.'

His voice died away. The gaslight flared up and showed joy on his face, and some surviving grains of gold on the wreaths stamped on the olive wallpaper. He continued, 'and as to the synthesis, the third organisation, which will be born of the other two, my friend won't be there to see it. He'll only have the satisfaction of knowing that he has controlled history.' He retreated again into the thicket of silence.

'Where is he now?'

He shifted in his chair, quite comfortably. It had not crossed his mind that she was mocking him. 'He . . . it's impossible to say what he's doing at this actual moment. We must wait for news.' He laughed to himself. 'There's one thing interesting I can tell you about him. If we're to believe his own account, he's undergone a peculiar change. It's as if the dialectic process doesn't operate only in the world of ideas and of events, but on matter itself. For years my friend put his strength under a double strain by giving prodigally to two organisations, day in and day out, and he'd grown stale and slow, one might almost say old. But now that he's come through the stages of thesis and antithesis he's emerging into what I can only call his own personal synthesis. Oh, it's extraordinary. Apparently – though, of course, I've nothing to go on but his letters – he's become a young man again. He can't believe it, he's never tired, and when he looks in the glass he sees a man years younger than himself.'

She wondered if she had after all been mistaken. Perhaps he had not been talking of himself when he spoke of his friend, perhaps someone of the sort really existed. For he had not changed since she had first seen him, except to grow slightly older, and he did not look a bit like a young man.

'It's also that he feels the blood racing through his veins, at a new speed, with a new drunkenness . . .' Hesitantly and softly, as softly as if he were talking of some delicate personal matter, he breathed some words, which she thought she had not heard correctly, and asked him to repeat. 'I said, my friend's account of his emotions reminds me of Hegel's description of reality, when he likens it to a Bacchic dance in which there is not one of the elements which is not drunk.'

'I'd like the image better,' said Laura, 'if I hadn't so recently seen the landlord of this hotel.'

His voice went on, low and sibilant and dry, making the same sound as the autumn leaves one scuffs off garden paths in autumn. 'What's so remarkable is that all my friend's life he's dovetailed every moment of the day to make patterns that will fit into the complicated design of his great innovation. In a short time there'll be hardly a fragment left of the solid structures he's spent his life in building, structures which, there's no denying it, gave him a certain position. They've collapsed, soon it'll be as if they'd never been, but he doesn't care, he's full of joy, he's making no plans at all.'

'Hush,' she said, 'don't speak so loud. You mustn't wake poor Madame Verrier.' She did not want him to go home till he had told her more.

'Forgive me. The poor virtuous woman, toiling for the sick.

313

Yes. Well, my friend's joyously persuaded he need take no thought for the future. He's got a trade and the world's wide. There are whole continents in which a European can start afresh.' There was another of those silences like retreats into the undergrowth. He raised his trembling hand and loosened his collar. 'I tell you, the dialectical process manifests itself not only in what is thought but in what is lived. In even the most personal experiences.' He passed his handkerchief across his forehead. His voice was not sweet any more, it was hoarse. 'The negation of life, that's death.'

She repeated the phrase in wonder. It was so commonplace that it was odd to hear it uttered except on some occasion when platitude was privileged, in a pulpit or at a prize-giving. Yet he had spoken it with agony. He was speaking of death as her grandfather had spoken of conspiracy and the fear of madness. Surely he had not really loved Nikolai, so that just knowing he was dead pierced him through and through. He took off his spectacles, and she put out her hand for them, saying, 'Let me polish them,' so that she could stare into his naked eyes. But in the half-light they were merely circles of lustred darkness, and in any case they would never have told her anything. They had their own shutters.

Looking back into her eyes, he whispered, 'What's the negation of the negation here? What's the negation of death? Ah, you can't say. Only I know the answer. Perhaps nobody else has ever known it before. Our circumstances are terrible and unique. But perhaps I'm wrong there. History is terrible, possibly other people have been burned to the bone by such an obligation – such a —' Gently his fingers forced the spectacles out of her hand, he put them on again as if the nakedness of his eyes had suddenly become shameful to him. Unsteadily he told her, 'It's so awkward, not being able to explain to you. But you wouldn't understand, at least not with your mind. Your whole being might grasp the meaning of what's happened, of any action that was determined by necessity. The poise of your head, the elegance of your movements, they speak of consent to the force which makes the earth move round the sun, the same consent that's given by all the great statues of the world. But in the meantime you must take my word for it. For what happened to my friend. There was life at its best. There was beauty, the still focus on earth of this force which keeps the stars shining in their place like icons, that sends forth the planets like processions on Holy Days. Then death came, or rather the threat of death. It seemed that life at its best had to go down to the grave. Beauty had to go into the darkness like a shooting star. Perfection had to rot. I accepted that. I even willed it. It had to be. But I felt such horror I thought I would fall dead myself, a crumpled heap of clothes, nothing inside them when they picked them up, myself ground to dust by my heartbeat. Then suddenly my horror turned to something else. Thesis, antithesis, and synthesis. There came happiness. Such happiness. A glory for which there are no words. The spreading of pinions. The flight up to the sun. The fearless flight. Knowing that the sun will not consume one. Knowing that one will consume the sun with one's own fiercer, purer fire.' His voice broke, though his lips went on moving.

Watching him she was troubled by the suspicion that he was silently saying her name over and over again, as if he were practising some kind of magic against her. To get him back to talking she forced out the words, 'What can death have to do with happiness?'

'Nothing at all, if you are thinking of happiness as it's been known till now. But this is something new. I said, flying up to the sun. Within sight of the Absolute. There are no words for it. There could not be. For it has not existed till now.'

'So that's how it is,' she said, and composed her hands on her lap. She had worked so hard to make Kamensky believe that she had not heard what Chubinov had told her grandfather, and had thought she had succeeded. But this raving could mean only that she had failed, that he intended to kill her, and that killing her would give him such pleasure that it was useless to hope he could be deflected from his purpose. He was sitting quite still, in a tense dream of action like a cat before it springs, and on his lap his bandaged hand pointed towards her, as if under its pretended helplessness there was a weapon ready to discharge. Somehow she was sharing his secrets. Quite well she knew that he was imagining with joy the act of shooting her, or piercing her body with a knife, or throwing a bomb that would scatter her to fragments. If she could keep going till the morning, her father would come and save her. But the tears formed in her eyes, for she doubted if she had so long. He was so clever, and he wanted so much to kill her.

Kamensky rose and stretched himself and smiled down at her, as if she were something he were going to eat. Slowly he strolled towards the window, brushing by the hunched body of Madame Verrier, without taking care not to awake her. He was a cruel man. If it had been Chubinov who was here, as soon as his eyes had fallen on the nurse she would have become his sister, and her grandfather would have harshly classed her as an inferior, and then been tender with her. But to Kamensky she was no more than a chair or a table. Probably he could not relate her to anything he had ever read in a book.

With his back to the room he said, 'I am here, nowhere else but here, how wonderful that is,' and drew back the curtains. The music from the Ball stopped, and silence pressed into the room from outside. 'What a pity. I thought it would be dawn. I expected the first sunlight and the first birds, but it's still night. Only such an unstained night, I shouldn't feel aggrieved. Look at the stars. They might be tapers lit for your grandfather's death, the beeswax tapers you and I will be holding as we stand together at his funeral. Up there space should be smelling of beeswax, of honey.'

She wondered if that meant he planned to let her live until her grandfather was buried.

'And look at the white light over to the east, where the sun will rise. Such a pure light, against that blackness. Oh, Miss Laura, take me now to your grandfather. Let me kneel beside him and pray.'

She found herself on her feet. 'You can't do that.'

'But I must. I have so many things to tell him while he lingers on the threshold. I want to give thanks for all he did for me, and they'll not be ordinary thanks. Generosity like his dispenses special powers along with its other gifts. Now in this hard hour I can render them back to him.'

She told herself that she must do everything Kamensky

316

asked of her, until her father came. But she found herself standing in front of the folding doors. 'No. You can't go in there.'

'But why not? You and I could kneel side by side and join our prayers together. I'm a man of the new age, I am a technologist, but I belong also to the world of old and magic things. All, all is within the Absolute.'

She repeated, 'You can't go in there,' and he repeated, 'But why not?' There stirred within the gentleness of his voice a subdued suspicion, as if the conspiratorial elements in him had revived, though not at full strength. If he were still in any doubt as to whether she knew what Chubinov had told her grandfather, if he could yet be convinced that she did not know what he was, it might save her life if she let him pray by the dead as friends do. But she felt obliged to bar his way, and what was worse, to bar it in a way which showed she thought he was unfit. She had stiffened into the attitude of a priestess defending an altar from desecration, or rather, of a bad actress playing such a part. She had thrown her head back as far as it would go, her chin was sticking out, and her arms were stretched across the folding doors behind her like pump handles. But she could not hold herself naturally, perhaps because she really wanted him to know what she was thinking. If she could save her life only by sucking up to Kamensky, it was not worth saving. Yet the whole thing was silly. It could make no difference to Nikolai if Kamensky chose to go on acting the hypocrite for a few minutes beside his discarded body. But that was nonsense, she could not face the shame of letting him into the room where that body lay, yellow, finished, empty, but still invested with a kind of honour which would be spat on as soon as that sweet voice began to call on God and the Birthgiver. 'No,' she said, 'you can't,' and sighed deeply, for part of her wanted to live at any price.

Kamensky came even closer to her, his spectacles aiming point-blank at her face, stretching out his hands. She stared at them, revolted by the spurious bandage, and expecting him to perform some deadly conjuring trick, to bring some small murderous object down from his cuff into his palm. But he made them into a cradle. So, in the next room, her grandfather was holding the icon on his dead breast. He murmured, 'I see what it is. Your nature is so sweet. I suppose your grandfather's last seizure disfigured him, and you want to spare my feelings. Oh, Miss Laura, thank you for that thought. But death and I are not strangers —'

'I didn't think so.'

'No, indeed. A man of my age —'

He stopped, and looked over his shoulder at the door into the corridor and turned his back on her. There were sounds of cautious movement and whispering from outside, and a scratching round the lock. Someone was trying to get in, and furtively. It could not be her father. Perhaps it was some of those idealistic young men who went such beautiful mountain walks near Montreux, come to help Kamensky by killing her and running and leaving him appalled; everyone would believe him. But that could not be right. He meant to kill her himself and when they were alone. The joy was to be private. On the other hand, it might be Chubinov with some of his lot. It would be like him to have difficulties with a door that had opened easily enough for everyone else. She leaned back against the folding doors, resting against her grandfather's strength, while Kamensky took up his stance nearer the door, his knees slightly bent, his body twisted, his right hip forward, his hand deep in his trouser pocket. His gun would be there. At least he was not sure who was trying to get in; and indeed they could not be conspirators. They did not want people to hear them, but for some other cause than fear. A deep voice panted, 'But it's not locked,' and the door swung open, a woman was pushed in by the tall man behind her, who had a blacksmith's majesty. Coming out of the lit corridor, they were blind in the half-darkness and stood breathing deeply like spent runners, without knowing they were seen.

The man's great shoulders were a wide frame behind the woman's head, his great arms were about hers and crushed them to her sides, his great fingers went on kneading her bodice until his eyes grew accustomed to the muted light. The woman's dress was honey-coloured, shining too gently to be satin, and a veil of the same dim brightness flowed from a wreath of pale flowers on her straw-pale hair, falling about her shoulders and her breast, where a fold of it was caught between two of the man's fingers, one loaded with a thick sombre ring. The vacillating gaslight made her skirt and veil tremble like a settling moth, and about her neck ebbed and flowed the blue shimmer of old diamonds. Colourless and vague and shaped like a fine vase, she stood there in an attitude of resignation, as if she found what had brought her there so strange that her capacity for surprise was exhausted, and she could accept passively the further strangeness that in this room, which she must have expected to be empty, there should be a woman asleep in a chair, a young girl in a peignoir, who had thrown herself back against a door, and in the middle of the room a man standing in a contorted position and speaking to her peremptorily in an unknown language. She continued to inspect them with a dazed curiosity as if they might move, and by their movement tell her what she ought to be thinking about what had happened to her.

For a time the tall man stood as she did, shocked into waxwork stillness, while through the open door there came the noise of the people in the ballroom below laughing and clapping, followed by a silence, and then more laughter and a rolling volley of applause. Then he came to himself and made an embarrassed and impatient gesture which his shaking shadow repeated more widely across the corner of the room. The woman stirred, and a tremor ran down her long gloved arms. Slowly she moved her pale flowered head from side to side, and as if drowsily throwing off drowsiness, uttered a sound of distress, pleasant in tone but not interesting, and shrank into the arms of the man behind her, who grasped her as he had done before, and drew her backwards. It was impossible to know how he felt about her from the way he touched her. He might have been moving a piece of furniture. The door banged, cutting off the first bars of the *Marseillaise,* it was softly reopened and softly closed.

Laura began to cry. Now Kamensky would probably start all over again wanting to pray by her grandfather, and she could not go on and on being brave. Also an irrational grief was hurting her chest. Surely there was no reason why those two people should make her feel humiliated and deserted and passed over, why she should have had a sense of loss and guilt because she had not clearly seen the tall man's face. In the half-light it had been only a dark mask. She would have liked to hurry along the corridor and catch them up, and lay a hand on the man's arm, so that he would turn round and look down on her. Yet she did not think she would have liked his face. She wished she had never seen the two of them, she would have liked to break them as in her childhood she had broken dolls which had seemed to her frightening. But all the same Kamensky was talking shocking nonsense about them. He had taken her hand and was calling them disgusting beasts and angrily repeating over and over again how terrible it was that they should have come in when she, she was there. But they had meant no harm. It was improbable that they had read dangerous books in which they had found a command to kill her.

'Miss Laura, you must stop crying. Forget that shameless couple. Oh, you are so free, so intelligent, so brave, so affectionate and so innocent, above all so innocent. To think that they should breathe the same air, it's insufferable —'

'I'm not crying because of those people. I'm crying because I want to go to sleep.'

'Oh, Miss Laura, I will leave you now. But I will not go far.'

'I'm sure you won't.'

'No, indeed, I will take a chair and sit in the corridor outside until morning.'

'Thank you. Thank you very much. My father will find you there.'

13

LAURA WOKE INTO a dream which was a memory. When she was quite little the whole family, her grandfather and grandmother as well, went to stay with a cousin who lived in Scotland. One day Nanny had taken her and her brothers into the dining-room where the elders were sitting over their dessert at a long, bright luncheon-table surmounted by a pyramid of pink and white carnations and asparagus fern. Nikolai called her to his side and held out to her a marron glacé, impaled on a fork. She had lifted her mouth to it, feeling as if her constant dream of being an animal had come true, and she had been changed into the tame fawn kept by the children of the house, which every morning after breakfast waited at the foot of the steps leading down from the terrace to the park and lifted its muzzle for scraps of bread-and-butter. It might be that if she could hold her breath for five minutes or pass some other magical test, her grandfather would speak to her in animal language and that she might understand and answer in the same tongue. He must have divined that she was telling herself a fairy-tale, for when she had swallowed the marron glacé he gave her a long, secret-sharing gaze and put down the fork with a sorcerer's gesture.

Her heart melted with love; and she became aware that she was being shaken, and pulled up and out of the bedclothes by the strong small hand of Madame Verrier, at whom she smiled, forgetting all that was disagreeable; the woman had such an amusing flavour, sweet and acid at the same time, like raspberries.

'Your father's here. In France. In Grissaint. In this hotel. Third floor down. In the landlord's office.'

Laura took her hand and kissed it, she was glad she was abroad where one could do such things. She looked towards the folding doors and said in Russian, 'Grandfather, I'm safe, my father's here,' and repeated to herself in English, 'he's here, he's here.'

Madame Verrier said slowly, their hands still gripped, 'You rely on your father a lot, don't you? How pleasant for you.'

'I was frightened,' said Laura, and under the nurse's clinically inquisitive gaze, she explained, 'frightened at seeing my grandfather die.'

'Naturally. Now get up and dress.'

'But can't my father come up here?'

'He didn't want to. I mean, he couldn't. He's talking to somebody from the Town Hall. About the return of your poor grandfather's body to Paris. You know what we French are.

Papers, papers, papers, always papers. If you're in a hurry to see him, jump out of bed.'

'Please wait a moment.' She was shaken by her renewed fear. 'Where's Monsieur Kamensky?'

'Ah, him. He's gone out into the town.'

'Did he meet my father?'

'Yes, as soon as he arrived.'

'Did they talk?'

'Yes. For half an hour, I'd say.'

'And then he went into the town?'

'Yes. Why, you're more like a judge than a young girl, asking all these questions. Do get up.'

'Did Monsieur Kamensky say where he was going?'

'Not a word. But he and I, we don't feel any great need to communicate. When I left this room to go to the *cabinet de toilette* I found him asleep in a chair outside the door. Well, if that's how he likes to spend his nights, I've no objection. But he woke up and told me about two people bursting into the room in the middle of the night, and what an affront it was to your innocence. I bit his head off. Very tiresome those two coming in like that, but it sets my teeth on edge to hear any man talking about female innocence.'

'Did he say when he would be back?'

'Not a word. But do get up. The place is upside down after that Ball, and you'll have to wash in this basin, you can't have a bath. All I could get is this crock of hot water, and it's not too hot either. I'll bring you some breakfast once you're downstairs with your father.'

But when she said that she was ready Madame Verrier denied it. 'No. Your stockings are not straight, and your hair, you haven't brushed it properly. You may be going downstairs to see you father but there's nobody, but absolutely nobody, of the opposite sex before whom we can safely appear at a disadvantage.' The poor woman was always making remarks suitable for printing on a calendar designed to prove that no day in the year was worth living. Her father would never have cared that her hair was too bushy, he did not judge her as if she were a stranger; and when he heard that her life was in danger he would run his hand through her hair, as he had done when he had saved her from the sea, like a man counting the coins of his treasure.

Expectation of the rage he would feel made her tingle as they went out into the corridor, going through the alternating tunnels of darkness and the shafts of light slanting out of open bedroom doors, which had pails and brooms on the threshold or chammy leathers hanging on the door-handles. Out of one room there suddenly protruded a gaunt old head under a mob-cap and a voice whistled through gaps left by missing teeth, addressing nobody in particular but with a personal vehemence, like a prophet crying in the wilderness, 'Hurry up after four-twenty, they've just this moment gone down, they've left some of their rubbish.' A nightgown too weightless to take the air flew hesitantly out and sank on the carpet in a rosy transparent quoit. 'No use to me,' the old voice cackled, and another old voice from another room cackled a comment which Laura could not understand and made Madame Verrier cry out a wordless laughing admonition. Nikolai was dead but not much else was wrong.

When they got down to the landing at the top of the great gilded staircase they had to wait. The double doors into the ballroom were ajar, and beside them stood a stout elderly woman with a moustache, her pomp and her lax black skirts suggesting the cassocked priesthood, in spite of her loaded bodice. She was holding a large bunch of keys with a ritual air, and out of the ballroom there filed, sober as nuns, all the women in blue-grey cotton gowns who had the day before been polishing the parquet floor so dutifully. Beyond them could be seen a narrow vista of the lovely room, quiet as if it had never throbbed to the clumping rhythm of the dance-band, given over again to the pure light from the high windows. Apollo and his nymphs had a simple morning look, as if they too had stripped to wash out of a basin, as she had just done; the figures in low relief on the ceiling were vague as the pattern on a damask cloth; and the chandeliers were back in their holland bags. After the last servant had passed down the stairs, the moustachioed woman locked the door with an air of deter-mination, and followed them with a heavy step, slower than theirs. It was the sort of thing which makes historians write, 'So ended the something or other'.

That fitted well enough. She would not choose to come back to the town where her grandfather had died and where she had had to sit the night through enveloped in Kamensky's murderous sweetness. It was a pity that this meant losing this ballroom, with its air of elegant fashion and eternal peace, and a worse pity that she must also lose Madame Verrier, whose arm round her waist felt protective, but not in a humiliating way, it was as if they were sharing an adventure. Had they been two women soldiers, two Maids of Saragossa, this is how the one that had not been wounded would have supported the one that was. Her heart ached as it used to at the end of the summer holidays, when she had to leave behind her at the sea-side all the people she had come to love, particularly the blacksmith's mother and the oldest of the fishermen. It hurt worse if, at the actual hour when the dog-cart came to drive them to the station up on the moors, the tide was out, the sea a blue bar far beyond the yellow sands, withdrawn from the bastions on each side of the cove. One way or another, there was too much loss in life.

She said, 'Madame Verrier, you must come to London and stay with us.'

'You're very kind. And you're a great charmer. But alas, my work is here.'

'But surely you take a holiday sometimes.'

They were not going all the way down the great staircase. Madame Verrier stopped in front of a panel which looked like all the rest, turned a gilt knob which might have been an ornament, and led the way into a dark passage. 'Holidays,' she said, in sudden dreaminess through the dusk, 'I always spend them in the same place. A little village in the Dordogne. Nobody knows of it. There's nothing there but an inn and a river, not a big river, quite a little river, running between rocks. There are pools under the rocks, and hills above, covered with woods.'

She was still smiling when they came out into the daylight again, on a glassed-in gallery round a large courtyard, where much was going on, full of a bustle of coaches and gigs. Now Laura knew she was going to see her father she was at ease and took her time, amused because the glass was so thick that not a sound came through, and so full of flaws that every few yards the vehicles and the horses and the ostlers and the travellers were elongated into rippling shapes, as if they were doing all their bustling far down under water.

Before the last door in the corridor Madame Verrier said, 'Here,' and they entered an encumbered room which was half-dark. It did not need to be so, for the window was high and wide enough, but the dingy damask curtains had fallen away from some of their rings and hung loose from a bent rod, not to be drawn clear. On the walls hung a misty mirror or two and some crumbling gilt frames enclosing squares of darkness, in the depths of which floated white wigs and shining crosses and medals, bits of necks and bosoms, half the branches of a tree and the midriff of a palace; and two newer pictures of an elderly man and woman, garish but insubstantial, portraits of coarse ghosts. There was a tall and rather splendid bookcase, choked with books in fine bindings, some crammed in across the tops of others, and on the chimney-piece was an ormolu clock, also rather splendid, surmounted by Father Time, with a wad of letters stuffed between him and his scythe. At a flat desk, littered with papers, her father was sitting, bright in the dusky room. He did not see his daughter, he was settling something; the two Professors stood in front of the desk, like prefects called before their headmaster, and a fourth man, probably the official from the Town Hall, was standing by the window, his back to the room, scrutinising some papers and putting them one by one into an envelope.

It was delightful to look at her father when he did not know he was being looked at, to enjoy his quiet handsomeness, and recognise the quality her mother often mentioned as his peculiar virtue. Tania often told her children that never once in all their life together had she seen him jealous of another man's success. For that they should look up to him, because it meant a triumph over his own ambition, which was strong; and men were more prone to jealousy than women, since they were not teased out of it when they were little boys in the nursery, as little girls were. Simply his admiration for what was admirable in other people flowed so strongly that it could not be dammed by any selfish consideration. And there Laura saw him at the desk, leaning forward in the chair, enjoying the quality of the two doctors who stood before him, a smile crinkling the skin round his eyes, his hand lying open before him, palm upward, as if ready to catch a ball when it was thrown.

Professor Barrault was saying: 'I agree with my colleague. Nothing more could have been done. Not, I think, by any doctor. The state of the patient was outside the pattern for which the practice of medicine and surgery prepares us. I am probably not expressing myself with what I hope is my usual lucidity, for I have, I don't know why, a terrible headache this morning —' it seemed to Laura that both Saint-Gratien and Madame Verrier silently giggled – 'so I will simply say that the wonder was not that we failed to keep him alive when he got here, but that he got here alive. It was, I suppose, a matter of a formidable will, which we recognised, transmitted in a graceful form, in your most remarkable daughter.'

'Yes,' said Saint-Gratien, with a catlike edge to his voice, 'A pity she had to go through this ordeal alone. The episode made me understand how wise it is that we doctors have always to leave word where we are, no matter how inconvenient it may be.'

Madame Verrier said severely, 'Mademoiselle Laura is here,' and they all swung round. Her father pulled himself up from the heavy Empire arm-chair and came round the desk, drew her into his arms and kissed her on both cheeks, then pushed her gently away, laid his hands on her shoulders and scrutinised her uneasily. She told him, 'Oh, I'm all right. It wasn't so terrible as you'd think. He was very good about dying.' Turning towards the doctors, she said, 'It's kind of you to worry about me, but really I didn't mind except for the sadness, and that had to come some time, he was old, I realise that.' She wanted to get them out of the room so that she could tell her father that she was in danger, she had begun a social smile of dismissal, when she became stone. The man at the window had turned round, and he was not an official from the Town Hall, he was Kamensky.

'Please,' she said to her father, 'please.' She herself felt that her beseeching stare was almost a grimace, but his hazel eyes

326

which, though brilliant, were always vague, as if he did not care to notice what was close at hand, were surely vaguer than usual. Altogether there was something strange about the meeting. It was as if a cloud had taken her in his arms and not her father.

'Yes, I expect he made a good end,' he admitted, 'but nobody would have wished you to share in quite such a heroic experience at your age, my poor girl.' He spoke calmly, but as if he had forgotten there were other people in the room. 'We must get you out of this atmosphere, give you a change, send you somewhere cheerful. What about going to stay with your cousins in Florence? It won't be too hot till July and then they go to their place in Portofino. You haven't seen Italy yet.'

She exclaimed, 'But I don't want to leave my mother!' At once she added, 'Or you.' But he should have understood that. Sometimes her nurse and governess had told her she was unkind because she made more fuss over her father than over her mother.

Yet he was looking as if he had been wounded to the quick by some tactlessness on her part. He said, and it was evident that now he remembered that there were other people in the room, 'And Monsieur Kamensky says there was some queer business with a man in the train. Who was he?'

'Well, he was a Russian —'

'He would be that,' her father said, with a shade of grimness. Then with an apologetic glance at Kamensky he repeated it as if simply commenting on a matter of fact. 'Yes, he would be that. But you've no idea who he was, or what it was that made your grandfather collapse?'

'Not the slightest,' she lied. 'Didn't Monsieur Kamensky explain about that? Grandfather sent me into another compartment. I wish now I hadn't gone. But how could I tell what was going to happen? The man was just mousey. You couldn't have dreamed he would do anybody any harm, though I gathered he was mixed up with Grandfather's disgrace, and, to be just, I don't believe he meant to upset Grandfather so badly.'

Her father said to the other men in the room: 'It's all very disquieting. My wife's father had, as you saw, this magnificent physique. You may not have grasped that his mind was as remarkable as his body. When he was young he was a very good soldier. If he had cared to stay in the army he could have ended up as Chief of Staff. He chose instead to be an administrator, and he was superb in his field, granted how different his country was from ours; and he had a statesmanly way of looking at things, very surprising, all things considered. He had great possessions, for what that's worth.' She thought she saw mockery on Kamensky's face. But she knew her father was speaking sincerely. He had been brought up among the Anglo-Irish gentry, most of them bone poor. 'Then things went wrong for him. As apparently they can very easily in Russia, if I may say so without offending you, Monsieur Kamensky. So someone whom my girl here can only describe as "mousey" could corner him in a train, and it's all over, the huge body, the six languages, the Ministries that worked like Swiss watches, the mines in the Ural and the oil-wells down at Baku, the intellect. Disgrace can work all that out without a shot fired.'

The three men murmured sympathy, and Laura stepped forward and said, 'Please, Father,' joining her hands under her chin in petition. Surely when he saw how wildly she was staring at him he would have the sense to say to them all, 'Forgive me, but would you leave us alone for a few minutes. I want to be alone with my daughter.' But he said to her with a false air, which made her think him still hurt by her tactlessness, whatever form that might have taken, 'In any case, I was horrified when I got in from the House of Commons and found your telegram and realised what you'd have to go through before I could reach you.'

'Oh, poor Daddy! You were at the House?'

'Yes, we had an all-night sitting.'

'How funny. Professor Saint-Gratien sent two telegrams for me, one to the House and one to Radnage Square, didn't you, Professor Saint-Gratien?'

After the Professor had uttered his faint assent, a silence fell.

It was broken by Barrault. 'How young you are, Mademoiselle. If you were as old as we are, you would know that of two telegrams, one very often goes astray.' They all followed him in laughing at nothing, and Madame Verrier said with soft roughness, 'Professor Saint-Gratien, may I speak to you for a moment about that case of yours that's booked for tomorrow?' The little silvery man bent his head over Laura's hand, and his eyes looked into hers, not ignoring her, seeing her as her father had not yet seen her. When he left the room with Madame Verrier she called after them, hardly caring if they were busy and she was plaguing them, 'But we must say good-bye before I go,' and they answered as if they had known her a long time and would not think of forsaking her, 'Oh, yes, oh, yes, but certainly. We're not going far, we'll be out in the gallery, there's just something we must settle.'

Professor Barrault cleared his throat and began to speak. 'I have heard, Mr Rowan, that the members of your Houses of Parliament are far more given to classical quotations than our Deputies and our Senators.'

Kamensky had moved across the room and was standing beside her. She shuddered back from the threat of him, and mastered herself, and moved closer, to show her friendship. Her father answered Barrault absently, searching on the desk for a pen and finding it, smoothing out a sheet of writing-paper in front of him. 'Gladstone and Robert Lowe seem always to have been at it, but that's a long time ago. Still, Asquith comes up with a tag now and then. He tries very hard.'

If Professor Barrault was going to talk about the classics she had better sit down. When she had settled in a chair, Kamensky bent over her, murmured, 'I haven't said good-morning to you yet,' and kissed her hand. She was determined not to flinch, but found that an effort. Other men barely brushed her skin with their lips, but Kamensky laid his whole mouth on her knuckles, and the man must have a fever, it was so hot. 'I raised the subject of classical quotations,' the Professor continued, 'because this family tragedy of yours, in which my colleague and I have played so unhappily ineffectual a part, has often recalled lines from our dear masters in the antique world. The vision of our race accorded to Virgil showed it at its most refined, its proudest, and its least perturbed. What does he tell us the noble ask for as they stand

329

beside their dead? *Manibus date lilia plenis.* Give lilies with full hands. *Purpureos spargam flores.* That those bright flowers I may scatter. I think "bright" is a legitimate translation of *purpureos.*'

Kamensky had gone back to his place by the window. Mr Rowan asked him in an irritable undertone what he had done with the blotting-paper, and then said civilly, 'Yes, yes, Professor, phrases no less marvellous for being quoted and requoted.'

'They came into my mind as I watched your daughter at her pious duties beside her grandfather's death-bed. She was a truly Virgilian figure. Her youth might well have been appalled by his sufferings, but she listened to his lamentations as calmly as if they were sitting together in his study or in his garden. Her appearance never became disordered, and several times I saw her grandfather regarding her with pride and the pleasure with which one salutes a woman who, when the wind is no longer tempered to her femininity, yet remains feminine.'

He had hit, Laura thought, on one of the thoughts least likely to occur to her grandfather on his death-bed or at any other time of his life. But there was no harm in it. Of course it was in a way maddening, that he was not talking about her, but about her looks. He was shutting her into a book because he liked her appearance in the same way he liked the book, and he had no eyes for her real troubles. He was not sorry for her because in some way she could not understand she had offended her father, and she did not want Kamensky to kill her. Now she was trembling with fear of Kamensky. He had found the blotting-paper and returned to his chair and even after she had turned her face away from him, she was aware that he was regarding her with an alarming intensity. He reminded her of the gardener in Radnage Square, who in summer burned his initials on any new spade or fork he got by focusing the sun-rays on the wooden handle with a magnifying glass. This was surprising. She would have supposed the desire to murder ice cold, not burning hot.

'An unavailing service, Virgil called the scattering of these lilies on the dead, and of course they are. But it is only if mourners perform such unavailing services that the grave loses

330

its terror. Good-bye, Mademoiselle, I shall never forget you. Good-bye, Mr Rowan. I'm uplifted by having met a representative of English Parliamentarianism.' Barrault hesitated before letting go Laura's hand, and said sorrowfully, 'Look, the child is pale, far too pale. Good-bye, Monsieur Menshikov, may you have a pleasant journey back to your country.'

The door closed and Edward Rowan took up his pen and then set it down, to say, 'Laura, a very charming speech has been made in your honour. If it should later occur to you that it was not quite spontaneous, and that he had perhaps written it out before he left home and learned it by heart, don't think less of the compliment but more.' He looked at her quite kindly. Whatever her fault had been, it was forgiven. He always liked to hear her or Tania praised.

Gaily she said, 'Yes, we must tell Mummie about it.'

She had inflicted the wound again. Coldly he turned to the paper on his desk. Surely things had not gone so badly that she could offend him simply by speaking of her mother.

Edward Rowan was about to take up his pen, but turned to Kamensky. 'By the way, surely your name is not Menshikov?'

Kamensky gave a restrained smile, amused, but not presuming to invite a superior to share his amusement, yet indicating that it was there to be shared, should superiority condescend. Her temper flared up at the joke this powerful man had played on her grandfather for years, in St Petersburg and in the apartment in the Avenue Kléber, that he was now preparing to play on her father, by building up, brick by brick, a huge construction of lowliness.

'No,' he said, 'that's not my name. To a Frenchman one Russian name is the same as another. At least, I hope that's the reason why the Professor made the mistake, for I wouldn't like to think anything about me had reminded him of the most celebrated of the Menshikov family, the Marshal who had the temerity to cheat Peter the Great out of a hundred thousand roubles over a wheat swindle. Anyway, the Professor must be pardoned for forgetting the quite uninteresting fact that I'm Alexander Gregorievitch Kamensky.'

Edward made a slight inclination of the head. 'I'd not forgotten it. I hope the Professor doesn't get his medical facts as mixed. I suppose the old gentleman did get as good medical attention as he needed.'

'You needn't have a moment's anxiety on that count. Not one moment. I have friends in the town. I went to see them early this morning. They tell me that Professor Barrault, the one with the inordinate affection for the classics, is the Dean of the medical college here, and has a high reputation, and that the other, Professor Saint-Gratien, has an even higher reputation. He is a Grissaintois, but was a distinguished surgeon in Paris till his father died and left him the old family house in town and a property near the coast, which influenced him to take a chair in the college. The only thing against him is that, unfortunately, he is a supporter of Captain Dreyfus.'

Laura and her father stared at him in sudden unity. 'I'm not likely to think any the worse of him for that,' said Edward Rowan drily.

Kamensky was taken aback. He jerked up his head and there was surprise and irritation and shame on his face. She could see him, when he got back to that little room in the Hôtel de Guipuzcoa et Racine, or it might be the Hôtel San Marino, whichever he got back to first, sitting on his bed and writing in a little note-book, probably in code, that English reactionaries were for some reason not anti-Dreyfusards, his mouth resentful under his beard, because for once an insincerity had misfired, and also he had been misinformed. She could have laughed aloud, she was not sure she had not done so. Kamensky neatened his face and said in tones of melancholy sweetness, 'Also, Professor Saint-Gratien is known to have an unfortunate attachment.'

After a pause Edward said slowly, scribbling on the blotting-paper, 'Ah, an unfortunate attachment.'

'To a most unsuitable person. So my friends in the town tell me. It has caused quite a scandal. Many say he is finished, his career ruined. Our hypocritical society does not forgive. I believe it's so in your country too.' He sighed and dropped a single monosyllable as if it were a tear-drop. 'Dilke,' he said.

Slowly Edward tore up the blotting-paper and dropped the fragments in the wastepaper basket. 'Well, if the doctors are really first-class men, it can have made no difference that I wasn't here.'

'None at all,' said Kamensky. Then the words forced themselves out of his mouth. 'Except for Miss Laura.'

'I was all right,' she told him coldly. Again her temper rose against both of them. Kamensky was exploiting her to torment her father; and her father was being stupid about Kamensky. He was being taken in by Kamensky more thoroughly than she had ever been, accepting him on his own terms as a little underling, a bottle-washer, a nobody. Even she had had the wits to guess from time to time that he had crossed the line and won a place among the people who mattered, though she had been fooled into thinking that he had earned it by loyalty. He had not noticed that Kamensky's annoyance at being wrong about their attitude to Dreyfus was that of a man who finds himself wrong and is accustomed not only to being right but to being told that he is right. Just for the moment he had been like one of her father's grander friends, Cabinet Ministers or Ambassadors, if at Sunday luncheon somebody worsted them in argument. Then in revenge for having been proved wrong, he had said that thing, that poisoned thing, about an unfortunate attachment, and her father had not seen its malice. She must separate the two men. She leaned forward and said, her voice cracking, 'Don't you want to see Grandfather? Let's go up together.'

'Yes, it would be a good thing to get it over, we must leave for the station some time soon.' Edward pushed back the heavy chair, took a step towards the door, halted and turned to Kamensky with a courtesy obviously framed to put an inferior at his ease. 'Since you've been such a good friend to my wife's family, and so kind to my daughter, I should be glad if you'd accompany us.'

Kamensky bowed his head modestly. 'You are doing me a great honour.'

Laura did not move. It was not fair. Not only was she not going to see her father alone, Kamensky had got his wish and would invade her grandfather's room. By now Nikolai would be further on his way to God, he might not mind so much. Yet surely his honour, vulnerable to insult as it had been to injury

333

by the Tsar, would cling about his body till it disappeared, till it was dust, so long as it was remembered. There came a knock at the door, and in her absorption in questions of where her grandfather's soul might be in eternity and his honour in time, she expected a messenger to enter who would be charged with precise answers, probably a priest of the true church, bearded and wearing a high biretta. But it was the landlord, followed by a waiter carrying a tray.

'This coffee is for the young lady,' he said to the waiter in an advisory tone, as if the poor fellow would have made some foolish use of it unless directed by a superior intelligence. 'Good morning, Mademoiselle. Hardly can I venture to hope that you slept well, simply I must ask you to believe that I wish you had. Madame Verrier ordered this breakfast for you, she has an excellent heart in spite of everything, and I beg you not to believe all you hear. No, not a quarter of it. Where are you going with that tray, Leon? Ah. How odd I haven't had that table-leg repaired. I cherish that table. Part of the original furniture left here by the aristocrats who gave this great house its tone. Never mind, Leon, put the tray down on the little table. But what's that? What's that on the little table?'

They all turned to see. He sounded as surprised as if he had caught sight of a hooded cobra.

'A bottle of cognac. How extraordinary. Ah, the mysterious things which happen even in a perfectly conducted establishment. Who can have left a bottle of cognac in my office? Not me, I swear. Wine I drink, from time to time, but not brandy. I rarely touch the stuff, not more than two or three times a year.' He weighed it in his hand. 'Empty,' he murmured, 'Empty. How can that be? But as I was saying, Sir Rowan —'

Kamensky was bending over the tray. 'I'll pour out your coffee, Miss Laura. Princesses should be waited on.'

She thanked him and watched closely to see he did not put anything in it.

'You see, I know how you like it. A little milk. No sugar, unless there should be a tiny lump like this. Yes, you're quite right. I've never before seen you drink coffee in the morning. But I've sat beside you as you drank coffee after luncheon and after dinner, and on my observations I've based a theory regarding how you would take it at breakfast, and the theory's correct, isn't it?'

She knew that behind this meaningless patter there was a meaning: 'I've watched you so carefully that I can predict anything you might say or do at any moment of the day or night. You won't get away.' Out of pride she managed to return his smile.

'You won't like this coffee. It's not as you get it in Paris. There's chicory in it. But take plenty of butter on your croissants. It's the best in the world, here in Northern France.'

Again it was as if he were a cannibal and meant to eat her.

'Yes, yes,' her father was saying to the landlord, 'we've got all we want, your staff has looked after us admirably; please don't trouble about us any more.' Though he was an impatient man, he often lost his impatience under provocation as other people lose their tempers. He would show an astonishing forebearance to drunken cabbies, slow railway-porters, crazed beggars, which he said he had learned when he was a young officer. Old soldiers, he would say, who were drunken and slow, might have some very good qualities, such as courage and comradely kindness; and he had never been sorrier for anyone in his life than for the men who enlisted in the army because they were too eccentric to follow one of the usual trades, and were thrown out because the army found them over-eccentric too.

The landlord replied: 'You'll excuse me for making all these enquiries about your comfort. But I'm moved partly by Christian sympathy with the bereaved, which I hope is as strong in me as it is in the next man, and partly because the death of his Highness the Duke on my premises was, if you know what I mean, a challenge. I am a frustrated man. I would have loved to spend my life in the service of glory.' He looked round the dim and disordered room and put his hands to his forehead. 'Nobody would believe what a headache I have this morning. But why should that be an occasion for surprise? I ran backwards and forwards from the dawn of yesterday until the dawn of today, preparing for the Ball, seeing that the Ball achieved itself, doing this, doing that, eating nothing, and, of course drinking nothing. In my position a man cannot drink.'

'No, indeed,' said Edward Rowan, 'and now my daughter and my friend and I must —'

'Spare me but one more minute,' said the landlord. 'Among all the rich Englishmen who form your circle, do you know one who would like to buy this hotel?'

'By some odd chance, no,' said Edward Rowan, impatiently.

Kamensky had started fussing about Laura's breakfast tray again. In a low voice, as if he were offering her some confidential service of a grave nature, he told her that as he was sure she would not like the strawberry jam that had been sent in on her tray, and as there would be no marmalade in the hotel, he would be delighted to get her honey. She told him bitterly that he need not trouble, too much sweetness of any kind made her sick. He answered: 'How wrong that you should not want honey. When we used to sit in the little drawing-room and you and your mother chose seats far away from the lamp, in case your grandfather should want to take up his book, your hair and your mother's reminded me of that honey, the specially rich honey, we get in Russia.'

'Of course, of course, I realise,' the landlord was continuing, 'that even the resources of such Englishmen as would be your friends must be strained by the beautiful castles you all possess, the vast studs of race-horses, your fleets of yachts, the week-end parties you give for the Prince of Wales – or is he your king? But even so I would think that among your friends there must be one, perhaps of the Byron sort, who will say to you one day as you sit together in the Turkish baths of your magnificent clubs, magnificent but not ostentatious, "I'm tired of drawing my income from prosaic stocks and shares, I would like a financial adventure, I seek an investment with more fantasy to it, more panache"; and you will reply, "My friend I know the very thing, a hotel, but a hotel which is more than a hotel, the hearth of one of the greatest families of France, a hearth still warm, never allowed to get cold, tended by persons insignificant, yes, in themselves, but not without sentiment." Your friend, believe me, will answer, "I can hardly believe that such an opportunity exists", and he will not wait till you have brought him here.'

His spreading arms and upturned eyes suggested that he was standing in some immense hall, but as his gaze followed his expository gesture, his face fell. 'Seeing all these papers scattered about this office, you might suppose them bills. A pardonable error, none of us can help being infected by the cynicism of the modern world. But an error all the same. These papers are receipts. Oh, there may be a bill or two among them, one here or there, but all the rest are receipts so many that the stamps on them must go far to paying the salaries of all our local officials. Ah, that reminds me. My primary purpose in coming here was to bring you the papers which have been sent along from the Town Hall this very moment – this very moment —'

Edward Rowan sighed and sat down again. His good humour was wearing thin. 'Hand them over, there's a good fellow, we're in a hurry, we must be getting on to Paris.'

The landlord stood by the desk for a moment or two, but Edward Rowan did not look up from the papers. 'It's of no consequence,' said the landlord at last, in a bright voice. There was no response, and he tried a second time. 'It doesn't matter at all.' When there still was no response, he shook his head and made his way to the door. As he passed Laura his moist eyes looked into hers, and she smiled and said, 'The croissants are delicious.'

The landlord waved his hand towards them, as if encouraging them in their deliciousness. There came the mince-pie smell again, but not as strong as it had been yesterday. 'Ah, Mademoiselle, it's only an accident which has caused me to offend Sir Rowan. All would have gone well if Napoleon had been allowed to live out his life. These papers, these papers, these insupportable papers, he would have rid France of them by one of those simple edicts with which his genius so often inspired him.' He slunk out soft-footed as a beaten dog.

Kamensky had drawn his chair close to hers, and though his head was bowed she knew he was looking at her obliquely. He muttered that it was a long time since he had breakfasted, and he would be glad if he might finish what she had left half-eaten

337

on her plate. That was surprising. The pale-gold feathers of the bitten pastry merged into a streak of the more golden butter among the crumbs on the china, and she would not herself have cared to eat anything like that from anybody else's plate. 'Shan't we ring and get the waiter to bring you a fresh one?' she suggested, but he shook his head, saying with a curious bashful obstinacy, 'It's that one I want.' It occurred to her that he really felt faint after his long fast, and that he feared it would take a long time to get hold of the waiter, and then she gave it to him gladly. It was pleasant to give food to anybody hungry, no matter who it was. She forgot for the moment that he meant to kill her.

At last her father pushed away the papers, saying they were in order. 'Thank heavens for that. I shall be glad to get away from here. That landlord's in a bad way, poor wretch. This must have been a fine place till he got hold of it. But now the wreck's complete. It's an odd thing, I've noticed it not only in hotels and inns and shops that are running down, but when I've had to call on men who've been unfortunate in one way or another; something goes wrong with the buildings where they live or do business. It's like going into a vault. All disgrace smells alike. Differences in ruin are only matters of degree.'

So that was why he had not liked visiting the apartment in the Avenue Kléber. She supposed she could not blame him. It frightened her too, that the shadows in the passages seemed a kind of dust.

Her father pushed back his chair and stood up. 'Now, Monsieur Kamensky, we'd better go upstairs and do our last duty. Just one or two things I want to settle.' He looked across at Laura and said, 'Monsieur Kamensky is not coming to Paris with us, he is waiting here till your grandfather's coffin is ready and will bring it back to Paris by a late train.' She sighed with relief. In a little while she would certainly be alone with her father, watching him change to what he used to be, as he heard her story and made plans for her safety. But he went on, 'You're quite sure they'll be able to have the funeral the day after tomorrow, as they wish, they don't suddenly change their plans?'

'It's not a matter of the family's wishes,' answered Kamen-

338

sky primly. 'It's our fixed custom to bury our dead on the third day after death.'

'That's good news,' said her father. 'It's important I get back to London as soon as possible. We politicians aren't free agents, you know, and my Party's run into some special difficulties lately. There's a division coming on when all of us will be needed. So I'm glad that so far as I can see, I can count on leaving Paris the day after the funeral, or the day after that. There should be nothing to keep me. All I have to do is to get Laura off to her cousins in Florence or take her back to London with me. I must get her out of this atmosphere at once.'

He spoke with passionate insincerity, as if he felt he had suffered a wrong which gave him a right to say what he knew to be untrue, and rantingly too, as if he hoped to start an argument in which he would exercise that right still more freely. That was why she stayed silent, though it was in her mind to say, 'Well, I don't really like the atmosphere of Radnage Square much as it is just now,' or 'It isn't my mother's fault that her father has died in inconvenient circumstances, and it might have happened even if they hadn't been Russian.' But Kamensky uttered a sharp exclamation before she could speak, and she turned on him in surprise. He had lost all his self-possession, his face was white. 'Excuse me, Mr Rowan – I'm sure you know well what you're doing but – would it really be worth your while for you and your daughter to return to London for so short a time?'

'So short a time? But I will be staying in London. I've no intention of returning to Paris in the near future. I'm not my own master. I'm tied by my Parliamentary duties.'

'Your Parliamentary duties,' echoed Kamensky, nodding politely, but after a second incredulity got the better of him. 'You're really quite sure that you don't mean to attend the Requiem of the Ninth Day?'

'What Requiem?'

'The Requiem held on the ninth day after death. If I may say so, we Russians regard it as very important.'

'What, another service!' exclaimed Mr Rowan sinking back into the arm-chair. 'From all I can find out, the funeral is interminable, but is that not the end of the business? On the

339

ninth day, did you say? That's seven days from now. I can't stay till then,' he said miserably, 'I really can't.'

'A pity,' said Kamensky, still polite but awkwardly so, as if he did not wish to correct a superior, but he still thought that there was a misunderstanding here which had to be put right. 'You must understand, this Requiem has an overwhelming religious significance for us. We have three supremely important Requiems for our dead which we think correspond with three stages in the soul's journey towards judgment. On the third day after our beloved's death we bury him, and help him with our prayers and rejoice with him because he has broken his bond with life and has been guided by his angels into the presence of God. There he is shown the wonders of Paradise and the beauty of righteousness —'

'Let me get this clear. You are now talking of a Requiem?'

'Yes, the first of the major Requiems.'

'Good God, is this an extra service, in addition to the funeral service?'

'No, it is the same. Or rather it is part of the funeral service.' He cleared his throat. Laura saw that he was going to make the whole thing even longer and more boring than it was just out of spite against her father. She tapped her foot with impatience at his malice. 'I can explain how it fits into that—'

'No, no, continue about the Requiems.'

'As I was saying, on the third day after the death God shows the soul the wonders of paradise and the beauty of righteousness and he is allowed to contemplate them for six days. It is then that we gather together to celebrate the second Requiem, for the soul is about to face a fearful ordeal, since it is to be conducted to hell, to watch the torments of the damned for thirty days —'

'The proportions are familiar,' said Edward Rowan. 'Six days in Paradise, thirty in hell. But do you really believe all this?'

'Yes, we believe it, no, we do not believe it. Not all of us take the story literally, but it is sixteen hundred years since it was told to Saint Macarius by his angels, and it has been repeated and believed ever since, and now it is embedded in our minds and fulfils some function there; and so we don't think about it very much any more. The question of belief hardly arises. We simply feel that when we attend the Requiem of the Ninth Day we are supporting our loved one in a time of anguish, and discharging an obligation which it would be shameful to repudiate – I don't know if I'm making myself clear —'

'I understand perfectly.'

'No, Mr Rowan, I don't think you do. Not the whole of what I'm trying to say. You can't understand it fully until you realise that people who attend the Requiem will not be the ones you expect.'

'Well, I suppose that my wife's brothers and sisters might manage to get to this second great Requiem. They certainly won't be able to get here in time for the funeral.'

'They will attend neither the funeral nor any of the Requiems. They will not be allowed to leave Russia.' Kamensky forgot and spoke with naked authority. Also with hatred. He was glad these people were not allowed to bury their dead. Laura felt a prick of contempt for her father, because he did not notice this lightning flash of tyranny. Immediately Kamensky corrected himself. 'At least,' he said, mildly and sadly, 'I don't think so. Though of course one doesn't know. But we can take it that they will not come, nor will any of his old friends, whether they be in Russia, or outside it.'

'I hardly see why this can be relevant, I simply want to get back to London, which is very important for me, but I believe there are some friends of his in much the same state of un-merited disgrace, a family living at Pau, a general at Nice —'

'They will not come to any of the Requiems. The Countess has spoken of what she meant to do if this tragedy befell her, and now Madame Rowan will do it for her. She will write to these friends and beg them to stay at home so that their loyalty to her father will not be remarked by the authorities and the lives of their relatives still in Russia be clouded by suspicion. These people will therefore mourn at home before their own icons. They will not mind it very much. It has been the Tsar's will to alienate them from all that is dear to them, and it has been God's will that the Tsar's will shall be so, and they will submit, even with gladness —'

'Yes, yes. You are telling me that some people would like to come to the services and will not be able to, but for some obscure reason will be satisfied as much as if they did. But what has this to do with me? Who will in fact attend the Requiem?'

'The Ambassador and all the senior members of his staff,' said Kamensky, with a relish her father ought to have recognised. 'Yes, and all the most distinguished Russians resident in France or visiting it. They will not attend the funeral, they won't hear of it in time, but the Requiem, yes.'

'The damned hypocrites,' said Edward Rowan. 'I am sorry Laura. I shouldn't use such language in front of you, but they hounded the old man to his death.'

Kamensky gaped for an instant. 'I may get away from him, he's not so clever as I imagined,' Laura thought, 'anybody who takes it that Daddy will be impressed by a bunch of diplomats can't be very bright.' She wondered why Kamensky was working to keep her father and her in Paris till the Requiem of the Ninth Day. Perhaps he had not planned to murder her till after that date.

Kamensky started again: 'If I may say so, Mr Rowan, since England is a monarchy you should be more sympathetic in your view of the situation. The Tsar has destroyed the Count, true. But it's also true that the Tsar could not destroy the Count, since he was part of the Tsarist structure sanctified by God and immutable during time. The Count was born in honour and he must die in honour. Also, it must be concealed that it was necessary to destroy the Count, because the public does not understand that the Tsar, as the protector of the Russian state, has sometimes to commit acts which would be culpable if committed by a private person. Therefore the Russian Ambassador to France and his staff will attend the Requiem of the Ninth Day after the Count's death just as if the Count had died in full enjoyment of the Imperial favour.'

'Good God,' Edward Rowan exploded, 'what has the fact that England is a monarchy to do with this sort of thing? And why, because these vultures convince themselves in Double Dutch that they're justified in holding a religious service over the bones of my father-in-law after they themselves have picked them clean, why should I lend myself to the occasion?'

Again Kamensky was at a loss and had to feel about and had something up his sleeve for a fresh start. But she had a feeling that he was convulsed by secret laughter. 'Well, it's as I said, difficult to explain – but the service, being considered so important by us Russians – if you were absent – I don't know how to put it – people might think – they might think —'

'What is it that they might think?'

'Well, I'm afraid that – I'm unfortunately quite sure that – though your family life is of course ideal – I understand that those who have the privilege of visiting your home feel positive awe – nevertheless it would be thought among us Russians, who are simple people, not at all sophisticated, really, compared to Westerners – it would be bound to be thought if a wife appeared at a Requiem held for her dead father, and her husband was absent, that all could not be well with her marriage.' In the silence which followed he took out his handkerchief and passed it over his forehead. 'And you know how it is with diplomats. If a story starts among them, it runs like wild fire.'

Laura looked downwards at her lap and braced herself against one of her father's rare fits of fury. But it did not come, and she raised her eyes again. On his face there was a shocking expression of prudence. 'I know the sort of thing you mean,' he said, easily, 'and we can't have that for one moment. So embarrassing for my wife. I'll certainly attend the Requiem.'

Kamensky was cleverer than she had judged him, or perhaps only very well-informed. He had known exactly what it was her father feared. Herself, she never would have guessed it. When Kamensky had begun to hint at a family scandal, she had expected her father to order him to leave the room. It might be that Kamensky would get her after all. For the first time she doubted her father's capacity to defend her. When she came to tell him about the plot to murder her, and how Kamensky was Gorin, he might not believe her, so thoroughly was he convinced that in Kamensky he had his hand where it had lain through his life, on a useful underling. She felt so frightened, and so tired of being frightened, that it occurred to her she might be looking plain; and she got up and looked at a mirror on the wall beside the fireplace. It was not much

343

use as a mirror. The glass was the colour of a pond overhung by trees on a dull day, it made her face greenish-white like a Christmas rose. But the thing was pretty in itself. Two little gilt sphinxes supported the oval shagreen frame, and she stood fingering their tiny periwigs, the twists in their tails, pretending that there was nothing else in the world. Then Kamensky's voice caught her ear, eager and young for his age, as it always was when he was turning the stalk of an apple ripe for falling.

'No, Mr Rowan, I'm afraid I can't tell you with certainty whether a letter you write in the train and post when you get to Paris will reach London tomorrow. My poor correspondence is so unimportant that I've never made any close enquiries as to the time it gets delivered. But as it happens, I think you needn't bother yourself with the problem. I have friends in the town, and when I called on them this morning I heard that their young son is going to London by the night train. A priest, he's going to attend some sort of congress in London. If you should sit down and write your letter here, I'll take it to him later in the day and he'll post it in London tomorrow morning. He's a reliable young man, he won't forget. They are a good family, very responsible people. You have some writing-paper in front of you, haven't you. See, here's a better pen. And let me clear away some of this astonishing salmagundi of papers to give you some space. Now write at your leisure, and as soon as you've gone I'll take it straight down to my young friend, who'll feel himself honoured by the commission. An English Member of Parliament will seem very grand to him.'

Laura whirled about and faced her father. 'You can't write a letter. Not now. We haven't time.'

'Never mind about that. I must write this letter.'

'But we've got to catch the train.'

'If we lose it we'll catch the next.'

'But we should get back to Paris as soon as possible —' she was shaking from head to foot, she would never get him alone. But her father's rage was a hot blast in her face. Now his fury was breaking over her, as it should have broken over Kamensky, once he dared speak of what was private, hidden, black. 'Sit down and be quiet. I must write this letter. I knew nothing of this endless dragging out of ceremonies, that every sane person would want to get over as quickly as possible. I'll have to change my plans for days ahead, put back engagements that involve other people. I'll have to write and warn them, don't you see? This is the last straw. Do you want to drive me mad?'

Her answering rage streamed out of her. She choked because she could not say, 'You idiot, don't you see this animal has got your letter in his pocket before you've even written it?' Kamensky's hand was gentle on her arm as he led her back to her chair and sat down beside her, closer than anybody could wish their prospective murderer. In her ear, irritatingly hard to hear, he murmured, 'Don't be so disturbed, Miss Laura, I can't bear you to be disturbed. And how terribly disturbed you are! It's natural I suppose, with all that happened to you yesterday, and those horrible people who came into your room last night, they must have frightened you.'

'I'm frightened of a lot of things, but not of them.'

'But I can't bear anything evil to come near you. You should be taken care of properly. I would not wish to do anything in the world so much as to protect you, so it is dreadful what I have to say to you. Though I will be in Paris tomorrow, I can't be with you in the morning. Or, indeed, in the afternoon, until four o'clock. I will simply perform my sad mission very early in the morning, and then leave. Then I will be with you. I will come on the hour.'

It might be, of course, that her father was simply going to write to his secretary or to the Party Whip, and that would be just male stuff which would take only a moment or two. But it was not so. He was going to take his time. Slowly he wrote the beginning of the letter, Dear Whoever-it-was, frowning slightly, and then he raised his head and stared straight at her, straight through her. She was simply part of the space between him and the image of another person.

'I feel it a terrible betrayal of trust that I won't be with you. But, dear Miss Laura, I had prepared everything I can for the arrival of our dear one. The Metropolitan will be there to receive him, and what your mother does not know about the ritual he and the servants will recall to her. This morning when I telephoned your mother she and I agreed that the most fitting person to recite the Psalms over your grandfather's body – you know, we call them in our church the candlebearers – would be a very devout woman well known to us both, who's very grateful to the Count for the charity he bestowed on her for many years. So there will be nothing for you to do except strengthen his soul with your prayers.'

'I shall be praying to God to tell me why he allowed so good a man to be persecuted to the very edge of his grave.' Now her father was writing, writing quickly, smiling down at what he wrote, dipping his pen in the inkwell and writing again. He looked happy to the point of deafness and absent-mindedness, as he used to do when there had been an election and he and her mother had just come back from the constituency and his majority was bigger than ever. It always was.

'Ah,' Kamensky exclaimed, 'if any of us could be vouch-safed the explanation of that mystery! But don't you want to know why, feeling as I do, I'm not going to be at your side tomorrow morning?'

Her father had raised his eyes from the paper and was again looking at the person he saw behind her face. He could scarcely credit that there existed such perfection. He had to stare and stare at the remembered image, to make sure it was so perfect. The crinkles round his eyes showed how amused he felt that the perfect object would walk, and talk, and laugh, and all that perfectly too. Her father must be writing to Susie Staunton.

'Of all people,' Kamensky was assuring her, 'you have the most right to know what I'm going to do tomorrow. I'm quite simply,' he said, gravely and smugly, 'going to secure my future.' She nearly laughed aloud at the ferocious irony of his words. They were so true nobody could accuse him now of lying. By killing her he would do just that, secure his future. He evidently felt he had to explain away what he had said, for he went on, 'You see, I'm not without means. Professionally, I've always been very lucky, largely through your grandfather's influence. But now I must find more lucrative employment if I'm to enjoy what's every man's birthright. You know very well what I mean by that, Miss Laura.'

'I know what I'd mean by it. The right to live.'

'Yes, indeed. The right to live. To live fully. To have a home. To have a wife. Whom I would love and cherish. The right to have —'

She could no longer hear what he was saying. 'The right to have what?'

'The right to have my children growing up around me.'

Well, snakes and bats could reproduce their kind, so she supposed he could and she was glad that she had a good chance of preventing it.

'Oh, forgive me. Please forgive me, Mademoiselle Laura. I didn't want to embarrass you. I feel quite ashamed —'

Her father had taken a second sheet of writing-paper. What could he possibly find to write about at such length, if he were writing to Susie? 'You are very beautiful you are very beautiful you are very beautiful you have marvellous hair you have marvellous hair you have marvellous hair you have a curious mouth you have a curious mouth you have a curious mouth.' That was all there was to say about Susie, except that she looked poor and was not, and that one would hardly be able to tell her. Anything else would be rubbish. She was glad that Kamensky would certainly read the letter and that Susie might never get it. For once she was grateful to Kamensky because he was evil, and she turned to him in thankfulness.

He bewildered her by saying, 'I'm happy that that makes you happy.' She must have missed some essential part of his twaddle. Apparently he was telling her about the business which had kept him running about Paris all the day before, between the time she and her grandfather had left him at the chemist's shop and his arrival at the apartment in the Avenue Kléber. 'Well, I can assure you that the salary the French Company offers me is beyond anything I had expected. It wouldn't mean riches, of course. There's no way by which a man like me can acquire a fortune such as comes automatically to those who have pillaged the people for many generations —'; too late he checked himself.

'That's not the way we used to talk in the drawing-room in the Avenue Kléber,' she said to herself, 'you slipped there.' Again she told herself that her chances of escape were good because Kamensky was not as clever as she had thought, again

347

she rebuked herself for over-confidence, because her father was stupider than she had thought. If he could go on and on writing to Susie Staunton, he had changed into someone else, someone else too obtuse to understand in time that Kamensky was Gorin. Again she wished that Chubinov was sitting beside her, the one man who knew the whole story, who was kind.

'That sounded as if I were a Liberal! Don't misunderstand me. What I meant was that it is God's Will that some should be rich and some should be poor, and it is not for us to kick against the pricks. But if I take this post abroad I shall have enough. Enough to make plans which intoxicate me.' He stopped and drew his handkerchief across his lips. 'You must not mind if I draw nearer to you. I don't wish to distract your father's attention while he is trying to write his letter.'

'You couldn't,' said Laura, bitterly. She would have liked to go back to the salon upstairs and lie down on the camp-bed and bury her face in the pillow. It was terrible to sit so close to one's murderer, while one's father went on and on making a fool of himself.

'I believe Rio de Janeiro is a delightful place to live. There's a magnificent mountain by the sea, a huge sugar-loaf. Living is expensive, but my salary, as I say, should be enough. I should be able to give my wife a home. Not a palace. But a home where I could make her happy. We would not have many servants, but we would have some servants. We could not have great stables, but we would have a carriage and pair. An official of the company whose superior I would be tells me that he keeps his carriage. I chose well, becoming a hydraulic engineer, though little did I know. The climate, I believe, is agreeable and healthy.'

Edward Rowan lifted his head from his letter and again stared into and through his daughter's face. She could not bear it, and she rose in her chair, and called to him. She knew he had heard her, but only because he frowned and looked away into the corner of the room. There was a faint smile on his lips, which brightened into silent laughter. Then it was as if his face were burning. It might have been that tears came into his eyes, he looked down at the paper again and paused before he began to write again, and then was solemn as he wrote. He must have been remembering some happy time he had spent with Susie.

But he should never have been happy with Susie, not for a second. The proof of that had come that afternoon when Tania had been trying on hats, and the bedroom floor had been covered with round yellow buckram hatboxes and clouds of tissue paper, and Susie had sat quiet as a mouse in the background beside the bed, while Tania sat at her dressing-table and Hélène brought her hat after hat. Tania had sprung up from her chair and held out to Susie a hat she thought would suit the fine small bones of her face; and as she threw out her arm in the gesture of giving, one of her shoulder-straps broke, and she had had to clap her hand against her chemise to prevent it falling clear away. As it was, she seemed almost as naked as a painted goddess on a ceiling, for the lace top of her chemise fell forward over her fingers, showing the rise of her breast, and in the triple glass behind her there was reflected and re-reflected, golden under the sunshine pouring in through the high windows, the cord of her spine, her strong shoulder-blade like a wing cut off near its base, her long waist tapering down into her satin corset. 'If the other shoulder-strap goes,' Laura thought to herself, 'she'll be left there all Elgin marble, and the silly dear won't notice, she's so keen on giving Susie that hat.'

She looked over to Susie to share the joke. But though Susie had seen a joke, it was not the same one. Her mouth was no longer vague as it trembled and twisted, as she altered a smile of derision to a smile of compliance, and with difficulty kept it so. She was wearing a black dress that covered her from neck to wrist and ankles, and it was an ambush from which she watched Tania making a fool of herself, romping like a school-girl, flinging out her arms so that she ended half-naked in front of her daughter and a servant. It was not mollifying Susie at all that if Tania was half-naked, it was simply because she had wanted so much to give her a present. It could not be the spectacle of accidental nakedness which had thrown Susie off her balance; nobody could call Susie common. Of course it had to be allowed that Susie was finickingly neat by nature, and that untidiness always seemed to strike her as a

349

threat, a hole in the dyke that kept the waters out. But it came to Laura suddenly that Susie had some large, coarse reason for despising Tania at that moment. Her lips went on twitching when Tania cried out, in a voice made pure as a blackbird's by her ecstasy of giving, 'Quick, try it on, we're longing to see you in it. There was never anybody who had so many different ways of looking lovely as you!'

Susie had at first not responded to the invitation, modestly shrugging her shoulders and shaking her head, as so often before miming her role of one doomed to go without, to go without what, to go without almost everything, while her narrow hand passed backwards and forwards, out of time with her other movements, over the Venice-point counterpane on Tania's broad bed, just below the pillows, for a foot or so. Ultimately Susie had been persuaded to come forward and take Tania's place before the dressing-table, to try on the hat, and to accept it, eyes enormous with surprise. She went on sitting there for some time, while Tania set the hat this way and that on her pale golden head, infatuated with the delight of making her beautiful friend more beautiful, preoccupied with it, so that she never paused to put on the négligé which Hélène was patiently holding ready for her; while in the triple glass Tania's bare arms, bare shoulders, half-bare breast, and all the rest that was too little obscured by her cloudy chemise, wove a pattern of rosy flesh round Susie's black figure, still covered to the throat. Laura felt that at any moment Susie might push back her chair and stand up and burst into laughter unnaturally loud and long and cruel. This had not happened. Yet Laura could never recall the scene without thinking that it had, and that Tania had then turned into a statue, her hands above the little hat, while she grew pale and rocked on her feet under the force of the insult. Now Laura knew her memory to be only slightly mistaken, and that through being too intelligent. This was what had nearly happened. Her father should not have been able to be happy with Susie for a single second.

Till then she had not known that she had stopped loving her father, that he was nothing to her. She said aloud, 'There shall be no more sea.'

So strong was her sense of loss that her fingers closed on her

350

handbag lest that went too. Everything seemed gone from her body except her heart, which felt as if it were made of glass and had cracked into a thousand sharp-edged fragments, which were holding together, as the pantry-window at Radnage Square was still holding together, though Osmund had sent a cricket-ball through it in the spring. 'I feel as if my heart would break,' Dolly the housemaid had said, when her brother was killed at Spion Kop, and Laura had thought she simply meant that she was very sad. But Dolly had been telling the literal truth: real grief meant a feeling of fracture inside one's body, on the left side, just above one's waist. What happened when the pieces of glass fell apart? There must be a crucial ending if people were as wretched as she was, abandoned, feeble, betrayed, unjustly sentenced, exiled, taken for less than they were, put below others who were their inferiors. She supposed they died. Well, she hoped that, dead, her father would realise that he had killed her. With that for prize, her mind went down into the pit. But it came back to her that for the last twelve hours at least she had been under threat of death, and that real death was quite different from the sort of dying she had been contemplating, which was like death in a picture or a poem, not death at all, just something about it. If there was one thing she had learned from that threat it was that she did not want to die, and that the sense in which her father might kill her was unimportant compared to the sense in which Kamensky meant to kill her.

She had relied on her father to save her from this real death. Now she doubted whether he could do it. He was on his third sheet of writing-paper now, and his half-smile of happiness was still on his lips. Now she came to look at him, he did not seem remarkable. Leaving out the Irish Members and Keir Hardie, he might have been any other Member of Parliament; when girls at her school had asked her to their homes their fathers had always looked much as he did; he was even like the people he sometimes invited to luncheon or dinner at Radnage Square, hoping they would not be able to accept. Apprehensively she remembered what she had always respected in him as a sign of wisdom, his habit of probing any crisis with quiet questions. When she told him of her danger he would ask —

But did your grandfather tell you quite definitely that he believed Chubinov? Did he say whether he had had any reason to suppose he was truthful and responsible, beside this acquaintance in the remote past? I don't understand why your grandfather and Chubinov attached so much importance to this horrible business about the man found hanging in the villa kitchen. Try to tell me more clearly. No, Laura, you have not yet given me any really satisfactory evidence that Kamensky, who seems a very decent fellow, is the same as this scoundrel Gorin. Go back to that point about the blind man. She would have to go back to point after point, while time was running out; and she felt relieved because the people in the story had such simple names as Gorin and Kamensky and Chubinov, for her father always muddled up Russian names of more than three syllables. That in itself was odd for a man who spoke and read Russian, who had visited Russia several times, and had been married to a Russian wife for over twenty years.

It could only mean that he had turned his face against Russia. He wanted to reject the wild mating of consonants and vowels which made the Russian language, he would be unkind to the confusion of good and evil, of imagination and obtuseness, of delicacy and coarseness, which made the Russian character. He wanted to reject everything Russian, and she was half-Russian, so of course he would reject her and her way of thinking. When she had told him as much of the matted story as she could understand, he would say something contrary to the Russian way of living. He would say, 'Well, anyway we can clear up the whole matter if we can get these two scoundrels, Gorin and Chubinov, under lock and key. Then we'll see who Kamensky is. I'll get on to the police as soon as I reach Paris.' Chubinov must not be put in prison. He was a good man. Though he had been accomplice to so many murders it was only because everybody round him was talking of murder as if it were a virtuous act, and he loved virtue, and had not too much sense. But he was of good will. He reminded her of a fairy-tale someone had told her, about a frozen city in the North, and a little draggled bird that hopped about the snowy streets in search of crusts put out by kindly householders, but not to peck at them itself, only to fly with them in its beak, one by one, and drop them in the laps of vagrants huddled in doorways. Her need for Chubinov was so strong that for a moment it seemed to her that it was he who was sitting beside her, and she let her body go loose towards him, turning her head and shutting her eyes to take the kindness of his imagined words.

But the quick furtive undertones of the other one were still skeltering on. 'Apart from all the pleasantness of the beaches, there's much agreeable that happens just because one's living there. The nights are warm. The stars, I'm told, are astonishing in their brilliance. There's the Southern Cross. Only think of seeing the Southern Cross. Think of changing one's whole life, even to the stars above. Under this new night sky, I'll sit beside my wife, my dear wife, in the courtyard of our house, all the houses have courtyards, and it seems that they grow a number of flowers out there which exhale a strong scent after nightfall, a fountain will play —'

She murmured 'A fountain, I like fountains,' lest he should guess that rage was flaring up in her, as savage rage as she felt against her father, a pure flame of hatred. It was so grotesque that he should be telling her how he meant to enjoy himself after he had killed her, when the worms were eating her or she was fine dust on the wind. Her rage turned into bewilderment and disgust, for Kamensky had passed into a state of silent excitement like a fit. He had been staring at her with this impudent burning-glass intensity, but now he turned aside, his head jerking, and rubbed the trembling knuckles of one hand on the trembling bandaged palm of the other. His chair was set near hers at such an angle that he could not quite hide his face from her, she could just see that between his neat moustache and his neat beard his mouth was wild, pulled into a twitching square, his upper lip raised so that his small white teeth were visible to the gums. His hands separated and became fists that clenched and unclenched, grinding the air between them. It was natural that he should want to get rid of her, the supremely inconvenient witness, but it was unjust that he should hate her so. She had never chosen to learn that he was vile. Yet he would have liked to go on and on tearing her to pieces, she could tell that from the flexing and unflexing of

353

his fingers. A blackness came down on her, and she began to breathe deeply, since she had heard that was the way to keep from fainting. When the light came back she found that Kamensky was breathing deeply too, and in the same rhythm as herself. They were in horrid physical agreement. It came into her mind that Chubinov had offered to rid her of this man.

Softly she asked Kamensky, 'You will be coming to our apartment at four o'clock tomorrow afternoon?'

He had to struggle for control before he could answer her. 'Yes. At four o'clock.'

She had thought she could not possibly let Chubinov save her his way. But, if it were the only way, she would not reject it now.

'The apartment will be crowded with mourners. But we can go into that little drawing-room at the end of the corridor.'

It was hard to think how he meant to kill her with so many people about. Perhaps while he was sitting with her, the door would suddenly open on strangers who were his friends – as she had thought the man and woman who had come into her room the night before, but who had proved innocent.

'Be there when I arrive so that we can talk. You know the room I mean. Not the big drawing-room and not the little drawing-room with the picture of the pinewoods under snow and the Verestchagin of the Cavalry charge. The other one. Where we sat one evening while your grandfather slept and the petals fell from the roses in the vase on the table.'

That evening her grandfather had slept so soundly because his trusted young friend, Kamensky, had told him that in his sober opinion there might be a conspiracy at work. It was time he died.

She stood up murmuring, 'I shall be there. I have got to go now —' she felt for a reason and found it just in time – 'I must go upstairs and see that my grandfather's things are not left behind.' He rose and kissed her hand, and over his bent head she looked at her image in the mirror on the wall, and was distressed because her body was not keeping up appearances, her eyes were blazing, she was flushed, even her lips seemed too bright, she might have been an actress ready to go on the stage and play a tragic part. At the door Kamensky said softly, 'Miss

Laura, don't worry yourself, I'll see that you don't miss the train.' She glanced over her shoulder at her father; he was still scribbling.

In the dim room she had forgotten it was a fine day. She walked blinking through the sunshine to Chubinov without the knowledge of her father and Kamensky. She bracketed them now as enemies. If she went down to the desk in the hall and got the porter to send out a boy to the post-office the landlord would be sure to rush forward as her party was leaving the hotel and recite to them the service his staff had done for her, with his air of recommending himself for a decoration. She was planning to slip out into the streets and ask the way to the post-office and send the telegram herself, when through the glass wall she saw on the opposite side of the gallery, straight across the courtyard, two figures which, though the glass seemed thicker at this point, looked like Professor Saint-Gratien and Madame Verrier, standing side by side and looking down as if there were a table in front of them. Now that she had made up her mind to take Chubinov at his word she felt proud and powerful; she might have compelled by her will those two people to be there where they could help her.

They did not see her till she was close to them. The table at which they stood was hardly that, it was more like a gardener's bench and on it stood some sickly potted plants. The glass had seemed thicker at this point because it had been built out to overhang the courtyard by a foot or two, in a sort of greenhouse, fitted with shelves on which there were more of these bleached and drooping plants. A sheet of paper was spread out on the bench and Madame Verrier, head on one side, was letting a pencil wander over it, and both were watching what it traced, as if the lead in itself were by its own volition spelling out a message settling some shared perplexity of theirs. But when they saw her they smiled as if they had no cares.

'So you've got what you want,' said Saint-Gratien. 'Papa is here. Forgive me if I speak to you as if you are a little girl. But you were so last year. I'm old and I can't keep pace with the times. So I say, Papa is here, and may you always get what you want as quickly, by waiting a single night.'

She could not say anything to that. She felt her eyes blaze even brighter, her cheeks grow hotter.

'And we,' said Madame Verrier, 'are behaving more like little children than you ever would. The Professor has an operation at half past two, I must go to a new case this afternoon. So we have some spare moments. But we're always telling ourselves that if only we had a spare moment, we would do this and that. And now here we stand, wasting our precious time.'

'In an appropriate place, the folly constructed by the landlord's wife,' said Saint-Gratien. 'It looks full south, and she adored her plants, so she smashed up this gallery, which is very old, older than the rest of the house, part of the Louis Quatorze building that was originally here, and built this sort of conservatory. But never mind, she looked very nice in her peignoir, about ten in the morning, wielding her watering-can. She had pretty arms.'

'Where is she now?' asked Laura.

'In Lyons with a commercial traveller who took her there last spring.'

'Oh! Is that why her husband is as he is?'

'Well, the landlord's wife is in Lyons because her husband is what he is, and he is as he is because his wife is in Lyons. That's what St Paul meant when he said that marriage was a mystery.'

She need not have worried because she was looking strange. They were so happy that they saw nobody but each other. It was as well, perhaps the whole idea of sending a telegram to Chubinov was a mistake. Perhaps she was tired and overwrought and had only imagined that, in these days, in a civilised country, murder was possible.

'What are you doing?' she asked Madame Verrier, who was still playing with her pencil.

'Spoiling a temperature chart. Defacing it with an ill-drawn dog, an ill-drawn cat, an ill-drawn church.'

'To which the dog would go,' said Saint-Gratien. 'But not the cat. All cats are Voltaireans.'

'But they're not ill-drawn,' said Laura. 'They're awfully good and very funny.'

'She loves to draw,' said Saint-Gratien. 'She steals all my pencils.'

'You steal all mine, so in the end we're where we started.'

The courtyard had been empty. But now two men brought out of the stable underneath a large piebald coach-horse, dragging on its check-rein ring with their full weight. The great round buttocks, like two stupid and indecent faces, rolled about while its four hooves scrambled and slipped on the cobblestones, as if the beast were too enraged to keep its balance. It swung round and they looked down on the long vicious fiddle of its head, the empty eyes rolling as hatred rushed in to fill the vacuum, the green-and-yellow teeth showing to the gums, the nostrils suddenly dilating and the whole convulsed by the spasm of a neigh. It was the worse because no sound came through the thick glass, even when the hooves struck a spark from the cobbles, even when the neigh blew out into discoloured froth. The stillness made the frightening brute frightening like a ghost as well.

'That monster's called Caesar,' said Saint-Gratien. 'Last year I operated on a groom he'd kicked. The operation could hardly have been less successful.'

It had come to Laura that she was wrong in changing her plan. She asked, 'Please can you help me? I want to send a telegram.'

Saint-Gratien answered: 'Of course. Write it down and I'll give it to the porter when I go out.'

'Ah, no! I'm sorry, that won't do. What I'm really asking for, and I'm ashamed to ask you so much after all you've done for me, is to send it yourself, or through a secretary, or somebody at the hospital, who wouldn't know it came from me. Nobody,' she said, desperately, 'nobody, nobody at all, must be able to trace it back to me.'

'My darling little Mademoiselle,' said Saint-Gratien, 'if this is an affair of love I can have nothing to do with it. You are too young. I am all for love. I adore it, if I could I would pass laws in its favour, I would set up a Ministry of Love with an enormous budget. But all the same, you are too young.'

She could not help laughing. 'Love doesn't come into this, from first to last.'

'You'll have a fine time convincing him of that,' said Madame Verrier. 'He thinks all women fall into love when they're sixteen, as they might into a muddy pool, and all their lives long never succeed in washing the mud out of their hair.'

'If you're in a difficulty, dear child, why don't you consult Monsieur Kamensky? He seems devoted to you.'

Laura began to tremble, she could not answer him. It was supernatural, Kamensky's power to deceive the subtle, the worldly, the experienced.

'It is odd, I've always told you you're nothing like as good as a diagnostician as you are an operator,' said Madame Verrier, 'and in ordinary life it's a shame to take your money. Can't you see she doesn't like this Kamensky? And neither do I. Why should a man pretend to be less important than he is? When he speaks to one he is a little country schoolmaster. If one comes into the room quietly and he doesn't see one, there he is with his head jutting forward, the Chancellor of the University, the President of the Republic, the Pope. What's the meaning of all that? Send the telegram for her. She's a sensible girl, and intelligent.'

'I always wanted to do what she asked,' said Saint-Gratien.

She borrowed Madame Verrier's pencil, she was given a leaf from Saint-Gratien's pocket-diary, she found in her bag the scrap of paper on which Chubinov had written the address of the hotel where he was hiding, and the name he would be known by there. But she could not bring herself to write the message that would kill a man. Her pencil hovering over the paper, she listened to the talk the others were carrying on in undertones.

'Yes, perhaps. But I thought he talked of her with such protective feeling about the couple that came into the little salon last night. You didn't see them, did you? Who do you think they were?'

'From the description this Kamensky gave, the man would be de Sancy. The woman any one of a number of fools.'

'Poor de Sancy, mewed up in that run-down property, with no money to keep it up. What can he do but chase women?'

'He would chase them if he had twenty millions. But is the place in such a state?'

'Very shabby. The sort of property where all the game-keepers look like poachers.'

Madame de Verrier said suddenly, 'Little one, don't send that telegram if you don't want to. Wait till you get to Paris, and you've had the chance to think it over in the train.'

But Paris was the place where Kamensky meant to murder her, in the little room where the petals had fallen from the roses. To fight this kindness which would kill her, Laura said, 'But I must send it now.' Again she found a lie at the tip of her tongue. 'There is trouble in my family. I want a friend to come and help my mother with his advice. My mother trusts him. But my father and Monsieur Kamensky don't like him.'

'Ah, if it's an affair like that, you're probably right, one should always mind one's own business,' said Madame Verrier.

'Yes, let's restrict our diagnoses to our profession,' said Saint-Gratien. He searched in his pockets and found another pencil. 'Now take your time over the telegram while Madame Verrier draws me another little cat on that temperature chart. All the little cats you draw remind me of someone; I can't think who. Creatures who scratch but have their claims to be considered domestic pets, for those who care for little animals about the house. There are some.'

Laura wrote quickly, 'Baraton, Hôtel de l'Independence, Rue des Nomades, Paris. Nikolai died yesterday, my father and I return to Paris this afternoon, please call at the apartment at four o'clock tomorrow, L.', and handed the paper to Saint-Gratien, and then rested her elbows on the table and covered her eyes. She heard him say, 'Mademoiselle, Mademoiselle,' and took no notice. But he repeated, 'Mademoiselle,' and she dropped her hands and saw that he was holding the paper out to her. She had known all the time that he would not send the telegram. He did not want her to die, but something did.

He was not giving it back to her. He said, 'My dear young lady, you know all about life, but you do not know that you should never use the word "tomorrow" in a telegram just by

359

itself. You must mention the day. "Tomorrow Thursday" is what is needed. Look, I have written it in.'

'He's fussy,' said Madame Verrier, her pencil going, 'but he's right about that. One comes in and finds a telegram telling one to go to a case tomorrow, the date stamp's illegible, one takes it for granted that as it wasn't there by noon it must have been sent that morning, and one puts one's feet up, and then there's a banging on the door, and they want one at once, and it turns out that the telegram's been lying at the post-office for twenty-four hours. Life's very boring, except, of course, when it's not.'

'I'll send your telegram when we leave,' said Saint-Gratien. 'The post-offices are closed now. Ah, yes, I like the way that little cat's tail stands straight up. One has to mind one's manners with that little cat.'

If she sat there any longer she would ask him to give her back the telegram. She must go back and look at Kamensky and refresh her hatred of him. When she got up Madame Verrier and Saint-Gratien smiled at her out of the haze of their contentment, and told her they would be there when she left, she must come and say good-bye to them, they were sorry they had met her in such sad circumstances, but age must die, and they had known many people suffer more painful deaths than her grandfather. Her heart was beating so that she felt sick, her cheeks were burning again and she knew her eyes were staring, but their kind glances slid from her face back to the temperature chart, unperturbed. As she walked slowly back along the gallery she was astonished because nothing happened to prevent her from becoming a criminal; no stranger, looking like a doctor, came out of a doorway and said, 'It is all a mistake.'

She expected that she would find her father still writing his letter. That was all he was fit for, to sit in the wrecked grace of this inferior room, behind him the fine bookcase with the fine unread books tumbling off the shelves, in front of him the fine desk with its mulch of bills. But when her eyes got used to the half-light she saw that her father and Kamensky were standing face to face in front of the desk and at that very moment her father's long and elegant fingers, looking foolish in the same way that faces do, were handing over the envelope to Kamensky, who gave it a little pat, a quiet, squeezing, satisfied pressure, before he slipped it into his pocket. It no longer caused her pleasure to know that he would be reading the letter within an hour or two. She wanted that letter to be burned at once, destroyed absolutely, not allowed any survival at all, even to the small degree of living in a man's mind during the day or so he had still to live.

As she came in her father was saying something about the importance of posting this letter in the centre of London, was spelling out St-Martin's-le-Grand. He looked shamefully ashamed when he saw her and cut himself short. 'Ah, my dear. Now we're going up to pay our last respects to your poor grandfather. Do you want to come with us? We'll have to hurry.'

She shook her head.

'Then wait here. I got the chambermaid to bring down your hat and coat. We won't be long. We cannot be long.' He spoke as if it were somebody else's fault they were short of time. 'Don't wander off, be sure to be here ready to start the moment we come back.'

Once they had gone she stood in the dimness, her eyes shut, her hands joined, begging her grandfather to forgive her for not having been able to protect his dead body from being seen by these men who were his enemies. She had to take part of that back. Her father was not Nikolai's enemy. Yet he was; he had offended against Nikolai's daughter and granddaughter. Then she heard a step beside her, and she opened her eyes. Kamensky had come back and had left the door open, they both stood brilliant in a shaft of sunlight piercing the dusk. She stared at him. She was fascinated by everything about him: his sleek head, his face half-hidden by spectacles and moustache and beard and very bland where it could be seen; his neat but inelegant body; because it was all about to perish. And he was staring at her, and it must be for the same reason: he was contemplating what was now bright in the sunshine, what, according to his plans, would soon be nowhere. For the first time she noticed a faint scar running from his hairline down to the middle of his left eyebrow, and she thought with the concern which springs up automatically at the sight of any injury, 'An inch further, and he'd have lost the sight of that eye,' and then thought again, in fear, 'How did it happen that someone got so near to killing him and failed? How did he get away?'

Hoarsely he said, 'I had to come back. You're looking so wonderful. They say in poems that women look radiant, but you really do, you're giving out light. But you're agitated. I can see you're agitated. Strangers might think you're quite calm, but I, I understand you, I see under the surface. Your heart's beating far too fast. Oh, be calm. Realise that there's nothing but peace and joy in the future.'

She nodded. 'Nothing but peace and joy,' she repeated. It would be true, once he was dead.

'And tomorrow I'll be with you at four o'clock, I promise you.'

'Please, please, be there,' she said.

'And tell me, what are your favourite flowers?' She looked at him in amazement, and he added, 'They should be white.'

Yes, she supposed they should. Flowers at funerals were nearly always white. It must have been Professor Barrault's twaddle about Virgil that had made his mind run in this direction. 'Not lilies,' she said, smiling at his impudence. 'Lilies are pi.'

'What is pi?'

'An English word. An English slang word. It means humbugging of a special sort, to do with religion, with pretending to be good.'

'You must explain it to me some time. We have so many things to talk about. But if not lilies, what then?'

'This is difficult. I'm quite overwhelmed by being allowed to make my own choice.' She remembered the petals that had fallen on the table in the little drawing-room, while her grandfather slept. 'Oh, let it be white roses. Yes, that would be fitting, white roses.'

14

ON THE RAILWAY platform at Grissaint, before the Paris train came in, Kamensky said to Edward Rowan: 'Don't thank me. To bring the dear Count back to Paris will be a great consolation. Once more, and for the last time, I will be alone with my master, my teacher, my exemplar. We will travel through the night to the same destination, the grave, though, by the great paradox, we shall arrive there at different times.' But the greater paradox was that, once again, there was what sounded like real affection in his voice. He turned to Laura and told her gently: 'You who love the customs of our Church may be distressed because the psalms are not yet being recited over the body of your poor grandfather.' He turned back to Mr Rowan. 'It is sad that no other person belonging to our Church was here with your daughter. Certain errors have been committed. The dear Count is holding his icon, whereas his hands should have been crossed on his breast, and the fingers of his right hand bent, as though in the act of making the sign of the cross. Had I only been here! But as to the recitation of the psalms, I will discharge that duty at the first moment possible. I will get a psalter. I have friends in the town who will find me one, and as I sit by the coffin in the guard's van I will read the psalms. He will not be without the services that we Russians love to render those we love at this time.'

In the train Edward Rowan hardly spoke. When they had travelled a quarter of an hour or so he explained to her, with an air of having been insufficiently praised for his self-sacrifice, how he had got to Grissaint so soon. When he had found the telegram waiting for him at Radnage Square – he paused again to wonder what had happened to the one sent to the House of Commons – he had telephoned to the Admiralty for help and the night-clerk had made arrangements. So when he took the tediously slow first morning train to Dover there was a steam-launch waiting to take him over to Calais, and there the stationmaster had been warned, and was holding back the fast train to Grissaint for his arrival. At each stage of the journey on the English side, porters and dockers and sailors must have gaped, recognising him from the newspaper photographs and cartoons, wondering why someone they had supposed fortunate through and through, for twenty-four hours a day, was out so long before decent breakfast-time, on a slow train or in a little boat. They would be puzzled and admiring, for the likenesses would not have prepared them for the unlined white skin, the eyebrows drawn by a fine brush over clear eyes, the easy walk that showed he could still run. He could not have changed much since he was young, only he had developed this power of settling things which for all his lightness made him seem weightier than an ordinary man, weighty like a statue of someone famous. All these men would have trusted him to give them good advice, to tell them how they could keep the house though the landlord said they had forfeited the deposit, who was going to win the Derby, whether they had got the right pension. She saw him through those strangers' eyes and leaned forward and said across the carriage, 'Papa, about Monsieur Kamensky.'

He was looking out of the window at the skyline, at what he saw beyond the skyline. 'Yes, Kamensky, Kamensky,' he answered absently, 'a very decent fellow. I expect you've been thinking what I have, that we must do something to show our gratitude, I wonder what on earth that sort of man would like as a present. Perhaps your mother would know.'

It was no use. He had become stupid. If she told him the truth, his disbelief would change into a rage which could get Chubinov into prison. 'The first thing is to find out who this fellow is.' She would be left unguarded. For distraction she turned to the magazines her father had bought her on the station, but they were of the same sort that Kamensky had bought her in Paris, *pour les jeunes filles*. She tried to lose herself in an article called 'Two Fair Portrait-Painters', comparing the art of Madame Vigée le Brun and Madame Nelly Jacquemart-André, and others concerning the home life and the poetry of Carmen Sylva, the Queen of Roumania, and the process by which stalactites and stalagmites are formed. What

364

she wanted now that she had sent that telegram was a magazine not *pour les jeunes filles* but *pour les jeunes assassines*. But she had hardly a mind. Fear, she had found, was a sliding of the bowels, and grief an illusion that the heart was made of glass and cracked into a thousand pieces, about to fall apart; and now her guilt was a heavy stone in her stomach, and a lump in her throat she could not swallow, and diarrhoea that sent her several times along the corridor to the lavatory. Also she had a sense of being connected with her father, on the other side of the railway-carriage, and with Kamensky, who was further away from her every moment, by twisted ropes which were her nerves. A camera behind her eyes took picture after picture of her father as he sat opposite, and compiled an unnecessary album of photographs of this man for whom she felt only indifference, faintly flavoured with hope that it was not simply that. Once she slept, but woke in a few minutes, seeing an image of Kamensky against a blood-red background, his neatness cast away, in his shirt-sleeves, more violent in gesture and expression than she had ever seen him. For the rest she watched her father; as he comfortably slept, or stared out of the window at villages and churches, grasslands and ploughed fields, woods and ponds, with that blind half-smile.

When they were nearing Paris she leaned over and touched his hands. 'Look. We're coming to that deep valley where the woods go sheer down to the Thève. Mummie always makes sure she doesn't miss this, she thinks it's lovely. She gets quite excited.' When he said nothing, she persisted, 'Grandfather knew it too. He told me there's a hunting lodge down here. He went to it long ago. With his brother. When his brother was Ambassador here.'

No matter how thickly she peopled those woods, with how many men and women nearly of his blood, he would not enter them. Only for a moment did his eyes leave the distance, which he had peopled with all the company he wanted. 'I never knew that brother. Dead before my time. A good man. He had a famous row with Holstein, Bismarck's man, when he was Ambassador at Berlin.'

At the Gare du Nord the carriage was waiting, with a red-eyed Vissarion, a red-eyed Louison. When Vissarion looked down on her from his box, weeping, she was just able to make a show of sympathy. Kamensky had confused the moment. He had told Chubinov that Pyotr was a spy, and that was certainly untrue, but it could be the truth that the spy was Vissarion, of whom Chubinov had possibly never heard, so that he probably had not enquired into his loyalty. As Louison opened the carriage door for her, again Kamensky confused her. She remembered how he had pretended the boy had slammed the door on his hand, but now wondered if he and the boy might not have been working together. She would live in a maze of suspicion till Chubinov had rid her of Kamensky. After that everything would go right, even the loyalty of these servants, had that been disturbed. They were simple people who could not be expected to resist the persuasion that had deceived Nikolai; and once the persuader was annihilated they would be themselves again.

They drove off through an evening identical with the one which had received her when she had come from London a few days before. The same sort of sunset was painting a bloom on the buildings and making the hurrying crowds sparkle like rivers under summer. Yet the city had changed. Then it had had an advantage over her. Everyone looked as if they knew more than she did. On that first journey from the station the horses had had to be held back at a street-corner where there was a café. At one of the tables a young woman, with a huge fair chignon under her broad poppy-laden hat, was sitting comfortably settled in her own flesh, her plumpness shown off, offered, self-praised by a starched white blouse and a black skirt; and a young man, self-praised too by his wavy black hair and his flowing white cravat, bent over her table and spread his hands with apologetic gestures. The girl had an easy air of anticipating exactly what he was about to say, and the young man had an easy air of anticipating all her anticipations. Looking out on them Laura had felt an innocent and awkward fool. Now she knew so much that they did not; they might know that if they crossed the river and went along the Rue de Grenelle they would pass the Russian Embassy; they would not know that in one room a diplomat sat at his desk and thought himself another Judas because he was reading the private papers of a man superior to himself, bought from a man despicable by trade, but need not have troubled, because he was already punished, his loved son across the Channel at Oxford being his own Judas. The world was encrusted with layer upon layer of these secrets, coloured and intricate like jewellery, but horrible. Only mercifully the world was nothing when one considered death. The spread sky above the Champs-Elysées was a pure, unearthly, shining green void, with a white sun sinking. Nikolai had gone an infinite journey through such landscape, and would pass planets from which the earth would look as little as the moon seen from earth, capable of being reflected like the moon in quite little ponds. In wonder at the world she laid her hand on her father's; but he was frowning and biting his lips, and answered only by an abstracted murmur.

Aglaia and Katinka opened the apartment door and fell stiffly on their knees, one a pace to her right and the other a pace to her left, and each seized one of her hands between both theirs, and covered it with kisses, while they wept noisily yet formally. She felt the hot tear-drops roll over her knuckles down her fingers, while her own tears ran down her cheeks. It was all sincere but controlled by design. It was as if the three of them had receded out of life into the surface of the painted wall which hides the holy place of an Orthodox Church. Grief lost its horrid immediate character.

Her father said wearily, 'Can't you tell them to stop?'

'Please let them have it out. This is their way of taking things. They need the relief, and it's terrible for them. They've been through so much for Grandfather, coming to France when they hate it so. Now they must feel' – she paused, but had to use Kamensky's phrase, there was no better one – 'masterless dogs.'

'I would have thought that ordinary self-control helped people more.'

He must be very unhappy to talk like a headmistress. It struck her that she had not heard him say anything amusing for quite a long time. It was as if Mummie had lost her looks. 'Oh, Daddy. Just let them go on with it a little longer. They're quieting down. In a minute I'll tell them that I'm tired. But just give them a little more time.'

He uttered an exclamation of disgust. But there was a new cause for that. Over the Venetian mirror facing the front door there was hung a fine sheet, over the smaller Dutch mirror at the beginning of the passage a net curtain.

'Oh, that. We do that when there's a death in the house. Mummie's told me about it before.'

'We?'

She recognised what he was doing; piling up grievances to kill his sense that he was in the wrong. She often did it herself, but had hoped that she would grow out of it. 'I mean the Russians. It's hard for me to keep straight on the word "we", being a mongrel.'

'Do you mean to say educated Russians do it?'

The question angered her. She felt nearer Aglaia and Katinka than to him. There was a case for the custom. Looking-glasses in a house reflect what happened to the people who live there, and life is so strange that often when these people die it must seem intolerable that they should have had to endure what they did, so one would want to seal off the mirror that had carried the images of what they had to bear, as one might beg the witness of a painful scene to say nothing about it. This Venetian mirror must often have reflected Monsieur Kamensky giving up his hat to Pyotr (of whom she would never again be quite sure), and being helped off with his coat before he went in to comfort the unfortunate Diakonov family, and Monsieur Kamensky being given his hat and helped on with his coat after he had comforted the unfortunate Diakonov family. She pressed the sheet close against the mirror surface.

Hélène, yellow-faced and much older, came down the passage and greeted them respectfully over the heads of Aglaia and Katinka. 'Madame is with the dressmaker at the moment. There's tea in the drawing-room, and she'll join you there. If only I'd been with you, Mademoiselle. You must have felt it strange when you had no clean things to put on this morning.' Her voice cracked. 'Forgive me, that is a trivial remark. I'm talking according to my trade. Permit me to offer you my humble sympathy. Your loss is immense. So is mine,' she added, with an unexpected desperateness. She had never appeared desperate before. 'I am an orphan, one of the attractions of this situation was that the Count always made the family seem so secure.'

It was not Edward Rowan who had made Hélène feel secure; it was Nikolai. Noting it coldly, Laura went and washed, and then went to the red drawing-room and found her father there. The great mirror over the chimney-piece was shrouded too, and he had pushed his chair to a point where he did not need to see either that or the icon and its lamp in the corner. She wondered if she could find a way of suggesting he should take a room at the Ritz.

'Surely nobody's coming?' he asked. 'All this school-feast spread, I mean.'

On the table there was one of the oldest of the samovars, a number of the fragile tumblers etched with gold for those who like to drink their tea in glasses, and some Meissen cups, all set out on the great tray made from the coins which one of her great-great-grandfathers had brought back from the countries where he had campaigned. Around it were several jam-dishes, plates covered with slices of bread-and-butter, and cream puffs, sand-cake, almond-cake and several other kinds of cake.

'Didn't you ever go to a funeral when you were in Russia?' she asked him. She knew he had, he had told her so. 'I would have thought you'd have known it was always so, the servants go mad and go on making more and more food.' She paused and decided that it was not the time to tell her father, what he might not have heard, that the servants imagined themselves to be providing for angelic guests as well as the visible company. 'It's part of the treatment, part of the system worked out for relieving everybody's feelings. You do, don't you,' she asked disagreeably, 'have Irish wakes?' He looked so tired, so shabby, so uninteresting. 'But please try to eat some of it. That cold chicken they gave us from the hotel wasn't much. Have some *plyoomkek*. They call it that because they think they're copying our plum-cake, but it's much nicer.'

She cut him a slice, and he ate it silently and dourly, a child awaiting punishment.

'The tea's good,' he said.

'There's a panic in the household if the bricks don't come

through from Russia and they have to fall back on the tea Mummie sends from London.'

She heard the door-handle click. It was turning backwards and forwards, as if another apprehensive child stood outside.

Tania came in slowly. She was wearing a tea-gown of pale satin, fastened at her breast by one of those great brooches, large in itself and made of large stones, which she did not like to wear publicly in England, where jewellery was small, and therefore used about the house for casual purposes. The diamonds were throwing out bright rays, she was so shaken. Her hair was not dressed but was coiled on the nape of her neck. Along the opening of her gown there ran a line of smooth, short, glistening rosy feathers, curling back on themselves, and these were trembling. She threw her arms wide to Laura and gave a dry sob under her kiss, then pushed her away so that she could search her face, and said, 'So it was horrible. But you could stand it.'

'It was horrible,' Laura agreed. But not so horrible as the feeling of her mother's body in her arms, pulsing like a bird one had just saved from the cat. 'But nothing, really, to fuss over.'

'Fortunately there were a number of helpful people there,' said Edward Rowan, 'though of course it was regrettable she was alone.'

There was a long silence. 'Goodbye, Edward,' said Tania, and went to the door.

Laura followed her mother and on the threshold turned to say, 'Excuse me, Daddy.' He should not have sat at that desk in the landlord's room and written that letter, that long letter, while everything between them perished. But in case he had something to say she waited. But neither his voice nor his face said anything. The cruel text came back into her mind: 'And there shall be no more sea'.

Her mother had walked so quickly down the corridor that she was going into her bedroom when Laura caught up with her. She slipped her arm round her mother's waist and kissed her wet face and led her to an arm-chair and put a coverlet round her as if it were cold, and knelt at her feet and called her the silly pet-names Nanny had called them in the nursery. She had comforted Nikolai with them the night before. It had not occurred to her they would come in handy so soon again.

Letting the tears run but speaking steadily, Tania said, 'Now tell me about your grandfather. Did he suffer much?'

'It didn't hurt him to die, not at all.'

'How wonderful. I thought God's cruelty might pursue him to the very end. How strange you should have seen someone die when I never have. It makes you older than me. Oh, that you should have been alone, to bear this horror!' She wept, the harsh, hacking tears of rage.

'Never mind that. Never think of it again. There wasn't anything I couldn't manage. Listen, it was easy for him. He thought the gas wasn't on, and he bullied the doctors and nurse for not lighting it. "Need we talk in the dark like gipsies," he asked. Then he was dead. Like this.' She snapped her fingers.

'Thank God. Thank God. But he will be angry with me, where he is. He'll think I've behaved badly to your father.'

'If he knows anything about it, which is doubtful, after all if the Church is right he's a lot to do just now, if he knows anything about it. I should think he would feel that Daddy has behaved quite badly to you.'

'But I should have done more than just say, "Goodbye, Edward", to him.'

'Well, it did seem a bit terse.'

'But I can't say anything of the things I really feel.' Now her tears were gentle again. 'What's unbearable to me is that I'm still beautiful. If I were old and ugly, then what's happened would be natural. I'd be in no sort of disgrace, I'd simply be in the same position as a singer who retires when age destroys her voice. But I'm beautiful and if he leaves me now, and our life is nothing but a form of desertion in which he both deserts me and is at my side to see how much I'm hurt at being deserted, then it means that he's rejecting my beauty, and my beauty is me, and I'm being rejected. But I can't say that, it sounds like vanity. That shows how impossible it is to be a woman. One's whole life depends on one's looks, but one mayn't speak of one's own beauty and one mayn't say either that it's specially galling if one's husband leaves one for a woman who isn't as nice as one is oneself. That would be counted as vanity too.

371

Did your grandfather have a heart-attack when he was spoken to by this strange man on the train the Professor talked about?'

Laura wished yet once again that Professor Barrault had held his tongue. 'No. He was just irritated, upset, bothered by seeing this man. Who seemed rather nice, really. I don't think that meeting was anything much to do with his death.'

'But wasn't that why your grandfather got out of the train? Another thing I can't say to your father is that what I mind is that she never tipped people properly. It's so pleasant, it's such fun, to give money to people who need money. She didn't like it. I thought it was because she was poor and then it turned out she had all that money, but it was just that, she didn't enjoy it. But I thought your grandfather got out at Grissaint because he was feeling ill, after this man had said something to upset him. Tell me, Laura, tell me everything. I loved him so.'

'Well, it wasn't quite like that. Grandfather told me to go into another compartment because he wanted to talk to this man, without me, and then just before we got to Grissaint this man came down the corridor looking into every compartment to find me, and —' she stopped. So often had she gone over the story that she now came near to believing it. She seemed to remember, not merely imagined, what Chubinov had looked like as he pushed back the compartment door and bent his spectacles toward her and told her that Nikolai seemed not very well, she had better come quickly. Perhaps this was the way Kamensky had begun his lying. 'He told me,' she went on, 'that Grandfather was ill. But I don't know whether that wasn't just his way of putting it because he was in a hurry. Grandfather wasn't feeling well, and of course, he wasn't well, but I think the real reason he wanted to get out of the train was that he felt he had to get back to Paris, because the man, whoever he was, had reminded him of something he thought might help him clear his name with the Tsar. You must remember, Mummie, that it didn't really matter what was making Grandfather ill, he was hardly conscious of it, he was so preoccupied by the other thing, the row in Russia. And he'd got excited about something to do with that.'

'But the Professor thought he was taken quite ill in the station. Wasn't he suffering then?'

'It wasn't quite like that. Grandfather was sitting on a bench and waiting for the train to Paris, and then suddenly he couldn't move.' It sounded incredibly bare. She wanted to pour out the truth, the whole truth about Chubinov and Kamensky and who Kamensky was. She grasped her mother's hand and was about to tell her to get ready for a shock. But even her mother's hand was wet, her tears were everywhere, and her eyes were full of grief, but not quite full, there was still room in them for a spaniel's sad hope. If her mother heard the truth, she would use it as an excuse for running to her husband as if he were still her husband, and annulling that goodbye. 'Edward, Edward! Listen to what Laura's told me!' If that happened, her father would take ordinary measures for her protection which would be quite wrong, since the man from whom she had to be protected was extraordinary and had caught her in the mesh of an extraordinary way of life. She had been certain of that at Grissaint. She was more certain now. Also her father lacked the thought-reading love which would have made sense of the long, involved story; instead he would produce a deadly common sense. He would tell the police and Chubinov would be arrested and would be in prison when Kamensky came to kill her. She went on distracting Tania's attention from the truth. 'And Grandfather was quite delirious. He kept on talking about a little girl blowing a toy trumpet.'

'One of us, perhaps? My sister Varvara, or perhaps Olga – or perhaps,' she just dared to suggest, 'me?' She averted her eyes quickly so that she need not see Laura's embarrassed shake of the head. 'Of course not. He wouldn't speak of any of us, even at the very end. Any more than he'd speak of his fingers or his toes or his ribs. He thought of us as a part of himself. And not a very important part. Dear me, a little girl blowing a toy trumpet.'

'At a children's party.'

'It must have been something that mattered to him.'

'What?'

'What the man told him on the train.'

Sometimes people thought her mother was silly. They were wrong. She could have wished that they were more right.

'It must have been really very important,' Tania went on, dreamily, 'to have sent his mind running all the way back from his greatness to a little girl blowing on a toy trumpet at a children's party. That's yet another thing I can't say to your father. I am so terrified that if I go back to London my mind will run away from what happens to me there now. I might act so strangely that people would think I was mad or drank or took drugs. I might start gambling. It's our Russian way of taking misfortune. There's some sense to it. At roulette or baccarat one can strip one's luck bare, and see if it's bad or good, and if it's bad one can give it a chance to take pity on one and change. But I couldn't admit to your father that what he has done has hurt me so much that I can't stay in the world of sanity and face it, he'd think I was simply being jealous and hysterical, and that's not what's happened. It's like being obliged to take up a cross and nurse the afflicted in prison, this being strange, the whole of one has to give the part of one that's suffering a chance to live outside the world of logic, where it's been scourged and thrown into a dungeon. But about your grandfather, you're sure he didn't suffer —'

'That reminds me. How's Grandmother?'

Tania smiled triumphantly. 'Ah, I've no need to worry about her. She's in pain now, but she won't be for long. It's this treatment they are giving her. Something called radium. She didn't like the treatment, she was frightened, that's why, as I told Kamensky to tell you, I had such difficulty over my telephoning. But she's bound to get better. But tell me about my father. This other professor, not the one who telephoned to me, the one the stationmaster brought to you at the station, he took you to a hotel. What was it like?'

'Quite old. It had a beautiful ballroom in it. I looked in from the landing and they were getting it ready for a ball. Why am I telling you that?'

'When awful things are happening one's sometimes grateful for the way the chairs and tables and carpets look. But he had a good bed, there were kind servants?'

'Oh, lots. Particularly one called Catherine. And the bed

374

seemed comfortable enough, he lay and talked and talked. Oh, about all sorts of things. About the South. About a place where there were olive-terraces and wine-cellars running far out under the sea.'

'The Four Towers, Leon Galitzin's estate. The Tartars built those cellars. Tartars in their white robes and their turbans. When I was little I thought they were captive jinns. Why should my father think of the Four Towers, at the very end? He was not often there.'

'Because he was talking about the Russians being a southern people as well as a northern. The descendants of the Greeks. Our great crimes. And then there was the olive oil. The holy oil. He went on and on about that, reciting great chunks of the Office of the Holy Unction, and that other one – the Office for the Parting of the Soul from the Body.'

'Oh, dear God, dear God, and there was no priest.'

'Well, if there had been a priest about, he wouldn't have got a word in edgeways. And Grandfather didn't really worry about that.'

'He wouldn't. He must have known he should have got absolution for his sins, but he wasn't much given to self-reproach. Some people aren't, but your father's not one of them. That means there's another thing I can't tell him. He's afraid I'll ruin his career by divorcing him. But I won't do that. All I feel is that I can't live with him, and divorcing has nothing to do with it. A woman can't in England or anywhere else divorce a man because he left her old father to die in a strange place, with nobody there but their daughter, a girl of eighteen. And remember, it didn't happen but it might have, the terrorists might have been there. That's the real reason why I can't go on living with your father any more. Laura, I tried to help you and my father. I couldn't leave my mother, she was frightened, being ill in a clinic was new to her, and she was too ill to take something both new and painful. Whenever I could get out of her room I rang home again and again, and told them to find your father, and they tried at the House, and rang back to tell me the Whip said he's paired, and then I humbled myself and rang up her house. But she wasn't there. Then I was tortured. Somebody once sent me an anonymous letter, and I read the beginning and then tore it up. I'd read enough to know yesterday that if I'd finished it I would have known where your father was. I was punished for obeying the rules I've been brought up to keep. But your grandfather, go on about your grandfather.'

'There's not much to tell, not that you can really tell. He recited these services by the yard, and then said he understood everything, and that he wasn't God but man, and had made far too much fuss about having been disgraced by the Tsar, because nothing that happened to him, or anybody who wasn't God, was of the slightest importance.'

'That's the sort of idea we Russians enjoy.'

'He enjoyed it immensely.'

'Possibly we enjoy it because it's true. But after that?'

'After that, I've told you. He asked, "Must we talk in the dark like gipsies?" and the next moment he was dead. Then they gave me some supper, the Professor who had found us at the railway station, and a nurse he had got in. They were really very nice.' She paused, and would have given anything to continue smoothly, 'so nice that afterwards they helped me send off a telegram to the man in the train telling him the hour at which he could most conveniently murder Monsieur Kamensky.' But her certainty came back to her: if she said that, in seconds her mother would be starting to her feet, eagerly crying, 'I must tell your father at once,' and then some witless, shrewd, conventional action of her father's would grind on its way to her death, amid a number of French policemen competently mobilised by the British Embassy. She said, 'Then I went to bed, but Monsieur Kamensky arrived, and was in my room for hours while I told him all about it.'

Her mother sat up straight. 'Was that – all right?'

Perhaps she knew everything after all. 'Do you imagine,' Laura asked, 'that it couldn't have been?'

'Was it?'

'Quite. He just sat about and nearly cried and said how much he had cared for Grandfather, and I got sleepy, and then some people barged into the room, and I asked him to go —'

'He was in your bedroom? It seems so improper.'

'Oh, Mummie! They'd put up a camp-bed in the salon

376

and the nurse was sleeping in an arm-chair. But, really, Mummie!'

'Forgive me, I'm not very clever just now. The little Kamensky couldn't have been kinder. He telephoned me this morning, and had thought of everything, he even reminded me that the nice wife of that blind man who comes here is a qualified candlebearer, and that it would be pleasant to have her as one of the two candlebearers who have to recite the Psalter over your grandfather's body. You know that the Psalms have to be read as soon as he's brought here late to-night until he's taken to the church the day after tomorrow for the funeral. The second candlebearer I don't know, he's sent from the church, but the Berrs have often been here, and, of course, they're special people. If she reads the Psalms there'll be some reality in that dreary ceremony.'

'The Psalms do twaddle on.'

'An angry savage in a tent, sometimes calming down when there's been a good haul of desert antelope, and there's been enough rain for the grass. Boring God like an ill-bred guest who will chatter about his own silly little misadventures to a host who has great affairs on his shoulders. How did we come to take this cross on our back, to repeat over and over again these barbarian curses and blessings, when our hearts are full of a clear image of the one we loved?'

'Sometimes you sound like your father.'

She shook her head. 'Not at all. I am moderate, rational, ordinary.'

'I wonder why it is,' Laura said, 'that when people make a statement such as you've just made, other people say to them, "Tell that to the marines".'

'Ask your father,' said Tania, absently. Tears came into Laura's eyes and she wondered if when Berr came into the apartment his powers would be excited and released by grief to the point of working miracles, and that time would run backwards, and then start again and keep itself undefiled. Let Kamensky's mother never have had him. Let the old days start again, let Tania and herself at this very moment be sitting on the terrace outside the drawing-room at home, watching the tennis-players tangle their feet in their own long shadows, while the windows of the houses opposite blazed with the reflected sunset, and let them be talking of a possible visit to Russia, which should be sooner rather than later, since Nikolai was so old and was never likely to leave his own country again. Let there be no Susie Staunton, but let that be done not by the simple racing back of clock-hands, but in some way that hurt her. Laura shut her eyes and offered up an enraged prayer.

'Don't, don't,' said Tania. 'Don't pray, I mean. We Russians are so frightful, dropping in on eternity all the time, without waiting to be asked. God must be so sick of us. Give Him a rest. Come and see the little dressmaker, she has your mourning almost finished, it only needs fitting.'

In the sewing-room, in air sour with the smell of black cloth, Hélène was stitching a dress which flopped over her lap like a second grieving skirt, while a young girl and a sewing-machine were involved in a common fury which sent another dress twitching off the table towards the floor. Calm set in and the two women looked at them kindly. 'This is our little Noémie, who's come to help,' said Tania, stroking the girl's dark curly head. It appeared she was the daughter of Hélène's best friend, Juliette, who sometimes came over and stayed at Radnage Square. What a lot of people would miss it if that house belonged to some other family.

The two of them took off Laura's dress and till they brought her the new one she looked at herself in the cheval-glass, and tried to master her annoyance at her breasts. She had to have them, it would be too odd if she did not. But they were silly things, and all the names for them – breasts, bosom, bust – were silly too, soft and credulous, as if they would believe anything they were told. They were certainly round and white and pleasantly hard, and the blue veins twisting prettily enough over the whiteness like sweet-pea tendrils. But they were tiresome additions to the useful body she had started with, and she had read somewhere if women's breasts were bruised they might get cancer. It was absurd to be exposed to such a risk on the off-chance one might some day have a baby, almost as absurd as the fatuous business of menstruation. But when the two women drew the black dress over her head she disliked it

378

more than her body. It covered her from neck to wrist and ankles.

But her mother seemed not to be reminded of any other black dress. She said, 'That's very nicely made. Only this one dart needs alteration. It's not as long as the one on the other side and it's at a different angle. Hélène and Noémie are very clever at this sort of thing, we know, but what's so wonderful is the way they've worked like beavers. Now the rest of it.' They draped over Laura's shoulders a black cape bound with white and set on her head a cap of black net. 'Oh, my dear,' sighed Tania, 'how our hair won't go into mourning. But otherwise it's all perfect.'

She made no move to rise and leave now that the business of the clothes was finished. The two women started gossiping, out of charity, offering her their affairs as a distraction, muting their quality out of respect for the occasion, making life more childish and innocent than it is. Hélène and Juliette had been at school together, in the parish of Poissy, outside Paris, and now the girl was engaged to the son of one their schoolfellows, Annette. They were going to be married in the old church, as old as old, at Poissy. It was a great joke, they laughed at it with reverently diminished laughter, because Annette was a twin and her other son had had twins. The young couple were looking for a house at Fontenay-les-Roses, where he worked, and it was being pointed out to them that, with his family tendency in view, they'd better choose a big one. Tania turned practical, asked whether they meant to rent or buy the house, and on hearing that it was to be bought with a legacy, told them they could use the services of the Diakonov's family lawyer, if they had none of their own. A phrase stirred in Laura's memory.

'Mummie, who were the lace-makers? When Grandfather was near the end, he told me to ask the lace-makers not to sing so loud. He said he liked to hear them at their hymns, but they kept him awake.'

'Well, there were lace-makers on every big house in the country. The cleverest women did that. But enough of them to make a choir? Ah, I remember – but that was a long time ago. Something had driven him far, far back.'

379

'What was a long time ago?'

'The trouble is I've forgotten. He told me about it several times but only when I was little. It was on the estate of someone who was quite elderly when he was a child, I think a grand-uncle of his. A river burst its banks, or was there a forest fire? Anyway a little village was destroyed and some dozens of serfs were homeless. The man who owned them couldn't afford to rebuild the village, so whoever it was, your grandfather's grand-uncle or whoever, bought the villagers, though he had too many serfs already, and put up some extra wooden houses and workshops for them. It turned out that in this particular village the people had been very clever. The men were good millers. Oh, it must have been a river burst its banks, if the men were good at handling grain, they couldn't have been forest people. And the women made beautiful lace and had divine voices. The estate-owner's wife was musical, and she trained them. Yes, my father told me how he used to eavesdrop outside the workroom where they made lace, to listen to them as they sang hymns, and also they used to come into the drawing-room and sing to the guests. My father remembered the look of their bare feet on the parquet floor on the Savonnerie carpets.'

'What happened to them all? Could one find their descendants do you think?'

'Ah, no. They were dispersed even when my father was still young. The owner went bankrupt and the estate had to be sold.'

'Bankrupt, when he owned a lot of serfs?'

'Well, owning serfs didn't stop people from going bankrupt. When the serfs were emancipated, it turned out that most of them were pledged to the banks. But where can that estate have been? And what was the disaster?' She stood up, picked up the black net and fitted it over her hair. 'And now I remember something more. My father said the women were beautiful with slanting eyes and high cheekbones, higher than the Russians have, Asiatic high. He said there was Mongol blood there. But where isn't it? It's even here in this cheval-glass so long as I stand in front of it. We both of us have a golden background to our skin, Laura. No, that doesn't give us a clue to where the village was.'

She shuddered, said brief good-byes to the two women, bade them remember about the lawyer and went out into the corridor, and burst out: 'Laura, we're being swept away by a dark river. That village gone without trace, we are like that. It's our custom to have a Book of Remembrance, in which there's written down the names of everyone united to a man by a bond of a certain strength, a certain good will. All his relatives, all his close friends, everybody whom he had helped, his blind, his lame, his idiots. When he dies it's the custom to read this Book in the Church at the funeral. But it must not be read for my dear father, because he died in disgrace. A young officer might have to leave his regiment, a girl like you might be sent abruptly away from her place at court, if the name of a father or mother was read from that Book at the service. We could read out the names of our beggars, but that would be to insult them, to state publicly that they cannot rouse respect enough to be taken seriously and persecuted. All I can do with that Book is to hide it, and who knows, when it is safe for it to be found, nobody may recognise it for what it is, or care if they do.'

'Surely it doesn't matter, considering we go on living after we're dead,' said Laura.

'Of course it doesn't. I am lying. I am a hypocrite. I'm talking nonsense about my father, whom nothing can hurt, when I am really thinking how I'm hurt, how the best of my life has been swept away by a dark river. Because of what has happened I can't bear to remember how I have spent my life between my eighteenth and my thirty-eighth year. Laura, you are my pride, my treasure, I love you more than anything else in the world, but I can't face thinking of how you came to be. It isn't only living people who die, it is great stretches of living, which can die even when the people who lived there still exist. Life drains away from itself and goes into nothingness. Now I understand why in our services for the dead we sing over and over again just the two words, "Everlasting Memory, Everlasting Memory". But come, let's see how the preparations are going on in the big drawing-room. They should be finished now.'

The room was as different from itself as the last few days of Laura's life differed from those that had come before. Folding doors she had never noticed had been closed, and nothing was left of the ordinary furniture in the remaining half except another veiled mirror over the chimney-piece. In the middle of the room, low on the four rounded supports, was the empty coffin. It was not like an English coffin, it was broad at the head and tapered straight to the feet, and very shallow, and it was covered with cloth-of-gold. It lay askew, the head turned towards the icon in the corner of the room, and at each end of it were two candlesticks, not yet lit, rising high above it, with lengths of white muslin like petticoats tied to them with black ribbon. Facing the icon across the coffin was a lectern, only a little more solid than a music-stand in an orchestra, covered with a piece of fine linen, with a large leather-bound volume resting on it. Close under the icon there was set a dark crucifix, nearly the height of a man, with a scarf of muslin twisted round it as if for decency's sake. It could have been a critical onlooker, deeply involved but not taking control, not offering active help. The rites to be performed here should be useful enough to make any special intervention unnecessary.

Words that she had heard her grandfather speak and had instantly forgotten sounded in her ear again. He had told her it was her Christian duty to dissuade Chubinov from murdering Kamensky. It did not deeply distress her that she had disobeyed, for after all God killed everyone by decreeing the existence of death, and it would be unfair if He did not occasionally permit a human being to kill in self-defence. Certainly she ought to defend herself. Apart from her own desire not to die, which might be sheer prejudice, she could not go away, so irretrievably away, from her mother at this time. But Nikolai had told her a Christian duty was invariably disagreeable, and the aspect of this room, the pattern described by the tall crucifix and the low coffin set aslant, confirmed that she expected to do something which would cause her pain. She had already some vague notion of what it was, and had even known she was holding her thoughts back from their proper end. Now she admitted to herself that if Chubinov killed Kamensky and was caught she could not let him take the whole blame. She would have to confess to the police that she had asked him and aided him to commit the crime. The drunkenness of self-sacrifice ran through her veins, but the room kept her sober. She looked again at the flickering light of the icon, the veiled mirror, the tall cross, the coffin set askew, the lectern with its Psalter, the four petticoated candlesticks. They were not demanding self-sacrifice of her, but the same grim ingenuity which, placing these things thus and so, made possible the performance of the useful rite. Perhaps Berr would show her what to do.

15

'IF MY FATHER had been in his own home in Russia,' Tania said bitterly to Laura, 'we would not have been with him, but he would have had three sons and two daughters and fourteen grandchildren to kneel by his side. Now, because he was exiled by our most pious, autocrat and puissant Tsar of All the Russias, as the prayer-book calls him, he is alone with you and me. So one or other of us will have to spend nearly all the day with him and we will keep vigil with him tonight. It's a lot to ask a girl of your age, but think of yourself as going out to meet the Tsar on the field of battle and humiliating him with your prayers. Oh, don't look at me in that English way. You English sing, "Onward Christian Soldiers", there can't be so much to feel strange about in this.'

'You don't understand. I was wondering about something else. Quite different. Feeling like that about the Tsar, could you join the revolutionaries?'

'Of course not. Let's leave out the question of whether a revolution would do any good or not, whether it isn't so alien from the Russian people that a revolution would mean that they ceased to exist as what they now are, it's not possible for people like you and me to become revolutionaries. Tyrants have to be deposed by subjects who have broken, whose nerves snap under tyranny, who are seized by frenzy. But people like us don't break. It's not specially to our credit. Indeed, it's a form of misfortune. Now I must go and receive General Dukingen. I am dreading it, he's very deaf.'

Laura went slowly down the corridor to the room where the coffin lay, noting that her mother was out of date. She was thinking of the French Revolution. Now revolutionaries sat quiet in their enemies' arm-chairs, and handed the ladies of the household their coffee and their cognac, and sat well-brushed and dapper while their thoughts went out and did their work for them. In the room, she found Berr's wife still standing at the Lectern and reading the Psalm, though she had begun in the early morning, and it was now afternoon. The other candlebearer was quite ready to take her place. Laura had just seen him in the kitchen, eating pickled mushrooms and reading back numbers of Russian newspapers, and he had spoken of Berr's wife with humorous sympathy, as a professional might speak of an amateur intractable in her enthusiasm. But Berr's wife meant to use her stocky strength till it ran out, Berr was kneeling in prayer beside her, because they could make no other sign of gratitude to the old man in the coffin. She was chanting the Holy Writ in the quick monotone the priests had taught her, so that the words ran together into an incantation such as tongue and lips might have woven before words were invented. But her round peasant face confirmed the sense. When her face crumpled as if a milking-pail had fallen on her toe, then King David was crying that God had cast him off and had given up his armies as sheep to the slaughterers, and sold them for nought and made them a scorn and derision for their neighbours. When happiness lifted her cheeks high like little shrunken russet apples, then David was naming the Lord his light and his salvation, the strength of his life, in whom he delighted, and who gave him the desires of his heart.

The incantation, the upward reflection of the Psalter on her face, did not cease when visitors came into the room to pray by the coffin and sometimes to lift the pall and look on Nikolai's face. There were more of them than Tania had expected. She had known the Countess von Krehmunden would come. It was in the chapel of her house in the Champs-Elysées that Sonia had been worshipping of late. The old woman had drawn the exiled family as close to her as she could, saying that she was too old to fear anything the Tsar could do; but moved, Tania said, by a far more interesting consideration. 'She's Russian only by marriage, being a German by birth, but she's the more Russian for that. She's a member of the house of Anhalt-Zerbst which never forgets it sent Catherine the Great to Moscow. So she thinks of the present Tsar as having let a flourishing family business go to pot. And when Germany had the luck to send another Tsarina to Russia in our time, she can't bear to think it was the present poor little thing.' It was indeed deep shame which possessed the Countess as she advanced into the room, small and stout, dwarfed by a hat covered with black birds on the top of a crimped mahogany wig, her short neck built up solid as a fortress with a dog-collar of black and white pearls, her black dress armoured with jet, her hand just able to beat the air in an attempt at a reverent gesture, since arthritis had made her rigid. The skill of her maid had covered her old face with some powder or lotion which did in fact soften her wrinkles with something like the bloom of youth, and this incongruity was not incongruous. She was an octogenarian grieving stoically for a lifelong friend and for a dynasty, but she was also pitifully embarrassed, as a young person might be when confronted with the fatal results of an act committed by a discreditable relative. The wrong that Nikolai had suffered was so great that, not only for the Countess but for all the other visitors, it competed with death in its power to awe. The Countess must have been the only one of them who had not had to overcome at least a moment of cowardice before determining to disregard Tania's advice and pay the customary visit of condolence; for all the rest murmured, 'We felt we had to come', and moved with the dandyish air given by consciousness of bravery, the men holding their tall hats high against their pearl-grey waistcoats, the women curtseying slowly right down to the floor. When they lifted the pall from Nikolai's face they did not sigh at its sudden revelation of the peace of eternity, they breathed quickly, angered by what had been done to him in time, and what might, perhaps, be done to them also, in a small measure, simply because they had made this act of presence.

They came and they went; but there were not many of them, and there were long stretches when Laura knelt by the coffin and tried to pray. But her mind constantly wandered. She did not know where her father was. She had not seen him since the evening before, when Tania had bade him good-bye, and she had no idea whether he was in the apartment or not. It might be that he had gone down to the Ritz, and had taken a room on the pretext of keeping Aunt Florence company after she arrived that night from Mûres-sur-mer. But it was also possible that he was travelling across Northern France, staring out of the window at the brassy cornfields and smiling that obsessed half-smile, passing through Grissaint without noticing it, going on to the Channel Boat and off again, without sense of the sea, sealed in his contentment. If he had started last night or early this morning, he might already be back in London. She was thinking of him as a short, correctly-dressed figure, walking with a false, uneasy springiness, small, as if she were looking at him through the wrong end of an opera-glass. It was beyond her understanding why she wanted to know where he was, or why she thought of him as short, when he was really quite tall, or of his gestures as trivial, when they were so decided and so sensible. But then she now thought of Kamensky, who really was small, as large and coarsely-made, and on the point of some gigantically violent gesture for which he would not really have had the strength.

Her hatred of Kamensky blazed up, and she begged God to do just one thing out of the many He could do for her and her family, and kill Kamensky. She would not ask Him to raise Nikolai from the dead. By now he must have reached the presence of God, and if he turned round and came back he would still have to deal with the Tsar, and it would need a vast revision of earthly affairs to make that other than an inconvenience, because the next Tsar would probably be a stupid grand duke who would be just as bad. But she would ask God not to let Kamensky kill her and Chubinov and to spare them the necessity of killing him by doing it Himself. 'You created him,' she said into her hands, 'we didn't. So you ought to kill him. Let him drop dead in the street, and then send someone in here to say so. You should kill him for Your own sake.

What's the good of our praying "God's will be done in earth as it is in heaven," with people like Kamensky about?' The word 'heaven' took her thoughts back to Nikolai. Now he must be happy, even if he had to spend some time in hell, because nobody was reading his letters any more, and he would never have laid on him again the duty of reading other people's letters. The diplomat in the Russian Embassy, too, the one with the son at Oxford, he would be fortunate as soon as he died, and he no longer need read stolen and tear-stained diaries, while his son stole the sight of them from him. The idea of eternity captivated her. It would be candid life, it would have the special beauty of flowers which open wide in their moment of perfection, like the wild rose.

Chubinov's wife being dead, she would not like to remember how she had spent her life making dynamite at Kamensky's behest, for surely one learned the truth about everything as soon as one died, and she would long have known Kamensky's treachery. Also she could not wish that her husband should run the risk of being guillotined. Laura was praying to Chubinov's wife to intercede with God and make Him kill Kamensky, when her thoughts passed to that appalling overcoat made by the female dentist at Lausanne. There could not be another like it in Paris. If Chubinov got away after he had shot Kamensky, the police would be able to trace him easily by that unique garment. Of course the day was too warm for an overcoat, but it would be like Chubinov not to notice that. She should have warned him to leave it at home, but it would have been an odd thing to put in a telegram, and she had wanted to stick to the point. Remembering what that point was, she was delivered over again to fear, and her bowels writhed once more.

Laura had no hope that God would answer her prayer and kill Kamensky. The aspect of this room the night before, with the tall cross and the coffin set aslant, had warned that this was not the sort of prize it offered. But it had been Chubinov's opinion that Berr had received from God some sort of plain, straightforward kindness such as a kind man might show to the victim of misfortune. She looked across the coffin into Berr's blind face to see what that might be. She found that Berr's wife was not only reading the Psalms as an incantation and living out their meaning in her mind so that they worked their full exorcising power on the old man in the coffin, she was doing other magical work as well, by sometimes stretching out her hand and touching her husband, without interrupting her chant. She looked a very simple woman, who would find it hard to go much beyond the most elementary drudgery, who would be able to do little more than scrub a floor and cook *kasha* porridge and cabbage soup, but she was practising some intricate and supernatural art in partnership with her husband, though he looked as simple, and stupidly so. Here he had lost his disagreeable air of arrogance, which was natural enough; since it was God who had made him blind, it was no use pretending before God that he could see. But he had a sheep's head, his forehead sloped, his nose was long, and so was his upper lip, and his chin receded. Much of the time he looked not just slow-witted, but even a little drunk, for he jerked his head about and muttered to himself in complaint. It was then that his wife, without ceasing to chant, put out her hand and grasped his shoulder, and at that he grew still, raised his head, stared at something in front of him, panted, and struggled on, to think a new thought. He might have been wrestling; thought was not his trade. But his thinking brought him deliverance, and then his features became firm and intelligent, sometimes he laughed, and his blind eyes looked as if they saw, and saw a glory. Then too his wife put out her hand and touched him, but to stroke his head, laying her hand on it reverently, as she might have touched the paten that held the altar-bread or the chalice that held the Communion wine. It seemed conceivable that if there had been no men on earth a vast immaterial heart would have ached with want. She did not doubt that the Berrs had wisdom such as she would never possess, if only because they were superior in equipment, having gifts of which she had so little that she could not even name them. But the Berrs could not help her. Their wisdom was rooted in their experience, which had nothing in common with hers. She tried to frame a question she could put to them which would convey her difficulty to them, and failed. Her mind wandered to her

388

father, and to Chubinov's overcoat, and she looked at her watch. It was a quarter to four.

She rose from her knees and stood looking down on the coffin, while she said good-bye to Nikolai. Perhaps this would be the last time she would be in the same room with him. She bowed to the icon, the cross, the coffin, and turned towards the door, to be checked by a thick black column rising high above her. It was Father Iliodor, a priest who had assisted the Metropolitan in the service held that morning. She had remarked him because he was so tall, and because he had a magnificent bass voice, like an opera-singer's, which was doubtless what had brought him into the Church. Otherwise he would have earned his living by his strength, probably as a soldier, and he still called to mind the fact of fierceness, for he had the light eyes and vigilant mask of a lion. But he was removed from the natural world by the cross on his breast and his long black robe and the tawny-gold hair glowing over his shoulders and his long tawny-gold beard, both undulating in the fine waves which came of keeping them tightly plaited all night. After the service, when Tania had given the priests and the mourners some food and drink in the dining-room, he had moved about in an indifferent, unemployed way, as if to him everyday life was merely the margin of the Liturgy, the unused portion of the paper it was printed on. Now he was as glad to be in this room of mourning as most people would be to leave it. It was through him and his kind that the Berrs had gathered their wisdom, but he could not help her. A saint might profit from an encounter with a lion who could sing hymns, but she could not.

After Laura had been to her room and combed her hair and washed her hands, she went down the dark corridor towards the hall. As she passed one door she heard Tania's voice, fatigued by the effort of shouting graciously, 'But I can assure you, General, that my father quite understood why you had not been to see him lately. He spoke of you only a few days ago with the warmest affection.' It was monstrous of her not to warn Tania. But her mother would try to stop her, and anyway she would be able better than most people to cope with what would happen afterwards, for she was always at her best in unforeseen circumstances. It was a long strain, which her mother could not bear. Laura let herself out of the front door, leaving it open, and slowly went down the four flights of broad, shallow steps, through the dusty darkness, rehearsing what she was going to do and say during the next half-hour or so. It was her intention to hide in the archway, peering out of its shadows into the avenue, just as Kamensky had hidden there when the actress and the three young conspirators went by, and to wait till she heard the noise of the shot. Then she would hurry into the street and see where they both were. If a policeman had got there already and had caught Chubinov she would go up to him and, imitating Tania as much as possible, tell him that the killed or wounded man was a Russian terrorist, that he had threatened to kill her, and that Chubinov had shot him only to protect her, and at her request. But French crowds sometimes lynched assassins, and she saw their point; she could only wish that some crowd had lynched Kamensky long ago. But if a mob were closing in on Chubinov she would pull her hair down and scream, 'Leave that man alone, he's innocent, I am guilty', over and over again, and perhaps tear her dress a little down the front, to look more dramatic. They would think her mad, but if that distracted their attention until the police came, she could put up with it. Still, she wanted to do none of these things. The world was choked with death and she did not want to add to it; and the goose-pimples rose on her flesh as she thought of strangers laying hands on her in the street.

On the last landing she stopped and stared at the broad mahogany door of the first-floor apartment. With its brass knob in the centre of each panel and the brass plate on the wall announcing this to be the Paris office of the Anonymous Society of the United Enterprises of Tokyo-Caracas-Tananarive, while the elevator thudded and clicked and squeaked past her up to the floor above. Rather than die out in the street she would choose to live the natural term of her life standing there on the spinach-green carpet, which had the matted texture of carpets not privately owned, in hotels or theatres or concert halls, and looking through the unsunned twilight at the gross door and listening to the whine of the elevator rope. She had thought like that at Grissaint station, sitting beside her grandfather, deliberating on Chubinov's warning, and looking out at the stained and sordid masonry of the railway-cutting just beside the platform. It was disgusting of her to want to live as much as that. A neighbour of theirs in Radnage Square had become a drunkard when quite an old man, and Dolly the housemaid had told her that when he found the sideboard and the cellar locked against him by his family he went down to the kitchen by night and stole the methylated spirit. She was behaving like that. Quickly she ran down the stairs into the hall and past the concierge's lodge into the courtyard and the lazy warmth of the afternoon, and had to smile when her eye caught sight of the plaster naiad on her pedestal in the circle of shrubs. The basin into which she poured her vase had been filled with potted plants by someone anxious to avoid the trouble of watering them. Bending over them with a languorous air of self-surrender, she seemed unusually fond of geraniums.

The smile went from Laura's lips as she walked towards the archway. Beyond its shadow, a few yards of the sunlit avenue were shown like a lit stage. In the apartment she had not realised how fine a day it was. In the background the cabs and carriages were rolling by, the horses' heads proud or humble, their hooves ringing on the metalled road. A low branch of a tree rose and fell with the breeze just below the span of the archway, drawing a dark pattern against the sunshine without. The air scintillated with summer. In the foreground a tall blonde young woman, wearing a large purple hat of transparent material, wired to stand out like an aureole, and a pale-mauve dress that, glistening, seemed to be rigid in anger at an affront. Her face was vibrating as if someone had just slapped it. Then her eyelids drooped, and she grew still as a wooden figure under her floating clothes, and fell back into the arms of a bearded young man in a frock-coat and striped trousers. As he caught her his monocle flew out of his eye and swung in a drunken circle on its black ribbon, at the same time that his top-hat slid off the back of his head; but this ridiculous double misfortune did not embarrass him, he was grey with nausea. Laura could not see how these people could be involved in the story of her grandfather and Kamensky and Chubinov and wondered whether they were what they seemed, or were conspirators, and if so on which side. But of course the young woman might have been fainting in front of this house by sheer chance, as she might have fainted anywhere else in Paris, and the man might simply be unused to handling unconscious women. But an elderly man in a light suit, with a red face, very round, under a bowler, was standing at right-angles to the couple with his back to the traffic, staring down on the ground with an astonished expression. It was on the same spot that the young man's eyes were fixed. Both men were looking at Kamensky. He was lying on his back on the pavement. Laura recognised him only by the polished black toes of his small shoes, which were pointing straight upwards. Where his face should have been, there was a bunch of white roses. He was gripping it with both hands, and these rested on his throat, just covering his beard. There was a spreading red stain on the paving-stone beside him, coming from somewhere near his left arm-pit.

An elderly woman, wearing an old-fashioned black bonnet tied with strings under her chins, came to a halt beside the man in the light suit, gaped at what she saw, crossed herself and stood blinking and praying. The next minute there were people standing on each side of these two, all looking down at Kamensky as if, once he had done this extraordinary thing of lying there dead, he might be expected to do something else as extraordinary. The woman in the pale-mauve glistening dress had sunk to the ground, and had twisted round and pressed her face against the young man's legs, so that her hat was a purple circle covering the knees of his striped trousers. Some of the cabs and carriages slowed down, others kept on their way. Above the noise of the traffic there could be heard curiously wistful shouts and sounds of running feet, and the street hummed as if it had an insect life of its own. From the archway she watched more and more people curdle into a silent assembly, looking down on the body through the bright light; and she slipped out of the shadow and joined them.

Suddenly there was amongst them a policeman, a sallow man with an angry blue-black moustache, waving his truncheon in a threat so general that it threatened nobody. The strap gave, and it fell from his hand, but he caught it in mid-air, nearly falling over as he stretched for it, and at once he had to fumble for his whistle, which had swung on its cord to the back of his neck. All his movements were going wrong, as if he were an actor in a harlequinade. He knelt down by Kamensky, felt his pulse, and then shouted to the crowd, 'Who put these roses on his face?' It sounded as if the unforgivable irregularity in the proceedings was the gross mishandling of the white roses.

'Nobody, he put them there himself,' said the man in the light suit.

'What?' exclaimed the policeman. 'A dead man decorated his own corpse with flowers?' He lifted the whistle to his lips, and the blasts ranged overhead like the call of furious birds.

The man in the light suit clapped his hands over his ears. 'If you'll stop that row I'll tell you what happened. No, I didn't see it done. But I think it must have been done just before, because I saw this poor man on the street-corner down there, where the Rue Belloy runs into the Avenue. I noticed him myself because he was carrying these white roses and was dressed as if he were going to call on a lady, and looked most respectable, and yet he was reeling, I thought he'd had a drop too much. When I saw he was going up the Avenue the same way as me, I kept well to the rear, for he was staggering worse, I didn't want him staggering on to me. Then I saw that his left trouser-leg had a dark line on it, as if it were wet, and then there was a red smear on the pavement. I felt ashamed, I should have known there was something wrong, he was too respectable to be drunk. I ran forward and said, "You've been hurt, sit down on a doorstep and I'll get help," but he only said, "I must get there, I must get there." Then he nearly fell, and I put my arm round him and said, "Lean on me," but he wrenched himself away, muttering that, "The flowers mustn't be crushed." But then the blood gushed out, see, it's here on my sleeve, and he called out something I couldn't understand, and he gave a cough and sagged into my arms and fell flat on the pavement and stretched himself out as if he were on a bed, and his hands went up, and that's why the flowers are over his face.'

The policeman sent another blast screaming overhead like a gull, took out a notebook and began writing, asked some questions, blew his whistle again. A bus came to an uneasy stop at the curb, the horses scuffling and slipping between the shafts, because the passengers inside and on top had all rushed to one side to see what was the cause of the commotion. On top several young men with angry faces leaned far over the side and howled abuse of the police, and slogans about freedom and Captain Dreyfus. The silent crowd turned and looked up at them in bewilderment, the policeman dropped his notebook. Then one of the young men shouted a prolonged denunciation of the authorities for preventing the sons of the people from honouring brave men on a sacred anniversary. The white roses had evidently been transformed by the group's preoccupations into a memorial sheaf, torn from the hands of libertarian demonstrators. The silent crowd turned back to their original position and went on looking at Kamensky as if he might know some other conjuring trick as well as lying there. The policeman, after blowing a few more blasts, began again to question the man in the light suit. Laura did not know what to do. The sunshine was very strong, it picked out in the pavement and the buildings the blue grain which summer discloses in stone, and the flecks which sparkle like lump sugar. The glare made her feel sick and stupid. It was all quite different from what she had expected, and she felt she might as well go back to the apartment. But when she turned towards the archway she found Chubinov standing behind her. He did not see her because his eyes also were levelled on Kamensky in that sceptical, precautionary stare. He was wearing the overcoat, but perhaps it was for the best. If anybody noticed that his face was shining with sweat they might think that the reason.

She said softly, 'Vassili, let's get out of this,' but he showed no sign of having heard her, and she repeated it. But at that moment the man in the light suit pointed straight at him. 'Yes. That's the gentleman. I don't think he can have seen the assault, but he may have seen the assailant, for he was standing only a few yards from the poor victim when I first caught sight of him. Not,' he added, 'that he can have anything to do with the stabbing, for he was yards away.'

If Kamensky had been stabbed, then someone else had murdered him. Liberated, she took her stand beside Chubinov without furtiveness and was unperturbed while the policeman came nearer and asked him, 'Did you see this man stabbed?'

Chubinov raised his eyes from Kamensky's body and said in a weak, bewildered voice, 'Did I see a man stabbed? What man?'

'Why, this one, of course, the corpse on the pavement.'

'No,' breathed Chubinov. 'No. I certainly never saw him stabbed.'

'Do you know him?' the policeman looked over his shoulder at Kamensky's body, and paused with a sudden and naïve movement of self-criticism. Plainly he was thinking, 'Good God, what have I been doing to leave those roses where they are? I should have had them off first thing, someone might have recognised him by now.' He went over to the body and knelt beside it, and Laura turned away and covered her eyes so that she need not see Kamensky's face. In her private darkness she heard the policeman ask, 'Do you know him?' and Chubinov answer, 'I don't know anything about him. I know absolutely nothing about him.'

Laura, keeping her head averted and one hand over her eyes, plucked at Chubinov's sleeve, and said, 'Vassili, Vassili, take me to the apartment.'

'Miss Laura!' he exclaimed, and his arm closed tightly round her shoulders, she felt his breath near her face. 'Miss Laura, I didn't see you were there. Oh, what must you have thought of me for leaving you like that at Grissaint. Not for one moment would I have gone off like that if I had known that Nikolai was to die.'

"Stay there, both of you,' said the policeman. 'What's this about Nikolai? If you don't know the man, how do you know his name was Nikolai?'

She could not imagine why Chubinov had not spoken to her in Russian. Quickly she said, 'The man lying there isn't called Nikolai. So far as I know. The Nikolai this gentleman means is my grandfather, who's lying dead upstairs.'

'How did that happen? When did it happen? Are the police with him?' He sent one whistle-blast after another soaring over their heads. Apparently a police-whistle had the power of a musical instrument to convey the emotions of the performer, for these blasts sounded more desperate than the earlier ones.

'No, no,' explained Laura, shouting through the blasts, 'my grandfather is Count Diakonov, and he was very old, he died of old age and a heart attack, two days ago —' she pointed at her black dress – 'and the funeral is to be tomorrow.'

'I have come to mourn the Count,' said Chubinov.

'Can't I take this gentleman up to our apartment?' asked Laura. 'We're on the fourth floor, in here on the left. You can come and question him afterwards. When you're ready.'

The policeman's attention had left them. Appalled, he was listening to a sound coming from further up the Avenue towards the Étoile. Another policeman was whistling for assistance, with blasts not less desperate than his own, in the very quarter from which he was hoping help would come. A boy ran by, laughing and shouting, and when the policeman stopped him he reported that disputes had broken out among the passengers on a bus, and some had alighted and were fighting it out on the side-walks, regarding a nearby demonstration which had been suppressed by the police. The elderly woman in the black bonnet, who had been lost in prayer ever since she had come to a halt by Kamensky's body, suddenly returned to time, said harshly to the policeman, 'What is happening to the amenities of this district?' and walked away, tossing her head.

Chubinov met the policeman's glazed look of grievance by a sympathetic pat on the arm and said, 'You heard what the young lady said. Count Diakonov's apartment. On the fourth floor. In this house. This very house, here. My name is Hippolyte Baraton, of the Villa des Mimosas, Rue Corneille, Nice. I'll be up there, ready to show you my papers.'

They hurried through the archway and across the courtyard. 'A typical historical event,' said Chubinov pedantically. 'Itself definite enough, yet surrounded by confusion apparently not connected with it. It is as if a drop of the extraordinary added to the ordinary produces a chemical explosion.' They got into the elevator and as it heaved and grunted upwards he took her in his arms and kissed her on the forehead. He moved and spoke as if he had grown much older since she had last seen him. 'Now you're safe. Now that all things are settled you can go on being a beautiful Russian girl, and become a beautiful Russian lady, and finally, long years ahead, a beautiful Russian old lady. I am quite content. My life has not been altogether wasted. I have saved Nikolai's granddaughter.'

She cut into her own murmurs of gratitude. 'But who stabbed Kamensky?'

'Oh, my dear!' He had to steady himself against the wall of the elevator. 'Why – nobody stabbed him. I shot him.'

She broke into sobs. She could not believe it. Angrily she thought of the crucifix in the room. 'What do you mean, you shot him? You can't have. That man said quite clearly he was stabbed.'

'Only because he didn't hear the shot above the noise of the traffic. This type of revolver – I've got a silencer on it – makes just a thud. Also he didn't see me shoot Kamensky, for I shot him from the pocket of my overcoat, through a slit in the seam, with my arm braced on my hip. It's one of our techniques, which I have practised without ever expecting to use it. Please, Laura, don't cry.'

'Oh, I hoped, I hoped so much that we wouldn't have to kill him. I prayed in the room. And out there on the street, I thought that what that man said made it certain someone else had done it, and I thought we were innocent. It's too awful, having thought it was all right, and now finding it isn't.'

'But it wouldn't have been all right if someone else had done it. It would have been illogical. I was the person who had a truly moral reason for killing Kamensky. I knew he meant to kill you. If anybody else had killed him, it was almost bound to be for a lesser reason. That would have shown a defect in the moral universe.'

She wished she could tell him to shut up, but it would seem ungrateful; and he looked quite dreadful. 'Did we really have to kill him?'

'I killed him. Not you. It is no use shaking your head. Those are the facts, Miss Laura. And I had no choice. While Gorin

397

was still in Grissaint a comrade and I went through all his papers in both his rooms. They were in code. In four codes. But I knew three of them, my comrade the fourth. Miss Laura, you will try to forget all this, you will not make yourself miserable by dwelling on it. You promise?'

'Oh, tell me quickly.'

'In one of his diaries, kept in the fourth code, there was written, "I fear I will have to kill Laura". It was an entry made just before he started for Grissaint.'

She shuddered. 'If you knew how he went on and on that night he got to Grissaint. Telling me I was as beautiful as my mother. And I was dying to get some sleep. And what about you? Had he got it all worked out for you?'

His mouth twisted. 'The plans were perfect. I have to admire them. He was going to leave the country, and before that I was not only to be killed but utterly discredited. None of my friends would have doubted the justice of my execution, or cared to think of me again.'

The lift had been stationary at the fourth-floor landing for some moments. They heard people moving about in the hall below, and Laura felt afraid. Out in the sunlight, when she had believed that someone else had killed Kamensky, she had felt weightless with innocence. Now the leaden heaviness had come back again. She hurried him through the still-open door of the apartment and there in the hall it came on her that they were trapped. She cried, 'But the gun. The gun. If you shot Kamensky, where is the gun?'

'Why, here in my overcoat pocket.'

'Vassili, what are we to do? They know where you are. We told them. Why, I hammered it in, I was so sure we had not killed him. But as soon as that policeman gets help they'll examine Kamensky and find that he wasn't stabbed but shot. And they'll remember what the man in the light suit said, that you were near Kamensky at the street-corner. They'll think of you. They'll come up here. Oh, if I hadn't thought someone else had killed Kamensky, I'd not have told them you were coming up here, I would have thought of something else. Now they'll search you, they'll search the apartment.'

'My dear, I'm prepared for all this, just take me to some room where we can talk,' said Chubinov, gently.

If Hélène had kept her promise and all the mourning dresses had been finished that morning, the sewing-room would be empty. It was the only place where she thought they would be safe from Tania. The air there was still acrid with the scent of black cloth, and though she threw open the window, it gave on a well, and admitted only another sort of stuffiness. Now she had time to look at him she saw that what he had done, what they had done, had worked some awful damage on him. It was impossible to detect what had changed in his appearance, but if one had seen him among a group of patients in a hospital one would have said, 'That one won't get better'. It might not be his body that would die, but something would. She wished she had not had to bring him into this horrid little room, without an arm-chair in it. But that hardly mattered, for he had shown his natural bent by going straight to the most uncomfortable chair in the room, where the seamstress sat when she worked the sewing-machine.

He said pedantically, fingering the maple cover of the sewing-machine, 'Ah, a Singer. What is American technology not going to do for humanity! No more fatigue. A life of abundance. No more tired eyes for the kind women of the world. My dear Laura, you must be sensible. I knew quite well when I came up here that the policeman would come up and question me as soon as they found out that Gorin had been not stabbed but shot, and that I would not be able to get rid of the gun. For of course they will find it, whatever we do. Nobody can succeed in hiding a gun from the police. You can't imagine what a house looks like after the police have searched it. They tear up everything by the roots. So we will not even think of trying to hide the gun, and there will be no question of my trying to evade arrest. I wonder if I might ask you if I could have something to eat? I'm not sure when I had my last meal.'

'I'll go and get you something.'

'And when you come back I'll tell you how to disengage yourself. Oh, it's quite simple. I'd better tell you now. Own that you met me in the train, say that your grandfather had asked me to go to Mûres-sur-mer with him, you didn't ask why, you only knew that I was an old tutor of the family, that I went back to Paris when your grandfather determined to go no further than Grissaint, and that you sent me a telegram telling me of his death and asking me to call at this hour. That's all.'

'Right. But when I come back let's go over it again if we have time. I might not get it word-perfect.' She picked up his overcoat, and hung it upon a peg on the door, and took the revolver out of the pocket and went out of the room.

A revolver was such a little thing. As she walked along the corridor, she kept it pressed under her hand against her thigh. It might never be noticed by Tania if they came face to face. And that was unlikely to happen. Tania's voice shrilled from behind the door, almost maniacal with sustained good will, 'No, I wouldn't go home now if I were you, General. You wouldn't have time to go and come back and be with us at the service this evening. That's going to be later than usual, but not so very much later.' When Laura shut herself in her own room, its pleasantness seemed foolish. It smelt sweet. The cream and pink peonies in the gold Meissen vase on the round table lay in the path of the sun, and the scent rose strong above them. The silver brushes and the cut-glass bottle of lavender-water were fourfold on the dressing-table, with the triple mirror behind them, and the sunlight cast patterns across the intricately ruched white muslin counterpane and ended by blazing back from the brass cartwheel bed-head. One of the wardrobe doors had swung open and showed the many-coloured dresses Tania had bought for her. But what she needed was a flat box just big enough to hold a revolver. There was nothing of that sort here.

Her trinket-box was long enough and broad enough, but too deep. She tipped the necklaces and brooches out on the bed-spread and lifted out the tray, and laid the revolver on it. Then she slipped the scissors out of her manicure set and took them on the tray over to the chiffonier where her underclothes were kept and found a pair of knickers and ripped out the elastic from the waist and snipped it through. She wound the elastic tightly round the tray and knotted it so that the revolver would not fall out. Her business now was to find some grand material. She was willing to cut up one of her dresses, but that would give her no more than a strip of plain silk or fine wool, and she wanted something far grander than that. With her knuckles to her lips, she stood trying to remember what she had brought from London, and out of the corner of her eye caught sight of her image in the mirror, fierce-eyed and desperate, an offence against the calm girlish room. She was much more afraid than she had realised. 'It's the room that's wrong, not me,' she said aloud. 'I have to get wild and frightened if I am to do the right thing.' It came to her that Hélène had said she would pack her orange Spanish shawl. It was in the lowest drawer.

Laura was sorry that it was too bulky and she had to hack off a broad strip with the flimsy scissors, for it was really very pretty. She supposed that by now Kamensky's white roses would be trodden into the dirt. It was hard to saw off the thick fringe of the shawl, but when she had folded in the butchered edges and fastened the fabric round the revolver with a safety-pin hidden inside the fold, the parcel looked quite important, quite solemn. It would not be disrespectful to take it anywhere, and nobody could guess what was in it. But when she got to the room where Nikolai lay, she had to hold herself back on the threshold and count up to twenty, for her fingers shook on the door-knob and she must be looking quite mad.

Berr's wife was still pouring out her strength in the incantation, her husband was still kneeling at her side. Father Iliodor was just completing his reverences to the icon and the crucifix, and turned about to go to the door and ran into her. She detained him with a murmur, and the lion-mask bent down towards her.

'Father, there was something my grandfather wanted buried in his coffin. He told me that I would find it in a drawer in my room, but it's only now that I've found the key. I know it's the right thing. It's just as he described it.'

There was uncertainty in the pale-amber eyes. A lion in a zoo must spend much time pondering on the incomprehensibility of the human life that goes on around it. He held out his great hands. So that he could not guess her panic she laid the parcel in them with exaggerated, hieratic slowness, looking up at him with a fixed gaze as if she saw things unseeable. The lion-mask became troubled. Perhaps her hieratic gesture was a mistake, and he was perhaps feeling uneasy lest she was asking him to perform a rite till then unknown to him. But he took the parcel from her and bowed low over it, paused for a moment and muttered 'Well, whatever it is, it can't do much harm in a coffin.' Laura thought this the most sensible remark she had heard for a long time. They stood side by side while he folded back the pall and the inner coverlet over Nikolai's feet and laid the parcel against his soles. The priest murmured a farewell to Laura, and the necessary reverences again, and was gone.

Laura said to the crucifix, 'As I said, You created Kamensky, and someone had to do something. And if Chubinov and I did the wrong thing, remember you created us too.' She let the silence settle. But the crucifix seemed to be having the last word. Wearily she conceded, 'Not that I think that can possibly be all there is to it.' But she felt guiltier towards her grandfather. She had to force her eyes to rest on the pall where it rose slightly over his face. 'Yes, I know you said that it was my Christian duty to do everything I could to discourage Chubinov from killing Kamensky. But can you blame me for wanting to live as long as you did? And about it being my Christian duty, I don't know how far you really meant that. You so often didn't really believe what you believed, did you? Or rather you sincerely believed some things that you didn't, or I should say don't actually believe in, though you believe in other things.'

But she would have to leave that till a time when she had quite a long time to go on her knees and talk to him, and when she was not so hag-ridden by the idiotic fear that the parcel would hurt Nikolai's feet, and by the sense that she had been presuming, irreverent, vulgar, by putting anything under the pall. Her grandfather had brought it out of Russia, fearing he might die in exile; it would have to be taken back to Russia. It was of pale and shimmering brocade, decorated with a cross made from pieces of the same stuff joined together, and sewn on lengthwise, and it was embroidered round the edges with texts from the Gospels. It was the work of a woman of the family who, centuries ago, had been imprisoned for many years in a fortress deep in the marshes, because a lesser prince had accused the prince her husband of seeking to betray a greater prince to the barbarians. To have a pall in readiness she had cut up a gown she had brought back from a crowning in Byzantium and sewn it with a needle made from a nail. The thing was beautiful, unpurchasable, inimitable, an inheritance such as the present or the future could never hope to bequeath. Laura felt ashamed because she had used it for a cover for that ugly killing metal thing, which had killed a traitor, and was tied up with elastic ripped out of her knickers inside a rag of fabric bought in a shop. It was the meanness of the disaster that she minded. This outrageous act had been forced on her by an accidental contact with a pack of shabby fanatics, who would die when they died and never find refuge in a paragraph in the history books. She would not have been able to go back and talk patiently to poor, dear, silly, futile, for ever insignificant Chubinov, had not Berr suddenly raised up a face clever with glory, and his wife, the flow of the Psalter never drying on her lips, stretched out a hand to touch his grey hairs, damp with prophecy, her face glorious too, though still not clever.

In the kitchen Laura told the servants she wanted a tray sent into the sewing-room for a mourner who was tired and hungry, and specially sad over the Count's death: coffee and a slice or two of fish pasty and cold chicken, and she added, for the servants' pleasure, some of the beggars' food. For they had cooked a mountain of that, although it had been explained to them – and indeed they were so intelligent that they must have grasped it already – that there would not be the customary beggars' dinner tomorrow, since there were no beggars in Paris, at least not such as could be relied on to attend a lengthy funeral service in a proper state of cleanliness and piety. The *clochards* who slept under the Seine bridges simply would not do. As she left the kitchen she said over her shoulder, as carelessly as she could, that she understood there had been an accident outside the house, someone had been hurt, the gentleman in the sewing-room had seen it, perhaps the police would be calling to question him. If they did, they were to be taken to the sewing-room and her mother was to be asked to come and talk to them.

When she got back to Chubinov he had slumped forward in the uncomfortable chair, his face pressed against the maple cover of the sewing-machine. He sat up and wiped his eyes with what he evidently thought was a handkerchief, but was some sort of kitchen-cloth; she thought the muslin through which one strained cottage-cheese. She wondered where on earth he had got hold of it, and how it had been so well washed, but cleanliness was his only point of contact with physical order. He said unsteadily, 'I've lost the two friends I loved most in the world. It's illogical that I should complain of this, as I've just shot one of them after I've for years assisted him to make the other one's life unendurable. Yet I'm weeping.'

'Well, Nikolai will understand everything now.' Yes, but Nikolai would still, even if he were actually in the presence of God, consider Chubinov as fundamentally a fool. It was impossible to imagine conditions in eternity which would have led him to modify this view. 'And some food is coming along in a minute. And I took your gun out of your overcoat when I went out of the room and I wrapped it up and gave it to one of the priests. He put it in my grandfather's coffin.'

Between his sparse moustache and beard his mouth was open.

'You can't be shocked!' she cried, in sudden loneliness. 'Oh, no, you daren't be shocked.'

'Oh, I'm not shocked at all,' he breathed, 'but startled. It's so exactly what your grandfather would have done in your place.'

'Well, will it work? Was it the right thing to do?' she demanded. 'Are we safe?'

He deliberated. 'I think we are. You despise us revolutionaries. But we've this much of a case. The police of this or any other country are a great deal less likely to search the coffin in which there lies a dead aristocrat than if he was a pauper.'

She flared up in rage. 'You have no right to blame society for anything, anything at all. If you put up people like Kamensky on a pedestal and lie and kill at their command, so that if the police feel suspicious about what's gone into a coffin they are probably right, it's sheer impudence to complain if when they search a coffin they don't do it with perfect self-control and self-command and justice.'

She had to turn aside and disguise her anger when Aglaia brought in the tray, and then her heart softened towards him. For it was when she lifted the silver dish-cover off the beggars' food that he cried out in nostalgic greed, '*Lapsha,* it's really *lapsha*! Oh, how good it used to taste when I sat on a high stool beside the fat cook in our kitchen and ate with her, and my elders never knew! I used to think it so much better than the veal and the chicken and the venison we had at the family table.' Really it was not so nice as all that, it was just like macaroni, only heavier. But he had loved his home and everything and everybody about it. This man of all men should never have got infected with this disease of the mind which sent people running out into exile like fever patients deliriously rising from bed and running out into the cold.

After he had cleared the plate and drank a cup of coffee, she put her hand on his and said, 'Forgive me,' and he murmured that it was nothing, he had understood how she felt. Then she said, 'Now go over the story again, I want to get it word-perfect.' But he held up his finger. 'Dear Miss Laura, it's too late. They're coming now. Be sure you let me do most of the talking, and remember that you don't know Gorin was shot, you think he was stabbed.'

The unlucky policeman with the black moustache came in with two others, one a man of his own age, also in uniform, but fair and smart and at his ease, and the other an older man in plain clothes. They were not getting on well together. They might even have had an altercation up till the very moment they entered the room. Their faces were untidy with disagreement. She poured out vodka for them, and sent Aglaia for more chairs. Till they came the three men stood wide apart, eyeing the room over the rims of their glasses. The unlucky policeman kept on looking at her hair.

When they were all settled down, the older man took out a notebook, put it down on his knee, licked the point of a pencil, and did no more, for his attention had been caught by the watch pinned to Laura's breast. Her grandmother had had it made for her by Fabergé, and thought it was inconspicuous, simply a niello watch-face sunk in a circle of pearls, it had been enormously expensive. Her father had thought it a ridiculous present for a child. Laura was sure this man knew exactly how much it had cost. Then his gaze moved to Chubinov, from his face to his clothes, from his clothes to his hand. Faintly he raised his eyebrows. The unlucky policeman inspected Chubinov too, with the gimlet of a hostile stare.

The man in plain clothes alluded briefly to the unfortunate incident in the street below, disregarded Laura's enquiry as to whom the victim had been, and went on to show an unexcited curiosity regarding Hippolyte Baraton of the Villa des Mimosas, Nice. He accepted the papers of identity which were handed to him and passed them to his uniformed assistant, who bent his head over them, raised it and nodded, while the unlucky policeman watched with under-lip protruded. Chubinov answered the questions with an excited verbosity, passing into an impersonation of a fool, a bore operating under no stress at all, in favourable circumstances such as he rarely enjoyed. He had four strangers to listen to him. Familiars, he must have learned long ago, do not listen. It appeared that Hippolyte's grandfather had been a Russian, and was tutor to both the Count Diakonov and his brother, who was Ambassador in Paris for some time.

'Oh, an Ambassador?'

'My Uncle Ivan,' said Laura. 'He was Ambassador at Berlin too.'

'And had been appointed to London at the time of his death.'

The man in plain clothes and his uniformed assistant looked very hard at the unlucky policeman, whose under-lip protruded still further. There was a faint shrug of his shoulders.

The grey stream of denatured facts went on. One winter the Diakonovs wintered in Nice, and brought Grandfather Baraton with them. He married a Frenchwoman, whose father was engaged in the manufacture of crystallised fruits: a description of the process, which demanded more care than the public usually realised, was with difficulty cut short. The couple's son had in turn tutored the Ambassador's children, here in Paris and down at Nice, and some of the Count's older children, when they spent any length of time in France. Once three of them had been down in Nice for several months, convalescent after suffering in Russia from a peculiar form of measles, not at all like ordinary measles, oh, no; differing from it in several of the symptoms.

'Yes, yes.'

The grandson, Hippolyte himself, had tutored the younger children of the two families and some of the grandchildren; and the Diakonovs had always been very kind to the Baratons. They had bought for his grandfather the little villa at Nice, which was small but commodious. They had given his father in his turn some shares in Russian mines and railways which had risen enormously in value. Thanks to them, he himself was quite comfortably off, not rich but never in need of a franc, and it was for this reason that he had been able to spend the last twenty years writing a book on Lord Byron.

'Has it been published?'

'Oh, no. It isn't nearly finished.'

A look of trust passed over the faces of the three men. The unlucky policeman's lower lip ceased to protrude. They could not believe that a man would say he had spent twenty years writing a book if it were not true.

'Is it a very long book?'

'No. It will be very short.'

The confidence established was nearly complete.

'It is because of the book, really, that I'm here, with this dear young lady at this moment.' He had taken a post as a French teacher in England, in order to do some research on Lord Byron. Sometimes he felt as if his studies had only just begun. When he broke his journey in Paris, he had rung up the Count, suggesting that he might call on him. This had worked out unfortunately, for the Count had explained that he and his granddaughter were leaving for Mûres-sur-mer the next day, and had proposed that he should travel with them on the Calais train, and when they had got off proceed on his way to England. He had felt obliged to fall in with the Count's wishes, but had not wished to do so, for his purpose in breaking his journey in Paris had been to inspect some letters, apparently by Byron, but possibly not genuine, owned by an old lady living at Versailles. It was very important that the authenticity of the letters should be proved or disproved, for they bore on a crucial event in Byron's life.

'I have the vanity to believe that I would know, I might claim at a glance, whether they are genuine or not.'

'Yes, yes. Yes, yes.'

'Well, I had a pleasant journey with this young lady and the Count. Who was a great man, great in body, great in brain, great in soul.'

He began to weep. His tears were real. They were true. Laura saw him change back from Baraton to Chubinov, and feared the truth was going to burst out of him. She handed him a glass of vodka, not daring to speak. Hell was this, being afraid of hearing someone tell the truth. She begged Nikolai's pardon, but could not see how she could have avoided being in this room, with these sordid things happening around her.

'But before we had reached Mûres-sur-mer, at Grissaint, to be precise, the Count felt ill and decided not to proceed to his destination and to stop the night in a hotel there, and return the next morning to Paris. Then, gentlemen, I was guilty of a grave error of judgment, a dereliction of the duty owed by the Baraton family to the Diakonov family. Tempted by the opportunity it gave me to inspect, after all, the Byron letters in the possession of Madame Jellinek, I took the first train back to Paris, and left this poor young lady alone with her grandfather, who died shortly after I left. I cannot forgive myself.' He could hardly get the lies out because of his terribly honest tears.

'But it didn't matter,' Laura said, 'I've told you it was all right. There were doctors all over the place. If it had mattered, I wouldn't have sent you that telegram inviting you to come here at four o'clock for the service.' She was enraged against him. Some of his tears were certainly for Nikolai, but some were for Kamensky, who was wicked. It would be that unnatural sorrow which was not of God, which would break him, if he should break. To give him time, she said to the policeman, 'Monsieur Baraton was exceptionally kind to my grandfather and me in the train.' But the eyes of all four men had gone past her. Her mother was standing in the doorway, her skin glowing because she took her grief indignantly, the bright hair the brighter because of her black dress. 'Good evening gentlemen,' she said, 'I'm sorry to hear of ——' a wave of her long white hand saved her the trouble of clearly recollecting what this tragedy, not relevant to her own, might precisely be – 'all this. Have you everything you want?'

Chubinov rose clumsily, not with the clumsiness of Chubinov, but with the greater clumsiness of Baraton, who was not so wellborn, knocking over his chair. Bringing Tania's hand to his lips he said, 'I would have known you anywhere. All the ladies of the Diakonov family look as if they were covered with diamonds, even when they are wearing none. This is no time for diamonds, but still you shine. You dispel the darkness of the spirit.' He was within a hair's breadth of breaking down and telling the truth. But painfully he forced himself back into the deception he was practising so cleverly, for all his foolishness. 'I am Hippolyte Baraton.'

'Ah. And I'm Tania, the one who never had the good fortune to be taught by you. But so often when the family photographs are brought out, all those of the garden at Nice, it always was, "Who is the boy who looks so shy, who's trying to hide behind his neighbour", and the answer was, "Oh, that was our dear Hippolyte".'

The man in plain clothes said, 'I'm sorry we have to intrude on you in your time of grief, Madame. But there's been a man killed on the street just below, and we thought that this gentleman, who was passing by at the time, might be able to tell us something about the incident. But first, just as a matter of routine, may I ask you some questions about yourself and your household?'

The unlucky policeman gave up his chair to her and stood leaning against the wall and staring at her, under puckered brows, while she gave the answers. The man in plain clothes finally said, 'That's all, I think. To sum up, this is the apartment of Count Diakonov, formerly a Minister of the Tsar, and brother to a former Russian Ambassador to Paris. You're his daughter, and the wife of an Englishman, a Member of the

House of Commons. And this is your daughter of eighteen. And you remember Monsieur Baraton from seeing him in your family photographs.' He and his assistant looked over at the unlucky policeman with an air of malicious triumph. 'And we didn't really need to ask who the young lady is, for her hair makes that evident.'

At that the assistant nearly laughed aloud, and the unlucky policeman bit his lip. It was plain what he had been telling them. 'There was something fishy about the couple. I think the man might have done the job, and the girl with him looked strange, and I believe her hair was dyed, as a decent girl's hair wouldn't be.'

'Now Monsieur Baraton, you told the officer here that you didn't know the man who was killed. When did you first see him this afternoon?'

'On my way here, at the corner where the Rue Belloy runs into the Avenue Kléber. I noticed him because he was carrying those white roses. Just afterwards I remembered I'd not packed any toothpowder, so I went back to a chemist's shop I'd just passed, and bought a tin of the stuff. It's in the pocket of my overcoat, there on the door. Then I made my way up the Avenue, but the Count being dead, I had my own preoccupations, and I didn't think of this man again, until suddenly, I saw him lying on the pavement.'

'And then our officer here questioned you, Monsieur Baraton. Since then he's thought over your answers and we'd like them clarified.'

'Well, I'll tell you what I can. But I really didn't see anything.'

'It isn't quite a matter of what you saw or didn't see. It's a matter of what you said. Our officer thought the man had been stabbed. He was told so by a witness who had formed a false impression. He therefore asked you if you had seen a man stabbed. You replied that you hadn't seen anyone stabbed, and twice you laid a slight emphasis on the word "stabbed", as if you were surprised by the notion that that was the way he had died.'

'That's quite wrong. What surprised me was that someone should be murdered, by any means at all, in the Avenue Kléber. It doesn't seem appropriate, someone being murdered in a Haussmann Boulevard. Down by the Marais, that would seem much more suitable, if you know what I mean. Not that I want to take issue with our friend here, for it can't be an important point.'

'But it is. For the man who was lying on the pavement had been shot. The man who murdered him would, therefore, have been very much surprised, if he were asked whether he'd seen the victim stabbed. Wouldn't he, Monsieur Baraton?'

The blood was racing in Laura's ears. She did not hear Chubinov's faint answer.

'The victim must have been shot just about the time when you and he were within some yards of each other on the corner of the Rue Belloy. Are you a revolver shot, Monsieur Baraton?'

The nostrils of the unlucky policeman were distended, his profile looked noble and triumphant.

The answer came loudly and confidently: 'Yes, I am an excellent revolver shot. The Count himself taught me. I am still quite fair. It would have been child's play for me to shoot this man just before I went into the chemist's shop. I couldn't have missed.' He took another drink of coffee and slopped it down his waistcoat, gaping about him in hurt astonishment, as Tania and Laura, the man in plain clothes and his assistant, burst into nervous laughter. 'If you ask your brothers,' he told Tania, 'they could confirm what I say.' Then his eyes fell on the unlucky policeman who was still leaning against the wall, still pouting in implacable suspicion. 'I suppose what I have just said sounds foolish,' said Chubinov stiffly, 'but I'd like to point out that I could hardly be accused of shooting this poor man, as I haven't got a gun nearer than Nice. I'll be only too pleased if you'll search me.'

The man in plain clothes smiled down at his notebook, and there was a pause. Tania said, 'There's been a lot of coming and going in this apartment this afternoon. I see you might quite well want to be assured that nobody here, either of my household or among my visitors had anything to do with this horrible business. Please search the apartment. But I'd be obliged if you'd let the servants help you. If you're going to turn out this room, for example, I'd like the servant who sees to the mending and the care of the linen to be with you, so that she can put things back.' She spoke placidly, as if in the interest of abstract order. But then her voice shook. 'And of course, you won't go into the room where my father is lying.'

'Of course not,' murmured the man in plain clothes, bowing.

'In any case it couldn't interest you, for in our church the Psalms have to be recited perpetually over our dead, and two people have been there all the time.'

'Actually we won't search that room or this room or any other in the apartment,' he said, 'at least not now. If this gentleman will come down to the police station, I'm writing down the address, and make a statement later tonight, that's all we need for the moment. If we need more help, we'll call on you again. But I hope we'll not need to intrude on you.' He spoke, as men often did when they met Tania, in the character of a man more elegant and fortunate than himself.

When Tania had thanked him she did not rise and leave. She asked gravely, 'Who was the man who was killed?'

'We've no idea, beyond the fact that he was middle-aged, dark, short, and healthy. He was one of those men of mystery we sometimes find on our hands. He must have been quite wealthy, and had a secret to keep. All the labels on his clothes had been carefully unpicked, even the tailor's marks which customers don't usually know about had gone. But coat, suit, underclothes, they're all of good quality. His shoes must have been quite expensive. Hand-made, of the best. Handkerchief of fine lawn, but no monogram. A silver cigarette-case, but no monogram. No papers of any sort, no letters. Only a considerable amount of money in francs and sovereigns. And these.' He held out a pair of spectacles, lying flat on his palm. 'But you will be surprised. The lenses are clear glass.'

'What horrible sinister things,' sighed Tania. 'Sinister because they're useless.'

'Not wholly useless. If he wanted to change his appearance quickly when he was pulling off a fraud.'

'Well, fraud is uselessness,' said Tania. 'I wonder who he was. You know, I thought we might know him. My father, like all Tsarist Ministers, was persecuted by the terrorists. I was afraid that one of the friends who came to mourn my father,

412

a general, perhaps, or a high official, had been shot down by one of these misguided men. But none of our friends would have had the labels on their clothes unpicked, or carried such spectacles in their pockets. I also wondered whether the dead man might have been one of the terrorists. They're always having feuds among themselves, my father used to say. But in that case his clothes would have been shabby, and he wouldn't have had all that money on him. These revolutionaries live very poorly. To do them justice, they're idealists.'

'It wouldn't be anybody of that sort. I would put him down as a criminal whose efforts had been crowned with considerable success. A jewel-thief. Or a bank-robber. Or a share-swindler.'

Still she lingered. 'How dreadful that we don't know his name. I'll have a prayer offered up for him by the priest at our evening service. And think, we'll have to pray for him as a man, just a man, an unknown person. Imagine destroying one's own identity as that poor creature did! Every day throwing away one's past. Annihilating one's self. What strange, strange things people do with their lives!'

Her soft gaze passed from face to face of the strangers, asking each if he could explain to her how this might be; and all gently shook their heads. The unlucky policeman, still leaning against the wall, impatiently shifted his position. His angry eyes said to Laura, 'You and your buffoon of a friend know all about this job, and the poor lady's in the dark.' Laura jerked her head high, enraged by the false accusation. But then she remembered that it was not false.

16

WHEN LAURA AND Chubinov were alone, she said, 'Now tell me what really happened.'

He was breathing heavily. 'If Gorin had not coached me so often in how to behave when one is taken by the police, we should have been lost. But, poor Miss Laura, you must take a glass of vodka. You look so white.'

'We're not allowed to drink in our family till we're

twenty-one. Now hurry up. Tell me. I want to know exactly what it is we've done.'

'Well, it began, you know how it is, with all my sense of time going to pieces. I left my hotel near Les Halles, with my gun in my pocket, and the seam of my overcoat properly slit, at what seemed to me the right hour. "Now you must go," I said imperatively to myself, "you haven't a moment to spare." But when I got off the bus at the Étoile I looked at my watch and it was an hour and a half too early. So I walked down the Avenue Victor-Hugo and across by the Rue Malakoff and up to the Place d'Iena, and I had three lemonades at different cafés, and the day was empty of everything but dust and warmth and glare, and what I had to do drained out of my mind, leaving nothing but the intention to do it. No more than my gun did I visualise the deed. Then I saw that the hour really had come, and at a quarter to four I went along the Rue Belloy towards the Avenue Kléber. I meant to go up to the Avenue till I came to this house, and then take out my note-book and fumble in its leaves, as if I were verifying an address, and every now and then stare in a foolish way at the neigh-bouring houses, keeping my face turned away from the en-trance, and looking at a little mirror held in the palm of my hand to see who was approaching it. But I didn't really care if Gorin did catch sight of me. He could hardly prevent me from accompanying him into the courtyard and after that I could shoot him as he got into the elevator and send it up to the top floor, so that I could get well away before anybody knew for sure there was a corpse in it.

'But almost as soon as I got into the Rue Belloy I found myself walking beside him. He was marching along as if he hadn't a care in the world, carrying these white roses. I can't remember ever having seen him look so happy. It's wonderful to witness a really intelligent man in a moment of real blissful-ness. Always when I walked with him I had to shorten my stride, my legs being so much longer than his, and I followed this habit, though it was the last thing I should have done just then. I should have dropped back and followed him. But with an insane rashness, I kept up with him, because I was almost sure I had recognised the way the white roses were wrapped;

and so I had. There's a florist in the Rue du Faubourg St-Honoré, whose wife comes from the Crimea, and she has a distinctive way of preparing bouquets for gentlemen to present to ladies. She puts them in a cone of thick white shiny paper, cutting holes in it with a pair of scissors to make a pretty pattern, and scalloping the edges. It's a craft peculiar to her native town. I was right, that's how those white roses were wrapped. It seemed so unlikely that he would be taking such a bouquet to a house in mourning, that I imagined he might not be coming to your house at all, and I feared I might have to alter my plans radically.'

'No,' said Laura. 'Those roses were for me. He asked me at Grissaint what flowers he could bring me when we got back to Paris, and said they must be white. White flowers for the dead. He was being funny in a horrible way.'

'How incredibly cruel. Anyway I was so puzzled by this bouquet that we went on walking side by side, in step, just as if we were out on one of our friendly strolls, say at Clarens. Then suddenly he turned his head and exclaimed "Vassili!" quite loudly. Not at all in a conspiratorial way. Then he repeated my name very softly, and we continued at our easy, comradely pace, "You're not in England. I thought you were in England. There must be an explanation."'

'That means he'd grasped that I'd lied to him when I said I'd seen you get into the Calais train at Grissaint,' said Laura. 'I'd have had no chance at all, if he'd ever got into this house.'

'None. For listen to my story. I said to him, "Gorin, I know everything. You've handed over many, many of our people to the Secret Police." I didn't speak of your grandfather. I didn't want to defile him. Gorin didn't reply. We just walked on, by now maniacally careful to keep step, you'd have thought it was a trick for avoiding arrest. Presently Gorin said, "You've been meddling, Vassili. Tchk, tchk. You've been meddling." And, do you know, I felt guilty. But I said, "It's as well that I have." He made another chiding noise, and told me, patiently, "Vassili, it's true that I've been obliged from time to time to do some very strange things. But what I've done for the revolutionary cause outweighs by far what I've done for the Secret Police." I simply replied, "Korolenko, Primar, Damatov." I

415

was shaking. I remembered that on occasions I had used the same cake of soap as Gorin.'

'Yes, and he used the knives and forks and spoons, drank out of the same cups and glasses as we did, here.'

'When I had got over my nausea I said, "Judas". Then he stopped and faced me. Not only was I looking directly at him, we were in front of a pharmacy which behind the wares in its windows had panels of mirror-glass, and in these I saw reflections of him from various angles. All of them showed a man of integrity, perhaps a little too stolid, a little too ob-viously moral. Fondly, as if speaking to a stupid son, he said, "But you can't compare what I've done for the Secret Police with what I've done for our revolutionary cause. Work it out for yourself, my poor Vassili." He spread out his arms. "I organised the assassination of many great men, such as Sipya-gin, the Governor of Ufa, Plehve, and the Grand Duke Serge. And whom did I hand over to the Secret Police, I ask you? Korolenko, Primar, Damatov." I found it hard to interpret the gesture he was making, for he was still holding the white roses in one hand. But he repeated it, and the second time I couldn't mistake his meaning. When he spoke of Sipyagin, the Governor of Ufa, Plehve, the Grand Duke Serge, his hand went down and down. When he named Korolenko, Primar, and Damatov, his left hand and the roses went up and up, and wavered. His hands were scales in which he was weighing the one set of his victims against the other; and for him the weight of his martyred comrades was so insignificant that the scale that held them would fly up. My mind was numbed but my skin thought for me. My disgust was said in sweat. My pores opened all over my body. Now you will not believe what he said. Surely with real kindness, with unaffected concern, he said, "You look quite ill, Vassili." I answered, "I am perfectly well," as if it were a curse. The hatred in my voice must have reached him. He said uneasily, "Also, I was working out a new principle." Think of that. A new principle!'

'He told me about that,' said Laura. 'It was something he got out of a book.'

'What book, I wonder?'

'Hegel.'

'Oh, no, it can't have been that. You must have been mistaken. Not Hegel.'

'It's what he said.' And that was natural, she thought, Hegel's your lot's *Old Moore's Almanack*.

'Strange. Well, there we stood, and suddenly, he looked over his shoulder towards the Avenue, and said, "But I can't wait. I have an appointment to keep." He ran his eyes over me, and I think it passed through his mind that I might be armed and could shoot him through my overcoat. But an expression of contemptuous trust came over him, he might have been a clever thief and I a toothless old watch-dog. "Good dog," he might have said. But then again, he frowned and shook his head, as if he didn't want to part from me like this, leaving me with a poor opinion of him. Reproachfully he said, "Oh, Vassili, you have prevented me from offering the movement a farewell gift which would have been my greatest contribution to the cause. I was about to arrange for the disposal of him." Solemnly he repeated the word. "Him." Miss Laura, you've been speaking as if the responsibility for his death was partly yours. You needn't feel a shadow of guilt. For the reason which made me shoot him when I did had nothing to do with you. It depended on what he did after he said the word "him".'

'Don't be silly, you're only trying to be kind. I told you he'd be coming at four, and that's how you cornered him.'

'Miss Laura, you're not regarding the matter from a proper philosophic standpoint —'

'You asked me when he'd be here so that you could shoot him and I told you he'd be here at four, and you came and you shot him. That's enough for me. Now go on.'

'Well, by "him", of course, he meant the Tsar. And I realised he was telling the truth. He had put into motion a plan for killing the Tsar which would be completed if he were to live. My helper and I had found in one of his rooms a telegram from a man called Sartrin, a leather-merchant in St Petersburg, which acknowledged the receipt of an order for so many hides, and saying that these were ready for dispatch whenever required. That is a phrase which among our people means all preparations have been made to carry out an operation as soon as the signal is given. Sartrin is an activist member of our organisation, who, among other duties, is our contact with a member who is a groom in the imperial stables. As this member is very young, and as any attempt he might make on the life of the Tsar must certainly result in his death, we have as yet hesitated to exploit the advantages of his position. I was about to stammer out some question about the regularity of the proceedings, whether the Battle Organisation had in fact been fully informed regarding this important operation, when Gorin backed away from me and again spread out his arms in that revolting gesture. He repeated the word "him" a third time, and his left hand and the roses jigged high in the air, but his right hand went down and down and down, far lower than before. This was his supreme act of treachery. He was not merely conveying that the execution of the Tsar would be of great service to our cause. He was acquiescing in the system of values we had spent our lives repudiating. He was claiming that the Tsar is all-precious, and outweighs all other human life, being a particle of human substance transmuted to the superhuman by its function, just as would be believed by the most bigoted priest and illiterate peasant. What was still more horrible, it was Gorin's recognition of the supreme value of the Tsar which had made him resolve to murder him. There was a huge solemn snobbery about him. He had the air of a vulgarian who asks one to dinner, though you do not know him very well, and holds out as bait that among the guests there will be a Countess. But the solemnity was real. He believed in the holiness of what he was about to kill.' Yes, Kamensky believed in the holiness of the Tsar. And also he did not believe it. But she could not explain this to Chubinov now, or perhaps ever. It was too silly.

Chubinov poured himself out a glass of vodka. 'I found myself performing the routine I'd often practised with the others. I turned on my heel, walked several paces away from him, gripped my revolver firmly in the depths of my pocket and braced my arm against my hip, spun round, squeezed the trigger three times, spun round again, and went on my way as if nothing had happened. I found myself passing the pharmacy again, and I went in and bought a tin of toothpowder, calmly enough, I think, for the pharmacist seemed to notice nothing unusual about me. Every minute I expected to hear a clamour in the street outside, and the sounds of shouts and running feet coming nearer and nearer, until, if my luck had gone against me, the shop-door would be burst open. But the afternoon was like any other. I concluded my purchase and, to gain time to think what could have happened, I chatted to the pharmacist for a minute or two about his little dog, which was snuffing about my ankles. Suddenly it occurred to me that I might have grossly overestimated my prowess as a revolver shot, and missed Gorin. Immediately I went out into the street, and was humiliated to find that this was the truth. For he was standing stock-still on the corner of the Avenue, just where I had left him, and nothing seemed odd about him except that he was clutching the roses to him very tightly, as if he feared someone might take them away from him. But then he moved off, too slowly, and as he entered the Avenue, he reeled. I saw I hadn't missed him. And I was in agony.'

'Why should you be in agony because you'd hurt this abominable man?'

'It wasn't quite like that. My agony went deep. I went back to my boyhood. When your grandfather taught me to shoot, he told me it was a sin, a real sin, he would have had it included, if he could, among the sins one had to confess and wipe out by penance, to shoot something and wound it without killing it. "Think of what it must be," he used to say, "to be a bird with a shot in its breast, unable to fly, unable to get to water, unable to fight off the hawk or the carrion crow, think of what that must mean for a deer, and the bear, who have nervous systems like our own and can suffer as we do. If we kill these creatures outright, they die as we would like to die, but if we wound them and leave them to a lingering death, then we torture them, and torturers are savages." Now I was torturing Gorin in this way. I followed him up the Avenue, and as he staggered on and I saw the blood he left on the pavement, he became innocent as a wounded pigeon, a pheasant, a deer, a bear. As for the staggering, that's not the right word. His body jerked about as if it were trying to evict his soul, and the soul wouldn't consent to be evicted, it seemed to be weakly angry with the body, to be feebly bludgeoning it from within.

Perhaps that's why it's such a sin to wound and not to kill, perhaps there are such struggles between soul and body when there is no muting of the sense by disease. Then the man in the light suit went to his aid and I felt jealous of him, and ran forward to share the precious burden, and then Gorin whirled round, still clutching those roses and exclaimed, "I must get there, I must get there." You know how sweet his voice was. Sometimes it was particularly so, with a hungry sweetness, though hungry is the wrong word, for he was eager not to take but to give. That's how it sounded then. Only it was more melting, more pathetic, more like the sound of a harp, than I have ever heard it. Then he cried out in Russian, "There must be some explanation", just as he'd done when he'd showed surprise I wasn't in England. After that his body and his soul wrestled for another second, and then he slid down into the arms of the man in the light suit, and through them on the pavement, landing softly, like a sack with hardly anything in it, and he lay stretched on the stones, quite easy, quite untroubled. Only his hands struggled to the last and they were convulsed among the flowers, so that he died with them covering his face. I walked slowly towards him, praying that he was not dead and would sit up, or that at least someone would uncover his face, so that I could look on him for the last time. But there was only the neat suit and the roses and the blood.'

'Don't cry. Oh, Vassili, you shouldn't cry. It couldn't be helped. We couldn't just let him kill us.' But she knew that would not comfort him. The murder was necessary, but that did not prevent it from staining them both. If hooligans threw one into the mud, that was not one's fault, but one's clothes would be muddy. This was the blackest mud.

When he had stopped weeping, he asked, 'And Berr. Have you seen Berr?'

'He is here now. He is here all the time his wife is a candle-bearer.'

But Chubinov would not let her fetch Berr. He started one of those distressing disquisitions about the working and counter-working of the machine his friends controlled and the machine his enemies controlled, which had to be respected, since he was intelligent and had studied this subject and nothing else for years, but which were ugly. Man could not have been born for this. Russians, he said, lived in a labyrinth of suspicion, whether they were in Russia or abroad, and he did not want anyone drawn into its dark core because of him. There would be a brief period when the murder would be considered by the French police as an ordinary crime, with nothing to show that victim and assailant were not inhabitants of Paris. But as soon as he had gone away, and he assured her that his plans for getting away would surprise her, it would be intimated to the landlords of the Hôtel de Guipuzcoa et de Racine and the Hôtel San Marino that a client of each, who would by then have been absent from his room for some days, was to be found in the police morgue; and in case either landlord felt reluctant to involve himself with the law, the police were to receive the same intimation. Then when it was realised that Gorin and Kamensky were one and the same man, and this a Russian, then the detectives in charge of the case would recall the unlucky policeman's suspicion of Hippolyte Baraton, and for a day or two everybody known to have spoken to him would be examined and cross-examined, held at police headquarters, threatened, perhaps imprisoned. Even Laura herself and her mother would be questioned, he thought. But that would be no ordeal. The Diakonov family was too important, and the British Embassy would protect them; and anyway her story was perfect, she had only to go on saying that her grandfather had introduced Baraton to her on the train.

This persecution would last only a day or two, even before they had time to recall him, in his role of Baraton, for examination. For the Russian Embassy would recognise at once that the dead man was not only Gorin and Kamensky but also Kaspar, their chief police agent, and by this time Chubinov and his helper would have seen to it that there had reached them material proving that most of the conspicuous terrorist accusations in recent years had been planned by Kaspar. It would be a Day of Judgment for the Russian Secret Police, particularly the staff of their Paris bureau. Also the French and Swiss Secret Services would be embarrassed, for they should have detected Gorin both as a terrorist agent and a Tsarist agent in their territories. The Quai d'Orsay would have to act in the interest of discretion. The Press would be silenced and the police investigations would be abandoned. It annoyed Laura that he foretold this with pride. For if he and his friends had not been making this cat's-cradle of mischief through the years the police investigations would never have begun in the first place.

Yet his gentle voice rang quite loud with pride, when he leaned forward and said, 'But, Miss Laura, the matter will not end there. We of the revolutionary movement will make the truth known. In our own way. On our own terms. Russia will be aflame.'

That was too absurd. This shabby row had no spark within it to kindle any fire. A man with a talent for lying had used it to buy himself power and devotion, pleasant quarters by a lake, and fine clothes, while his doting and obedient disciples wandered homeless, shorn of their own kin and their identities, clad in garments such as the product of the female dentist's skill which Laura could see over Chubinov's shoulder, hanging on the door in abstract deformity. It was so badly cut that it did not even fit the air.

'But for a day or two the authorities will carry on a merciless harassment of everyone who met me as Hippolyte Baraton. And though the file is closed, a black mark might remain against the name of those questioned, if they were poor and helpless. I'd not choose to do that to anyone. But it gives me the pleasure of making a gift to a beloved friend, not to do it to Berr. So I'll not see him. Anyway, it's a great thing to sit here, under the same roof as Berr, as Nikolai, as your mother, as you.'

He should be in Russia, working as a doctor or a teacher in some town where generation after generation could profit by his sweetness, and rejoice to pay him back in kind. Her eyes were wet, and she saw that his were too. He had better be left alone for a time. She put the coffee-pot and the dish of *lapsha* on the tray, since they were cold by now, and they seemed all he wanted. She carried the tray to the kitchen and asked that some fresh coffee and some hot *lapsha* should be ready in a quarter of an hour, and sat down in a corner, watching the first stage of the sombre domestic carnival which, her mother said, would reach its height the next day. The servants were all dressed in black cotton clothes, and they were still cooking, as they had been since dawn, the meal that would be served to the mourners after the funeral. The kitchen table was covered with cold birds, and the cook was slowly moving round it decorating them with slices of lemon and sprays of herbs. There was a smaller table set up not far from it, spread with a fine cloth, on which a woman Laura had never seen before, who must have been brought in specially, was rolling out pastry into huge thin sheets; rolling them thinner and thinner till they were bluish, folding them up and setting them aside, and beginning all over again. Nothing could stop the servants preparing this feast for mourners who were thousands of miles away, and who, even had they been present, would probably not have dared attend. All of the servants moved slowly and hieratically, but the kitchen echoed with their quick cries, which, as always, performed a linguistic miracle: the Russians were talking Russian to the French, the French were talking French to the Russians, and although neither knew more than a few words of the other's language, the conversation was coherent. But though it was coherent it was wild, for they talked as if there were taking place in their midst, in this apartment, even in the kitchen, an event which was a cross between a circus and a harshly-conducted Day of Judgment.

Little Louison went by, staring down into the small wooden bowl he was carrying, pressing up and down a cutter shaped to its inner sides. He saw her, halted, and pulled up a stool beside her, as if they were two Westerners sticking together. She saw that the bowl and its cutter were a tool for chopping up herbs, and exquisitely made. She felt the smooth sides of the bowl, admired the way the cutter fitted into them. Human beings were never so exquisite as the things they made. She pulled out a fine frond of the parsley which had escaped the blade. Human beings were never so exquisite as the earth they lived on and the things that grew on it. Louison leaned towards her, and asked her to tell him who the people were in the pictures painted on the big iron panel round the kitchen clock. The French servants, he said, did not know, the Russian servants tried to tell him, but he could not understand what they said.

'Those are scenes from the life of St Serafim of Sarov.' They showed him standing before the altar and seeing the Son of Man coming down a path of gold between the kneeling worshippers; prostrating himself in the snow by his hermitage in the forest; walking among the pines with a maimed wild-cat in his arms and a wolf and bear beside him like happy children; being beaten by unbelieving robbers but saved by an angel from the final blow; receiving in his tiny cell the Queen of Heaven, attended by her twelve hand-maidens, two angels, and St John the Baptist and St John the Divine.

'Ah, superstition,' nodded Louison, his blade going chop-chop in the bowl. So it was. But only such legends, which were not true, had prepared her for the strangeness of life. What the newspapers and books gave as fact pretended that events and people were the colour of photographs, and predictable. She did not know how she could explain this to Louison; but how useful it would be if she had the power. She stiffened with rage as she remembered the cruel trick that Kamensky had played by pretending that the boy had slammed the door on his hand. Perhaps poor Louison might still worry about this at nights, particularly if he heard that Kamensky had come to an ill end. She wished she could tell him that a devil from hell had come to plague him for that minute.

When the quarter of an hour was up she took the tray along the corridor, feeling sick, for it was as if she would find in the sewing-room both Chubinov and the thing they had done together.

But he looked so gentle, so helpless, so spent, that she forgot everything in her concern for him, and listened sympathetically to his plans, for which he expected praise, though they sickened her. He was going to wander still further away from his home, on an errand which would be empty of any purpose but deception; his very name would be a colourless blob, because it was assumed and there was no childhood or youth or manhood behind it. He was going to England, not to London, where Gorin's people would still be hunting for him, but to England. For he had been much impressed by the advice she had given him at Grissaint when she had said that if he became a teacher in an English school he would be safe, for if members of the Battle Organisation came to kill him the headmaster would simply send for the police and the matter would be at an end. He thought she was taking too simple a view of the situation. It could not be, he said, smiling, that England was so unaffected by the march of progress. She saw that he thought there was something slightly disgraceful in the idea of a society where, if someone with political ideas wanted to kill a teacher in a school, the staff might be able and willing to prevent it. He was so silly as to be mad, she reflected. But he had considered that in England the process of extraditing him might go so slowly that he would probably not get fetched back to France until the authorities had stopped looking for the murderer of Gorin. So he had gone to a scholastic agency which had once found him a post in a Belgian school when he was in need of cover, and found there was an emergency call from an English headmaster who had lost his French teacher in midterm. So, tomorrow morning, after he had made his statement at the police station, he would take the train to England and make his way to St Aloysius' College, Bournemouth.

'I think it will be an agreeable hiding-place. They tell me Bournemouth is surrounded by pine-woods, and I imagine it resembles Finland, where I spent some happy summers when I was a child.'

'I shouldn't count on that.'

But the future was to be wholly glorious. The next time her mother went back to Russia she would be received with the highest honours, solemnified by the remorse of the imperial family, for her father's memory would have been rehabilitated, indeed enhanced, by the material he and his helpers would by that time have put before the authorities. 'I have been able to clear your grandfather quite finally, thanks to the help of this comrade, who, as I mentioned to you, so greatly aided me to search Gorin's two rooms. It's ironical that we were brought together by Gorin's own determination to destroy me.'

She had to listen. Of course she had been fully justified in conniving at the murder of Gorin. Yet she felt a strange hunger for still further justification.

'I can't tell you this comrade's name. But he's wholly

dedicated to the cause of revolution, that I must say for him, and highly intelligent, a former journalist on the staff of a Moscow newspaper. He came to me because when Gorin decided to kill me he had also to make my killing a respectable act by proving that I was a traitor to our organisation. That's where this man came in. Gorin was going to allege that I was secretly an adherent of a Marxist group which does not approve of terrorism and are not, like us, strictly democratic. Correspondence was to be produced between me and a man named Ulyanov, or Lenin, who's been for the last two or three years in Siberia, and has just returned to Russia and is on the point of being exiled and coming out into the West. This comrade who is helping me was commissioned by Gorin to forge the correspondence. But he came straight to me, and told me everything. For he himself is actually a secret member of Lenin's group.'

'Let's get this straight,' said Laura. 'I haven't understood. If this man was a member of the group, why did he tell you what he'd been asked to do, because if Gorin had to forge evidence proving you were a member of this group, you obviously weren't?'

Chubinov looked uncomfortable. 'Miss Laura, we aren't in the nursery. We are making a revolution. Therefore we don't, I freely admit it, act always with perfect candour. It's possible, if it should happen that the revolutionary cause seemed to be in danger and the leaders were quite certain that this was due to one particular member, but they had no actual proof, they might feel under an obligation to provide forged evidence to convince the rank and file, who are bound to be their inferiors in intellect and intuition and experience.'

'But you wouldn't have done that. Vassili, you couldn't have done that.'

'No,' he said wretchedly, 'it is not in my nature. But perhaps that is a weakness. And, as for Gorin, I thought that he was so clever, so harmonious, that such problems never existed for him, that he always found a way of avoiding them.'

The grief in his voice was so great that she stretched her hand across the table and stroked his cheek. 'But this friend of Ulyanov, Lenin, or whoever he was. What happened when he came to you, thinking that you were one of the Marxist group and heard you weren't?'

Again Chubinov looked uncomfortable. 'I didn't feel bound, in view of the very pressing circumstances, to tell him the exact truth. Then in the morning, when the import of Gorin's papers was quite clear, I was frank with my comrade. And by that time it was obviously in the interests of both of us to work together for the purpose of exposing Gorin's villainy. For when the truth is out we will be able to purify the revolutionary movement, which he has left honeycombed with treachery and mistrust, and to prove to the whole world the rottenness of the Tsarist government. This will certainly be to the benefit of our organisation, and by a pardonable error, which I find quite pathetic, my poor comrade thinks that it will benefit his little Marxist group. Though heaven help us, if it were to be so, for Lenin and his followers present the idea of revolution with all the poetry, all the spontaneity, all the natural grandeur, subtracted from it. Though, mind you, this Lenin is a clever man. He knows how to get people on to committees and off them against the will of the organisation, indeed without anybody in the organisation realising what is happening till it is too late. But a courageous deed, the sublime defiance of authority, these things mean nothing to Lenin. Such a man can never change the course of history. That is for our organisation to do, for to a man we are idealists.'

She poured herself out some coffee. She felt the need of something warm inside to counter this feeling of hollowness. Why did these pathetic waifs and strays think of themselves as idealists? An idealist did some good to somebody. But these poor pantaloons could do no good by this endless masquerading under false names, this spying, this stealing of private papers, this fuss about being sent to prison or to Siberia or into exile, though obviously the authorities had to find somewhere to put people who thought themselves at their best when they were engaged in assassination. Of course, millions of Russians were hungry, but she doubted if one of them had ever been moved nearer a square meal by anything Chubinov had ever done. He was not sufficiently sensible about getting square meals for himself. And of course millions of Russians were oppressed, but she doubted if the practice of continual crime was likely to cause a reduction in the police force. 'I've made that problem worse myself, now,' she said aloud, but he was too absorbed in his recital of future glory to ask her what she meant. Looking across the table and hearing this babble, she was moved by his shabbiness, his fatigue, his dry, lined skin, his sparse hair and beard, his spiritless and nicotine-stained hands, his air of shock. He had spent all his life turning into something which was to ordinary people's lives as straw is to grass. He was not doing anything for anybody. Conspiracy was for him – as she had already recognised – what cricket was for her father and her brothers. It was the game he happened to enjoy. It was his kind of fun. There was no more to his revolutionary passion than that. If he had really been doing anything for the sake of helping other people, he would sometimes have got bored with it, for it was everyone's instinct to live for themselves, and he would have gone off and done what he really enjoyed doing. She had found out that, by working to raise funds for Indian Famine Relief, there came a time when one simply had to stop embroidering those night-dress cases and go to the theatre. But this lot kept on and on being revolutionaries, year in, year out, and could not think of anything else, showing that they were simply serving their own pleasure.

'Lenin,' Chubinov was saying now, 'can be very insulting. He has called our movement childish, thoughtlessly provocative, frivolous.'

'I'm for Lenin,' thought Laura. Yet she liked Chubinov, she liked him very much, she even loved him, as if he were one of the family, the nice fool of the family. When he rose and took that overcoat down from the door, her heart ached.

It was so ingenuous in its malconstruction that she even had to guide his arms into his sleeves. Then he said, 'Never forget that Kamensky loved your grandfather. In his diary he expressed great satisfaction because he would be able to attend the Ninth Day Requiem before he left France.' He fell into reverie. 'What a mysterious story. I still don't fully understand the pattern. There's a piece missing. Why did Gorin leave himself off guard by going to Grissaint, when he should have been in a defensive position, and make it possible for us to go

428

through his papers? After a lifetime of carefulness, how could he be so careless?'

'Well, he was looking forward to going to this new job in South America.'

'Also he may have been distracted by his affection for this woman he was about to marry. How wretched, that in performing a necessary act of justice I have had to bereave a woman, about whom I know nothing, who can never have committed any offence against me.'

'Oh, her. Surely they were married already? He spoke to me about his wife.'

'I think not. We gathered from his diaries that he was much in love with a girl whom he had known only a short time. At first he had doubted whether she could possibly love him, then he realised from unmistakable signs that she returned his passion.'

'Well, I think she was his wife. He talked a lot about what they were going to do together in South America.'

'Strange. We knew nothing of a wife. Taking him as Kamensky, had you any idea he was married?'

'It never occurred to me. You don't ask yourself whether somebody like that is married or not.'

'Well, anyway he had tickets for himself and his wife on a ship sailing for Rio in eleven days' time. Just after the Ninth Day Requiem. I must face the facts. Through me a woman has lost her devoted lover.'

'I shouldn't worry about that,' said Laura. 'What sort of woman would Kamensky love? Only a woman like himself, capable of treachery and murder.'

They went out into the corridor and he paused on the threshold to say softly, 'Tell me when we pass the room.' When she laid her hand on his arm and said, 'Here', he laid his cheek against the door. They could hear the quick low monotone of the Psalms, very indistinct now, for it was still Berr's wife who was reading. Chubinov murmured, 'In there. Nikolai and Berr.' She would have told him that if he went in, both her grandfather and Berr would turn back to him from the presence of God out of loyalty to their own kind; which God in His peculiar way would probably regard both as a virtue and

429

a sin. But she assumed it to be a point of honour with Chubinov not to take grace poured out generously. He would prefer some mean trickle among the rocks. She prayed that the whole story of the world might blaze up like the Northern Lights on the other side of the door and put an end to people being foolish; but if she had learned anything during the last three days it was that miracles do not happen. When he drew his cheek away from the door, he said, 'This I have done for Nikolai. I've given him back his splendid shining name, and you and all his family will be treated like royalty for the rest of your lives. The Tsar will be ashamed. He will grovel,' he added, for a second full of hate. 'But to Berr I can give only this little, little present of not seeing him. Not bringing a further trial upon him. All I can do. I'm a beggar, really. Destitute. Not a spiritual penny in my pocket.' She put up her hand and stroked his cheek again, and he kissed her on the forehead, and with his arm about her shoulders they went along the corridor. On the threshold he paused. 'All the same, the future is mine. No other organisation can stand against our spirit.'

The twitter of exclamatory Russian rose up from the hall below, the elevator door banged. So Chubinov put his finger to his lips, and he became a descending shadow on the shadowy staircase. But as she turned to go back into the hall he recalled her in a loud whisper. His spectacles shone through the dusk with an air of urgency.

'Miss Laura, I don't want you to think worse of me than I deserve.' She went out on to the landing, hoping that he was going to tell her that he had not killed Kamensky, that out of chivalry he had taken on himself the guilt of a comrade. But he said: 'It may occur to you that I have got this post in Bournemouth on Hippolyte Baraton's academic qualifications, and this may seem to you like a fraud practised on a schoolmaster who is perhaps not very successful. But I can assure you that my own academic qualifications are much higher. Good-bye, dear, dear Miss Laura.'

But still he lingered. 'If you could find some way,' his weak voice stuttered, 'of speaking about me to Berr . . .' The elevator was grunting its way up, he slipped quietly down into the darkness. She did not suppose, as she turned away to avoid the newcomers, that she or anybody else would ever hear of him and his great plans again. Probably he was right enough in foretelling that the Russian and the French Governments would throw a pall of silence over Kamensky's death; but surely his own life would be as silent. She could see him, years hence, mum at the end of a crocodile of mocking schoolboys, as it wound under the dripping pines of Bournemouth down to the broken-spirited sea; while his Marxist helper was as mute, the post never bringing anything to the point, at Westgate; and Ulyanov, who was also Lenin, said not a word at Eastbourne. Yet she could not forget that once at least it had passed through her mind that Kamensky spoke like a man of power, used to being obeyed on large issues, although his apparent role was to obey; and Madame Verrier, whose eye was always on the target, had railed at him as a Chancellor of the University, the President of the Republic, the Pope. Anyway it must cost a tremendous amount of money to keep all these people running about. She did not really know what to think.

She felt a great desire to be with her mother. She had not heard her go into the room, and there was some time to go before the evening service began. She went to Tania's bedroom, but it was empty, and the air too heavy with the scent of gardenias. Her mother, who was careless now, or rather too full of care to do the little things that the fingers ordinarily do without care, had left the stopper out of her scent-bottle. As Laura pressed it down, wishing she were married and could use really interesting scent instead of just lavender-water, a voice called to her through the communicating door into Sofia Andreievna's bedroom, which was ajar. 'Is that you, my darling? Come and talk to me. We've a few minutes before the service, and there's something I must ask you.'

Tania was stretched on Sofia Andreievna's bed, in the shadow of her taffeta curtains, her cheek resting on a pile of covered pillows. 'I don't know why, I felt like lying on my mother's bed,' she said, as Laura pulled forward a chair. 'How I want my mother. And how glad I am she does not have to go through all this. Did I tell you that when I saw her at the clinic she sent you her love and was sure you managed splendidly at Grissaint, and thanked you for it?'

Laura murmured her acknowledgements, and found she had to raise a question which had occurred to her several times. 'I say, how clever of you to recognise that Monsieur Baraton from the family photographs. He must have changed a lot.'

'Of course I didn't recognise him. But if a grand duke or a Cabinet Minister tells you that you've been together on some occasion, it's all right to say, "I'm so sorry, my memory is bad, at the moment I've forgotten." But if it's somebody less important than you are, then you say "Oh, of course, but I remember perfectly," and you fudge up something agreeable. And a tutor would be bound to be in the family photographs.'

It had all worked out very well, Laura thought.

Tania put up her hand under the corner of a pillow and tweaked it so that it hid her face. Her voice cracked as she asked, 'Would you feel it terrible if we didn't go back to England? We would stay here for a time till your grandmother is cured. Then we would go to Russia.'

'For good, you mean?'

'For good.'

Laura was in the drawing-room at Radnage Square as it was on autumn evenings, when the smoke curled up blue from the heaps of burning leaves in the gardens, and the reflected sunset was tempered scarlet and gold over the roofs of the houses on the opposite side of the square, and the street-lamps blossomed primrose-yellow one by one, and the parlourmaid drew the faded gold-green damask curtains that had come from the Rowan house in Ireland, and they were all shut in with Tania, and the bowls and vases of bronze chrysanthemums, and the crackling new-lit fire. The noonday sun blazed down on the sand in the cove, burning it white, while Nanny rubbed her down after her swim in the icy blue-purple sea and gave her a ginger-snap. Her father took them all to the Zoo on Sunday afternoon, each with a tin of Lyle's golden syrup to give to the bears. She did not exactly want to cry, but her eyes stung. But what she was regretting was not there any more. Tania had not been very good about the chrysanthemums lately; Nanny had gone, having stayed on as a sewing-maid but leaving suddenly six months ago after she had been suddenly rude to Mr Rowan; and if the bears had relied for their golden syrup on the Rowan family they had been out of luck for quite some time. It was hardly for her to decide to leave England. England had left her.

She supposed she should consider what it would mean to her father if her mother and she went away, but she found it hard to consider that. It was irrelevant that at the moment he would not really notice whether they stayed or left, except for appearances' sake, since she understood this sort of silliness cleared up after a time. But she could hardly bring herself to think of her father. For an instant it seemed to her that it was he whom she had seen lying on the pavement outside the house, his face blotted out by roses. Even when the hallucination left her, and she knew he was alive, he did not live for her. But she saw her brother Osmund as he was when he was out on the cricket-pitch bowling, an archer who was his own bow, changing a clumsy ball into a keen searcher like an arrow; she remembered his blue eyes, solemn with recognition that as little fuss as possible should be made about everything particularly his own excellences. She saw her brother Lionel, bouncing his top-hat on his head as he walked through the water-meadows on the Fourth of June, with his hands in his pockets, laughing because he was aware that it was ridiculous to be wearing such clothes in a water-meadow on the Fourth of June, but not getting indignant about it, he hated Eton but he lived it. She understood why her mother had forgiven Nikolai for not sending messages to her and her sisters and brothers, saying that he had regarded his children as parts of himself like his fingers and toes. She hardly ever thought of her brothers when they were not there, but she found herself crying, 'Mummie, you can't just walk off and leave Osmund and Lionel!'

'That's just what I'm afraid I must do. I told you before if I go back to England, I'll behave strangely. Your father's left me so completely. And for her. I haven't the strength to bear it. I don't think Osmund and Lionel will suffer as much pain at losing me as they would if they saw me disgracing them.'

Speaking like that, like someone who had gone down to the

tomb and come back for some other reason than that she wanted to, she was probably right. 'I'll come,' said Laura. In any case, right or wrong, her mother could not go away alone.

'I know I shouldn't do this. It isn't fair I should have to do it. Because something wrong has been done to me, I'm being forced to do wrong,' Tania went on.

Laura reflected that there seemed a good deal of that in life.

'You're sure, Laura, darling, it won't break your heart to leave England?'

Laura shook her head. She would cry if she spoke. Also she was so strongly tempted to tell her mother that, to judge by the last few hours, there was much to be said for leaving a country where, if one asked the vicar to hide a revolver in a coffin, he might raise objections. But she felt the victim of injustice. Everyone would think she had chosen to go to Russia. Yet she had no choice. Life was making her do it.

'Then we'll talk no more of this till after the funeral,' said Tania, swinging herself off the bed on to her feet. She had crumpled her dress by lying on it, and she raised her hand as if to ring for Hélène, dropped it, and frowned down on the creases, as if longing to get to the end of a period in which she could not use the prop of elegance. She sat down in front of the dressing-table and smoothed her hair, and asked, 'By the way, has the little Kamensky turned up?'

A shudder ran through Laura. 'I've no idea.'

'That sounds rather cold. Laura, nothing – nothing happened at Grissaint?'

'Well, I should have said quite a lot. But what exactly do you mean, Mummie?'

'The fact is, I don't want to seem absurd, but since we got here from London it had crossed my mind once or twice that the little Kamensky was taking too warm an interest in you.'

'You mean,' asked Laura, 'that you thought he was in love with me?' She laughed aloud at her mother's simplicity. 'No, indeed. Sometimes he flattered me and told me I was a stunner like you, but one could see it was humbug a mile off.'

'It might not have been.'

But even if it had not been true that he feared and hated her to the ultimate point, the notion was ridiculous. She thought of reminding her mother that Kamensky was old enough to be her father, but that now proved nothing. But there were other considerations. 'Why, I don't believe he's as tall as I am. I should think he'd be a full inch shorter.'

'Oh, I'm probably wrong, I'm not very clever just now.' Tania put down her comb and rested her chin on her hands and looked at her reflection in the triple mirror. 'I'm not so clever as I was. I'm not anything as much as I was. I've been destroyed.' But she pushed her chair away from the dressing-table so that she could no longer see herself in the glass, and spread her hands out as if she were wiping out of the air the words she had just spoken. 'But I'm being absurd. Yes, I've been destroyed. Yes, I am maimed for life. But for other people, for the whole world, it isn't so. For them life's getting better and better all the time. Look at Russia. It's coming out into the light, every year the sun shines on it more brightly. Oh, we still have pogroms, but we know whose fault that is. Everybody who isn't old or mad is against the persecution of the Jews, the next Tsar will put an end to it. How I wish your grandfather had lived longer, he hadn't realised yet that you're of an age to enjoy serious talk. He would have told you such stories of what Russia used to be like when he was young. The serfs were so ignorant that when there were cholera epidemics they thought the doctors who came to save them had given them the disease by poisoning the wells, and they killed the poor dedicated creatures. And the police went round the markets squeezing bribes out of the poor stall-holders so that they'd only a few copecks to take home. And the army took their recruits by kidnapping them, and if there was a village where too many of the boys escaped into the forests, then every house was burned down. The prisons were filthy and the prisoners were sent there without proper trials, and day after day the chain-gangs dragged themselves along the Vladimirovsky road to Siberia, and God knows how many never even reached there. But all those horrors are done with and over. It's true they lingered longer with us than in other countries, but we got rid of them more quickly, in less than a lifetime. And when all our peasants understand the new ways of farming, and all these new factories and railways are working, and when all the men who are liberal like your uncles – you will like your uncles – have forced the Tsar to grant a constitution, nobody'll be poor, nobody will be oppressed. And everywhere in the world the old stupidities are going to die. I don't believe there'll be another war after this wretched South African business, we've all too much to lose. And people are getting so clever, there's science, it's going to do wonderful things, indeed, it's doing them already.' She threw back her head and laughed as if she knew a wonderful secret. 'Think of it, in ten and twenty years, with this radium treatment, nobody will ever die of cancer. Oh, my darling, unhappiness has touched us, but you are young, you are going to live in a happy age.'

There was a knock on the door, and they delayed only long enough to smile at each other, and to exchange a kiss.

Piers Paul Read
Polonaise 95p

Count Stefan Kornowski, born in 1914 on his father's Polish country estate, is destined for the comfortable, if limited, life of the Catholic aristocracy. By the time he is fifteen, his mother has died, his sister has been seduced, his father has been declared bankrupt and gone mad . . . This rich and complex novel traces the fortunes of the Kornowski family through the troubled mid-century years as they face crises of family, faith and political involvement which lead from Warsaw to a country house in Cornwall.

The Junkers 80p

'A young Englishman in the Foreign Service is posted to Berlin in 1963. He pursues and beds Suzi, who is related to the von Rummelsbergs, a family of expropriated refugee Junkers from Pomerania. One of his tasks turns out to be an investigation of the Rummelsbergs' activities in the Nazi era. The absorbing and contrasting back-history of the three von Rummelsberg brothers is gradually teased out . . .' PUNCH

'Full of cold wit, coldly compelling realism and sentences so stylish they're a joy . . . one of the most promising writers of his generation' GUARDIAN

Monk Dawson 80p

Edward Dawson had three mistresses, and they all betrayed him . . . Jenny betrayed him in the ordinary way, with another man. Theresa's betrayal was more subtle: she married him. But the Church was the cruellest mistress of all . . . *Monk Dawson* won both the Somerset Maugham award and the Hawthornden Prize for 1970.

'A remarkable novel . . . profoundly moving' GRAHAM GREENE

Nevil Shute
A Town like Alice 90p

A magnificent, moving and invincibly readable story of bravery and
endurance, of enterprise and love – in war and the aftermath of war.
Out of an English girl's faith in humanity and an Australian POW's
quiet courage comes 'a harrowing, exciting and very satisfying war
romance' HARPER'S MAGAZINE

Round the Bend 80p

Tom Cutter gambles his life and his money to pioneer a charter air
service from the Persian Gulf to the Near East. To help him comes an
old friend – Connie Shak Lin, a Eurasian mystic, and his beautiful sister.
Their three destinies interlock as events move swiftly to a compelling
climax . . .

Marazan 75p

The first of Nevil Shute's brilliant novels – a story of prison escape,
murder and smuggling blended with all the drama and romance of
flying that the author came to make so much his own.

'He is an honest, exciting adventure writer who blends narrative gift
with a fine power of description' DAILY TELEGRAPH

Landfall 70p

An unforgettable dramatic story of one man's agony and of a woman's
devotion which springs from the bitter air-sea battle of World War II.
A grim naval tragedy leads a young Flying Officer to volunteer for a
highly dangerous assignment. Even then the antagonism of the Senior
Service threatens his future . . .

'A first-class fighting story and a first-class love story'
NEW YORK HERALD TRIBUNE